PATENTING THE SUN

D0729540

PATENTING THE SUN

POLIO AND THE SALK VACCINE

JANE S. SMITH

ANCHOR BOOKS
DOUBLEDAY
NEW YORK LONDON TORONTO SYDNEY AUCKLAND

AN ANCHOR BOOK
PUBLISHED BY DOUBLEDAY
a division of Bantam Doubleday Dell Publishing Group, Inc.
666 Fifth Avenue, New York, New York 10103

ANCHOR BOOKS, DOUBLEDAY, and the portrayal of an anchor
are trademarks of Doubleday, a division of Bantam Doubleday
Dell Publishing Group, Inc.

Patenting the Sun was originally published in hardcover
by William Morrow and Company, Inc., in 1990.
The Anchor Books edition is published by arrangement
with William Morrow and Company, Inc.

*Acknowledgments for permission to quote from
copyrighted sources appear on page 414.*

Library of Congress Cataloging-in-Publication Data
Smith, Jane S.
    Patenting the sun: polio and the Salk vaccine /
Jane S. Smith.—1st Anchor books ed.
        p.   cm.
    Reprint. Originally published: New York:
W. Morrow, c1990.
    Includes bibliographical references and index.
    1. Poliomyelitis—United States—History.
2. Poliomyelitis—Vaccination—History.
3. Poliomyelitis vaccine—History.   I. Title.
    [DNLM: 1. Poliomyelitis—history—United States.
2. Poliomyelitis—prevention & control—United
States.   3. Poliovirus Vaccine—history—United
States.   WC 556 S651p 1990a]
RA644.P9S553   1991   91-14425
614.5'49'0973—dc20   CIP
DNLM/DLC
FOR LIBRARY OF CONGRESS
ISBN 0-385-41868-X

To Carl

CONTENTS

Illustrations   9

CLOSE-UP
FEAR, COURAGE, AND THE CARE
OF LITTLE CHILDREN   15

PART ONE
PARALYSIS, POLITICS, AND MONEY   27

PART TWO
LABORATORY LIFE   89

WIDE-ANGLE
PARENTS AND CHILDREN   151

PART THREE
LINING UP FOR THE PARADE   165

WIDE-ANGLE
POLIO PIONEERS   261

PART FOUR
PROOF BY NUMBERS   275

PART FIVE
POLITICAL SCIENCE   331

CLOSE-UP
THE HEALTHIEST GENERATION IN HISTORY   379

Acknowledgments   392

Notes   396

Index   405

ILLUSTRATIONS

Unless otherwise indicated, all illustrations are reproduced courtesy of the March of Dimes Birth Defects Foundation.

Between pages 256 and 257:

Quarantine, Brooklyn, New York, 1916 (courtesy of the Bettmann Archive)

Epidemic toll, New York, 1916 (courtesy of the Bettmann Archive)

Franklin Roosevelt and children, Georgia Warm Springs Rehabilitation Center

Franklin Roosevelt and Basil O'Connor, 1928 (courtesy of the Franklin D. Roosevelt Presidential Library)

Roosevelt and O'Connor counting dimes at the White House

Roosevelt waving giant check, February 1934 (courtesy of the Franklin D. Roosevelt Presidential Library)

Eleanor Roosevelt and Hollywood stars

The rush for care, North Carolina epidemic, 1948

Hospitalized twins, Texas epidemic, 1954

Emergency hospital, North Carolina, 1948

Iron lung patients, Rancho Los Amigos, California, 1952

March of Dimes, Lexington, Kentucky, 1952

Mothers' March on Polio

Howdy Doody supports the March of Dimes, 1955

Virus Research Laboratory Team, University of Pittsburgh

Tissue-culture production of poliovirus, Jonas Salk and associate

Cargo of monkeys, 1954

March of Dimes poster children, 1946–55

Dr. Jonas Salk

Dr. John Enders (courtesy of Harvard University News Service)

Dr. Albert Sabin

Vaccine Advisory Committee

Dr. Thomas Francis, Jr.

Basil O'Connor

Jonas Salk vaccinates son Jonathan

1954 Salk Vaccine National Field Trial, Jackson, Mississippi

Polio Pioneers, 1954

Thomas Francis, Basil O'Connor, and Jonas Salk, April 12, 1955

Press release under guard, April 12, 1955

Press room, University of Michigan, April 12, 1955

Salk family at Inglis House

"Rush" shipment of Salk vaccine

Jonas Salk receives citation from President Dwight Eisenhower, April 23, 1955

"Conclusion," May 13, 1955 (© 1955 by Herblock in *The Washington Post*)

Elvis Presley receives his polio vaccine, 1956

Making history in the classroom, 1955

Jonas Salk and Randy Kerr, the official "first polio pioneer"

Edward R. Murrow: Who owns the patent on this vaccine?

Jonas Salk: Well, the people, I would say. There is no patent. Could you patent the sun?

—*See It Now*, April 12, 1955

FEAR, COURAGE, and the CARE of LITTLE CHILDREN

The Things that never can come back, are several—
Childhood—some forms of Hope—the Dead—

—Emily Dickinson

A buried fear is hard to resurrect. To many people today, paralytic poliomyelitis seems as distant as leprosy, as remote a danger as the bubonic plague. Mention the word "polio" to people born after 1955 and you often draw a blank. Some have a dim awareness that it used to be a disease. Some think it might be a kind of cookie, or perhaps a South American sport. Mention polio to someone born before that crucial year of 1955—and especially in the twenty years before—and you get a quick, startled glance of recognition, as though you've confronted them with proof of an old crime they've gotten away with for so long they've almost forgotten their guilt. "Polio," they say, drawing out the first long o into something that's almost a whistle, not quite a gasp. "Pooooolio. I remember polio."

Then the tales tumble out. First the memories of childhood summers spent in protective detention, exiled from city, shore, swimming pool, amusement park, movie theater, and wherever else the all-powerful adults thought contagion might lie in wait. Children were taught to be afraid of polio, to regard it as a fierce monster that lurked in the damp hollows of their experience. "Don't go to the beach," their parents warned, locking the bathing suits in the hall closet as an extra precaution. "Don't lean too close to the water fountain. Don't play in the puddles after a rainstorm. Don't go near the pond. Stay out of the pool. Get away from that hydrant." Polio will get you. It will creep in your window at night and you'll never get up in the morning. It will spring out at you from the sewer grate and drag you down below.

And the children knew it was true. Everyone could recall at least one foolhardy soul who had defied the bans—sneaked off to the ocean, gone swimming in the river during an epidemic, taken a drink from a dirty fountain—and sure enough the next day came down with polio. Everyone had a tale of a friend who was stricken, a classmate who died, a favorite aunt or brother or cousin whose life was broken in its prime. The reminders of vengeance were everywhere. How could you escape thinking about polio when you lived with a father who wore shorts despite his withered leg, or an older brother who insisted on having his arm amputated rather than enter high school carrying a shriveled, useless object in a sling? Living through a polio epidemic was like living in a city in the bombers' path. Each night you wondered if you'd wake up the next morning; each morning you checked to see if any of the neighbors had been hit.

Thirty years after the last of the epidemics, people still have polio stories to tell, with an urgency that is first amazing and then no less moving for being completely predictable. After that first gasp of recognition, after the tales of caution and retribution that gain them entry into the select generation of people who really do remember polio, the confessional whispers grow stronger and the really scary memories comes out. You hear about the juvenile sadist who assured the younger children in the neighborhood that they were all about to get polio and sent them home in the middle of the afternoon to lie down and await their fate; of the aunt who insisted on sweltering through hot summer nights, warning that polio would slip right in the window if you left it open; of the neighbor who said that polio was a Communist plot brought in by foreigners and only families with bomb shelters would be saved. You are reminded of the terrifying features in Life *or* Look, *with full-page pictures of perfectly ordinary children entombed in iron lungs. If an epidemic was going on—and when wasn't there an epidemic, some-where, in the forties and early fifties?—you could see these living dead in the local paper, children snatched from the crowd and stacked up in respirators, each metal cylinder with a little hole in the end where the identifying head stuck out. The pictures of the polio wards were just as effective as the starving faces of Auschwitz for introducing the youth of the postwar decade to that most modern of psychological burdens, the guilt of the survivor.*

June through September, the polio season, people scanned the front page of the daily paper looking for the baseball scores and found another box giving the latest tally in the polio play-offs: how many hospitalized yesterday, how many paralyzed, how many dead. And so they waited, worried, and obeyed the strictures as best they could, until suddenly, miraculously, it was all over and they consigned polio to the locked chamber of childhood horrors, alongside the secrets of bedwetting and thumbsucking and the humiliating terror of losing Mommy in the store. When you bring it up again almost forty years later, they catch their breath in surprise and then confess. The hidden crime they have suppressed so long is fear.

•

Some time in the early months of 1954, when I was midway through first grade at P.S. 61 in New York City, my parents signed a form in which they requested that I be allowed to participate in the testing of a new vaccine that might prove effective against poliomyelitis. The form was part of the steady current of official papers that flowed from school to family—notices of conferences and scout meetings, school pictures, bake sales, visits from the dental hygienist and educational excursions to City Hall (bus money absolutely due before next Tuesday). In those days, before the time when every toddler had his own backpack, teachers would pin the notes to the children's clothes as they lined up for dismissal at the end of the day, and hardly a week went by without some important communication or other sent fluttering home on my sweater.

Perhaps this form got swept up in the stream, given the same routine signature as the papers agreeing to vision screenings and milk money and subscriptions to *My Weekly Reader*. I was only six, and I really don't recall, but I doubt the response was so casual. To the parents of the 1950s, there was nothing routine about polio. Everyone knew someone whose child had been stricken, who had gone to bed one day complaining of a headache and had never walked again. Everyone saw them—the valiant toddler learning to lurch across the floor with his leg in a brace, the speed demon who had traded in his first bike for a wheelchair, the teenager who would never dance at her high school prom—and everyone realized it could just as easily have been his or her child. The worst polio epidemic in history had been in the summer of 1952, only eighteen months before, with almost sixty thousand cases reported in the United States. It's no surprise that my parents, like millions of others, gratefully volunteered their child as a test subject for Jonas Salk's polio vaccine, disregarding any possible dangers in their desperate eagerness for protection. In all the literature that surrounded the effort, the word "permission" was never used. Neither were "volunteer," "experimental," or "test." Parents had to "request" to "participate" in a "trial." It didn't matter. Everybody knew what was meant, and they couldn't wait to volunteer. *Someone is giving out vaccine that might protect my child against polio? Where do I sign?*

Like many of the children who participated in the vaccination program, I have vivid but fragmentary memories of the field trial itself. I remember the exciting sense that we were doing something brave and important, and the thrill of realizing that the adults had to depend on children to complete the job at hand. I remember waiting in the hall outside the third-floor schoolroom where the shots were given, staring at a large, framed reproduction of what I much later learned was Renoir's portrait of Madame Charpentier and her children. I wore a plaid cotton dress with short sleeves, to provide the doctor with easy access to my upper arm. The Charpentier children wore blue silk, and their arms were bare except for the white satin bows that slipped off their shoulders in fetching disarray. The line moved forward, a doctor stuck a needle in my arm, my friend Nikki's mother gave me a lollipop, and I returned to my classroom in time for the afternoon snack of milk and cookies. A week later, I was back studying Madame Charpentier and her well-dressed children, and four weeks after that I was back again. After the third injection, I received a large souvenir button and a wallet-size card, both of which proudly announced, "I Was a Polio Pioneer." Summer came, the school year ended, and I survived another polio season without injury. The following spring, my parents were informed that I had received placebo, not vaccine, and I had to go through the whole series of shots again.

The school I attended happened to be large and well organized, with a picturesquely diverse student body and an address conveniently close to both the municipal offices of lower Manhattan and the national media headquarters of Midtown. As a result, it received more than its share of attention during the days of the vaccination clinics. It was only much later that I learned about the newsreel cameras that had been there, or of the ceremonial visits from Mr. Basil O'Connor, president of the National Foundation for Infantile Paralysis, and Dr. Leona Baumgartner, New York City commissioner of health. Lillian Ross wrote about my class in the *New Yorker*'s "Talk of the Town," and a number of other reporters were hanging around the halls picking up pearls of childish wisdom for the features that filled the papers for the next few weeks. I don't remember them at all. I remember the lollipop and the button, and the long wait in the hall. I remember wondering if I had gotten the "real stuff" or the sugar water, but I didn't wonder about it very much.

In fact, I rarely thought of polio at all. Unlike so many others, I had no direct contact with polio, no friends or relatives who were paralyzed. To me it was all very distant and very idealized. What I knew best was the beautiful little girl pictured on the March of Dimes fund-raising posters the following winter. How I envied her dress, with its crisply puffed sleeves and starched skirt belling in a perfect circle around the metal braces on her legs. How I admired her dark, smooth hair, held back with a ribbon tied in a perfect bow. Painfully aware of my own droopy socks, skinned knees, and crooked bangs ("Hold *still!*" my mother would hiss, struggling to trim my hair), I regarded the poster child's immobility as an advantage, a way of keeping her skirts unwrinkled and her shoes unscuffed. More than three decades later, when I saw the poster again, I was shocked by how well I remembered the dress and how thoroughly I had disregarded the braces and crutches.

It wasn't chance that had led me back to the picture of the pretty little girl on crutches. I had gone looking for it in the archives of what is now the March of Dimes Birth Defects

Foundation. The vaccination program of 1954, which I accepted so unquestioningly at the time, had begun to loom in my imagination as one of those vast public events that everyone remembers but nobody knows very much about. Whose idea had it been? Who was in charge? Who had paid for it? Who approved? Who volunteered? Why had they all done it? And once it was done, and the Salk vaccine was shown to be successful, how had that changed people's expectations about how things would happen in the future?

This book is an attempt to answer those questions. It is about the development of the first successful polio vaccine: funded by decades of small private contributions to the National Foundation for Infantile Paralysis; produced by a team of laboratory scientists working under Dr. Jonas E. Salk at the University of Pittsburgh; tested in the spring of 1954 on almost 2 million children in the first, second, and third grades of public and private schools across the United States; evaluated by a small, secretive group gathered at the University of Michigan under the direction of Dr. Thomas Francis, Jr.; chronicled by the largest phalanx of reporters ever then assigned to cover a scientific event; and thrust onto the agenda of a reluctant federal government as an urgent matter of public policy.

In a larger sense, this book is about a forty-year reign of terror that engulfed two generations, and about the different groups that mobilized that very terror to find a way to end the disease that caused it. Ultimately, it is about the children of the 1950s—the parents and leaders of today—who were the first to benefit from the new vaccine, and who grew up in what may well be the healthiest generation the world will ever know.

For the 9 million children who were in the first, second, or third grades in 1954, and especially for the 1.8 million who actively participated, the Salk vaccine field trials stand out as their first conscious mass experience, a moment of personal glory achieved by being part of a crowd. They talk about being Polio Pioneers the same way they talk about seeing the Beatles, going to Woodstock, marching on Washington, serving or not serving in Viet Nam. They remember the room where they got their polio vaccine the same way they remember where they were when they heard that President Kennedy was shot. Even those of that generation who didn't take part remember the

event. Some were jealous, some curious, some apprehensive—
but all of them, even at so young an age and so great a distance
from the centers of decision, were aware that they had been
singled out for a special destiny.

Polio was the last of the great childhood plagues. A century
ago, and for all the centuries before that, everyone knew the
bitter truth that many children were doomed to sickly lives or
early deaths, or both. As the first generation in history to take
health as a birthright, the parents of today assume that for every
physical problem there is a solution, and further, that the solution will appear quickly, be applied boldly, will require little
more effort than simply showing up, and that it will work. That
is the way it was when they were children, and they see no
reason to anticipate anything different now that they are adults.
    Still, nature is a canny adversary, and new dangers arise when
you least expect them. When we think about the things we fear
today, we often try to compare them with the terrors of the
past. The fast-growing library of books on influenza, tuberculosis, leprosy, plague, syphilis, and other ailments of the past
is, paradoxically, a search for comfort. What we seek is the
reassurance that just as these diseases were once mysterious and
incurable, and led to terrible treatment of the victims before
reaching a point where they could be controlled and even forgotten, so will the scourges of the present vanish in the mists
of time. The horrors of today are but part of the progress of
history, we want to think, and so we look to history for reassurance that other horrors have given way to a kind of blessed
tedium. In an age when AIDS, asbestos, radon, toxic waste, and
a host of other biological and environmental threats cloud our
consciousness, forming a dark haze of concern through which
we filter all our hopes, plans, and expectations, the reminder of
conquered plagues, including polio, gives us courage.
    In practical fact, however, the conquest of disease is not an
easy leap from horror to history, from ignorance and devastation to knowledge and control. Progress takes place in that great
muddy middle ground that stretches between perceived need
and accepted treatment, a murky zone where the paths are always changing but the going is always slow. Despite the great

advances that have been made in understanding AIDS, scientists have always warned that it will be extremely difficult to develop a vaccine against the infection, and even harder to put such a vaccine into use. The history of the polio vaccine, which was in many ways a simpler project, illustrates what they mean.

The question I keep asking myself is what I would do if it were my child? I was a Polio Pioneer. I led the vanguard of mass immunization. I grew up in the era of radiant good health and planned my family under the assumption that my children would all survive. Let us imagine for the moment that AIDS is spreading—as it is—and that the available treatments are all designed to slow the progress of the disease, not to protect against its arrival. Immunization would be preferable to containment, but the only way to immunize against viral disease is to take a vaccine before you're exposed. To know if the vaccine works you have to test it on a population that has not yet encountered a natural infection, wait for that encounter to occur, and then monitor the test subjects until symptoms of the disease would begin to manifest themselves, which for AIDS means several years.

Ultimately, this means children. I have a daughter—a feisty four-year-old who knows how to flirt, whine, dance, and count to fifty, and who has already announced she wants to be a space pilot when she grows up, and a princess. I don't know if she'll ever reach these goals, but I want her to live long enough to have the chance. In two years, she'll be the same age I was when my parents requested that I be allowed to test the Salk polio vaccine. What will I do, I wonder, if she comes home one day with a note from school: "Scientists working at the Advanced Research Center have developed a vaccine that may give lasting immunity to the viruses that cause AIDS. A nationwide field trial is being planned, and children in your area have been selected to be among those who will have the opportunity to take part. If you are interested in participating, please fill out the request form below."

Do I believe them?

Should I sign the paper?

Would you?

PART ONE

PARALYSIS, POLITICS, and MONEY

Contact with someone afflicted with a disease regarded as a mysterious malevolency inevitably feels like a trespass; worse, like the violation of a taboo. The very names of such diseases are felt to have a magic power.

—SUSAN SONTAG

New York, 1916

Cholera and typhoid were familiar enemies. People died of pneumonia complicated by malnutrition, coughed out their insides in a tubercular hack, came down with a fever and were gone by morning. But no one had ever seen a plague like this. It struck lightly at first—a summer cold, a headache, a mild fever that was scarcely more than the flush of playing outdoors on a steamy day. Then suddenly there was the faint crash of a small body falling, the cry of terror. "Mama, I can't move!" "My head, Pa, I can't lift my head!" There was the scream of pain as the little arms and legs twisted inward on themselves, or the most fearful sound of all, the choking rasp that came when the lungs forgot how to pump and the throat how to swallow, when before your eyes the baby grew still and blue and cold.

Other diseases had been fought with brushes and boiling water and good strong soaps. People had closed off the sewers, washed their hands, insisted on fresh air, clean food, pure water. It was the bright new age of public health, when cities opened Sanitary Fairs with the parades and brass bands that were usually reserved for the national holidays—and suddenly there was this horror, striking without visible source or pattern, appearing in the cleanest places and the dirtiest. Nobody had the slightest idea how to stop it. They didn't know what to call it. All they knew was that it was catching, and children seemed to be caught first.

The things they did were predictable. They huddled—behind doors to keep out strangers, behind screens to shut out insects,

behind the quarantine notices put on their walls and doors by
public health officials bent on keeping the sufferers to themselves. They fled, or tried to flee—suburbs set up roadblocks to
keep the pestilence contained within the city; hotels and farm-
houses refused to take in travelers. Those lucky enough to be
out of the city when the epidemic struck extended their summers
through September, moving from one resort to another as the
hotels of the Catskill Mountains and the Adirondacks closed
for the season. They searched for cures and nostrums, shared
information and misinformation on symptoms, looked to experts who didn't really know what they were doing and quacks
who didn't really care. Barred from the horse carriages and
trolley cars that crossed the city, parents carried children dozens
of blocks to the nearest hospital. They held meetings. They
prayed. By October and the onset of cold weather, over nine
thousand cases had been reported in New York City. Two thousand four hundred and forty-eight of the victims had died.

New Rochelle, New York, was the hardest hit of the Westchester suburbs, a fact many people attributed to its large immigrant population. Nonresident bathing was banned at the
Hudson Park beach, Sunday schools were closed, and children
under sixteen were forbidden to attend the local vaudeville theaters. Travelers were stopped at the city limits and issued transit
passes good for one-half hour. Ferry service from the Bronx
was suspended, and meetings were held almost daily for doctors
to inform parents how best to care for their children. Sutton
Manor, an exclusive residential enclave with a private marina
off the main harbor, declared itself in voluntary isolation from
the rest of the city. The local board of health printed quarantine
signs in English, Italian, and Yiddish. Joseph Mariano, mer-
chant, was arrested on the charge of assaulting Dr. Giovanni
Stella when Dr. Stella demanded an apology from Mrs. Mariano
for her critical remarks about his work with the victims of
infantile paralysis.

Still, life continued. Miss Hortense L. Schey was married in
a quiet ceremony in her mother's home. Three-year-old Isidor
Kalen was injured when a wagon wheel passed over his hand.
The Magnus department store announced its summer sale,
church groups made packages to send to American soldiers at

the Mexican border, and dancer Irene Castle went into mourning when her husband's plane was shot down over Germany in a world war that was still "over there." After much debate about which neighborhood would take it, a new contagious disease hospital went up in a little over a week. Professional builders worked overtime alongside volunteers; as the head of the carpenters' union explained. "Why, we will give you the men for nothing, if necessary, to hurry this work along. We want nothing to interfere with the care of little children who are afflicted with this dread disease." But by then, most of the children who survived had recovered, and those who hadn't were neither contagious nor likely to improve with any of the medical treatments available.

1

THE VIRUSES THAT CAUSE POLIOMYELITIS HAVE ALWAYS BEEN with us, but until fairly recently, nobody knew they were around. As early as 1789, doctors recorded small outbreaks of a mysterious disease characterized by fever, contagion, residual paralysis, and a cruel preference for children. Ivar Wickman, a professor of neurology and pediatrics at the Stockholm Pediatric Clinic, had charted a Swedish epidemic in 1905; Karl Landsteiner and Erwin Popper, working in Vienna, had shown that paralytic poliomyelitis was a contagious viral disease that could be passed from humans to monkeys. Dr. Simon Flexner, director of New York's Rockefeller Institute for Medical Research, published a series of papers between 1909 and 1913 that made him the country's leading authority on the disease that was beginning to appear in scattered pockets of the United States. It wasn't until the appalling summer of 1916, however, that the public began to pay any great attention to this new and terrible affliction.

Infantile paralysis was one of the earliest names they used, although many adults were also stricken. It sounded impressively Latinate, but it was really just a description of the symptoms and the most common victims, like calling cardiac arrest "midlife sudden death." Poliomyelitis was the term doctors preferred, referring to the characteristic inflammation (-*itis*) of the gray (*poliós*) anterior matter of the spinal cord (*myelós*). That, too, was a symptomatic description, but with a slightly more clinical view of the symptoms. It was only after World War II, when the disease was always in the news, that editors shortened it to "polio" to fit the headlines.

34

Symptoms were all they had to go on for quite a while. At the turn of the century, the science of virology was in its infancy, and the difference between bacterial and viral infections was not at all clear. Edward Jenner had found a vaccine for smallpox in the eighteenth century without knowing anything about viruses, and Louis Pasteur had developed the rabies vaccine in 1885 under the mistaken belief that the disease was caused by a very small bacterium. Experiments in Vienna in 1908 and in New York in 1909 suggested that polio was an infectious disease, but nobody had the slightest idea where the infection came from, or why it had suddenly arrived to paralyze little children. Certainly nobody realized that the source of these new epidemics was in fact the very advances in public hygiene that had so recently begun to conquer other killing diseases, such as cholera and tuberculosis.

Put simply, paralytic polio was an inadvertent by-product of modern sanitary conditions. When people were no longer in contact with the open sewers and privies that had once exposed them to the polio virus in very early infancy, when paralysis rarely occurs, the disease changed from an endemic condition so mild that no one even knew it existed to a seemingly new epidemic threat of mysterious origins and terrifyingly unknown scope.

Grasping for ways to deal with this new menace, baffled health officials clung to the very rules of sanitation that they would later learn had made the threat of polio so much more severe. For two generations, as summer epidemics came and went across the country with bewildering randomness, the guardians of public health advised against open drains and unscreened windows, and told parents to keep their children well bathed, well rested, well fed, and away from crowds. Whenever polio struck, schools and camps were routinely closed, movie theaters shut by authority of the public health commissioners, drinking fountains abandoned, draft inductions suspended, and all nonessential meetings canceled "for the duration."

Harmless strictures, by and large, but not particularly helpful ones. When used against plague or influenza these same precautions had an immediate impact, cutting the spread of disease. In the case of polio, the shunning of the fairground and the movie theater had its greatest meaning as a superstitious gesture, part of a ritual taboo against sensual indulgence in times of crisis. When people went out anyway, and did indeed contract the disease, they were always sure that it was in the danger zone of illicit pleasure that they had gotten sick. If they stayed home and obeyed all the rules and restrictions and still got polio, they wondered what transgression they had forgotten. They never doubted the value of the precautions themselves.

For decades doctors, epidemiologists, and laboratory researchers tried to discover how the disease was spread. Was it an outward sign of immorality, the sins of the fathers being visited upon their children, or an indication of innate social inferiority? Was it carried by flies, or fleas, or sultry breezes, by hand-to-mouth contact or inhalation or genetic predisposition? If the virus was carried in the air, would nasal sprays keep it from entering the body? Some researchers favored severing the olfactory nerves; others suggested treatment of the nose with picric acid or alum as a nasal spray, a plan that resulted in total loss of the sense of smell (though no protection against polio) for several children who participated in tests. George Washington Carver saw possibilities in peanut-oil treatments, and Dr. C. W. Jungeblut experimented with vitamin C. In 1940 came the disturbing news that children with recent tonsillectomies were for some reason more susceptible to polio, a finding that effectively suspended the nation's most popular elective surgery for the summer months.

Nobody has ever completely settled the question of how polio is spread, though the best evidence suggests the virus is excreted in the stool and passed through hand-to-hand or hand-to-mouth contact by people who don't wash their hands as much or as well as they should. During the polio years, when frustrated virologists struggled to solve the mystery of the disease's movement, the only sure progression was the steady march of officials from the local health department, marking doors and windows with quarantine notices at the first diagnosis, taking histories of every place the patient had been and everyone he had talked to, looking for clues in the plumbing arrangements, inspecting the drains and the garbage cans, and generally making it seem it was the victim's fault for getting sick. Keeping track of contagious disease was a big business in the first half of the twentieth century, but the swarm of health inspectors and visiting nurses couldn't hide the fact that they didn't really know what they were looking for, or where they would find it.

Doctors often resented the amount of fuss made about polio, and complained that the exaggerated fear of the disease diverted attention from other, more serious health threats. The overwhelming majority of people who had polio never even knew it, and of those who were diagnosed, most recovered with little or no disability. In the worst epidemic year, 1952, polio caused only three thousand deaths, compared to the half million people who had died of influenza in 1918. Accidents always killed far more children than polio.

Such thinking missed the point. We all have priorities in what we fear, and the order often has little to do with the actual levels of danger. Epidemic diseases that strike whole communities at the same time are more frightening than chronic diseases that kill individuals over a number of years. Diseases of unknown origin are more fearful than disease whose causes are understood. Diseases that strike the young and active are more terrible than those that prey upon the old and weak. In any case, mortality figures miss the true horror of polio. To many people, there were far worse things than dying of paralytic poliomyelitis. You could get the disease and live.

What was it like to have polio? For one thing, it was an insidious disease, with early symptoms not very different from those of a summer cold. Case after case recounts a history of feeling poorly for a day or so, but not so sick that you couldn't go to Sunday school, take part in the family picnic, play football, or do any of those things that seem so ordinary at the time but take on a terrible irony two days later when you stumble in the hall, lose control of your limbs and wake up immobilized in plaster or draped in the scalding packs of wet wool that might keep your muscles from going into spasm.

For the victims of the earliest epidemics, treatment was a matter of guesswork and recovery a matter of luck. As late as 1939, there were only three hundred hospitals in the entire country that would accept polio patients; everyone else had to make do with whatever care and equipment they could find at home. Many people survived a bout of polio with no aftereffects, but those who were left with residual paralysis found little to help them with either the burden of public pity or the nuisances of everyday life. The meager range of braces and crutches that existed were heavy, expensive, and often painful to use. Wheelchairs were more suited for boardwalk promenades than for the actual business of getting about, elevators were rare, and ramps were as nonexistent as the idea of handicapped rights. Doctors encased paralytic patients in plaster casts and splints; it was not until 1940, when Sister Elizabeth Kenny came from Australia to promote her "Kenny method" of hot packs and massage, that they realized the casts themselves could cause permanent damage to nerves and muscles.

The survivors who were crippled called themselves "polios," a name that merged their identity with their disease but was at least better than "gimp," or "four legs," or "hopeless case." They consulted faith healers, bone-crackers, herbalists, and quacks of every sort. Mostly they languished, shunted off to the inevitable back bedroom that was set aside for invalids. When polio first appeared as an epidemic malady at the end of the nineteenth century, people who were paralyzed were treated like the victims of a wasting disease, suddenly lifted out of the mainstream of life and transported to a special alternate universe reserved for those who are waiting to die. The only problem was, they weren't dying, or at least not any faster than their able-bodied contemporaries. They were simply crippled.

Nobody knew quite how to feel about these incongruously healthy polio survivors, bereft of both the tragic glamour of an early death and the hope of recovery that accompanied mysterious fevers. Victims of cancer, of heart disease, of reckless horses and polluted waters—those people died and were mourned, perhaps forever, but they did not need to be carried to the bathroom or fed with a spoon for decades. Their families grieved for them, but never lay awake at night wondering what would happen to their helpless dependents after they, the caretakers, were gone. Everyone knew how to behave at a funeral, but how do you conduct yourself when a living reminder of fate's cruelty drags himself down your street every afternoon? People had infinite sympathy for orphans, but what of those whose mother was a twisted cripple, whose father could no longer earn money for the food he continued to eat? What of the wife who in effect lost a husband and acquired another child, one who would never grow to independence? Over the years, better crutches and lighter braces were developed. Wheelchairs became more practical and less exotic. But nothing stopped the steady swell of people whose lives had been forever changed by a sudden fever on a warm afternoon.

After the terrible summer of 1916, there was not a year that passed without an epidemic somewhere. In 1930 an outbreak centered in Middletown, Connecticut, caused Wesleyan University to cancel its football season and prompted 141 students to quit school. That same fall, local health officials closed schools in Topeka, Kansas, and banned public meetings in Los Angeles, California. Six deaths were also reported in Rumania, and cases appeared in France and Egypt, but there could be little quarrel with the 1930 report that found "undue prevalence" of the disease in the United States. In 1931 there was another epidemic in New York City, in 1932 in New Jersey and Pennsylvania. That same summer, Los Angeles witnessed an epidemic so severe the city health services began to break down. Ambulances and stretchers blocked the streets in front of Los Angeles County Hospital, where patients were turned away by frightened hospital employees. In 1935 Boston was hit, the entire city of Annapolis, Maryland, was quarantined, and President Roosevelt, himself a polio victim, called off a national Boy Scout Jamboree in Virginia. In 1936 churches and resorts in Alabama were closed, Chicago was swept by a large epidemic, and Tulsa, Oklahoma, shut down tight. In 1939 a woman gave birth while in an iron lung; by that time, it had been proven that you could survive in an iron lung for ten years.

Improved care cut polio mortality over the years, but it didn't make the acute stages any better. For the rest of their lives, parents would recall with perfect clarity the limpness of the baby's legs, the strange chill of fear that came when they realized their five-year-old early bird was still in bed, crying for a drink of water. In the days of house calls and bedside diagnoses, doctors had routines that helped them tell what was the matter. "What's that there by your belly button?" they would ask. If Susie could lift her head to see, she didn't have polio. If she didn't lift her head, that meant trouble. Usually, the doctor packed the patient off to the nearest hospital for the spinal tap that confirmed the diagnosis. Some performed their own spinal taps right there and then, stretching the child out on the kitchen table and having the mother or father hold him still while the doctor drew the fluid from the cord around the spine. Then there was the wait for the lab results and the horrible moment when you had to abandon your child—or your husband, or your wife—to the isolation of the hospital. Would they be able to breathe? Would they ever wake up? Would the muscle spasms subside and let the limbs recover?

Barred from the hospital by the rules of isolation, parents went out to buy new blankets and dolls to replace the beloved companions the nurses had insisted on burning. Patients who were old enough to write got blackboards, so they could write messages to visitors behind the glass windows of the contagious wards. Families who lived far from the hospital kept vigils in their cars, waiting for a signal from the window. Radios were a godsend for those who couldn't move, and the World Series in the fall became the background music for their recuperation.

Most polio patients were jammed together in the open wards of contagious hospitals, rigidly segregated by sex but otherwise jumbled together with no regard for age or temperament or the severity of their case. An infant in an iron lung would be put next to a teenager with a paralyzed arm, and beyond him lay a distraught postman wondering how he would support his family when he couldn't even stand up. A young girl just beginning to dream of dates would be sandwiched between a screaming toddler and a pregnant woman struggling to remember how to swallow so she could eat enough to feed her unborn child. Everywhere there was uncertainty about the future, everywhere there was the wheeze of the respirators and the smell of steaming woolen hot packs.

In the enormous charity drives mounted to raise money to care for the ever growing number of polio survivors, fund-raisers liked to show pictures of grateful patients smiling inside an iron lung, a lifesaver that came into use in the early 1930s. Nobody took pictures of the early stages, when the patient's lungs began to fill with fluid and doctors performed emergency tracheostomies, cutting a hole in the neck for suction tubes to be inserted. Doctors who worked the polio wards did a lot of those, and they knew the incision had to be higher up on the neck than the textbooks prescribed, to allow for the rubber collar, like a gasket, that was part of the machine. That first tube—some doctors called it "the respiratory toilet"—was used to suck mucus from the lungs. After the lungs were cleared, they'd put a second feeding tube down through the nose, to bypass the paralyzed muscles that prevented swallowing. That was how you ate in an iron lung, at least at first.

With luck, respirator patients could start breathing for themselves fairly soon and be released from the metal sheath that left them staring forever at the ceiling or at the reversed, distorted images reflected in the mirror hung at a forty-five-degree angle overhead. If they stayed in the iron lung for several days, they might begin to suffer a kind of hallucination that was peculiar to their treatment: the vivid conviction that they were moving, sometimes in the respirator, but more often in a car, train, or airplane. Even after they recovered and recognized these delusions for what they were, patients recalled their iron lung "travels" with extraordinary vividness, clinging to this imaginary locomotion when they most feared that they might never move again.

Once they were able to breathe outside the iron lung, the next stage was indeed a new kind of motion, though not the one imagined. Sometimes patients were transferred onto a device called a rocking bed, which worked like a seesaw and literally tilted a patient up and down so that gravity would help force air in and out of the weakened lungs. Sometimes they graduated to a smaller portable respirator that would wrap around the chest and push the lungs in and out like an accordion. And sometimes, of course, even heroic measures failed; the sickest patients needed iron lungs, and they were the ones most likely to die.

The best progress was when they regained the ability to breathe for themselves and could leave the iron lung entirely, though by that time they might well have become fond of their predictable, reliable, life-sustaining machine. "Wean" was the word professionals used to describe the process of getting patients out of an iron lung. They didn't want to make the change, any more than an infant wants to give up nursing at his mother's breast for the dubious pleasure of a cold metal spoon full of lumpy gruel. And like a baby, they were comforted as well as sustained by the overpowering presence of the machine. Nurses on the polio wards had their patter down, a combination of praise and punishment that cajoled a patient out of the machine, at first for a minute at a time, then five minutes, then gradually up to a few hours, until the final goal of a whole night away from the machine. It was terrifying to think of falling asleep without your security. What if you just stopped breathing and never woke?

Often a kind of desperate fellowship arose among polio patients. Every crisis breeds its own literature, but all suffering is in some ways alike; the memoirs of the polio wards share a powerful sameness that quickly overcomes the attempts to show how various the victims were, and how capriciously polio could strike. Children, parents, men, women, soldiers, civilians, rich, poor, urban, rural: anyone could get polio, that most democratic of diseases, but in that very leveling, all were made alike. Whatever their temper before, they all now had to find new reserves of courage, determination, sympathy, and spunk, the qualities that would get them through their current ordeal.

The very titles of the books about polio show the required dose of jaunty uplift. *Rise Up and Walk. My Place to Stand. On the Shoulders of Giants. No Time for Tears. Keep Trying.* What they really resemble is the most formulaic of war movies, the kind where a disparate crew is sent on a dangerous mission and, in the process, discovers the true meaning of fellowship. Every polio ward, it seemed, like every Hollywood fighter squadron, contained a wisecracking optimist, a poetic cynic, a hero, a traitor, a brave lad who died and another who made it home for Christmas. Every hospital had a beautiful nurse with soothing hands, a sadistic one who kept to the strictest of rules, and a doctor who would arrive to make the rounds and offer hope when morale was at its very lowest.

Most polio patients' treatment had fewer parallels to a Hollywood script. The lucky majority survived with little or no residual damage. The less fortunate stayed in the hospital, struggling for breath in the iron lung, straining to wiggle a toe or flex a finger, learning the routines of therapy, trying on a host of orthopedic devices. Lame or limber, they were all forever polios.

Everyone was afraid of polio, and especially those who saw it all the time. The nurses who worked in the contagious hospital wards were convinced at every moment that they were coming down with the disease. Working double shifts during an epidemic, lugging around the paralyzed patients, wheeling in respirators or huge vats of hot water, endlessly wringing out heavy wet towels, they were always exhausted, but exhaustion was one of the symptoms they were told to watch for. Backache? Headache? Stiff neck? Fatigue? Before you got up from your cot in the nurses' station, you could just run through your muscles, see which ones responded. Were they really working? Well, then, up and at it for another day. In at least two instances during polio epidemics, hospital staff were felled by their own contagion of what turned out to be hysterical paralysis, brought on by fear.

And then, as suddenly as the threat had appeared, it was vanquished. Paralytic poliomyelitis is a phenomenom of the twentieth century, a disease that went from epidemic appearance to near-extinction in fifty years. Twenty-seven thousand people were paralyzed in the epidemic of 1916, and six thousand died. There were twenty-five thousand cases of poliomyelitis reported in 1946, fifty-eight thousand in 1952, thirty-five thousand in 1953. In 1957, the first year the Salk vaccine was widely used, five thousand cases were reported. By 1960, a year before the Sabin oral polio vaccine was introduced, the number of cases had already dropped to three thousand. In many parts of the Third World, paralytic poliomyelitis is still a real and present danger, but in the developed nations a child is more likely to be struck by lightning than by polio.

II

WHAT WAS IT THAT GALVANIZED SO MUCH SUPPORT FOR THE polio cause? What made this disease, of all the ills that plague humanity, a community rallying point and an urgent subject for medical research? In part, it was the very suddenness of the threat—not an old familiar trouble, but a new enemy that had to be destroyed as swiftly as it had appeared. In part, it was the pathos of the little children, so young and obviously undeserving of their misery, and so very visible in their suffering. But most of all, at least at first, it was the single fact of a famous victim that moved the polio cause forward. If you want to understand how the Salk vaccine came into being, and how that process developed into a national and international event, you have to start with the shaping power of simple chance. Franklin Roosevelt happened to get polio, and he happened to be rich, ambitious, charismatic, a good politician, a bad investor, and a Democrat. If any one of these factors had been different, the whole course of the movement to overcome polio would have changed.

The Bay of Fundy lies just above the northeastern border of the United States, between the Canadian provinces of New Brunswick and Nova Scotia. The water is always cold, the tides are high as they rush in from the Atlantic Ocean, and the sea air comes across the bay to cool the evenings of even the hottest summer day. At the end of the nineteenth century, the islands that dot the bay were a favorite retreat for genteel people who liked to sail and swim and lead the simple, strenuous life that often takes a great deal of money to maintain. Rich families built summer houses there, huge wooden "cottages" with big porches and no insulation, a dozen bedrooms for guests and cousins and a back staircase for the servants, who crowded together in the tiny chambers under the roof. The climate was considered particularly healthy for children, who had to be protected from the diseases that raced through the city streets so terribly during the hot summer months.

Campobello Island, nine miles long and three miles wide, is at the mouth of the bay, one of a cluster of islands just off the coast of Maine. The Roosevelt house there was a large brown-shingled cottage furnished with wooden chairs and tables, iron beds, and oil lamps. The food was plain and the exercise was hard, which was the way they wanted it to be. Franklin Roosevelt had been coming to Campobello since he was a child. He knew the currents and channels of the bay, and the best routes to lead his children in chases over the rocks. He thought of the island as a refuge and had kept the children there well into the fall of 1916 to protect them from the polio epidemic that was sweeping through New York City; but in August of 1921, at the start of his first long stay at Campobello since the beginning of World War I, Roosevelt himself developed the acute case of poliomyelitis that was to leave him paralyzed for the rest of his life.

Just five years had passed since the terrible epidemic of 1916, but it still took two weeks and three doctors to even diagnose his complaint. When Dr. Robert Lovett, a specialist brought up from Boston, finally recognized the disease, he said that there was really nothing to be done. Hot baths might help, and sleeping potions would make Roosevelt more comfortable. For the rest, only time would tell.

Roosevelt was thirty-nine years old and deeply committed to politics when he was paralyzed in 1921. If he was ever to get the elected office he craved, he would have to work an extraordinary change in the public perception of cripples, starting with the insistence that he himself was a man of strength. For the rest of his life, the image of Roosevelt that the public saw most often was that of a healthy, vigorous man who happened to be seated at the moment—working hard at his desk, traveling to important meetings in the back seat of his automobile, or relaxing in an armchair next to his devoted wife, with children wreathed at his feet in a garland of familial devotion. If he stood, he leaned forward, braced against a railing or a rostrum, head thrown back in a gesture of smiling welcome to hide the fact that he could not wave without losing his balance, cigarette holder deployed to disguise the jaw clenched in effort.

It was a brilliant picture, directly opposed to the image of paralytics current at the time. When people thought about cripples, which was as seldom as possible, they were far more likely to envision a beggar in an improvised pushcart than a head of state. It is not surprising that the great movement to find a way of preventing polio began during the presidential administration of Franklin Roosevelt, the most famous and powerful polio survivor in the world. The real surprise was that he ever got elected—a triumph that demanded not only political victory but also a widespread change in attitude by which people could accept the idea of a crippled leader.

Roosevelt had been telling friends about his plan to be president since 1907, three years before he first ran for office as state assemblyman for New York's Dutchess County. He had doubtless begun considering it much earlier. Groton and Harvard had given him the education considered appropriate to his social standing as a member of one of New York's oldest families. Columbia Law School, a term in the New York State Legislature, and a prominent appointment in the Department of the Navy under President Woodrow Wilson were carefully planned stages in his political journey to the White House. The route took a slight detour, however, when he ran for vice president on the Democratic ticket in 1920, with Ohio Governor James Cox for president. Warren G. Harding won the election and Roosevelt found himself carried to political retirement on Cox's coattails.

Resettling his family in New York after seven years in Washington, Roosevelt joined the Fidelity and Deposit Company of Maryland, a surety bonding company, as vice president in charge of the New York office, and also returned to his old partnership in the law firm of Emmet, Marvin and Roosevelt.

The Fidelity and Deposit office was in the huge new Equitable Assurance Building at 120 Broadway, a forty-story tower of marble, limestone, and gilded plaster that occupied an entire square block and cast its shadow over both the Stock Exchange and the colonial burial ground of Trinity Church, across the street. The law firm was around the corner at 52 Wall Street, near where George Washington had taken his oath of office as the nation's first president. It was a simple matter for Roosevelt to move from one address to the other, particularly since his activities were not very strenuous in either place. In both offices, Roosevelt's contribution was to be a well-known name on the letterhead and a smiling face behind a desk, the jovial "generalist" whose prestige and connections would draw in clients who could then be passed on to less renowned but more active and capable agents in either firm's affairs.

In the summer of 1921, Roosevelt wasn't paying much attention to either law or insurance. A Senate inquiry into wartime misconduct at the Naval Training Base at Newport, Rhode Island, had focused on a secret vice squad that had used homosexual entrapment as part of its investigation. As assistant secretary of the Navy, Roosevelt had authorized the vice squad (though not its techniques), and the newly installed Republican majority fully intended to use the inquiry to smear the popular young Democratic politician. Shaken by the final report, which charged him personally with "an utter lack of moral perspective," and furious at the way he was kept from presenting a rebuttal to the charges, Roosevelt had rushed from the blistering heat of Washington to a crowded Boy Scout rally in New York and on from there to several days of strenuous exercise on Campobello, where the paralysis struck.

For weeks the Roosevelt household at Campobello was cut off from the rest of the world. No one dared to come in for fear of contagion, no one inside dared let the full truth of FDR's condition emerge for fear of destroying his spirits and ruining his career. The five Roosevelt children were kept from seeing their father and were instructed not to tell anybody what had happened. His wife Eleanor was his bedside nurse, doing the bone-wearying labor of massage and dressings, bedpans and catheters. Louis Howe, a shrewd, cranky former newspaper reporter and Roosevelt's closest political advisor for the last ten years, had come to Campobello with his family. Now he refused to leave with the rest of the guests, insisting Eleanor would need his help.

Forced into an uncomfortable alliance by the combined pressures of isolation and anxiety, wife and advisor put aside their mutual distrust and collaborated on the only common cause they shared—the need to preserve Franklin's political future. Starting with a report that he was suffering "a severe case of influenza," they began what was to become an unceasing exercise in omissions, evasions, and outright lies about Roosevelt's physical condition, fabricating a facade of health and well-being so sturdy that it survived Roosevelt himself by many years.

The first step was to downplay the severity of Roosevelt's illness. The remoteness of Campobello helped, but Roosevelt was too well known and too newsworthy to have a major illness go unnoticed. As soon as reporters heard that a doctor had been called to Campobello from Eastport, Maine, they, too, made the short trip out to the island to find out the latest story they could file under the always popular Roosevelt name.

For a month, Howe insisted that Roosevelt was recovering from severe chest congestion complicated by a touch of lumbago. When the patient was finally well enough to make the difficult trip back to a hospital in New York City, Howe cleverly diverted reporters from the moments of actual movement—the painful, humiliating arrangements of stretchers, slings, and baggage carts that were needed to hoist Roosevelt's helpless body from boat to train to private car. Only when Roosevelt was comfortably settled and suitably jaunty was anybody allowed to see him. Four weeks after Roosevelt's paralysis, Howe was finally forced to acknowledge the truth of his condition, but he emphasized that Roosevelt was recovering and no permanent damage was expected. Perhaps Howe even thought that was true. Certainly he knew it was essential to say so if Roosevelt's political career was to continue.

In fact, however, Roosevelt would never come close to full recovery. Whether from the severity of his case or from mistakes made in the early days and weeks of his treatment, he would remain permanently paralyzed from the hips down. Still, progress was possible. As his legs withered, the muscles shriveling from lack of use, he began to exercise his upper body, building up the broad shoulders and powerful chest that would later persuade millions of people to overlook his paralysis and see him as a robust, even athletic figure. For three years, while Eleanor made speeches for him and Louis Howe worked to convince the party powers that Franklin Roosevelt was still a force to be considered, Roosevelt himself continued to exercise, rest, and contemplate his future. Slowly, he learned to sit up, to get into a wheelchair, to walk on crutches, and finally to stand with leg braces concealed under his clothes.

For many people in his situation, it would have seemed a triumph to be able to do that much. For Roosevelt these steps were the beginning of a second phase of image-making in which his paralysis, while denied as a physical handicap, was at the same time glorified as a source of wisdom and political maturity. By 1924, three years after the onset of his paralysis, he was ready to step back into the political spotlight when he made his stunning nominating speech for Al Smith, "the Happy Warrior," at the Democratic National Convention held in New York's old Madison Square Garden in July.

Calling on will and ambition to simulate a mobility he did not have, Roosevelt was determined to reach the podium without using a wheelchair. In a hushed moment at an otherwise hot and quarrelsome gathering, he locked his leg braces so they could not bend at the knee, leaned heavily on his son James' arm for the journey to the speakers' platform, and then walked to the rostrum on crutches to place Smith's name in nomination. On the 103rd ballot the deadlocked convention finally turned to John W. Davis, who later lost the election to Calvin Coolidge as decisively as Cox had to Harding four years before. Roosevelt's appearance, by contrast, was a triumph that passed immediately into legend. Instead of being brought down by polio, it seemed, he had been elevated, rising above the shallow concerns of lesser politicians whose souls had not been purified in the crucible of suffering.

Newspapers that supported the Democrats caught the note of glorious martyrdom immediately, and held it throughout Roosevelt's career. A reporter from the *New York Evening*

World wrote the next day: "Franklin D. Roosevelt stands out as the real hero of the Democratic Convention of 1924. Adversity has lifted him above the bickering, the religious bigotry, conflicting personal ambitions and petty sectional prejudices." At the 1928 convention in Houston, Texas, when Roosevelt once again "walked" to the rostrum, this time without crutches, again to place Al Smith's name in nomination, popular historian Will Durant saw Roosevelt as "a figure tall and proud even in suffering; a face of classic profile; pale with years of struggle against paralysis; a frame nervous and yet self-controlled with that tense, taut unity of spirit which lifts the complex soul above those whose calmness is only a stolidity; most obviously a gentleman and a scholar. A man softened and cleansed and illumined with pain. . . . a civilized man."

Whether or not it was true was immaterial. What mattered was that the very paralysis that could have disqualified Roosevelt from office instead had been transformed into a special qualification for leadership. As they listened to the rhetoric of Roosevelt's early campaigns, first for governor of New York in 1928 and then for president in 1932, voters absorbed the message that the candidate had not simply survived polio, but through it had risen to become something nobler, wiser, and more appealing than he had been before. Polio was Roosevelt's log cabin—the necessary handicap, the humble state overcome but not forgotten, that keeps a president in touch with the common man.

By 1932, when he ran for president in the deepening financial depression that followed the stock market crash of 1929, there was a subtle inner logic to his election that proved more powerful than his opponents' many claims of Roosevelt's physical incapacity. Groping for terms through which to understand what had happened, the country as a whole turned to the language of polio, making an instinctive equation between the national experience and the personal tragedy that had struck Roosevelt eight years before. The nation was "stricken," the stock market had "fallen," business was "paralyzed," the economy was "crippled," people were "having trouble getting back on their feet." Did it not make sense, then, to turn for guidance to someone who had already learned to rise from adversity? There were a number of other forces at work, of course, not

least of them the large number of people who would have voted
for anybody to replace the Republican administration that had
afflicted them all. Still, it is hard to imagine Roosevelt even
being nominated if he had not first transformed his paralysis
from a physical weakness to a source of political and spiritual
strength.

As the years passed and Roosevelt rose in politics, the legend
grew richer in every telling. Watching the first inauguration in
the grim winter of 1933, the chief of the White House Secret
Service felt the new president "had somehow overcome more
than a physical illness. He had somehow acquired a vigor, an
optimism, a feeling of sureness in himself which he had never
before possessed." Frances Perkins, Roosevelt's secretary of labor and the first woman to hold a cabinet post, said she believed
that "Franklin Roosevelt underwent a spiritual transformation
during the years of his illness . . . having been to the depths of
trouble, he understood the problems of people in trouble." Louis
Howe, who had often made fun of Roosevelt's flighty enthusiasms, grew solemn when asked to consider the consequences
of immobility. Being paralyzed, he said, gave Roosevelt time to
think: "His thoughts expanded, his horizon widened. He began
to see the other fellow's point of view. He thought of others
who were ill and afflicted and in want. He dwelt on many things
which had not bothered him much before. Lying there, he grew
bigger day by day."

Even Eleanor Roosevelt, who was a fundamentally honest
person and well aware of the physical and emotional drain of
paralysis, credited the polio victim's suffering with bringing a
heightened sensitivity so great it could overcome the ogres of
boredom, frustration, depression, and exhaustion that rule the
center of any paralytic's life. When asked at a public meeting
if her husband's illness had affected his mentality, she adroitly
reversed the meaning of the question. "The answer is Yes," she
said. "Anyone who has gone through great suffering is bound
to have a greater sympathy and understanding of the problems
of mankind." For those who devoted themselves to furthering
Franklin Roosevelt's career, any suggestion of weakness was a
piece of useless baggage quickly discarded in their swift ascent
to that High Moral Ground on which their leader, sanctified
through suffering, would find his place to stand.

III

THE CAMPAIGN TO RECAST THE IMAGE OF THE CRIPPLE, THE necessary first stage in Roosevelt's personal political recovery, was so successful that it made possible the much larger change of attitudes by which people could be aware of the terrors of polio without being revolted by its victims. The humanizing weakness that took Roosevelt off his patrician pedestal was not something he sought, however, and it was far from being a handy or comfortable way to become "approachable." Roosevelt's popularity, visibility, and charm took the stigma out of polio, but for the sustained and successful search for a way of stopping others from catching the disease, we have to look elsewhere, starting with a small, imperious, Boston-Irish lawyer named D. Basil O'Connor, known to his intimates as Doc.

Daniel Basil O'Connor was born two generations after the great famine migration that brought so many Irish Catholics to America in the mid-nineteenth century. "Two generations removed from servitude," he liked to say, waving his cigarette holder to survey his suite at the Waldorf Towers, flicking the ashes off the carnation he always wore in the buttonhole of his custom-tailored suits. By the time he was thirty-five, he had made enough money as a Wall Street lawyer to support his taste for private railroad cars, limousines, a gentleman's farm on Long Island, and a ready table at the most expensive restaurants. What made him famous, however, was his unpaid position as the lifetime president of the National Foundation for Infantile Paralysis. "Basil O'Connor said today . . ." was the way he liked his press releases to begin, and for over forty years, up to his death in 1972, what Basil O'Connor said always made the news.

That hadn't been part of his original plan. Born on January 8, 1892, in Taunton, Massachusetts, the second son of a second-generation Irish immigrant who never earned more than eighteen dollars a week as a tinsmith at the local ironworks, O'Connor had none of the patrician aura of *noblesse oblige* that was so much a part of the aristocratic Roosevelt ethic. Nobody exactly starved in the O'Connor household, but there could be some lean days if they were laying off at the iron works, and the children were encouraged to remember that charity began at home. O'Connor started delivering newspapers when he was ten, and it wasn't long before he had outworked the competition to get a monopoly on the city's paper routes.

The O'Connors relied on education to bring them up in the world. John, the oldest son, went to Brown University, just over the Rhode Island border from Taunton, and then to Harvard Law School, which was known at the time as one of the few routes a Catholic or a Jew could take to a mainstream law firm. Daniel Basil went even farther afield, up to Dartmouth College in Hanover, New Hampshire, where he supported himself by playing the violin in a local dance band. He couldn't cut much of a social figure and he wasn't an athlete, but he developed the kind of passionate loyalty to his school that Dartmouth has always been famous for inspiring. When none of the fraternities asked him to pledge, he formed his own house, and he took it well when people saddled him with the nickname "Doc." Doc O'Connor, the football coach at Dartmouth, was no relation, but it was a good joke when you pretended to confuse him with a kid who was barely five feet seven and weighed all of 116 pounds. The joke stuck, though, and when you saw O'Connor's signature, with the large ornate capital letters and the tiny script for the rest, it looked like his name really was DOC.

O'Connor was smart and ambitious, and he caught the eye of Thomas W. Streeter, a Boston lawyer and a Dartmouth man himself. Streeter helped pay his way through Harvard Law School and gave him a job in the firm, but by 1919 O'Connor was ready to set out on his own. That summer he had married Elvira Miller, a nice Catholic girl from Louisville, Kentucky, and his goals were simple: to become a Wall Street lawyer, make a lot of money, and lead a comfortable life.

In 1919, even more than today, New York was *the* place for

an ambitious corporate lawyer. The Great War was over and a decade of prosperity and expansion had begun. Many of the country's biggest banks and corporations had their headquarters there, along with the shipping companies and the mercantile exchanges, to say nothing of the brokers of Wall Street, and they all needed lawyers. If you knew somebody at City Hall, there was a nice steady business in writing the contracts and selling insurance for the new buildings going up all over town and the subways being constructed underneath. O'Connor took an office at 120 Broadway, conveniently close to both the municipal court house and the Stock Exchange, and quickly began to prosper. One of his first acts had been to drop his first name for the more distinctive "Basil"—one look in the New York City directory had persuaded him that there were already too many Daniel O'Connors in town—but apparently that was not enough. By 1924 he was looking for a partner, someone whose name and connections would bring in new clients of a sort not always available to the unknown Mr. O'Connors of the world. He found Franklin Roosevelt.

The two men had met briefly during the campaign season of 1920, when Roosevelt was running for vice president and O'Connor's older brother John, now turned to politics in New York's Democratic party, had been elected to the state assembly, but there was little to draw the rising young star of the national party to the younger brother of a local candidate. Their professional acquaintance apparently began when oilman John B. Shearer, a client of O'Connor's, suggested him to Roosevelt as someone who could help with some legal questions. Over the next two years O'Connor helped Roosevelt with several cases, and by the fall of 1924 they were discussing the possibility of a new partnership. Years later O'Connor recalled the decision with characteristic terseness: "I was looking for a law partner. I had a couple of lunches with him. I asked him how he liked the idea . . . he liked it."

Over the succeeding decades, as O'Connor became famous as president of one of the world's largest and most successful charitable organizations, a foundation with a multimillion-dollar budget dedicated solely to the prevention and treatment of infantile paralysis, great significance was attached to the popular story that he first met Roosevelt when he saw him sprawled on the slippery lobby floor of 120 Broadway, the very model of a great man humbled by crippling disease. Similarly, in the burgeoning mythology of the National Foundation for Infantile Paralysis, which would eventually have its headquarters at the same address, much was made of the importance for Roosevelt of leaving Emmet, Marvin and Roosevelt for a law practice that was in the same elevator-equipped building as his other position as New York vice president of the Fidelity and Deposit Company. The true attraction, however, had nothing to do with polio, at least directly. Both men entered the partnership with the simple motive of making money, to which Roosevelt added the stipulation that he had to make it with as little effort as possible.

This was fine with O'Connor, since the Roosevelt name brought in business even when the man himself was off in Florida. Socially minded clients were reassured that the unknown Mr. O'Connor was associated with the right sort of person, one whose name had been listed in the registers of New York society since the seventeenth century. Politically minded ones, remembering Roosevelt's triumphant speech at the recent convention, were eager to have ties to a man who might soon be in a position to bestow favors. As for Roosevelt's continuing trade in the bond business, there was a pleasing synergy in the plan—a man with powerful political connections, perhaps a future office-holder himself, who could also write the surety bonds needed to back a commercial venture, would be a very attractive legal representative for anyone wanting to do business in the city.

The new partnership of Roosevelt and O'Connor appealed to Roosevelt's vanity—it was pleasant to have "my name at the head instead of the tail as it now is"—and it appealed even more directly to his pocketbook, especially when O'Connor added that he would guarantee his new partner $10,000 a year whether or not he did any actual work.

Despite his wealth, or perhaps because of the habits and expectations that wealth created, Roosevelt needed the money. In 1924 his oldest son was at Harvard, three other boys were at Groton, and Roosevelt was faced with the ongoing expenses of two houses, a yacht that was wrecked before it could be sold, substantial medical bills, and a portfolio of unprofitable investments—a sorry list that included dirigible service between New York and Chicago, a lobster factory in Massachusetts, and an oil company in Wyoming among other "guaranteed winners."

The freedom from work, however, was at least as attractive to Roosevelt as the money. From 1924 to 1928, the year he ran for governor of New York, Roosevelt spent most of his time away from New York in search of a cure for his paralysis. His early letters to O'Connor were optimistic about the potential new clients he was finding in his travels, but Roosevelt was always optimistic. Far more telling is the handwritten letter from O'Connor, dating from sometime between 1926 and 1928, that suggests in the most delicate manner imaginable that it would be both pleasant and profitable if Roosevelt would some day come and see the offices of his own firm:

> Dear Franklin:
> In connection with our law practice a thought has occurred to me which at first may not impress you. I am sure, however, that you will be glad to consider it seriously. The thought is this: If when you are in NY you could spend a couple of days at our office (or even more if such a thing were possible) it would impress much more forcibly all those who call on you that you really have a law firm and are active in it. It would also permit me to have people meet you here in the office. This I believe would make a great deal of difference over a period of time. As you know this is really a very busy office and I am sure that your acquaintances would be quite impressed with the reality of it.
> Of course you are used to the Surety Co office and the question of convenience may give you worry. So far as you are concerned we can give you better service in every way—that's that! It's a guarantee. In fact I think we can even give you more impressive service.
> Think it over . . . faithfully, DBO'C

In the margin, O'Connor added a conciliatory and tempting postscript: "Don't gather from this that I'm dissatisfied in any way. When I am I'll tell you! I can make money but I want you to make a lot of money. DBO'C."

There is no evidence that Roosevelt ever acted on the suggestion. The practice of law had never really interested him, and by 1924 even the lure of politics had to compete with his overwhelming desire to regain the use of his legs. In the three years since he had contracted polio, Roosevelt had experimented with both hot- and cold-water exercises, salt-water baths, treatments with ultraviolet lights and electric currents, osteopathy, and even Dr. Émile Coué's regimen of "positive thinking." None of them had shown any particular effect, but Roosevelt was still hopeful about his chances of eventually being able to stand and walk —not in the artificial lockstep he had perfected for the Democratic convention that summer, but like the hearty and athletic man he once had been. At the suggestion of his acquaintance George Peabody, Roosevelt set off in October to visit Warm Springs, Georgia, where a miraculous cure from paralysis had been reported.

Warms Springs is now most famous as the site of the presidential retreat, "the little White House" where Franklin Roosevelt died on April 12, 1945. No one who heard them can forget the first bare radio bulletins of the president's death, telephoned from the plain mountain lodge in the woods in the waning days of World War II. Like Moses and Lincoln, the leader had fallen on the eve of the final triumph he had made possible. Newsreels and photographs of the solemn journey back to the capital memorialized every detail, from the flag-draped train to the tears streaming down the cheeks of the accordionist playing "Goin' Home" as the coffin passed. What most people forget is that Roosevelt went to Warm Springs not to retreat from the pressures of the White House but to find a way to reverse his paralysis, and that the spa continued to operate as a polio rehabilitation center long after the presidential cortege had passed.

When Roosevelt first saw Warm Springs, it was a derelict resort, its overgrown grounds dominated by a crumbling Victorian hotel with an ominous four-story tilt. Undaunted by the decrepit state of the property or the pall of poverty that hung over the area, Roosevelt settled himself in a borrowed cottage nearby and began to devise a program of exercises in the in-vigorating waters of the thermal pool.

Roosevelt had already left for Warm Springs when it was time to sign the final papers for the new firm. When he suggested that his partner join him there, O'Connor took the long train ride south without any inkling that Warm Springs was more than an inconvenient place to clinch a deal. He was soon to realize the error of that view. By the time he arrived, Roosevelt was already talking about buying the place. O'Connor told him at once that it was a terrible idea, with a candor that was always a mark of their relationship. Roosevelt ignored the advice, be-ginning another pattern that would endure for the next twenty years. Eighteen months later, when Roosevelt acquired the prop-erty for $195,000—$25,000 down and the balance payable over ten years—O'Connor packed up his misgivings and came south again, this time to supervise the closing.

The early years of Roosevelt's ownership of Warm Springs are cloaked in a gray veil of chaotic mismanagement splashed with the vivid strokes of overoptimistic expansion that marked most of Roosevelt's investments in the 1920s—and many other people's as well. Convinced that the property could be made a fashionable resort as well as a health spa, Roosevelt proceeded to build a golf course, a riding trail, a new "cottage," and many other improvements that were paid for directly out of his own pocket. It was a combination of enthusiasm, greed, hopeful delusion, and the carelessness that comes from speculating with money you have not yourself earned. In the new era of minigolf, movie stars, and buying-on-margin millionaires, he somehow found it reasonable to expect that wealthy people would pay to relax at a resort that had already become a magnet for cripples visibly suffering from a contagious disease whose origins were as unknown as its cure.

Certainly he hadn't realized quite how soon those cripples would start arriving, which was immediately after the first news-paper interview on his own hopes for rehabilitation, and, plainly, he hadn't the heart to turn them away when their money ran out, which was usually quite soon. Instead, he hired a med-ical staff, organized picnics and card parties and endless games of "water basketball," fought for recognition from the medical establishment, and continued to subsidize patients who couldn't pay for themselves. The original purchase took over one-third of Roosevelt's fortune, though, and even a timely inheritance from his half brother in 1927 could not sustain the level of investment Roosevelt was putting into the Georgia spa.

Without Basil O'Connor, Warm Springs would have turned into yet another dismal listing in the Roosevelt portfolio. By 1926 O'Connor had taken over the financial management of the property; in 1927, after three years of steady losses for the resort, he persuaded Roosevelt to create the Georgia Warm Spring Foundation, a nonprofit organization qualified to accept grants or gifts. FDR was president, Doc O'Connor was secretary-treasurer, and Louis Howe was made a trustee. So were the fathers of the two resident patients who were actually in a position to pay for their own care.

If it had not been for the financial burden Roosevelt assumed when he bought the Warm Springs property, Basil O'Connor would never have started building the great fund-raising machine of the National Foundation for Infantile Paralysis. But to think of Warm Springs as a bad investment that had to be nurtured because it was too big to write off is in some ways as misleading as to see it merely as Roosevelt's presidential retreat, his hideaway from the burdens of state. Warm Springs was central to Roosevelt's life after paralysis, and for a time more important to him than politics. It was at Warm Springs that he had the first encouraging signs that he might regain some use of his legs, in 1924, and it was at Warm Springs that he consciously abandoned his therapy to reenter politics in 1928. This was the home he went to every possible Thanksgiving, the one place where people who couldn't walk were still allowed to flirt, joke, play, fall, and lurch about in ways too painful for the able-bodied to watch. Here he saw his friends and his advisors, drank his illegal cocktails, planned the horse trails he would never ride and the golf course he would never play.

For twenty years Roosevelt was drawn back to Warm Springs whenever he could go, and time after time, trip after trip, Doc O'Connor was with him. Whether they left from Grand Central Terminal in New York, from the station in Albany, or from the secret railroad siding under the Bureau of Engraving and Printing that the president used to conceal his movements during World War II, it was a long journey, almost twenty-four hours just from Washington, and full of transformations: away from the cities into the country, away from the centers of progressive social action to a village that had changed very little since the area was first settled in the eighteenth century, away from the seats of power to a community founded on the single attribute of paralysis.

The comfort of Warm Springs was not that it allowed Roosevelt to forget his condition, but that it was the only place where he could indulge it, free of the need to pretend to a health, vitality, and mobility he simply did not have. After he became president, Roosevelt convinced the press corps never to photograph him in the embarrassingly dependent moments of, say, being lifted out of a car or carried up a flight of stairs, and he could count on the Secret Service to destroy the film if anybody violated this gentleman's agreement on nonreporting. At Warm Springs, though, he could move from pool to lawn by crawling on his belly like a walrus, and everybody would agree it was a good joke and a fast way to get about. At Warm Springs Roosevelt could be a cripple among cripples, an inspirational example but not someone who had to stand up and fake it, locked into painful braces. To the very moment of his death, polio shaped Roosevelt's every gesture, and it was fitting and proper that Warm Springs was where he died.

Basil O'Connor recognized and respected this deeper value of Warm Springs. At first it had been nothing more than a necessary complication of his partnership with Roosevelt, the ugly stepchild who came with the marriage, but in later years he looked on Warm Springs as very much his own. Maybe he didn't love it, he boasted, but he knew Roosevelt did, and he kept it alive from the days when it needed its own financial iron lung. Eleanor hated the place, a seedy backwater that was diverting her husband's time and money from the family that needed him. Louis Howe, who was so unsophisticated about finances that Roosevelt had to teach him how to use a checkbook, shared the delusion that Warm Springs could be turned into a money-making resort. Only O'Connor saw it for what it was, drew up the papers for incorporation as a nonprofit foundation, and went to work.

"I thought he was crazy to want that big goddam four-story firetrap with the squirrels running in and out of the holes in the roof," O'Connor later observed. "I couldn't have been less interested in the project. But in 1926 he bought it and made a nonprofit foundation of it and in 1928 he ups and becomes Governor of New York and nonchalantly says to me, 'Take over Warm Springs, old fella: you're in.' I tell you, I had no desire to be 'in.' I was never a public do-gooder and had no aspirations of that kind. But I started enjoying it. Like Andrew Jackson at the battle of New Orleans, I found myself up to my rump in blood and liked it."

In all the accounts of Roosevelt's life, there is a strange little riff that runs through the endless chants of influential people present at this or that event. So and so was there, and so and so, and this kingmaker, and that king, "and also Basil O'Connor, FDR's former law partner." For twenty years, he was a part of every important Roosevelt gathering, present in the background of almost every election-night vigil, back-room conference, after-dinner political confab, or private railway journey. He was always mentioned parenthetically, always identified as "Roosevelt's former law partner," because the mere repetition of his name would never be enough to remind us of who he was. Yet he was always there.

But what was it O'Connor did? The law firm of Roosevelt and O'Connor was dissolved in 1933, when Roosevelt entered the White House, but by then the partnership that had started in a simple search for mutual profit had turned into something a good deal more complex. Basil O'Connor wrote all or part of many of Roosevelt's early speeches, including his acceptance speech for the presidential nomination in 1932. He helped recruit academic advisors for the Brain Trust and business leaders for the Cabinet, served as personal lawyer to the Roosevelt family, organized Roosevelt's papers into what would eventually become the first presidential library, and continued to be one of the most reliable contributors to Roosevelt's many campaigns.

Roosevelt trusted O'Connor as he did few others, and brought him into the inner chambers of power—a heady position that never kept O'Connor from following his own policies and interest, even when they disagreed with the president's. In 1932, when Governor Roosevelt was weighing the tricky administrative questions of how to deal with New York City's highly popular but flagrantly corrupt mayor, Jimmy Walker, Basil O'Connor was Walker's lawyer. In 1934, when President Roosevelt was praising the trustbusters, O'Connor was representing the Associated Gas and Electric Company, a giant holding company. In 1938, when Roosevelt campaigned aggressively against the reelection to Congress of O'Connor's brother John, whose own rise in the Democratic Party had often put him at odds with various White House legislative programs, Basil never discussed it with the president. When Roosevelt decided to run for a third term, O'Connor argued strongly against it. Four years later, exhausted and disinclined to hear bad news, Roosevelt knew better than to ask what O'Connor thought of yet another reelection bid.

To look for O'Connor's influence on Roosevelt in the political record is to choose the wrong sphere. Unlike so many of Roosevelt's other advisors, O'Connor had no interest in going to Washington and no ambition to be a shaper of public policy. His importance lay not in what he did for Roosevelt, but in what he allowed Roosevelt not to do. The original offer of a well-paid partnership had freed Roosevelt to pursue politics. The later assumption of the burden of Warm Springs liberated him in a far more fundamental way. When O'Connor "took over" Warm Springs, he assumed not only the administrative tasks of a rehabilitation center, but the whole complex of social, medical, and philanthropic concerns that came with it, enabling Roosevelt to shake off the pity and frustration of paralysis that could so easily have come to dominate his life.

Anyone who had any dealings with Roosevelt soon became aware of his tremendous capacity for concealing his true thoughts, taking on a chameleonlike interest in whatever lay before him but rarely revealing his plans before they were put into effect. What few observers recognized was how much this quality grew out of the special circumstances of Roosevelt's paralysis, with his simultaneous need to deny his own weakness and delegate others to do the many things he was unable to do for himself. As one term in the White House turned to two, and then the unprecedented three and the unimaginable four, the early habit of delegating tasks came to seem the attribute of a mighty leader, the powerful enigma who can hear all views while espousing none, while the members of his closest circle came to represent the facets of Roosevelt's personality he could not himself express. In this division, not just of labor but of being itself, Eleanor Roosevelt was the noble soul; Louis Howe and others after him embodied the canny instincts of the politician, the "gut sense" vital to any reelection; Raymond Moley, Rexford Tugwell, Thomas Corcoran and the other strategic advisors who followed them to Washington were the brains; and Basil O'Connor was the bleeding heart, custodian of the physical suffering Roosevelt could not acknowledge if he were to maintain his position as leader.

No one could have been less suited to the part. O'Connor was short-tempered, sharp-tongued, egotistical, and famously intolerant of other people's failings. When Roosevelt persuaded his partner to take on the administration of Warm Springs, he did not realize that he was handing O'Connor a sacred banner he would carry to the death. That was what happened, however, and in the process Roosevelt unwittingly started one of the century's most original careers in philanthropy.

IV

By 1954, WHEN PEOPLE ACROSS THE NATION MOBILIZED FOR the field trial of the Salk vaccine, the Georgia Warm Springs Foundation had given rise to the much larger National Foundation for Infantile Paralysis, which in turn had grown into one of the most successful voluntary health organizations in history, second only to the American Red Cross in the sheer volume of dollars it was able to attract each year. Operating without an endowment or a wealthy patron, the National Foundation raised enough money every year to pay for the hospital and rehabilitation costs of any polio patient who needed help, while simultaneously sponsoring training programs for nurses and physical therapists and supporting the laboratory research that led to both the Salk and Sabin vaccines. In its heyday in the early 1950s the privately supported and administered National Foundation for Infantile Paralysis spent ten times as much on polio research as the tax-supported National Institutes of Health.

From the annual White House introduction of the new poster child to the mothers who went door-to-door collecting money during the January "March of Dimes," the National Foundation was everywhere. Hard-pressed families coping with polio welcomed the foundation as a savior that provided help and hope at a time of uncertainty and terror. Medical-profession conservatives reviled it as the opening wedge to the much-feared socialized medicine. Many people regarded the National Foundation as a public institution and gave it the unquestioned approval usually reserved for motherhood and the flag. A few

64

condemned it as the tool of Madison Avenue fear-mongers who launched elaborate and expensive publicity campaigns designed to terrify people into contributing money. Nobody denied that it was a very visible part of contemporary American life.

In the more specialized community of people whose business it is to gather money and give it away, the National Foundation for Infantile Paralysis was famous in other ways. It was the first nationwide charitable organization to operate successfully as a democratic institution in the small-*d* sense. It collected dimes, not dollars, and it gathered them from people who had never been part of groups like the American Red Cross or the Junior League, where social standing often determined one's role within the organization. It was the first national charity that went to the middle of the middle class for its volunteer workers, appealing to young parents and small businessmen, to local citizens who were not yet leaders, to that vast reservoir of people whose vague desire to help the world, and maybe also get their picture in the papers, had not been tapped at all by existing organizations.

The operating structure of the National Foundation was even more distinctive. Starting in an era when most groups that cared for the destitute, the diseased, and the disabled in the United States were governed by socially and financially powerful volunteers who dictated the activities of a small, subordinate professional staff, the National Foundation had a chain of command that was straightforward and unique. All power was vested in National Headquarters, located in a suite of offices on the eleventh floor of 120 Broadway, just a few floors down from the law offices of Basil O'Connor. The three thousand local chapters, staffed by some ninety thousand year-round volunteers, were supervised by five paid regional directors, all of whom reported directly to National Headquarters. Money collected by the 2 million other volunteers who worked during the January fund drive went back to National Headquarters, to be distributed from there; it was only after vigorous protest from contributors that O'Connor agreed to set aside half the money they raised for the care of polio victims in their area—with the stipulation that they would give it back to headquarters if needed for emergencies in other parts of the country.

In each field the National Foundation supported, from breeding laboratory animals to the purchase of orthopedic devices, the executive committee sought out the advice of scientific and medical experts and paid them well for their opinions, but at no time were the experts given final control of the money-granting process. All major decisions were made by National Headquarters, which everybody knew meant Basil O'Connor. A high-ranking epidemiologist for the Public Health Service was outraged when O'Connor explained his philosophy in the bluntest of terms. "Committees are to help you do what you want to do, and if the committee doesn't do it, fire them and get a new one!"

The system was O'Connor's own creation, and whenever it was attacked (as happened fairly often), he would point out that it was extremely successful. At fund-raising banquets, he would dwell on the magnificent progress that had been achieved through the selfless efforts of local volunteers, and how grateful he and all his staff were to be able to be part of this triumph of the people. To staffers who came upon some bad press—perhaps an accusation of scare tactics or of misappropriation of funds, perhaps an attack on Warm Springs or on O'Connor himself—he would growl that he ran a multimillion-dollar business and ran it very well, and anybody who didn't like his way of doing things could just get lost. Whatever the critics might say, his methods worked.

But where did they come from? Everyone agreed that Basil O'Connor was a very smart man, gifted with a brilliantly incisive mind and trained to grasp the details of unfamiliar material without losing sight of the backbone of significance that allowed those details to stand and march. No one, however, regarded him as a creative genius. During World War II, when O'Connor served for several years as executive director of the American Red Cross as well as of the National Foundation, patriotic journalists would sometimes compare his leadership of both organizations to a general commanding his troops, overlooking the fact that O'Connor had no military training or experience of any kind. Staffers who had managed to get on O'Connor's bad side simply called him a tyrant and a bully, and saw that as explanation enough for the way the National Foundation was run. The truth was at once more obvious and more original. In shaping the operations of the National Foundation for Infantile Paralysis and in defining his own role as its president, O'Connor turned to the two organizations models he knew best: the Democratic Party and the Wall Street corporation.

Politics came first, as it had in O'Connor's own experience. For an Irish-American lawyer of O'Connor's generation, the Democratic Party clubhouse was as familiar and comfortable a retreat as the Catholic Church itself, and its rites and rituals were as familiar. The really unusual thing about the National Foundation was not its structure but its goal—a humanitarian effort to aid the victims of poliomyelitis and protect those who had not yet been afflicted. The structure was still quite common when O'Connor helped establish the Georgia Warm Springs Foundation in 1927 and was already on the wane when he used it to shape the National Foundation for Infantile Paralysis in 1938. It came straight out of the unwritten rule book for Democratic Party urban politics, in which patronage was cherished as a tool of efficient operation, high style in high places was accepted as a leader's due, and delegation of power was recognized only as long as the delegates were loyal to the boss, who was expected to have his finger in every pie.

After Roosevelt became governor of New York in 1929, O'Connor often railed at the influence of New York City's Tammany Hall, an archetypal clubhouse for urban political dealmakers, but that was mostly because the Tammany boys were often at loggerheads with his revered law partner. The personal conflict disgusted him far more than the Tammany style, which consisted of listening to the boss, being loyal to the system, watching out for the little guy (who would pay you back in eternal devotion), and returning a favor for a favor due. Not coincidentally, these were also the operating principles of the National Foundation.

The resemblance of the National Foundation to a well-run political machine was equally evident on the local level, "out in the field," as O'Connor would say, where the mass of workers was really called into action only for the yearly "campaigns" at which they "got out the vote." Whether election or fund drive, the razzmatazz fervor was the same and so was the paraphernalia, from buttons, banners, armbands, and posters to campaign dinners, torchlight parades, and late nights at the local headquarters. The wards and precincts were called chapters and districts, the clubhouse captains were local volunteer coordinators, the big campaign drive was in January instead of the weeks before the November elections, the patronage took the form of iron lungs and paid-up hospital bills instead of jobs, and the boodle was the small change of limousines for the executive director and expensive dinners for staff people on the road. It was still traditional back-room politics, though, turned philanthropic and nonpartisan.

O'Connor was not a politician, however, either in fact or in spirit. He started his career on Wall Street in the days of boutonnieres and pearl-gray spats, when tycoons ruled their empires from paneled offices where ticker-tape machines were delicately housed on pedestals under glass bells, and he kept that as his model for personal and managerial style long after it had become an anachronism on both fronts. He was a man who saw nothing incompatible in combining charitable intentions with conspicuous consumption, and his very real generosity in many areas was coupled with a keen enjoyment of power as an elegant pursuit in its own right. Autocrat, dandy, tough talker, and demanding taskmaster, he asserted his control by force of personality, and it was not the personality of a saint. What distinguished him from the president of U.S. Steel was that his shareholders were millions of anonymous contributors, his profits were measured in terms of public health rather than corporate wealth, and his loyalest customers were cripples, every one.

At the beginning, and for a good while thereafter, political connections were the glue that held the polio cause together. In the first five years of Roosevelt's ownership of Warm Springs, great improvements had been made. There was a new therapy pool and new cottages to house the "polios" in greater comfort and safety, and the dangerous old inn had been torn down. There was now an orthopedic surgeon in residence, a permanent director of nursing, and a trained staff of physiotherapists. Arthur Carpenter, former advertising manager of *Parents* magazine, had arrived as a patient in 1928 and stayed on to give the place the professional management it desperately needed. Wonderful things were happening at Warm Springs, but by 1929 hardly anybody, including Roosevelt, could afford the cost of keeping it going. The dream of turning the property into a fashionable resort had faded early, and the hope of getting large donations from rich supporters hardly lasted longer. What was left were debts, no endowment, and a need that grew more urgent as each summer's epidemics added the costs of caring for new polio survivors to the continuing expense of treating old ones. What was left was fund-raising.

They faced heavy competition, and not only from the hard times that had destroyed so many fortunes. In the first quarter of the century over seventy-five other groups were established to raise money for specific diseases. The National Tuberculosis Association had been founded in 1904, the American Cancer Society in 1913, the National Society for Crippled Children (now the Easter Seal Society) in 1919, and the American Heart Association in 1924. The Red Cross and the Salvation Army had become quasi-national causes during World War I, when they held rallies side-by-side with the sellers of government bonds and pledged themselves to care for the American soldiers overseas. It took considerably more than good intentions to focus attention on a small rehabilitation center in a remote town in rural Georgia. Only after Roosevelt's election as president in 1932 did polio become a national cause, with money raised by a public mobilization as bold in its conception as any of the New Deal programs coming out of the White House, but directed by and for the benefit of a private charity.

In 1929 O'Connor had hired Keith Morgan, a high-powered insurance super-salesman who was familiar with all the techniques of the burgeoning industries of advertising and public relations, to direct fund-raising for the Warm Springs Foundation. In 1933, when Roosevelt's popularity was at its highest, Morgan came up with the idea of "selling" Warm Springs with a series of parties held simultaneously across the country, a charity ball on a national scale. To establish the network of regional volunteers that would be needed to manage the events in each community, Morgan took a short cut through the back room of contemporary politics, tapping an organization of influential local leaders who had no known interest in polio, but who did have unparalleled access to all parts of their communities. The organization was nothing less than the United States Post Office Department, under the direction of James A. Farley, recently promoted to postmaster general after his success as Roosevelt's presidential campaign manager. In short order, the postmasters in each community were named as honorary chairmen of the local Birthday Ball Committees, with the double duty of drumming up support for the new charity and finding the local volunteers who would be needed to manage the details of each event.

Today there are laws against this kind of strong-arm recruitment of civil-service workers, but in November 1933, when the planners met in Warm Springs and decided to hold the fundraiser on Roosevelt's birthday at the end of January, everybody thought it was a grand idea. The postmasters were political appointees, loyal to Roosevelt by preference and out of gratitude for a good job in hard times, and it didn't take much to convince them that they should help the president's new charity as part of their patronage obligations. Wherever the mail went, which was everywhere, there went the polio cause. It is doubtful that any other charity has created a national organization in so short a time, and almost certain that none will again.

The results were far more successful than anyone had anticipated. By January 30, six thousand separate balls had been planned across the United States, ranging from an opulent gala at New York's Waldorf-Astoria, attended by the president's mother, to a party for wheelchair "dancers" at Warm Springs. Roosevelt, remaining at the White House, welcomed all the partygoers through a special radio hookup. As an operational model, the speed and scale of this first national fund-raiser foreshadowed most of the polio programs to come, including the Salk vaccine field trials.

The first year of Celebration Balls in Honor of the President's Birthday, as the birthday balls were officially known, brought in a profit of over $1 million, ten times what Basil O'Connor had predicted. There was no difficulty finding ways to spend the money at Warm Springs, where the needs were as obvious and pressing as a leaking roof and a broken set of crutches, but the surprisingly strong response to the call for funds to battle polio inspired the planners to look beyond their immediate needs. After almost two decades of polio epidemics, it was clear that prevention was the only way to stop the ever-expanding population of polio survivors. If somebody didn't find a way to keep people from getting polio, no amount of brilliant fund-raising would ever bring enough money to care for all the people injured by the disease. In November 1934, when the trustees of Warm Springs formally decided to make the President's Birthday Ball an annual event, they also decided to form an independent commission to distribute funds for research into the causes, treatment, and possible prevention of paralytic poliomyelitis.

Of the eleven prominent citizens who accepted Roosevelt's invitation to serve on this new commission—including Edsel Ford, Theodore Roosevelt's daughter Alice Longworth, philanthropist Jeremiah Milbank, and Under Secretary of the Navy James Forrestal—only one had any background whatsoever in medical research. His name was Paul de Kruif, and he was the sort of science advisor you picked if you knew very little about the business of research.

De Kruif had studied bacteriology at the University of Michigan and worked at the Rockefeller Institute under pioneer virologist Tom Rivers in the early 1920s before leaving to earn more money as a writer of mass-market books and articles popularizing the heroic achievements of medical science. His great talent was the capacity to put research problems in terms everyone could understand, and to make them thrilling, as he had proven in his best-selling *Microbe Hunters* in 1926. His virtue was that he knew everybody in the small world of microbiology. His weakness, which was not always apparent unless you knew the field yourself, was that his enthusiasms were rarely deterred by ordinary caution or the need for proof. A big bear of a man who liked to describe himself as a backwoods boy buffeted by city slickers, de Kruif was constitutionally incapable of moderation. He drank hard, talked loud, worked late, wrote long, praised to excess, and damned to oblivion, depending on where his current passions lay. Under his guidance, the President's Birthday Ball Commission funded rather more than its share of fascinating but flawed projects before the job of making grants was put into other hands.

As word spread through the small community of research scientists that Paul de Kruif was giving out money, he soon gathered a substantial file of letters from applicants who were very willing to keep him posted on the promising nature of their current work. Most were highly legitimate areas of inquiry, though their main product was a survey of the things people didn't know about poliomyelitis. Funds were given to support the study of how nasal sprays could prevent polio contagion (they can't), how vitamin therapy would improve immunity (it won't), and what the effect is of hormone changes on susceptibility (none).

By far the largest of the sixteen grants made in 1935 was to support a trial of a polio vaccine made by Dr. Maurice Brodie, working at New York University under the very reputable but increasingly doddering Dr. W. H. Park. Almost immediately, the Birthday Ball Commission found itself embroiled in serious problems. Brodie had tested his vaccine on twenty monkeys with no bad results, and now planned to give it to three thousand children—a precipitous move doubtless prompted by the jealous knowledge that Dr. John Kolmer, of Temple University in Philadelphia, was testing a differently produced vaccine. Hundreds of children were vaccinated with each product before it became clear that the Brodie vaccine was ineffective and could cause severe allergic reactions. Kolmer's vaccine was even more dangerous, having already caused a number of cases of polio and several deaths. Although Kolmer's work had no support from the Birthday Ball Commission, most people assumed it did, and blamed the commission for both. "Fiasco" was the word most commonly used when referring to the simultaneous trials of the two vaccines, and it was a word that came up fairly often, in a cautionary way, in the planning for the Salk vaccine field trials eighteen years later.

Partly because of the well-publicized disasters of the Brodie and Kolmer vaccines and partly because Roosevelt had been in office long enough to have lost a good deal of his fund-raising luster, the Birthday Balls made less money each successive year.

By 1937 O'Connor had concluded that something different was needed to raise money for polio—something that could draw on popular sympathy without seeming to be a specific endorsement of "that man in the White House." On September 23, 1937, at O'Connor's urging, Roosevelt announced the formation of the National Foundation for Infantile Paralysis, to be incorporated the following January. Funding for the Warm Springs rehabilitation center would continue, but the new organization would also pay the expenses of needy polio patients around the country and make grants for the basic research in virology that was needed before anyone could venture another trial vaccine. Affairs of state prevented him from taking an active role, Roosevelt explained, appointing Basil O'Connor the president of the new foundation.

Now that O'Connor was officially in charge, he moved the polio cause forward with the kind of sweep and efficiency that had made him such a successful lawyer. Once again, the first step was to use political connections to build a fund-raising base. This time it was not the civil service that was enlisted but the movie industry. Starting in 1935, Hollywood stars had been invited in growing numbers to come to Washington as decorative attractions at the Birthday Ball celebrations. Eager to assert their benevolence and their patriotism, and not at all adverse to currying favor with an administration that was in the midst of antitrust prosecution, the studio moguls gladly sent their stars off to work for the cause of infantile paralysis. Thereafter, several dozen stars made the annual trip for the balls, the radio broadcasts with FDR, and the luncheon that Eleanor would host at the White House.

In 1938, when the National Foundation for Infantile Paralysis took the fund-raising focus away from Warm Springs and into every town in America, the Hollywood community became much more involved. At a planning meeting in Los Angeles, comedian Eddie Cantor proposed that he and a few friends use their radio programs to urge people to contribute to the new charity. Playing on the popular newsreel feature "The March of Time," Cantor dubbed the January fund-raising campaign "the March of Dimes" and planned to ask each of his listeners to send a dime directly to the White House to help fight polio.

Cantor was best known for his bulging eyes, his blackface

minstrel songs, and his ever growing number of daughters, but he was also a shrewd and experienced charity worker and a loyal Roosevelt supporter. Three weeks younger than Basil O'Connor, he, too, was a child of the urban, immigrant, working-class environment that in those years bred lifelong loyalty to the Democratic Party, though in Cantor's case the nursery was the Jewish tenement district of Manhattan's Lower East Side. Children there learned early to associate politics with Democrats, Democrats with Tammany Hall, and Tammany Hall with free overcoats and buckets of coal in a freezing winter. Cantor had made corner speeches for Al Smith before he was old enough to vote, and had a career as a party fund-raiser that preceded his rise as a vaudeville star.

Cantor had also known Roosevelt before he was stricken, having been introduced to him during World War I, and so he had a vivid sense of the personal burden paralysis had brought to this vital young politician. Most important, he had a keen professional awareness of the power of radio to establish a special relationship between a performer and each member of his audience. Roosevelt himself used the magic intimacy of radio for his weekly broadcasts from the White House, his "fireside chats," but neither he nor anyone at the foundation had considered how powerful and profitable that magic could be for the National Foundation.

The first appeal for "the March of Dimes" aired during the last week in January 1938, to coincide with those Birthday Ball celebrations still being held. That same week, the Lone Ranger used his radio show to urge all the boys and girls listening at home to send their dimes to the president to fight the disease that had crippled too many of their playmates. Two days after Cantor's broadcast, the usual White House mail of 5,000 letters swelled to 30,000, the extra bulk coming entirely from March of Dimes contributions. The next day, 50,000 letters came in, and the day after that 150,000. "The Government of the United States darned near stopped functioning because we couldn't clear away enough dimes to find the official White House mail," the chief of mails at the White House later complained. "We got fifty extra postal clerks, but we still couldn't find anything but scrawled and finger-marked envelopes from every kid who could get his hands on a dime." When the litter was cleared, the officers of the new foundation discovered they had raised $1.8 million of which $268,000 was sent directly to the White House a dime at a time.

After that first great triumph, charity and showmanship were forever united in the battle against polio. It was an alliance that appalled the conservative souls of the medical community at the same time that it funded their hospitals and laboratories. Dr. John Paul, who for many years held Virus Research Grant no. 1 from the National Foundation for Infantile Paralysis while remaining sharply critical of the organization's fund-raising methods, likened the arrival of the new foundation to "the sudden appearance of a fairy godmother of quite mammoth proportions who thrived on publicity."

Whether the doctors liked it or not, the polio show was on. Radio stars made a point of working the March of Dimes into their routines. Jack Benny's trademark stinginess sparked a series of jokes about the difficulty of prying a dime from his hoard to send to the White House. Humphrey Bogart and Jimmy Cagney went on the air as "tough guy" dimes bragging of their power to fight polio. Jascha Heifetz played his violin for the March of Dimes, and Kate Smith sang. To lessen the annual near-collapse of the White House mailroom, the main source of collections moved from the mails to the movie theaters. The campaign was still called the March of Dimes, but now it was a blackout parade, conducted in the plush darkness of the local movie theaters, where the stars would appear "as themselves" in short films before the main feature, asking each of their dear friends in the audience to please contribute to the March of Dimes. Judy Garland and Mickey Rooney appeared together, Jimmy Stewart and Robert Young made separate appeals. Voices quavered, eyes watered, and the audience was told how, right now, each of them should reach into purse or pocket and get out some money. Then the lights would come on and the ushers would pass up and down the aisles with collection baskets, and only then would the feature begin.

On November 29, 1941, Franklin Roosevelt observed his long-standing custom of celebrating Thanksgiving at Warm Springs with the resident patients and staff. On December 7, the Japanese bombed the U.S. naval base at Pearl Harbor, Hawaii. It was "a day that will live in infamy," Roosevelt declared in what was perhaps his most memorable speech, and the United States entered World War II.

War sometimes mobilizes people in unpredictable ways. The plight of a few thousand people disabled by polio could have been lost amid the daily reports of carnage and devastation in Europe and the South Pacific. Contributions to the polio cause could well have dwindled in the face of the incessant appeals to buy war bonds, give to the Red Cross, donate blood, save cans and string and aluminum foil. For the National Foundation, however, the global crisis that might have overshadowed their efforts instead expanded the organization. Against all expectations, contributions rose in the midst of the many distractions and hardships of war. Rather than fighting for the same dollars, the new spirit—and the new prosperity—of wartime seemed to make people give more to everything. "Give 'Til It Hurts," the posters said—and people did.

The biggest threat to the January fund drives came not from lack of donors but from the loss of people to collect the money. Through the early 1940s the bulk of money raised during the March of Dimes came from movie-house collections; a few juvenile cynics would try to fish some coins from the can as it went by, but most people found something to put in the kitty. It was a regular part of going to the movies in January across the United States, but by 1943, thirteen months after the Japanese attack on Pearl Harbor, the ushers were in the army and there was no one left to collect the dimes. At this point, the collection boxes were handed over to the club ladies of America, women who wouldn't have dreamed of asking strangers for money if it weren't for the heightened atmosphere of war.

The creation of the National Foundation's Women's Division, like the original rehabilitation center at Warm Springs, was an improvisation endorsed by Roosevelt, foisted upon a reluctant O'Connor, and turned into a lasting success far beyond anybody's expectations. Sometime in the spring of 1943, Joseph Schenck, the powerful behind-the-scenes ruler of United Artists, had asked Roosevelt to appoint Mary Pickford to an honorary position at the National Foundation. America's Sweetheart, the darling of the silent screen, was by then forty-four years old and four years past the last movie she would ever make, but Pickford's enduring fame and popularity were still valuable commodities in whatever game of horse trading Schenck and Roosevelt were playing. The president blithely accepted her services and sent word to the foundation's headquarters that they had just acquired an honorary director of women volunteers—a category that had not existed until that moment.

Basil O'Connor, the least progressive of men, had little interest in women's activities and less in making any change in his organization. Months passed and nothing happened, but as summer turned to fall it became clear that they would have to think of *something* to occupy this famous new volunteer. To help their thinking, and to shepherd Pickford on the inevitable fund-raising tour, they hired a strong-minded, gravel-voiced creative dynamo named Elaine Whitelaw. Whitelaw had been active in war relief, first as a volunteer herself and then as a professional fund-raiser. Working with women's clubs across the country, and with local organizations such as hospital boards or Parent-Teacher Associations that attracted women members, she used the initial promise of a chance to meet Mary Pickford as a way to recruit a home-front army of money collectors who had both the time and the passion to work against childhood disease. From that time on, the main resource of the March of Dimes became women volunteers. The local and regional directors were generally men, but the people who actually worked in the chapters were women. Lots and lots of women.

The money they collected was put to use in ways that no one had anticipated when the foundation charter was drafted five years before. As the wartime military drained the hospitals of doctors and nurses, the National Foundation established scholarships and training programs in an effort to replace them. When Sister Elizabeth Kenny championed hot packs and massage for polio treatment instead of plaster casts and wooden splints, the National Foundation paid for special classes to introduce doctors and nurses to her techniques, and then paid for the additional staff now needed on the polio wards to implement the new methods. As more and more hospitals asked for emergency loans of heavy mechanical equipment like iron lungs and rocking beds, the National Foundation created epidemic equipment "depots" where the machines could be stored until shipped to a needy area, and paid for flying squadrons of doctors and nurses to travel to epidemic areas to organize emergency hospitals. Hospital waiting rooms and doctors' offices now had stacks of pamphlets and informational bulletins put out by the National Foundation, giving advice on everything from the payment of ambulance bills to the psychological problems of the siblings of paralyzed children. When in doubt, the final advice was always, "Consult your local chapter of the National Foundation for Infantile Paralysis. This service is made possible by contributions to the March of Dimes."

V

WHEN YOU ASK ABOUT THE GLORY DAYS OF THE NATIONAL Foundation, from 1941 to 1955, when they expanded in so many different directions and seemed to triumph in them all, people who worked there are likely to say something to the effect that the gods are kind to the dumb. "I don't know how we did it," is a constant refrain, along with "We'd never be able to do it again today." As for what they did, there is certainly something to be said for youthful energy combined with the flexible visions of a growing organization. As for not being able to do it again, it's also true that subsequent events, including some projects sponsored by the NFIP, inspired a great deal of regulatory legislation that would make it difficult to repeat their triumphs. Still, the modesty can be very misleading, because the people there were anything but dumb.

They knew the complex range of issues they were raising when they mounted a national campaign to conquer polio, and the serious consequences a wrong move could have. They were aware of their place in history; unlike just about any other philanthropic organization, they hired historians to record their activities, psychologists to help plan them, and statisticians to help chart where their money had gone and predict where it would be needed next. The board of trustees was drawn from the top ranks of major banks and boardrooms—people like Marshall Field, Henry Ford II, Juan Trippe (president of Pan American Airways), and Walter Gifford (president of American Telephone and Telegraph Company)—and the medical advisors were always the leaders in their fields. Dumb luck can't have been the whole story. But neither was brilliant foresight—not because that wasn't there, but because foresight alone won't smooth the road to success. You have to have foresight, good luck, and, most of all, a lack of competition in the field.

When Basil O'Connor became the founding president of the National Foundation for Infantile Paralysis in 1938, the federal government was only barely in the business of medical research. The National Institute of Health (not to become the plural "Institutes" until 1944) sponsored no programs beyond its own laboratories. The Communicable Disease Center, only later renamed the Centers for Disease Control, was a small outpost of the Public Health Service whose primary job was tracking malarial epidemics that threatened military bases in the southern states. Relatively few people had medical insurance and almost none had coverage for the extended care that polio required. Fewer people had gone to medical school in the lean years of the Depression, and those who did become doctors learned little about the various kinds of physical therapy that proved most beneficial to polio patients. Pediatrics was only beginning to be recognized as a medical specialty and childhood disease was accepted as a tragic but inevitable blight of mortality.

Into all these voids stepped the National Foundation, pushed forward as ever by the brilliant, impatient prodding of Basil O'Connor. O'Connor never designed the fund-raising campaigns for the National Foundation, any more than he devised the laboratory strategies for virus research the campaigns supported. If he wanted a thinker, he recruited one, and then hired another person to catch the bright ideas and put them in circulation, and a third to make sure the world was well informed about the wonderful show the NFIP was putting on. None of this was O'Connor's job. His mission, and his special talent, was to stand back and make sure that amid all this juggling nothing ever flew out of control, keeping in mind the goal that had set the great fund-raising circus going in the first place.

By the end of World War II, the National Foundation had become a very large, very slick organization. The single room O'Connor had set aside in his law offices for foundation business had been exchanged for a large suite several floors below in the same building, filled with scores of people devoted to the various aspects of getting and spending money for the polio cause. Dorothy Ducas, a longtime newspaper correspondent who had covered Eleanor Roosevelt since the first presidential campaign and sometimes helped write her popular column "My Day," became the director of public information, with a staff of forty helping her in her publicity work. The staff photographer traveled with Basil O'Connor, taking pictures of banquets and speeches, and went into the polio wards they visited around the country to get the pictures that tug on people's wallets. The Radio and Film Department, later expanded to include television, churned out dramatic scripts about the heroic people who struggled against the terrors of polio, the dedicated doctors and scientists who worked to help them, and the generous citizens who made it all possible. Reports of scientific "breakthroughs" were placed in popular magazines like *Reader's Digest*, and gossip columnists were fed items about movie stars filming appeals for the March of Dimes and socialites collecting change on corners. Meanwhile, National Foundation publicists were busy making their own films, cranking out fund-raisers that ranged from three-minute informational shorts to half-hour dramas of suspense and salvation recruiting audiences to the fight against this terrible disease.

The people who came to work at the National Foundation during and just after World War II had not joined the polio crusade because it gripped their hearts above all others. They were professionals: publicists, journalists, fund-raisers and salesmen who peddled polio the same way they could have sold cars or corsets or annuities. They called themselves flacks and handlers, and they charged their expense accounts as much as they thought fair, but their pitch was for health and research and rehabilitation—things they were proud to promote. For many of them, it was the high spot of their careers, if not their lives—contributing to something that was so obviously good, and helping to make it work.

What they lacked in medical expertise they made up for in skill, experience, and sheer physical stamina, the endurance needed to survive long speeches and large quantities of banquet food, and to spend a good part of their lives on the road. In most cases, they found themselves growing more committed to the polio cause than they had ever expected. They would come back to their hotel rooms after their first day of touring the hospitals on some fund-raising, fact-finding, filmmaking trip or other, and they would suddenly notice that their necks ached, they had a queasy feeling in the stomach, their legs felt weak. They would feel the terror of being alone in a strange place, sure they were coming down with polio, afraid they were going to die. It was a trial by fire they all had to go through, that moment when they stopped shooting pictures or making speeches or organizing shifts for other volunteers, frozen by the sudden vision of themselves paralyzed on a stretcher, in a respirator, dead. The moment passed and the job went back to being a job, but it was a very powerful conversion, that vision of what it meant to have polio, and it kept a lot of people working for the National Foundation far longer than they had ever planned.

The permanent staff of the National Foundation had creative people and dedicated people and people who just plain loved the joy of the hunt, and they raised astonishing amounts of money. The $1.8 million contributed in 1938 rose to almost $3 million in 1941, almost $5 million in 1942, $6.5 million in 1943, over $12 million in 1944, and almost $20 million in 1945. The means they used were not for the faint-of-heart or the easily embarrassed. The National Foundation brought the cripples out of the sickroom and into the limelight, but they did it using publicity techniques that made some people profoundly uncomfortable. They were accused of being manipulative and money-grubbing, of exploiting the worst-hit victims for their sympathy value and manipulating the better-looking ones for their appeal. They were accused of exaggerating both the dangers of polio and the progress that sufferers might make, all for the sake of driving up revenues.

Many of the accusations were true. Whether the fund-raiser was a professional showman like Eddie Cantor, auctioning off his shirt to the highest contributor, or simply a local citizen who had been transformed into a promoter by his position as chapter chairman, the understanding was that dignity had little to do with the enterprise at hand. A rational and dignified appeal wouldn't cover the cost of an iron lung or fund the shipment of a hundred laboratory monkeys from Manila. Dignity couldn't buy a gross of crutches or pay for the training of a single physical therapist. Energy and ingenuity were what counted, and old-fashioned tear-jerking sentimentality.

The appeals took many forms. A banquet speaker would describe a family's frantic rush to the hospital, show photographs of their child, gaunt and immobile in his hospital bed—and then introduce to effusive applause a happy, husky youngster who would make his way to the microphone swinging confidently on crutches paid for by contributions to the National Foundation. At another dinner, the lights would dim for a twenty-minute exercise in terror put together by the Radio and Film Department. One of the most popular was *The Crippler*, which opened with a dark cloud spreading over playground and farm, mansion and tenement, a cloud that takes the shape of a hunched and sinister figure who cackles over his many victims. The fearful shadow of the Crippler is finally dispelled by a National Foundation volunteer, played by a very young actress later known as Nancy Reagan, but the overall effect of the film was to terrify a great many people into making contributions. Guests at a ladies' luncheon would receive a more subtle but equally emotional greeting, on film, from actress Helen Hayes, whose daughter had died of polio and who now was asking each of her very special friends at the table to please, please give as much as they could to spare others that terrible tragedy.

The March of Dimes was not about solemn research in ivory towers, the fund-raisers would remind the people who objected to their high-powered techniques. It was not about the French Academy or Pasteur's tomb. It was about radio and money and sick little kids. The scientists want to be all pure and intellectual, and that's what they ought to be, they would say to each other. But dammit, we've got to raise the dough to pay for their work. You can't just issue a report every five years talking about the importance of basic research and expect every Joe in America to reach into his pocket and give you a buck. Research and professional training weren't the kinds of things that got people to dig down in their pockets. Cute little kids on crutches, kids from your home town, were what opened the wallets and the coin purses.

Just about any gimmick that worked was acceptable, and the

ones that worked best were those that were tied in some way to the moral duty of the able-bodied to help those who were not. The President's Birthday Balls flourished from 1934 through 1937 with the slogan "To dance so that others may walk." Starting in 1938, when the January fund-raiser became known as the March of Dimes, the fund-raising switched from the dance floor to the street, but the language of mobility remained, with its implicit reminder of the need to help all those who could not march, or walk, or dance. Relays of walkers brought money directly to the White House. Hollow canes were distributed that could be filled with coins. During the Mardi Gras festival in New Orleans, a mile-long strip of tape was laid out along the parade route so the throngs on the sidewalk could pass the time forming "a mile of dimes." Special tables were set up in railway stations and town squares across the country, with a narrow, twisting trough gouged into the surface. If every space of that trough was filled with dimes, volunteer workers explained, it would form a silver trail one mile long. A mile of dimes to fight polio.

Each generation was singled out for special appeals, reminded of what "we" have to do to lick polio. Parents were a natural source of both money and volunteer workers, but there were also special bulletins on the radio that would instruct grandparents to send the children from the room, at which point the older people would be reminded of what a terrible loss it would be if anything ever happened to those precious youngsters. Schoolchildren were urged to collect money, lured by the promise of getting on a special honor roll if they filled every slot in their collection card with dimes. Soldiers stationed overseas were shown movies detailing how the National Foundation would provide care for any of their dependents back home—and each film ended with a reminder that the National Foundation depended on their contributions.

The call for contributions started in the White House, but it descended very quickly to the grass-roots level of parish church and Boy Scout troop, and it didn't stop at the usual boundaries of class, color, or religion. The effort was not integrated, but pluralistic: separate appeals were made to the National Council of Catholic Women, the B'nai B'rith, the National Council of

Negro Women, and the National Federation of Women's Clubs, and separate rehabilitation facilities were funded at Tuskegee Institute to care for the blacks who were still not admitted to Warm Springs. But if the table was set with due regard for all the boundaries of prejudice and protocol, it was still true, and unusual, that everybody got a piece of the pie. Roughly half the money raised went back to the local community for care of polio victims in the area. The rest went for professional education, epidemic aid, and to support research to find better kinds of treatment and maybe someday a preventative or a cure. Anyone who needed help could get it. Anyone who resisted was an enemy of children, of hope, of life itself.

By enlisting so many people as active contributors to their cause, the National Foundation secured more than money. The principal weapon the foundation used in its war against polio was the tremendous loyalty people felt to the organization itself, loyalty that began with the first dime they gave and grew every time they read a progress report that told about what "we" have accomplished and what remains for "us" to do. Whenever a hospital got an iron lung or a child a new pair of crutches, there was sure to be a photograph in the local paper and a story reminding you that it came courtesy of *your* contribution to the March of Dimes. Whenever a polio scientist found something promising, foundation publicists made sure it was reported in the popular press as well as the scientific journals, and the very first sentence of every article always pointed out that the research had been paid for by the National Foundation for Infantile Paralysis.

After the war, the educational programs continued, and so did the rise in contributions. In the decade from 1945 to 1955, the years that saw most of the research that made the Salk vaccine possible, two unrelated movements came together to magnify the importance of the National Foundation. The first was a steady, visible rise in the number of cases of polio. The second was the postwar population explosion commonly known as the Baby Boom.

Polio came first, starting with the American soldiers stationed in southern Europe and North Africa who began coming down with the disease. The local people had developed immunity long before, in the mild infections of infancy that had protected most of the earth's population since the beginning of time; but the soldiers, living in close quarters with primitive sanitary systems, succumbed in force—and, some speculate, brought the virus home with them to fuel the rising epidemics of the postwar years.

Whether or not that was true, there was no disputing the unprecedented, inexplicable rise in both the number and the severity of polio epidemics in the postwar decade. In 1940 over ten thousand cases of polio were reported in the United States —a total that qualified it as a major epidemic by the standard set in 1916. From 1945 to 1949, the average number of cases reported each year was over twenty thousand. From there the numbers climbed still higher, with a peak of close to fifty-eight thousand cases reported in 1952—one new case of polio, severe enough to be diagnosed and reported to the local health department, for every three thousand people in the United States. The disease wasn't spread out evenly through the population, however. Most of those cases were children.

At the same time that the polio epidemics were increasing at such a terrifying pace, it escaped nobody's notice that the birth rate was rising even faster. From 1945 to 1946, the United States birth rate made the biggest one-time jump in history, and that was just the beginning: 3.4 million babies were born in the United States in 1946, 3.8 million in 1947, and over 4 million in 1954. In the five years from 1947 to 1953, the population of the United States increased more than it had in the three decades from 1917 to 1947.

To the biostatisticians who keep track of these figures, the parallel rise of birth rate and epidemic rate was an insignificant coincidence. Coincidence it may have been, but it was hardly insignificant. The emergence of what soon became known as the Baby Boom meant that a large segment of the population had returned from war to go on active assignment as parents —the group that has always been most concerned about polio and most willing to work for its control. The unprecedented surge in the birth rate, and the new national interest in the care and protection of children, made the goals of the National Foundation seem more worthy and more urgent than ever. More people were having more babies, and there is nothing like becoming a parent to focus your attention on childhood disease.

In their rhetoric, the people who worked for the foundation made it sound at times like a financial prospectus: your investment in the March of Dimes would pay off many times over in patient care should there ever be an epidemic in your area, they would say. By the time the Salk vaccine was ready for testing in 1954, the director of the Women's Division explained the high level of parental support by exclaiming, "They thought it was their vaccine! They had done so much volunteer work, each one of them felt she was a majority stockholder!" And it was true. People trusted the National Foundation, and supported the Salk vaccine field trial, because they had already invested two decades of their time, money, and interest in the cause.

PART TWO

LABORATORY LIFE

Bacteria, protozoa, viruses . . . About the only genuine sporting proposition that remains unimpaired by the relentless domestication of a once free-living human species is the war against these ferocious little fellow creatures, which lurk in the dark corners and stalk us in the bodies of rats, mice, and all kinds of domestic animals; which fly and crawl with the insects, and waylay us in our food and drink and even in our love.

—HANS ZINSSER

What every scientist knows, but few will admit, is that the requirement for great success is great ambition. Moreover, the ambition is for personal triumph over other men, not merely over nature. Science is a form of competitive and aggressive activity, a contest of man against man that provides knowledge as a side product. That side product is its only advantage over football.

—RICHARD C. LEWONTIN

Paris, September 28, 1895

Louis Pasteur, the scientific genius, was dead. Not quite three years before, his seventieth birthday had been declared a national holiday. This would be a day of national mourning.

Only at the end of his life had Pasteur received the honors he knew he deserved. Scorned for years for his unconventional theories and procedures, he had spent much of his career in makeshift laboratories performing experiments that were ridiculed in the newspapers and denounced in the academies of France. Abandoning his Paris laboratory to work in epidemic regions, he had developed vaccines to prevent chicken cholera and anthrax, a deadly disease of sheep. He had discovered the bacilli *that were destroying the silk industry of Lyon, and he had perfected a preservation process that he called pasteurization, first used for France's exports of wine, vinegar, and beer. At every stage, his work had been reviled and discounted, and only later grudgingly accepted. His father died. His children died. He suffered a stroke that left him partly paralyzed. His beloved France was ravaged by the brutality of the Franco-Prussian War. Still Pasteur continued his stubborn struggle to bestow the miraculous gifts of science upon an indifferent world.*

The change had come in 1885, when people everywhere were electrified by the news that nine-year-old Joseph Meister, attacked by a rabid dog, had been saved from a slow and painful death by a series of injections with Louis Pasteur's experimental vaccine. Suddenly, Pasteur became a national hero. Streets, boulevards, squares, and parks were renamed in his honor. Throughout the French Republic, private citizens rushed to give money to build a permanent laboratory to house his work. In 1888 the Pasteur Institute opened at 25 rue du Docteur-Roux, just off what was to be the Boulevard Pasteur, in Paris' Montparnasse district. Pasteur himself, increasingly frail, served for seven years as its director, and it is there that he is buried.

The chapel where Pasteur's body lies is at the center of the Pasteur Institute, surrounded by laboratories and lecture halls, a vaccination center and a hospital for the treatment of infectious diseases. The walls of his tomb are decorated with marble mosaics depicting his many fields of study: molecular asymmetry; fermentation; spontaneous generation; research in wine; diseases of silkworms; research in beer; virulent diseases; virus vaccines; control of rabies. There is a white marble altar, to be used for saying mass; in the vault overhead hover four large white angels representing Faith, Hope, Charity, and Science.

Pasteur himself is remembered not as an angel but as a sort of secular saint, the one to whom microbiologists and immunologists pray for intercession in their research. Were there a movement for actual canonization, it might well meet the strictures of the Catholic Church. During his lifetime, Pasteur was a martyr, having to bear the outrages of public neglect and the far more painful scorn of his professional associates throughout most of his career. He underwent personal torments, watching two daughters die of typhoid fever in 1866 and suffering his debilitating stroke two years later. He performed miraculous intercessions, rescuing creatures as different as silkworms and humans from diseases that had always before meant certain death. Honored at last in the final years of his life, Pasteur remained humble to the end. His last words were, "One must work; one must work. I have done what I could."

This is a hard act to follow, but also an impossible example to forget. Every biologist who has ever been rejected takes comfort from the story of Louis Pasteur, the innovative genius who had to battle the stupidity of the masses and the jealousy of his peers to bring truth and salvation to a world that remained ungrateful almost to the very end. Most ignore the way Pasteur courted publicity to spread the word of his triumphs, and how very commercial were the applications to which he turned his research. What they remember is the originality and the suffering, and the immortal fame that came as the final reward.

1

THE MILLIONS OF PEOPLE WHO GAVE MONEY EVERY YEAR TO the National Foundation for Infantile Paralysis did so because they shared its goals—the desire to care for polio patients and eradicate the disease that had injured them. The scientists who were to make those goals possible often saw their mandate in a somewhat different light. For practitioners of microbiology, biochemistry, or the newly emerging specialities of virology and immunology, the solution to the mystery of poliomyelitis was but an aspect of the larger search to understand the nature of viruses and the means by which they spread—which was, in turn, part of the *much* larger question of how all living organisms were created and sustained.

The difference in perspective created priorities that were mirror opposites of each other. To Basil O'Connor and the people who worked with him at the National Foundation, fundamental knowledge gained from basic research was a means to the end of taming polio. To the researchers who received National Foundation grants, understanding the deepest mysteries of life was the end and money raised for polio research was one important means by which it could be reached. At times the different perspectives were the necessary counterpoise that kept either enterprise from toppling into the abyss of self-absorption. At times they clashed like angry snakes climbing a single pole, hissing and biting as they struggled for dominance. But at no point could either group move forward without the other.

* * *

Poliomyelitis is a viral disease. So are measles, chickenpox, influenza, yellow fever, warts, at least some forms of cancer, and AIDS. The smallest form of life and one of the most recently discovered, viruses have entered the common parlance as the embodiment of belligerent stealth. The language of warfare is almost irresistible: viruses "invade" the body, "breach its defenses" and "attack" the cells until, with luck, they are "repelled" by the immune system as the host animal "fights off" the disease. In politics corruption is a virus, as is ambition when it overpowers considerations of the common good. Computer operators who in simpler days worried about "bugs" in their programs now hold emergency conferences on how to protect their systems against "computer viruses," insidious electronic signals that sneak into the system carrying a hidden command that will destroy essential programs and vital data.

The terms are graphic and powerful, but this vocabulary of aggression credits viruses with a conscious malevolence they quite obviously lack. Tiny parasites, less than one-millionth of an inch across, each virus particle consists of a bit of nucleic acid, which determines its nature, and a protein shell that coats that tiny shred of identity, protects it, and guides it in its journey within the living organism to the particular types of cell that can be its host. Moving through the microscopic universe in a kind of suspended animation, the virus particle springs to life only when it enters a living cell, where it usually multiplies at so mad a pace that it quickly destroys its nurturing chamber. Within minutes, hundreds of newborn viruses explode out through the cell's shattered walls to find new homes, new cells, new hosts to devastate.

The speed and strength of the individual body's immune system determine how far a virus will travel and how much damage it will do before this multiplication is stopped. The complex process may take several weeks; if too many vital cells are destroyed before the immune system marshals its forces, the infected person dies. Those fortunate enough to survive a viral infection are left with a system of antibodies and memory cells that are primed to stop that particular virus at once, should it ever enter the body again. This triumph of biological memory is known as immunity.

In protecting against viruses, the best defense is a good offense: fool the body's immune system into thinking it has encountered a dangerous virus so its protective force of antibodies will be already alerted when and if the real virus ever arrives. The agent of this deception is called a vaccine, in honor of the vaccinia virus used by Edward Jenner in 1796 to induce artificial immunity to smallpox. *Vacca* is the Latin word for cow, and Jenner's discovery that a deliberate infection with the relatively mild disease of cowpox could protect people against the much more deadly smallpox began the industry of vaccine production.

Like many good doctors, Jenner had no clear idea of why his treatment succeeded. Louis Pasteur, working a century later, is generally regarded as the father of immunology—although he produced his rabies vaccine in 1885 without realizing that he was mobilizing the body against a still-unidentified agent of disease. The name "virus" comes from the Latin word for poisonous slime, which is what Martinus Willem Beijerinck thought he had discovered in 1898 when he found something even smaller than bacteria that was causing disease in the tobacco plants he studied. Over the next ten years, it became clear that the "poison" was in fact a microorganism, smaller than the smallest bacterium. It was not until 1935 that Wendell Stanley, a biochemist at the Rockefeller Institute, identified the protein that marks viruses as a form of life.

At the beginning of the twentieth century, there were less than a dozen viral diseases known to afflict human beings. Smallpox, the greatest terror, had been tamed by vaccination long before anybody had any idea what they were vaccinating against. Chickenpox, measles, and influenza were all to be feared, but most people survived their ravages. Rabies, transmitted through the bites and scratches of infected animals, had meant a slow, terrible death until the first success of Pasteur's vaccine, made from carefully dried particles of the brains of infected sheep and rabbits. The search for a vaccine against poliomyelitis began in 1916.

Twenty-two years later, when the National Foundation for Infantile Paralysis began providing significant amounts of money for polio research, scientists knew that poliomyelitis was a viral disease, that it attacked the cells of the nervous system, that at least half of the people infected recovered with no residual paralysis, that children between the ages of five and eight seemed to be most susceptible, and that epidemics appeared to occur only in the so-called "developed" nations of the world. Before they could discover an effective protection against polio they would have to achieve two major changes in the state of scientific understanding. The first was to learn a great deal more about the virus that caused poliomyelitis and the course of the disease. The second was to adjust to the startling idea that the foundation that supported their work fully expected its investment to result in a marketable product that would justify their years of fund-raising.

During World War II, most of the National Foundation budget had gone to patient care and professional education, and there had been little progress on polio research. Many of the most original and energetic microbiologists were in the armed forces, working on the dangerous and unfamiliar diseases that threatened American troops in the Pacific and in North Africa, or were working as civilians on projects that had a higher military priority than polio research. Laboratories that remained in operation had lost both staff and equipment to the war effort, and those scientists who continued to pursue the problems of polio were often older people who were professionally committed to areas of experimentation that showed little hope of significant progress.

After the war, however, there was a great flowering of interest in all fields of scientific research. The atom bombs dropped on Hiroshima and Nagasaki introduced a new and lasting terror to the earth, but they also brought new prominence to the physicists who built them and created a surge of interest and respect for all areas of scientific investigation. Laboratory research, long regarded as a tedious occupation of little public interest, suddenly became a source of glamour, prestige, and national influence.

It had also become a very expensive enterprise. It is fashionable among the more avant-garde sociologists and historians of science to talk about researchers conducting a commerce in credibility, using their stature as expert investigators to negotiate for personal fame and fortune. Before they can trade on the value of their reputations, however, the people who work in laboratories have to deal with the far more common currency needed to buy the goods that build those reputations. Forty years ago, most research scientists were affiliated with a university or teaching hospital, but their salaries and operating budgets could not possibly pay for the expenses of sophisticated research. They needed money to free their time from teaching and other routine duties, money to buy the enormously expensive machines and materials necessary to modern research, and money to hire the lab assistants needed to run the machines. The era of the outside grant had arrived.

Many of these new grants came from the federal government. By 1947, NIH grants to outside investigators—scientists who were not members of the Public Health Service—jumped from the meager $180,000 of 1945 to $4 million—and in 1947, $4 million could still buy a great many microscopes and Bunsen burners. Little of this money went to polio research, however. The people at the NIH were far more interested in cancer (which still receives the largest portion of federal allocations for medical research), and they reasoned, with some justice, that the continuing enigma of poliomyelitis was receiving adequate attention from the National Foundation for Infantile Paralysis. In 1947 National Foundation research grants totaled slightly less than half the funds available from the National Institutes of Health —but the grants came with far fewer regulations, and they were all for polio research.

The result of this postwar resurgence of research was remarkably fast progress in the search for ways to combat polio. In 1946 the prospects for a usable polio vaccine were little better than they had been ten years before. By 1949 foundation publicists were openly predicting that there would be a vaccine ready for testing in three or four years. Dr. Albert Sabin, who published his first study of poliovirus in 1931 and introduced his own oral polio vaccine in 1959, protested that the statements were misleading and the program they described was hopeless and impracticable. With the support of other prominent researchers working under National Foundation grants, he convinced Basil O'Connor to withdraw the offending publications, but in this case he was wrong and the pamphlet writers were correct. After twenty years of scattered progress, people were beginning to find the answers to some of their most urgent questions about the nature and behavior of the poliovirus. Understanding the virus was the most important step toward developing a vaccine.

To appreciate what happened next, you have to go back to the confluence of science, money, and academic expansion that changed the business of research in the years immediately after the Second World War. More specifically, you have to consider how that confluence flowed through the rocky hills of western Pennsylvania, where the University of Pittsburgh is located.

Pittsburgh has spent most of the twentieth century climbing out of the sooty abyss of its own reputation for economic depression and industrial squalor, a civic revival so prolonged that local leaders have started numbering its stages like movie sequels. Amid the talk of Renaissance I and Renaissance II, it is hard sometimes to remember how very prosperous the area was in the half century after the Civil War. The buried riches of oil, gas, and coal that fueled the local fortunes are memorialized in the scarred landscape of mines and mills, and in the names of communities near Pittsburgh: Bessemer, Coal Bluff, Coal Brook, Coal Center, Coal Valley, Cokeburg, Energy, Nu Mine, Petrolia.

In the days when the steel mills were booming and the immigrants were pouring into western Pennsylvania to work there, Pittsburgh was a place of constant black skies and blacker buildings, and "filthy rich" was a simple description of fact. "Hell with the lid taken off" was one popular description of the local climate, where the soot could get so bad you needed to drive with your headlights on in the middle of a sunny day. There was a strong element of pride in the tales of suffering, and a firm belief in the miner's truism "Where there's muck there's money." Most of the residents got the dirt without the dollars, but they still recognized their soot for what it was, a mantle of prosperity that lay over the city as much as the endowments of the Carnegies, the Mellons, and the Fricks.

After World War II, though, a few people started having their doubts about being known exclusively for steel and smoke. More specifically, Richard King Mellon changed his mind and brought the rest of the city leaders—elected and otherwise—

over to his way of thinking. With the promise of backing from the city's donors, most of them Republicans, newly elected Democratic Mayor David L. Lawrence began to forge alliances with local industry and community groups to work together for the transformation of Pittsburgh, and in 1946 the city started an ambitious program of pollution abatement, urban renewal, flood control and plain old-fashioned washing that was designed to rescue the downtown triangle from the seedy wreck it had become and to turn the city as a whole into a promising site for a variety of businesses.

As part of this grand scheme of civic rehabilitation, the rather modest local institution known as the University of Pittsburgh was targeted to receive a great deal of money—money that was going to make it into a national power on the intellectual scene and also turn it into a training ground for the sophisticated scientists and technical workers who would be needed to push the local economy into the twenty-first century. The largess that had first gone to institutions of art and recreation—libraries, museums, public parks—was now ready to turn to the support and promotion of medical science.

Over the next ten years, the A. W. Mellon Educational and Charitable Trust, the R. K. Mellon Foundation, and the Sarah Mellon Scaife Foundation gave over $26 million to the University of Pittsburgh for various medical-related programs. Part of it went to create a new School of Public Health directed by Dr. Thomas Parran, the crusading former surgeon general who became notorious when he instituted public screening programs for syphilis and gonorrhea. Part went to establish a program in pediatric psychiatry led by Dr. Benjamin Spock, author of the book that was fast becoming the bible of childcare to the postwar generation of parents. Part went to improve the University Health Center and start new research programs, including one in virus research. Part went to fund a general mandate to hire as many bright young lights as possible and bring them to Pittsburgh, where they would be given every opportunity to bring honor and glory to themselves, the university, and the city of Pittsburgh. One of the first of these to arrive was Dr. Jonas Salk, who came in the fall of 1947 as associate professor of bacteriology and microbiology.

If you look at a current map of the University of Pittsburgh campus, you will see a building marked Salk Hall, which now houses the dental school. If you go there, you'll find a brass plaque that marks the building's first incarnation as Municipal Hospital, built for the city of Pittsburgh in 1940 by the New Deal's Public Works Administration. Designed for the care and isolation of people suffering from contagious disease, the hospital opened on the morning of the bright new day of sulfa drugs and antibiotics, the "wonder drugs" that made long hospital stays unnecessary. Soon there weren't nearly enough patients to fill the contagious wards. By 1947 the University of Pittsburgh had arranged with Mayor Lawrence to use some of the empty wards for the expanding medical school and the new School of Public Health. It was here that Salk and his associates at the Virus Research Laboratory developed the first effective vaccine to give immunity against paralytic poliomyelitis, an achievement that rightly catapulted Salk to the rank of international hero. For the second half of the twentieth century, Jonas Salk's career has stood as the measure for dedication, hard work, and brilliant success, all applied to the welfare of others. All of this is true, but to these qualities must be added the pull of circumstance and the guiding hand of chance.

Born in 1914 in New York City, the oldest son of Russian Jewish immigrant parents, Salk had been raised in the expectation that he would make his parents proud. He had graduated from Townsend Harris High School, one of New York City's highly competitive "elite" public schools, and went on to fulfill the classic immigrant dream of upward mobility by becoming a doctor. On June 8, 1939, he received his medical degree from New York University and the next day he married Donna Lindsay, whose father had insisted they delay the wedding until he could announce that his daughter had married a doctor.

Even before he began his two-year internship at New York's Mount Sinai Hospital, Salk had decided to forego the practice of medicine for a career in research. He had attended research seminars in medical school, and for several months after graduation he had done virus research in the laboratory of the highly respected Dr. Thomas Francis, Jr., who had recently left the Rockefeller Institute to become a professor of bacteriology at New York University Medical School. Francis soon left NYU to direct the new School of Public Health at the University of Michigan in Ann Arbor, where, in September 1941, he received a letter from Salk in which the young man stated his earnest and urgent desire to work with Dr. Francis when his internship was over.

For a research scientist, the choice of a first laboratory is a very important decision. Most research projects are group efforts, and the people who work on them are described as the laboratory team. The team you start with will often determine the direction of your research for quite some time, perhaps for the rest of your career. Even more crucial than the choice of subject, however, is the chance of getting a good mentor. A fledgling scientist is helped enormously by a project director who is able to get funding, and whose name at the top of a paper will command the attention of the editors of the most important professional journals. If you can find a director who has a national reputation but is still sufficiently aware of his assistants' needs to acknowledge their own work and allow them to develop their own reputations in the field, that is paradise indeed.

Thomas Francis' attitude toward Salk was characterized more by respect for his abilities and bemused tolerance for his ambitions than by the personal and intellectual kinship that makes for great creative partnership. Still he was perfectly willing to have him join the laboratory team in Ann Arbor, and welcomed the extra enthusiasm Salk would bring to his work.

If there had been an equivalent opportunity closer to home, Salk probably would have taken it. Many people had noted his interest in research and his willingness to work hard, but Francis was the only one who had encouraged Salk's hopes for a laboratory career. While in medical school, Salk had applied several times to the Rockefeller Institute for a research position, but had been turned down at each application. Other places he applied to made it extremely clear that they had no interest in hiring Jewish doctors. Mount Sinai Hospital, so closely affiliated with the Jewish community, could not be accused of the anti-

Semitism then so common in academic life, but the hospital was famous for never hiring its own interns.

For several weeks, Salk pondered his future. Although Francis had said they knew each other quite well enough to dispense with an interview, Salk went to Ann Arbor to discuss his best course of action. Should he start his career in a school of public health? Should he spend some time studying plant viruses first? Should he apply for one of the new National Research Council fellowships for young investigators that the National Foundation was funding as a way of training a new generation of virologists? It was all very confusing and, at the same time, very important.

Like almost everybody else, Salk had his plans rearranged by the fortunes of war. In December 1941 Congress declared war and the New York City draft board informed Jonas Salk that he had until March 1, 1942, to apply for a commission as a doctor in the armed forces, be classified 1A for induction into the infantry, or present the board with a letter showing that his research was vital to the national defense. Thomas Francis' laboratory, working under contract for the Armed Forces Epidemiological Board, was demonstrably engaged in war-related research, and other possibilities were quickly abandoned.

Francis' field of interest was influenza, a disease that had cast a long shadow on the minds of military planners even before the United States had entered World War II. The senior health officers of the army were all old enough to remember the devastating epidemic of "Spanish influenza" that had swept through Europe and the United States in 1918, when many soldiers were still on military bases awaiting discharge or transport home. More American soldiers died of influenza than had died in combat, and the army was understandably eager to support any work that would help develop a vaccine against that disease.

On April 12, 1942, Jonas Salk arrived in Ann Arbor, where for the next six years he worked on influenza virus research, experimenting with different methods of virus inactivation and vaccine production and mastering the skills that would enable him to develop—and test—a polio vaccine. Except for a summer at the marine biology lab at Woods Hole, Massachusetts, where he had met his wife, he had never lived outside New York City.

Donna Salk, also a New Yorker and already started in her own career as a social worker there, was astonished to learn that they were moving to what seemed like the middle of nowhere, and dismayed by the scarce, dilapidated, expensive housing in Ann Arbor. But if living conditions at the University of Michigan lacked the polish of New York, the special nature of Francis' lab gave Jonas Salk not only the grounding he would need in the technical intricacies of vaccine preparation and testing, but also in the politics and ethics of laboratory life.

Unlike many other virus workers, Thomas Francis saw himself first as an epidemiologist, concerned with the practical application of laboratory findings to the conquest of disease. Pressure from the army for a usable vaccine led to a great many experiments in ways to "kill" the influenza virus, which Francis considered a more promising technique for vaccine production than trying to breed less infectious strains. The extreme variability of the influenza virus itself, with over one hundred strains, forced his laboratory team to become experts in packing as many different strains as possible into a single dose of vaccine. As an added benefit, Dr. Francis was a very busy man, and as time passed he was happy to give his new associate administrative experience with the Army Commission on Influenza, of which Francis was director.

The relationship was not always smooth. The son of a lay minister who had emigrated from Scotland to Gas City, Indiana, Thomas Francis was a man of rigid standards who regarded a career in science, like a career in the church, as a vocation whose virtues justified a degree of self-denial. In a profession where rank and status are often determined by the order of names on published papers, Francis was more amused than offended by Salk's frank ambition to have his name at the top of the list, but he wouldn't tolerate the young man's desire to publish experimental results before Francis thought they had really been confirmed. Salk's occasional interest in taking on outside consulting jobs was even less acceptable, and on more than one occasion his director had to make it clear that if Salk could not make the financial sacrifices an academic career demanded, he would simply have to leave the laboratory. Forty-seven hundred dollars a year was quite a good wage for someone in his position, and Francis felt perfectly comfortable reminding Salk "that academic work never permitted the same affluence which many other activities did." He himself had turned down the offer of a very comfortable job as private physician to the Rockefeller family, complete with a house on the grounds of their estate at Pocantico Hills, to come to Ann Arbor, and he expected his associates to pursue their work in the same spirit of disinterested dedication.

When Salk had gone to Ann Arbor in 1942, he had been a young man seeking the apprenticeship that would start him in a career of laboratory research. By 1947, thirty-three years old and the father of two sons, he was eager to shape his own research and manage his own lab. In the jargon of the profession, he wanted to become a principal investigator, but to do that he would have to leave the shadow of Thomas Francis. Once again, however, the world was slow to acknowledge Salk's potential. He had applied for openings at one of the branches of the University of California and at Western Reserve in Cleveland, but was turned down for both. Negotiations to return to Mount Sinai Hospital to set up an immunology lab floundered when the hospital refused to provide the facilities Salk wanted. And then there appeared the offer to come to Pittsburgh.

In the delicate task of recruiting people to come to a lower-echelon school in a city with a reputation as a horrible place to live, William S. McEllroy, dean of the Medical School, knew what appealed to researchers: space, staff, equipment, and independence. Salk visited Pittsburgh in the spring of 1947, and McEllroy made large, airy gestures to describe the huge opportunities that beckoned there. Everyone in Ann Arbor thought Salk was making a big mistake, and Francis even offered to hold his position open for a year, in case he changed his mind, but the next fall the Salks moved to Pennsylvania, renting a house in the comparatively rural town of Wexford, a half-hour's drive from the university. When Salk got to the medical school, it was clear that McEllroy hadn't been exaggerating about the boundless possibilities presented by the job. Indeed, there was almost nothing there but possibilities.

Municipal Hospital did have a good deal of empty space, but the part rented to the Virus Research Lab was only a small area in the basement that would have to be completely remodeled before it was ready for laboratory work. Furthermore, despite McEllroy's assurances of independence, any changes Salk made would have to be approved by Dr. Max Lauffer, who was officially in charge of the university's virus research program.

Immediately, this created problems. Lauffer was a biophysicist with an appointment in the Physics Department, not the Medical School. His specialty was plant pathology, and while he had hired Salk, he neither knew nor cared a great deal about Salk's emphasis on the new science of immunology. He was also a somewhat fussy administrator, and the restraints and conditions he imposed had already driven off the first man he had hired for Salk's position. Details of professional etiquette had to be observed, like the impossibility of Salk's hiring a secretary who was paid more than Lauffer's, and every requisition Salk made, from laboratory benches to paper clips, had to be approved.

Looking back, Salk called the arrangement naive, and wondered at his own innocence in thinking it could have worked. Still, a laboratory of his own was a treasure not to be forsaken. Something wonderful could always happen. Soon there would be a School of Public Health that might provide a home for his lab, as the School of Public Health in Ann Arbor had for Tommy Francis. In the meantime, he began to maneuver, seeing what could be done to improve his situation. Salk had always been inclined to regard cumbersome regulations as technicalities that could and should be circumvented by a creative mind. It was an attitude that had led to friction with Francis and would create problems with other colleagues later on, but in this case, at least, he was right. Before many months had passed, Salk told McEllroy that he would need an independent appointment if they expected him to stay at Pittsburgh, and by the end of his first year he had left the Faculty of Arts and Sciences to become a professor at the Medical School, reporting directly to McEllroy, the dean.

It was hardly a prestigious appointment. In 1947 the University of Pittsburgh Medical School would not have appeared on anybody's list of top medical centers. Its students were all local people, it had few facilities, and its research program was almost nonexistent. Teaching at the Medical School was considered a marginal obligation of someone practicing medicine in Pittsburgh, and Salk was the first, and only, full-time member of the faculty. In terms of the kind of virus research Salk had been doing, Pitt was about as far from the center of the action as he could go without falling off the edge of the earth.

At least there was the chance of space and the hope of money. In the past, his work had been supported by the army and by the National Foundation, which had a longstanding commitment to the basic virus research done in Thomas Francis' lab, but neither of those sources was interested in the kinds of "bricks and mortar" grants needed to build a laboratory. Individual donors and private philanthropies, however, have an almost hypnotic attraction to buildings. Through the Sarah Mellon Scaife Foundation, Salk secured a $12,500 grant to renovate a forty-by-forty-foot space in the basement of Municipal Hospital. Coupled with the funding he had from the army to continue a long-term influenza study at Fort Dix, New Jersey, he now had enough money to get by.

Getting by was not quite what Salk had envisioned, however. He wanted the kind of success that leads to power—the power to attract grants and students and interesting projects. Nothing of note would come out of a forty-foot-square laboratory operating on an academic budget. With more outside funding, Salk could follow his own path, pursuing questions of immunology and vaccinology on a much larger scale than Max Lauffer or anybody else had envisioned. With enough outside funding, it didn't really matter what other people at the University of Pittsburgh thought of him. It's very hard to remain a subdivision when your space, your staff, and your budget are all bigger than the whole of which you are supposed to be a part. To give his laboratory the size and scope he wanted, Salk took on a well-funded assignment that was outside his immediate field of interest. He agreed to participate in the virus-typing project sponsored by the National Foundation for Infantile Paralysis.

II

THE VARIETY AND INSTABILITY OF VIRUSES HAS ALWAYS BEEN a problem for people trying to study them. Viruses can mutate, changing so rapidly that vaccination against a current strain offers no real protection against whatever may be coming along next season. This is why there is no vaccine that offers lifetime immunity to influenza. Epidemiologists track influenza outbreaks the same way meteorologists track tropical storms; if a particularly violent strain seems about to devastate an area, laboratories scramble to produce enough vaccine from that particular type of influenza virus to protect the most susceptible people.

Even a stable virus may have several strains, and for some time polio researchers had suspected that there was more than one type of poliovirus. By 1948 Howard Howe and David Bodian, working at Johns Hopkins University, and John Paul and James Trask at Yale, had completed separate studies showing at least three separate strains of poliovirus. Since every strain would have to be included in any successful vaccine, the question then became whether there were no *more* than three. The only way to answer that was to test the many different samples of poliovirus isolated from patients across the country over the years, to see if they all matched one or another of the three strains already identified. To lessen the possibility of error, four different laboratories were to test one hundred different samples of virus. Following different procedures, each laboratory would "type" the viruses, according to strain, and compare their results. The entire project was expected to last about three years.

The virus-typing project was an essential step in the under-standing of poliovirus, and a necessary precursor to the devel-opment of any future vaccine. It was also a job that was dauntingly, staggeringly, stupefyingly dull. Its main attributes were constant repetition of the same small procedure, endless waiting for results, painstaking attention to detail and method—and a clear certainty that no glory lay at the end of all the effort. It was the laboratory equivalent of sorting beans, and there's little wonder that the leading lights of the research community were happy to pass it on to others. People like Howe and Bodian at Johns Hopkins, Paul at Yale, Albert Sabin at the University of Cincinnati, or Thomas Francis at the University of Michigan—people whose names were immediately associated with polio research and respected around the world—were more than happy to design the project and evaluate the results, but they wanted nothing to do with the actual work. For that the National Foundation had to seek out laboratory directors who were either reliable, capable technicians without higher ambi-tions, or else were very young and very hungry.

Salk was in the "young and hungry" category. He worried about polio as much as any parent of young children—and by now Salk was the father of three young sons—but he felt no personal mission to save the world from its ravages. All his research had been in influenza, where he had had promising results in creating vaccines that protected against several strains of virus, and he intended to keep that focus. The National Foundation's virus-typing program would be menial but liber-ating, he told himself—a simple job that could run itself while he was busy on other projects, and a means to expand both the size and the equipment of his laboratory in ways that would remain long after the various strains of poliovirus were iden-tified, labeled, and forgotten. Then, too, he imagined it would be interesting to learn something about poliovirus.

The National Foundation directors who had chosen Salk's laboratory as one of the four virus-typing centers didn't mind a bit of careerist greed as long as it got the job done. In fact, they welcomed Salk's ambitions, overjoyed to find someone whose vision wasn't restricted to the small, cautious scale of academic research and who didn't freeze in terror when you mentioned the possibility of vaccination. Salk was proud of having maneuvered around a restrictive budget to find another source of money, but he was now working with people far wilier and more experienced than he. Their scheming was to get someone to find an end to polio. Dr. Salk fell gladly into their toils.

The first person Salk dealt with was Dr. Harry Weaver, who deserves much of the credit for steering the young immunologist into polio research. Weaver had been a professor of anatomy at Wayne State University in Detroit, where he had worked on various National Foundation programs. In 1946, when Basil O'Connor left the Red Cross and decided to give the considerable force of his full attention to the problem of polio, he brought Weaver to New York to be the foundation's director of research.

The National Foundation had never had a director of research before, and the scientific advisors on the Committee on Research thought it was a terrible idea to get one. There was a considerable difference, they told O'Connor, between choosing among existing projects for those that best deserved support, and "directing" researchers toward the projects the foundation wanted done. Any attempt to guide research, they felt, would stifle initiative, offend the independent thinking demanded of science, and alienate the most creative and productive scientists in a way that would defeat its own purpose. O'Connor, who had a somewhat lower opinion of the sacred independence of scientific research than did the members of his advisory committee, went ahead with the appointment anyway.

Like Basil O'Connor, Harry Weaver was a man of huge self-confidence. He also shared O'Connor's fondness for big solutions and grand gestures, and he matched this largeness of vision with a considerably deeper understanding of the way that scientists work and think. Weaver had a genius for balancing the individual needs, abilities, and egos of his many grantees with the larger question of what would need to be done in polio research over the near and distant future.

One of his grand designs—or at least it seemed grand in the somewhat confined world of laboratory science—was to cut through the isolation of separate laboratories and the slowness of communication that resulted when research findings were published in professional journals. He did this by persuading foundation grantees to let him publish and distribute their progress reports, and by instituting a series of round-table conferences on central areas of research—conferences paid for by the National Foundation for Infantile Paralysis, held in luxury hotels in attractive cities, and attended by stenographers who recorded the discussion for later reference. In a profession marked by jealousy and competition, where secrecy was simply a prudent defense against scathing attacks on theories not yet backed with the most extensive of proof, Weaver's round-table conferences were a revolutionary change. What made them possible was the fact that Weaver gave out huge amounts of money for research he liked—research that showed promise of having some practical effect on polio.

Scientists who were used to the measured pace of academic research, where even the most modest appropriation required a conference with the dean, were stunned by Harry Weaver's methods of operation. Some, eager to expand their studies, couldn't believe their good fortune in meeting up with this brusque stranger who gave them hundreds of dollars for chimps and cages and lab equipment just for the asking. Others, particularly those outside the polio field, regarded him as an agent of corruption who had arrived to seduce their best workers, luring them away from the cloistered pursuit of pure science and into the more aggressive world of result-oriented applied research. Weaver was all for basic research, but with the clear understanding that the basics were going to lead to results, and the sooner the better.

Not that he ever spelled it out in quite that way, or at least not to anyone but Basil O'Connor. Having dinner together at "21" or one of the other expensive restaurants O'Connor favored, Weaver could be as blunt as he liked. In the more public forums of professional conferences or site visits, he cultivated the scientists with the kind of close attention usually reserved for opera singers, racehorses, and other performers of great talent and unstable temper. He admired their laboratories, took them out to dinner, encouraged them to see him in New York and to use his office as a kind of central intelligence depot through which they could discover what other people were up to. In the process, he often "discovered" new areas of research the investigators hadn't quite realized they were pursuing until their own brilliant path was illuminated by the light of Harry Weaver's educated enthusiasm. The round-table conferences, with agendas and attendees chosen by the National Foundation for Infantile Paralysis, were an admirable way for researchers to air both grievances and progress, for Weaver to keep abreast of far-flung developments, and, most subtly, for him to plant ideas about new directions that would blossom in the hearts, minds, and laboratories of others.

Nonetheless, Harry Weaver was hardly Mephistopheles, luring innocents to betray loyalties and values so fundamental they could scarcely be spoken, any more than Jonas Salk was Faust, selling his soul for forbidden knowledge. Weaver was an able executive with a large budget and an eye for people who could produce. Salk was an ambitious young scientist and a good manager, juggling administrative work against laboratory work, career against family, fully aware that the commodity in least supply was time. Salk had been brought to Pittsburgh because he was promising, and it's hard for a research scientist to be promising after forty. You can be productive, creative, accomplished, wise, influential, and even original, but it's hard to sell yourself on expectations. When the virus-typing program came up, Salk's career clock was ticking loudly, and the offer was irresistible.

If Harry Weaver pushed polio research forward, the person who kept it from dissolving into acrimonious competition was Dr. Thomas Milton Rivers of the Rockefeller Institute, who would eventually become a spirited supporter of Salk's work. Rivers had worked as an unpaid advisor for the National Foundation since 1936, when the foundation was still known as the President's Birthday Ball Commission and he had been the loudest critic of both the Brodie and the Kolmer vaccines. A short, broad, blunt-spoken self-professed country boy from Georgia, Rivers had gotten his medical degree at Johns Hopkins in 1916, when that was one of the few "modern" medical schools in the country, and had trained as a pediatrician before deciding to abandon clinical practice for laboratory research. He had come to New York in 1922 to develop a laboratory for the study of viral diseases at the Rockefeller Institute, and was considered by many to have founded the independent study of virology in 1926 when he had asserted that viruses, unlike bacteria, were parasitic organisms unable to reproduce outside of living cells. By 1935, the Rockefeller Institute was the center for virus research in the United States, and a whole generation of virologists—the first—trained at Rivers' lab.

As chairman of the National Foundation's committee on research, Rivers had been quite vocal on the subject of how insulted and stifled the research scientists would be if O'Connor hired Harry Weaver as director of research. In his own way, however, Rivers was just as hardheaded as Weaver and just as interested in the bottom line of improving health. Like Weaver, Rivers was also bold and self-assured, a man who was able to keep things moving in the right direction. Where Weaver was suspected of trying to turn the National Foundation into a commercial research-and-development organization, however, Rivers was the official keeper of the flame of Sacred Science.

Rivers was a man of determined opinions, none of which he ever hesitated to express. Having come of age in an era when medical treatment was often more dangerous than the ailment it proposed to cure, he had a keen sense of the hazards of experimentation and the fallibility of diagnoses. His medical conservatism was the product of experience, however, not of a blind resistance to change, and his well-known tendency to doubt cures and anticipate deadly side effects was matched by an enlightened certainty that cures did in fact exist, and would be discovered through careful laboratory work. Tom Rivers had dedicated his career to finding laboratory solutions to medical problems, and when he became convinced that something really promising was out there, he was ready to let out the hounds and chase it down.

He and O'Connor had spent years jousting with each other over the direction of the foundation's programs, and they had developed a respect for each other's powers that made them the best of friends in those intervals when they were not the best of enemies. "That old man didn't know any more about science than my left shoe," Rivers said of O'Connor, "but he was willing to learn." "He was extremely learned," O'Connor said of Rivers, "but not what you'd call exceedingly bright." Rivers lacked the scintillating intellect that O'Connor admired, but he gave the National Foundation programs a scientific credibility that would have been hard to equal. One would have to be a very brave soul indeed to question the value of a study approved by Dr. Rivers.

Encouraged by the financial support of the National Foundation and the moral support of both Harry Weaver and Tom Rivers, Jonas Salk began to expand his laboratory team. Byron Bennett, a hard-drinking, self-educated Texan who had taught himself how to do virus research, had met Salk when Salk was acting head of the Army Influenza Commission, taking over for Thomas Francis. Despite his lack of advanced degrees, Bennett was an extremely talented laboratory technician, and Salk had persuaded him to leave the army's Walter Reed Hospital even before the virus-typing project began.

Bennett was soon joined in the laboratory by Dr. Julius Youngner, who came from the National Cancer Institute at the NIH to work as Salk's chief assistant. Youngner, four years younger than Salk, had also grown up in New York City and graduated from New York University. From there he had gone to do graduate work in bacteriology at the University of Michigan Medical School. The two men had never met in Ann Arbor, but a mutual friend suggested Youngner might be the associate Salk needed to handle the increased work of the virus-typing program. Not long after, the team was expanded to include Dr. L. James Lewis, a bacteriologist who had worked for several pharmaceutical companies. Salk himself did little work at the laboratory bench, but he was the engine that organized this group and got it going.

Salk sometimes had difficulty dealing with people of divergent scientific thinking, but he got along very well with those who agreed to make his interests and scientific opinions their own. Warm, authoritative, respectful of people's individual skills and talents but always comfortable with the responsibility of providing directions and decisions, he was in many ways an ideal boss, and he fostered an extraordinary degree of loyalty. Francis Yurochko, who became his animal technician in 1949, caring for the large colony of test animals that lived and sometimes died in Municipal Hospital, stayed with him for over thirty years. So did Elsie Ward, a lab technician who came to work for Salk in 1950. So did Lorraine Friedman, who arrived as his executive secretary in 1948 and still held that position forty years later.

In time, the Virus Research Laboratory would expand to cover three floors of Municipal Hospital and employ over fifty people, but this was the core team. All were young and eager, all were searching for the satisfaction of hard work well done, and none had any prior reputation to defend or prior defeats to justify. The research staff was also united in having all had experience in the practical application of biomedical research, whether for drug companies or in the army. Later the sense of fellowship would crumble, but for the six years from 1949 to 1955, the years when the first polio vaccine was developed and tested, they worked as a coherent and extremely innovative group, bringing together a wide range of complementary skills and, equally important, a liberating absence of convictions about what could or could not be done in making vaccines.

What followed next was a great deal of very hard work, much of it dogged, some of it inspired, all of it performed under enormous pressure. People who were working in the lab came in at all sorts of odd hours to tend the animals and check on their experiments. Saturday, supposed to be a half day, seemed to go on a good while after lunch, and five o'clock meant nothing when there was work to be finished.

New work required more space, and the carpenters were around so often it must have seemed at times that they should be issued laboratory coats. From a small space in the basement, once the site of the hospital morgue, the laboratory grew until it was renting several upper floors of the hospital building. Two large storage closets became temperature-controlled chambers for producing poliovirus: a warm room, lined with stainless steel shelves, where virus was incubated, and then a cold room next door, kept at a constant 32 degrees Fahrenheit, for holding virus samples stable. Down another hall was Salk's office, re-modeled from a staff lounge, and the original lab he set up in space that had been an auditorium. The monkey quarters were in the basement, on the site of some old storerooms; additional labs were three floors up. On the floors in between were the active hospital wards. People who worked at the Virus Research Laboratory saw the victims of polio every day, just by going about their business, and it gave a special urgency to their work.

Many of the materials Salk needed for his renovations were in short supply, their distribution still governed by military priorities, and much of what he was doing required equipment he had to design himself, and redesign when it didn't quite work, and reorder when the company sent the wrong thing, as seemed to happen so often. None of that obscured the joy of the venture. It was just plain fun to be able to build your own laboratory —to order the bottles and the test-tube racks, and the special desk where the file drawer had been fitted with a heating element for incubating cultures. What a pleasure it was to weigh the merits of wood shelves versus steel and finally go for the more expensive. What a marvelous experience to explain the real and urgent need for a new cage for a monkey and then have someone whip out his checkbook, just like that, and give you the money you needed. Touring the building for a television documentary a quarter century after he left Pittsburgh, Salk was thrilled to find pieces of his old laboratory still intact. "It's still here!" he exclaimed. "I spent so much money on this! I can't believe it's still here. When I got here, it was a dingy hospital with no facilities. Look at those stainless steel shelves! I designed it all myself."

Salk had imagined the virus-typing project as a dull but de-pendable investment of time that would produce a regular div-idend of money for his lab while he continued to pursue his prior commitments to influenza research. Being an obsessive fiddler, though, and working with other creative and accom-plished people, he soon saw its possibilities in a far more am-bitious light. A successful vaccine against poliomyelitis was at least as important as a vaccine against influenza. Influenza had killed hundreds of thousands of people, but polio had broken their hearts.

Before anybody could think about vaccines, though, they had to confirm that there were no more than three types of poliovirus. The first order of business was to improve the procedure set down for the typing program, a method of operation that was guaranteed to consume enormous amounts of time and huge numbers of monkeys. The stated plan was a textbook model of immunological testing: infect hundreds of monkeys with one or another of the three known strains of poliovirus, wait for them to recover, and then challenge them with standard doses of an unknown virus and chart their responses.

Since the unknown viruses differed as much in strength and power as any other living organisms differ, preparing these "standard" doses was a delicate, time-consuming, and frustratingly imprecise job. A monkey was to be infected with a virus of known type—say Type I. After it had succumbed and recovered (you hoped), it was then infected with a virus strain of unknown type. If it got sick again, the unknown strain was either Type II or Type III. That strain would then be injected into a monkey known to have recovered from an infection with a Type II virus. If there were no ill effects, the unknown strain was Type II. If the monkey got sick, it was Type III. Unless, of course, you had miscalculated your dose, which was very easy to do with virus strains of widely different degrees of virulence. Too weak a dose and you might mistake a very mild infection for prior immunity. Too strong a dose and you killed your monkey, which was a very inefficient use of animals. To guard against these kinds of mishaps and miscalculations, ten, twenty, or even thirty monkeys would be used for every stage of the operation.

Even worse than the difficult procedures and the imprecise results was the infuriating slowness of the process. As set down in the protocols for operation, the virus-typing project called for great stretches of waiting around: waiting for monkeys to get sick, recover, and get sick again; waiting for virus to multiply in blood samples; waiting for the titrations to be done; waiting for everyone else's results to come in so you could compare them with your own. It would be pure luck if the first group of monkeys proved to be immune to the unknown virus, meaning it was the same type as the virus used to infect them in the first place. More likely the whole process would have to be repeated with another group of monkeys that had been infected with another type of virus. Very possibly it would have to be done a third time, too, since the whole point of the project was to discover if there were any strains not included in the three types of polio against which the monkeys had been made immune. That would be big news, but nobody really expected it to happen. What they expected was three years of nailing down the proof of what they already believed was true.

As soon as Salk heard the plan for the typing program, he envisioned better ways of doing things. Perhaps mice could be used for some tests instead of monkeys. Perhaps antibody titres, the level of antibodies produced in response to a particular virus strain, could be tested at the same time that virus samples were being typed. Several weeks and dozens of animals could be saved by infecting a monkey first with an unidentified virus strain, and then "challenging" it with known strains. And then, most tantalizing of all, arose the possibility of doing without monkeys altogether for several stages of the work.

III

As far as anybody can tell, poliomyelitis is a disease that attacks only humans, monkeys, and chimpanzees. For decades scientists had been trying to give polio to mice, rats, rabbits, and other small, amiable, inexpensive, and readily available laboratory animals. Except in a very limited way, none had succeeded. If you wanted to do polio research, you had to assume you would be working with monkeys. Messy, silly, sickly, expensive, rare, and all-too-human monkeys. Leaving aside all the important questions of the ethics of animal research, working with monkeys was a true nuisance.

First there was the problem of supply. Although the breeding of animals for laboratory use was a well-established business, nobody had ever tried to breed monkeys. They were what suppliers call "random source" animals, as opposed to "purpose-bred" ones—which simply meant that the animal went about its business in the wild until someone with a big net came along and interrupted the party.

Capture was not always a simple affair, or free of outside considerations. Rhesus monkeys, the type most commonly used for laboratory research, are plentiful in India, but they are sacred to the Hindu religion, regarded as incarnations of the monkey god, Hanuman, an immortal hero who is also a fertility god and protector against whirlwinds. Only non-Hindus would work in the monkey-catching business, and then only during certain seasons. Supplies were unpredictable at best, and shipments halted altogether if the Indian government decided the animals were being mistreated in transit. This could easily happen, given the fact that the animals had to be shipped halfway across the world. Many died on the way, and more succumbed to unrelated diseases before they could be used for research. Cynomolgus monkeys from the Philippines suffered from polio in ways that were much closer to those of humans, and they were also much easier to work with. Cynomolgus monkeys can be taught to stand in line, for example, which is a trick that rhesus monkeys either cannot or will not master. Unfortunately, the cynomolgus monkeys were also much scarcer and more expensive than the rhesus, and just as susceptible to injury and disease.

Disease was the second major headache in working with monkeys. Even if by some miracle you had access to all the animals you needed, they were not always fit for the jobs that had to be done. Dysentery was a real problem, along with pneumonia, worms, and other parasites. Researchers supported by the National Foundation were always complaining to their funding committees about monkey morbidity. Committee chairmen then complained to Harry Weaver, and Weaver passed the problem on to Basil O'Connor himself. The estimate was that they would need as many as fifty thousand monkeys for the virus-typing program. If the monkeys that arrived from India were too sick to use, O'Connor decided, it was only an efficient protection of investment to see that they be nursed back to health.

Exercising his natural flair for large measures, O'Connor arranged for the National Foundation to establish a monkey conditioning center at a place called Okatie Farms in Pritchardville, South Carolina. The National Foundation would buy the animals and have them sent directly to Okatie Farms. There they would rest, recover their bearings, and recuperate from whatever diseases they had brought with them from home or picked up on the road. Only then would they be shipped out to laboratories around the country. Those that were too sick to recover would at least not take up laboratory time and effort. Although nobody thought of it in quite those terms, Okatie was in its way a little Warm Springs for monkeys, a rehabilitation facility that was also a center for research in the solution of problems nobody else cared much about.

People doing research under National Foundation grants were told they should buy all their monkeys from Okatie Farms, which was also happy to send along sacks of their scientifically developed dry monkey feed, along with instructions on how to mix it and tips on how to get the animals to eat it. A twenty-five-pound sack cost $2.50; a quarter of a pound, mixed with water to the consistency of friable putty, would feed one monkey for one day. Monkeys being monkeys, the experts at Okatie recommended dividing the daily ration into three portions so the animals would not have quite so much at any one time to fling around and mash in each other's ears and stuff down the drains and suchlike. On the other hand, it wouldn't do to mix a full day's batch in advance; the feed would harden like concrete if you left it around too long. In the collected correspondence of anybody working in polio research at the time, there were very fat files devoted entirely to the buying, shipping, delivering, housing, feeding, handling, and disposing of monkeys.

Once the monkeys were installed in the laboratory, their status remained a ticklish issue. On the one hand, they were there for experimental purposes, just another tool to be treated with no more sentiment or ceremony than the test tubes or microscopes or samples of horse serum taken from some poor dobbin stabled out in the garage. On the other hand, they were so *cute*. Children would be bribed with the promise of a visit to the monkeys in Daddy's lab if they would just hold still in the shoe store. Workers in other parts of the building would find excuses to drop in on the animals, just to say hello. At Municipal Hospital, patients and visitors alike were always asking the nurses to take them to see the monkeys. Everybody knew the animals were busy getting sick, or getting better, or eventually getting dead a good deal before their natural time. In the meantime, though, it was very cheering to watch their antics, and hard to feel outrage when you saw the wards full of paralyzed children upstairs.

The people who actually worked with monkeys had their own range of attitudes, less sentimental but no less complex. Jonas Salk arranged to have some of his discard animals donated to the zoo, but it was hardly something he fretted about if it wasn't possible. Tom Rivers was vehemently opposed to treating monkeys like pets, and he would get quite exercised if anybody referred to an experimental animal as "he" or "she." A monkey is an "it," Rivers always insisted. Thomas Francis bore with the monkeys as he did with many things, wryly. Over the years, he had sacrificed hundreds of monkeys and had written scores of letters to suppliers complaining about animals that arrived too sick to use, or about shipments that came on Sunday morning when no one was around to open the crates, or about feed orders that were so short they left him with a room full of starving, shrieking animals, but he retained a certain fondness for the beasts. On his desk he always kept a monkey skull, known to everyone as George, and the shelves of both his office and his study at home held a number of small stuffed toy monkeys, several carved wooden ones, and the classic triumvirate of monkeys hearing, speaking, and seeing no evil. Albert Sabin, who was rarely seen without his pipe, taught one of his monkeys to smoke cigars, and invited reporters to his laboratory to see this gentlemanly feat of scientific conditioning. There were lots of ways of handling the monkey question, but what you couldn't do was ignore it.

In designing his laboratories at Pittsburgh, Salk had spent a significant proportion of his time arranging the housing and feeding of his monkeys, as well as placating the assistants who had to work with them. Monkeys can be charming animals, but laboratory life doesn't always bring out their best humor, particularly under the rather Spartan conditions that prevailed forty years ago. It takes a special kind of person to work with monkeys—someone who can watch out for their welfare and keep up their spirits while also cleaning their messes and contending with the constant chance of bites and bashes, as well as the less likely but more frightening possibility of catching a deadly disease like encephalomyelitis. In 1949 Salk asked the National Foundation for money to buy a $10,000 life insurance policy "for each of the individuals who will be engaged in this extra-hazardous work." His request was denied, however, and his monkey handlers had to make do with whatever private insurance they could muster, and the first-aid help of the doctors in the lab.

Troublesome as they were to deal with, the monkeys deserved at least part of the credit for the massive support Salk received from the National Foundation. The initial decision to choose his lab for the virus-typing program was based not only on his ability and willingness to do the research but also on the important fact that the hospital where Salk had his laboratory had empty wards to house the animals. Although it was a rule they broke more often than they liked to admit, the officers of the National Foundation were opposed to spending money on construction. There was a certain irony, then, in the fact that Salk's biggest innovation in the virus-typing program was to reduce the number of monkeys needed for the project.

The virus-typing program was set up in 1948, to begin in 1949. That same year, Dr. John Enders and his associates Dr. Thomas H. Weller and Dr. Frederick C. Robbins, working at the Children's Hospital in Boston, succeeded in doing something that had been considered impossible: growing poliovirus outside the body in laboratory cultures of non-nervous-system human tissue. To understand this achievement, which won them the Nobel Prize in 1954, it helps to go back to the early years of virus study, when it had first become clear that viruses would not grow on the simple petri dishes and agar plates that made such comfortable homes for bacteria and molds. Harboring a menagerie full of sick animals as a source of viruses for laboratory study was neither pleasant nor convenient. How wonderful it would be to find some other way of maintaining living cells in which the viruses could thrive.

Alexis Carrel, the French biologist who worked at the Rockefeller Institute in the early years of the century, is widely regarded as the father of *in vitro* tissue culture, the process of growing living cells outside the body. His work with chick embryos, done in the years just before World War I, was the very stuff of science fiction. One did not have to be a biologist to contemplate with wonder the endless, infinite proliferation of embryonic cells he fostered, tiny pieces of life that would multiply but never mature. Carrel's original cultures were kept alive for many years after he himself left the Rockefeller Institute, partly out of curiosity to see if it could be done and partly, no doubt, out of reverence for these ancient bits of being, caught forever in a laboratory limbo between the chicken and the egg.

Carrel's discovery that he could take cells from the hearts of embryonic chickens, place them in test tubes in a nutrient solution and keep them alive indefinitely, provided the means by which it would be possible to produce viruses in a controlled laboratory setting. Translating possibility into fact was a tricky process that took a number of years, but by the mid-1930s several animal viruses had been cultured in laboratory flasks, as well as in the developing chicken embryos of fertile eggs. No one had succeeded in growing poliovirus, however, until 1936, when Albert Sabin and Peter Olitsky managed for the first time to cultivate poliovirus in test-tube cultures using human embryonic nervous tissue as their medium.

This was a dubious triumph, since their failure to culture the virus in other kinds of human tissue led to the erroneous but widely accepted conclusion that poliovirus multiplied only in the cells of the nervous system. It was a logical assumption, since polio damaged nervous-system tissue, but it raised major problems for vaccine research. Nervous-system tissue is notorious for provoking fatal allergic brain damage when injected into the human body—a fact that had been well established by none other than Tom Rivers. Since there was no way to be sure that all nervous-tissue cells were removed when "harvesting" virus from the culture medium, Sabin and Olitsky's findings made it seem highly unlikely that tissue-culture methods could be used to produce the large quantities of poliovirus that would be needed to make a vaccine.

John Enders was not particularly interested in polio when, in 1948, he showed that Sabin and Olitsky had been wrong. A tall, gaunt, laconic man who had a distaste for publicity and a fondness for slow, meticulous research, Enders was in some respects a throwback to the eighteenth-century tradition of the gentleman scientist, using the security of family money to pursue those subjects that interested him without having to worry about which would earn him the biggest salary. He had entered Yale in 1914, left to serve as an officer in the U.S. Naval Reserve Flying Corps in World War I, returned to New Haven to graduate in 1920, and had gone from there to do several years of work in the graduate program in English literature at Harvard. Instead of writing his doctoral dissertation, however, he transferred to Harvard Medical School, to pursue a Ph.D. in microbiology under the charismatic Hans Zinsser, whose lectures on bacteriology combined cosmopolitan wit with a crusader's fervor to conquer infectious disease.

Rising slowly from student to instructor, Enders eventually

became an associate professor of microbiology at Harvard Medical School, but grew restless with the demands of teaching and administration. During World War II, he worked for the Armed Forces Epidemiological Board devising diagnostic tests and methods of immunization for measles and mumps, and after the war he made yet another abrupt career change, resigning his position at Harvard Medical School to take a post of considerably lower prestige at Boston Children's Hospital, where he would be able to devote himself more exclusively to research.

In 1948 Enders had taken on two young associates, Tom Weller and Frederick C. Robbins, both graduates of the Harvard Medical School class of 1940 who had spent the war years as army bacteriologists. As so often happened in the small world of virus research, they had financial backing from the National Foundation for Infantile Paralysis. Enders' laboratory was supported in part by a National Foundation grant for basic research, and Robbins was paid through a National Research Council fellowship funded by the National Foundation. They were not working on polio, however, but on mumps and chickenpox, experimenting with the possibility of using tissue cultures to diagnose the many different infectious diseases their young patients carried. When Thomas Weller prepared a few too many tubes of culture medium for an experiment he was doing with chickenpox virus, Enders suggested he seed the extra tubes with some poliovirus he had in the laboratory freezer, sent by the National Foundation and shoved into storage some time ago. To everyone's intense interest, the virus grew even though the medium contained no nervous-system tissue cells. The exclusive affinity for nerve cells that Sabin and Olitsky had discovered would soon prove to have been a peculiarity of the type of poliovirus they had been using for their experiments. Using the advanced techniques of tissue culture Enders, Weller, and Robbins had developed, it would be feasible, for the first time, to produce enough poliovirus to make a vaccine.

Enders' tissue-culture techniques transformed virus production the same way John Deere's plow and Cyrus McCormick's reaper transformed agriculture. Before, polio researchers had to infect individual monkeys, coddle the animals until they achieved just the right degree of sickness, and then kill them to grind up their spinal columns and take the live virus within. A single monkey could provide enough virus to make only a few doses of vaccine, and there weren't enough monkeys on earth to produce sufficient virus for large-scale commercial production of vaccine. Now, however, laboratory workers would be able to prepare racks of tissue-culture tubes, each filled with a murky broth of tissue finely minced and suspended in a nutrient medium, "seed" the virus in the tubes, incubate them at a temperature between 96.8 and 98.6 degrees Fahrenheit, and "harvest" the entire crop at once. It took a fraction of the time and used only a small percentage of the monkeys required by the older methods.

Everybody in the polio business saw that Enders' breakthrough was staggering news. Astonishingly, only Jonas Salk began immediately to equip a lab for the new production techniques, recognizing at once that it offered a way of speeding the completion of the virus-typing project while simultaneously developing the means to produce a potential polio vaccine.

In growing poliovirus in glass tubes instead of in monkeys, Salk saved both time and money. Two hundred culture tubes could be prepared from the kidneys of a single monkey, whereas before a monkey could be used to test, at most, three samples of virus. Salk learned the trick from Enders, who took a few days instead of a few weeks to type a set of virus samples Salk sent him: seed a tissue-culture tube with unknown virus, challenge it with blood serum from a monkey or a human being known to have antibodies to one of the three types, and see what happens. Attacked by antibodies that match its type, the virus will die. This is the way the immune system works, and it's very exciting to watch the immune system duplicated under a laboratory microscope.

When Salk had first applied to the National Foundation for additional money to start a tissue-culture laboratory, his request had been denied. Undaunted, Salk marched his plan across the street to Dean McEllroy to see about getting another grant like the ones that had first helped him renovate Municipal Hospital. McEllroy had close ties to many Pittsburgh philanthropists, and by December Salk had $7,500 from the Spang Foundation. It wasn't a great deal of money, but it bought an incubator and roller drums and paid the salary of a technician, Elsie Ward, long enough for Salk to get started in the business of virus production through tissue-culture techniques.

On his next visit to Pittsburgh, when Harry Weaver saw what Salk was up to, he bought out the grant. Seven thousand five hundred dollars was a cheap price to pay for the phrase "financed by the National Foundation for Infantile Paralysis" that figured so prominently in the news releases about polio development. If Salk was going ahead with vaccine production anyway, reports on breakthrough developments "financed by the Spang Foundation" was not something Weaver wanted to have to live with for the rest of his life.

The question one asks now is why Enders himself did not proceed to make a polio vaccine, or why nobody else but Salk followed his lead. The answers are various, depending on the different circumstances of the careers of other people, but they all illustrate in one way or another the reason so many people in the academic research community resisted the applied science that making a vaccine entails.

Under the best of circumstances, making a vaccine is not a simple job. The object is to produce a form of the virus that will provoke a strong antibody response but not a powerful infection. The two basic strategies are either to kill the virus so it can no longer multiply or to weaken it until the infection it causes is so mild as to be harmless. Viruses are killed, or inactivated, by being heated, treated with radiation, or bathed in chemicals—most commonly formaldehyde—until they are no longer able to reproduce within the living cell. For a killed-virus vaccine, the idea is that the very presence of the foreign virus within the body will stimulate an antibody response, even without the galvanizing challenge of infection; the trick is to be sure that every single virus particle is really truly dead, and yet still have a product capable of causing immunity. By contrast, live-virus vaccines are made from viruses bred to be particularly weak. The "breeding," or attenuation, takes place in the laboratory as the disease is passed from monkey to monkey or from culture medium to culture medium. Proponents of live-virus vaccines believe that they create the most natural immune-system response; critics point out that a live-virus vaccine carries the small but very real possibility that the virus will at some point revert to its original virulent form and make somebody very sick.

Many people active in virus research were simply not interested in dealing with this kind of technical challenge. When Weller and Robbins had wanted to take that next step that making a vaccine entails, Enders had refused, saying his lab was not set up for polio vaccine production. Since no lab was, this can only be taken to mean that vaccine production was not something Enders wanted to do. Enders had no intention of submitting himself to what he correctly foresaw as a National Foundation juggernaut of promotion for any vaccine they supported. David Bodian, who probably contributed the greatest number of individual pieces to the puzzle of understanding polio, also dismissed the idea of vaccine production on the grounds that it was not his field. He was a pure scientist, and his colleagues in the Johns Hopkins group were all pure scientists, and they were not in the business of making vaccines.

Other researchers who *were* interested in making vaccines were delayed by distracting circumstances, or by their own failure to move quite as fast as Salk and his associates. Isabel Morgan, whose successful work in 1948 in immunizing monkeys with killed-virus polio vaccine had given her the initial lead in killed-virus vaccine work, had married in 1949 and left Johns Hopkins for the Westchester County Department of Laboratories and Research, outside New York City. Taking time out from her career to have a baby, she returned to find that Salk had overtaken her in vaccine production.

Some scientists rejected the idea of a killed-virus vaccine out of hand, and so had no incentive to plunge into the wholesale production of the virulent strains of virus then available. Albert Sabin was firmly convinced that the only vaccine that could provide lasting immunity was a live-virus vaccine. In time, he would become very interested in tissue-culture techniques for large-scale virus production, but in 1949 he was still working on virus passages and was hardly interested in starting in with a whole new method of producing something he didn't particularly need. John Paul and Joseph Melnick at Yale were experimenting with their own live-virus vaccine, and so was Hilary

Koprowski at the Lederle pharmaceutical company's labs, but no one's results had suggested that a massive field trial, much less mass production, was anywhere close at hand.

Without a clear need for large-scale production of poliovirus, few people were inclined to go to the trouble of setting up a tissue-culture production facility. Despite the homey language people use to describe the process, growing virus in a test tube is not as easy as growing beans in a garden. It takes a good deal of skill and practice to get a decent crop of virus from tissue culture. The cultures have to be kept at exactly the right temperature. The containers have to be the right size and shape, with the right kind of stoppers, and they have to be very, very clean. Before you sow your virus, you have to create the field in which it will grow, which for the early work with poliovirus was living cells of human tissue. The people who debated the ethics of using monkeys for laboratory experiments, and the politics of their import, never seem to have pondered for a moment the fact that the tissue used for much research was not monkey tissue but human, begged from maternity hospitals, mostly: the odd foreskins and placentas and stillbirths that had no use to the donors but were obviously much too valuable to discard.

Embryonic tissue grows much faster than adult tissue, and is much freer of disease, and so it is by far the preferred tissue for experimental work. The tissue Enders used for his cultures was taken from the foreskins of baby boys circumcised shortly after birth. They did not provide great quantities of tissue, but they were as close to embryonic tissue as the doctors could get, and they were at least in fairly steady supply. The only other sources were stillbirths and miscarriages—both unpredictable and controversial sources of laboratory material. Scientists working with tissue-culture techniques kept in close contact with the local maternity hospitals, and at the same time searched for substitutes less delicate and rare.

Once again, monkeys became the substitute of choice. Salk was jubilant when he could report that the testicles of a single monkey could produce as many as two hundred roller tubes of culture medium. By March 1953, the Virus Research Lab was producing poliovirus in cultures made from monkey kidneys, which seemed to offer even better results. When researchers at

Connaught Laboratories in Toronto developed a synthetic nutrient mixture with the romantic name of Medium 199, Salk was very happy to use it to reduce his need for animal serum in his florishing new business of growing poliovirus.

By the time other polio researchers decided it was worth investing the time, space, and money to equip their labs and train themselves and their staffs for tissue-culture work, Salk had a powerful production lead. The next step was to take his virus and use it to make a vaccine. Salk's work with influenza had convinced him of the value of killed-virus vaccines, and his latest experiments persuaded him that a killed-virus polio vaccine, its potency boosted with mineral oil adjuvant, actually produced better immunity than a natural infection. What one was after was immunity, he reasoned, not infection, and immunity could be had without infection if you could persuade the body's immune system to produce antibodies.

Very few scientists agreed with this conclusion, for a number of reasons that were not all as benighted as Salk liked to think. The hidebound traditions of immunology that Salk was trying to overthrow were in fact fairly recent discoveries, and they had the virtue of being proven effective. Based on their own knowledge of the relatively short history of vaccinations, many people felt that there was no evidence that killed-virus vaccines would provide immunity that would last more than a few months. Killed-virus vaccines were fine for travelers preparing for brief visits to unfamiliar areas laden with exotic diseases, but they had no place in protecting children against recurrent epidemics of poliomyelitis.

The objections took many forms. John Enders, whose work had provided the indispensable foundation for Salk's vaccine, opposed it out of a deep concern that the widespread use of a killed-virus preparation would interfere with the natural epidemiology of polio and end by creating a population more, not less vulnerable to the disease. Albert Sabin objected that a massive investment of time, money, and public faith in a vaccine of only temporary use would hurt efforts to find a live virus that would really solve the problem.

Tom Rivers feared that the adjuvants used in a killed-virus

vaccine might cause allergic reactions, local irritations or even cancer. And in the background there was the lurking memory of Doctors Kolmer and Brodie, forever linked by the shared disaster of 1935, the early vaccination program that had driven the National Foundation back to fifteen years of "basic research." Both had seen their careers ruined by premature polio vaccines. Kolmer had publicly wished the floor would open and swallow him up when his research was taken apart by Tom Rivers at a professional meeting; Brodie, despondent, died suddenly four years later, and many suspected he had committed suicide.

The people at the Virus Research Lab in Pittsburgh were not distracted by the issue of what had been, what else might be, or what other things could be done. Jonas Salk had been inactivating viruses since he had first joined Thomas Francis' lab in Ann Arbor. He had spent the last ten years producing potent vaccines packed with several different virus strains and testing them on large populations, and he was eager to press forward with polio as he had with influenza. A neighbor who also worked at Municipal Hospital compared Salk's work habits to the way he had seen him drive up one of Pittsburgh's steep cobbled hills during an icy winter storm. "He was going up, no matter what, and the way he was going up was, he'd drive his car, and his car would swing in to the curb, and he'd swing out and start back up. I don't know what that did to the car, but he was determined to get up. He had things to do, and he did. Other people were stuck down there."

Free of any qualms about the use of a killed-virus vaccine, Salk still had a huge number of technical problems to overcome before he would have any vaccine ready. Killing a virus is just as intricate a process as growing it, and the success of the results was a good deal more difficult to measure. There was the question of how long you needed to "inactivate" the virus for it to be safe without being ineffective, and at what temperature, and in what concentration. After you were quite sure the virus was dead, you then had to explore different ways to increase its potency, to avoid having to inject people with a quart of vaccine. Then you had to decide the best sites for injections, the best spacing for the multiple shots that would be required, and the best intervals for testing blood samples to see if antibody levels had risen and stayed elevated. There were usually about sixty variables being tested at once in the Virus Research Lab.

Still, work moved fast. In January 1950, the laboratory started tissue-culture production of poliovirus. That June, Salk wrote to Harry Weaver outlining the steps by which he planned to extend his research. After five single-spaced pages discussing the efficiency of applying tissue-culture techniques to the virus-typing program and the possibility of using "discard" monkeys to search for virus strains of low infectivity, Salk moved on to the interesting subject of "further studies on vaccination of animals and of man."

Salk's tests had shown that monkeys injected with killed-tissue-culture virus combined with adjuvant produced more antibodies than monkeys subjected to natural infection. To him the next step was obvious. "Without much further thought," he wrote, "I think we could consider inactivation of this material with ultraviolet light for [the] immunization of children. I have investigated the local possibility for such an experiment and find that not too far from here there are institutions for Hydrocephalics and other similar unfortunates. I think that we may be able to obtain permission for a study of immunization using tissue culture material . . . I think we might be able to transfer patients to the Municipal Hospital, keeping them under isolation and under very close supervision."

Salk acknowledged that his suggestion was unlikely to be approved anytime soon. "This is more of a dream than a reality," he conceded, "but something that might be considered. Some of the earliest experiments that might be tried, both in chimpanzees and in the institutionalized children, and, perhaps, inmates of prisons who might volunteer for such studies, would be vaccination followed by the administration of [attenuated] virus after the titre of antibody is increased and becomes stabilized."

Salk's dream was Weaver's nightmare—taking helpless children, wards of the state, isolating them in Municipal Hospital, injecting them with an unproved vaccine, and exposing them to live poliovirus, even in an attenuated form. Although Salk's proposal was not far from standard experimental procedures in 1950, Weaver knew better than to think the public would regard the test of any polio vaccine as a routine experiment. Far more work was needed before Salk would have a vaccine ready for testing. The last thing he needed was a reputation for premature experiments conducted without sufficient regard for the interests of his volunteers. If anyone was harmed during tests, the press would be accusing Salk and the National Foundation of medical atrocities.

Secure in his conviction of his careful work, his good intentions, and the infallibility of his laboratory results, Salk never even imagined such a response. He did anticipate objections to a killed-virus vaccine on immunological grounds from the conservative element of the profession, and he suggested a degree of "flexibility" by which his funding proposal might bypass the skeptical review of the Committee on Standards, but he was eager to push forward to the goal of ending polio, and impatient with any doubts or delays. He ended his letter with a stirring call to action: "I think that the time has come for initiating the critical experiments for immunologic prevention and more than that, the time has come for these experiments to be carried out in man."

Weaver disagreed strongly, and he responded to this part of Salk's plan by ignoring it entirely. Salk had great confidence in his results in typing virus samples using tissue-culture methods and thought it would be a waste of precious time for him to complete the typing program, but the National Foundation could not share his certainty. Writing on June 22, 1950, using the stately language that foundation officers master early if they are to stay in the game at all, Weaver reminded him that the current funding of the Virus Research Lab at Pittsburgh was for virus typing, using the methods approved by the original committee, and not for any other use. Privately, he suggested ways Salk might couch his research proposal in more acceptable terms, so that he could continue with vaccine experiments while completing the work he had first agreed to do.

Two years later, when the virus-typing project was officially completed, confirming that there were indeed only three types of poliovirus, Salk and his associates had done enough additional work on poliovirus inactivation to convince the foundation officers that his vaccine preparations were safe. The time had come to see if they were also effective.

IV

Who is the first to take an untried medicine, to undergo a novel treatment? Who helps in the most dangerous stage of medical development, after the laboratory animals have done all they can and the time has come to see how the experimental mixture works on human beings?

One of the hoary traditions of medical research is that you first try out your discoveries on yourself. It's the basic double dare of laboratory life: "What's the matter? Can't take your own medicine?" And who better than you can judge the effects of the potion you have so carefully, anxiously prepared? Sometimes you smile and live and go on to dose your wife and children and a goodly number of total strangers, as Jonas Salk did. Sometimes you die, a victim of overweening pride as well as of whatever ailment you meant to cure. Sometimes the results are more ambiguous: it was home testing, after all, that turned Dr. Jekyll into Mr. Hyde. Sometimes you try to hedge your bets: Dr. Daniel Zagury, of the Pasteur Institute in Paris, injected himself with his own experimental AIDS vaccine in 1986 and made international news when he reported that his antibody levels had risen. There, however, he drew the line. Asked if he would now inject himself with AIDS virus, to see how effective his vaccine might be, he responded, "Do you think I'm crazy?"

Officially, self-inoculation is frowned upon. It's hard to maintain the proper level of scientific detachment when your veins are full of the very stuff whose effects you want to measure. It's quite impossible to have a rich, full career in the lab if you die from the procedure you're supposed to be evaluating. On the other hand, self-experimentation is very tempting, not only for the glory that successful bravery brings, but also for the chance to get things done quickly and efficiently, with a maximum of cooperation and a near absence of paperwork. Even today, self-testing goes on much more often than anyone cares to acknowledge, and certainly much more often than is allowed in any research institution's current guidelines for "human subject" review.

Although he first denied it, Jonas Salk has since acknowledged that he tested his polio vaccine on himself and other members of his laboratory before trying it out on the population at large. Asked to comment on his actions thirty years later, Salk said, "I look upon it as ritual and symbolic. You wouldn't do unto others that which you wouldn't do unto yourself."

And so it is, ritual and symbolic. What we are dealing with here is as much magic as method; the ancient need to prove your bravery before you can claim any power or authority; the primal conviction that the experiment will fail if you don't mix a drop of your own life's blood into the final potion. Scientists who conduct experiments upon themselves are considered slightly mad but also quite heroic. When they take their experiments to others, a larger, stricter set of ethical questions enters.

The history of man's inhumanity to man is full of examples of unwilling volunteers, from the victims of the Spanish Inquisition to the "research subjects" of the Nazi Reich. Less barbaric, but equally common, are the neurotic martyrs who are eager to sacrifice their time, their health, and even their lives for the furtherance of science. These unsought guinea pigs are the last people any reasonable scientist would want to use, however. Whether or not they are otherwise suited to the project, they are disqualified by their very eagerness to help; the same mentality that makes them volunteer makes it highly likely that they will fake their responses in whatever way they think will please the doctor most.

The most reliable choices for human trials are people who are acting from self-interest. In low-risk studies, money is a popular motivational tool, especially since a cash payment for showing up carries no incentive to influence the results. High-risk studies are often carried out in prisons, where inmates are often sadly accustomed to weighing different kinds of dangers and see their participation in medical experiments as a way to shorten their sentences. Scientists always like to use what they call captive populations, which includes not just prison inmates but any group whose whereabouts and behavior can be monitored by others. Schoolchildren, who spend most of their time in large institutions that routinely keep track of their attendance and their health, are another favorite captive population.

By the end of 1954, hundreds of thousands of schoolchildren had served as willing guinea pigs for the Salk polio vaccine, but the first tests were done on small, isolated groups that were sometimes unaware of the other studies taking place elsewhere. If you talk to people who were living in Pittsburgh in the early 1950s, dozens of them will tell you, in considerable detail, how it came to pass that they, or their children, or their neighbor's best friend's cousin, were the first to receive the Salk vaccine. "I worked in the lab," they explain. "I was a family friend." "We were neighbors." "I was sick that day and had to come in early." *Nobody knows that*, they'll add, *except now I've told you. I was the first. Really. Me.*

In fact, there were many stages of trial and development, and many people in the vanguard. The very first group to try one of the killed-virus preparations was the staff of the Virus Research Lab. This made practical as well as symbolic sense, since they were constantly exposed to live poliovirus and had no doubts about their preparation's safety. No one knew yet how well the vaccine worked, but it couldn't hurt to try it. A highschool student who had a part-time job in the laboratory recalls the low level of ceremony attached to the process: after she had worked there for a few days, Dr. Salk came through the lab, told her to roll up her sleeve, and vaccinated her as though he were stamping a crate of fruit.

From there the chronology of tests depended on medical and ethical considerations, and also on the mechanics of getting approval and producing vaccine. Following his penchant for doing several things at once, Salk approached the directors of two nearby institutions for permission to conduct vaccine trials. The first to answer was the Polk State School, a residence for retarded males, children and adults, maintained by the Pennsylvania Department of Welfare in nearby Venango County.

Dr. Gale Walker, the director of the school, was all in favor of the program. Paralytic poliomyelitis had never been a serious problem at Polk, but there had been enough cases for Walker to argue with a clear conscience that the vaccinations would benefit the inmates. He also saw the great merits that Polk had for Salk: a place where patients stayed for an average of twelve years, living in isolation from the general community and its diseases, where very accurate records were kept on residents and strict controls of diet and activity could be maintained during the study. Although Walker was a physician, he had no prior theories or policies about polio that kept him from accepting Salk's assurances of safety, and while he was very aware of his own responsibility, legally and ethically, as the director of a state institution for people who were not capable of taking care of themselves, he saw the experiment as a valuable opportunity to raise the status of the Polk School while assisting in a worthwhile project. He was also a pleasant fellow, fun to relax with over drinks and dinner, able to hold his own in the war stories about fights for money and power, ready to give good advice in designing the kind of official forms and letters that get the answers you want.

As Jonas Salk has often remarked, it would be impossible to repeat his polio work today, when such ventures need to be passed by human-subject review boards and peer review boards and various other qualifying agencies. In 1952 you got the permission of the people involved and went out and did it, and then wrote up your results in a scientific journal. If something terrible happened, the blame would be on your head and the blood on your hands, and of course your career would be over—but in the planning stages, at least, life was a great deal easier for the medical experimenter than it has since become.

Still, the consent forms were no small issue. Unlike prisoners, that other favorite "captive population" in the temporary custody of the state, the inmates at Polk could hardly be expected to give anything like informed consent to the experiments. Because many of them had no family to sign for them, the request had to go all the way to the state Department of Welfare in Harrisburg. Harry Weaver took the drafts of the consent forms that Salk proposed and sent them to the National Foundation's lawyer, who suggested a number of revisions. Salk sent the revised draft to Gale Walker at the Polk School, who added his own changes—translations of legal language into common terms so people wouldn't be too terrified to sign. Walker's revisions went back to Weaver, who sent them to an outside lawyer, William Martin, senior partner at the law firm of Martin and Clearwater, to double-check their legality. Then he telephoned Martin, who was in Atlantic City, to triple-check, and asked him to put his opinion in writing. Then he sent the final version to the Manhattan branch of the Berlitz School of Languages, where for six dollars somebody translated it into Spanish.

The negotiations had lasted five months, but on May 23, 1952, Salk drove the eighty miles from his home to the Polk School to take blood samples from the people who would be receiving vaccine. It was important to know what their blood antibody level was to start with, before they received any vaccinations, so he could measure how much the levels later rose. Salk packed syringes and vials for the blood samples, index cards for the records, and lollipops for the one hundred inmates who took part. Even the simplest children like lollipops, and they would look forward to the doctor's return.

Despite its convenience, the Polk School was a difficult assignment. Lorraine Friedman accompanied Salk on his visits there, to keep the records of which blood sample went with which subject, and she doubted she would stay in the job much longer if they had to make many such trips. It was a long ride, a couple of hours in the car each way, and when you got there the scene wasn't pretty. Children and adults were housed at Polk according to their mental age, and it was hard to go into a building with men older than she was who had the mental age of children or even infants. It smelled bad, too, because the men didn't exactly take good care of themselves, any more than any other toddler does.

It was much more pleasant to work at the second institution Salk used for his early tests, the D. T. Watson Home for Crippled Children. The object here was to prove Salk's contention that his killed-virus vaccine created higher levels of immunity to polio than a natural infection, which could be shown by measuring the before and after antibody levels of children recovering from the disease. The unstated reality was that the children at Watson would not be harmed if the vaccine wasn't quite as good as Dr. Salk thought.

The Watson Home had not begun as a center for polio treatment, and its history was a reminder of the highly individual, idiosyncratic forms that philanthropy took in the early years of the twentieth century. Planned in the decade before World War I and opened in 1920, the Watson Home grew out of the bequest of a prominent Pittsburgh lawyer and his wife, who willed that their fortune be used to turn their country estate into "a home for destitute poor white female children between the ages of three and sixteen years, especially including and preferring children crippled or deformed." As the years passed, the trustees adjusted their rules to reflect the shrinking number of deformed and destitute white female children and the rising number of polio victims in urgent need of rehabilitation. By the time Salk came to Pittsburgh, the Watson Home for Crippled Children was a leading center for post-polio work in Allegheny County, with its own school to train the nurses needed for polio therapy.

Watson was a beautiful place, high on a bluff overlooking the Ohio River only twelve miles northwest of Pittsburgh, in the wealthy suburb of Sewickley Heights. The nurses lived in the original mansion, and passed the radiant portrait of Mrs. Watson and her pearls as they went to work every morning. The children lived in a large brick building that looked far more like a country club than a rehabilitation center. Most of the patients had come from Municipal Hospital, where Salk had his laboratory, but there was considerable psychic distance between the heat and tension of the contagious wards and the serene lawns and well-tended gardens of the Watson Home, where a resident farmer provided fresh produce, milk, and poultry for the children. If you had to learn to bear the burden of paralysis, this was a good place to do it.

The patients at Watson covered their walls with movie pinups and wore the same dungarees, cardigans, and bobbysocks as their friends at home. They put on shows, gave concerts, and kept up with their schoolwork as they were able. They had quarrels and crushes and goofed around at meals, but they never forgot what they were doing there, struggling through long hours of physical therapy in search of the tiny twitches and flutters that signaled that maybe, after all, this muscle or that one might be coaxed back to action. In the meantime, it was very exciting to take part in the first secret tests of Dr. Salk's new vaccine. The tests were secret because it would be wrong to raise people's hopes before knowing how well the vaccine worked, but even in secret it was clear that the children who helped were, every one of them, heroes. Salk explained very carefully that it was too late for his work to help them personally, though some, for whom hope was the sustenance of life, refused to believe him.

Salk was already negotiating with the director of the Watson Home, Dr. Jessie Wright, before he began the work at Polk. Wright was a leading authority on the rehabilitation of polio victims and well known to the National Foundation for Infantile Paralysis, which had given her many grants for programs to teach physical therapy and had appointed her to its advisory committees on post-polio care. She was a terrifying woman, well over two hundred pounds of iron determination, demanding of her staff and sometimes hard on patients who weren't putting forth enough effort to get their muscles moving, but she had no trouble accommodating Salk's experiments. Neither did Lucile Cochran, the small, soft-spoken superintendent of nursing at Watson since 1927, who really ran the home. When Jonas Salk brought his vaccine to the Watson Home, Cochran was the first to volunteer to take it, and it was she who convinced reluctant, heartbroken, guilt-ridden parents that they should be proud to let their children participate in his experiments, not fearful of bringing greater harm to these already burdened lives.

On June 12, 1952, two-and-a-half weeks after his first trip to the Polk School, Salk drove to Sewickley Heights to take prevaccination blood samples from forty-five children and twenty-seven members of the Watson staff. On July 2, having typed the blood samples to see who had antibodies to which strain of polio, Salk returned to give his first injections. Thirty children were injected with an inactivated vaccine prepared from Type I poliovirus, two with a vaccine of Type II and eleven with a vaccine of Type III. That night a very nervous Dr. Salk drove back to Watson from his home in Wexford to see for himself that nobody had gotten sick. Nobody had. Over the summer, he would return several times to take further blood samples. Antibody levels had risen, and were staying up. The killed-virus vaccine produced stronger antibody response than the original infection. The vaccine formula was far from perfect and it was still too soon to tell how long its effects would last, but, indisputably, it worked.

Compared to the problems and objections that arose when Salk went public with his experiments and the complications that came when he extended his studies to larger groups, there was a wonderful simplicity about the arrangements at Polk and Watson. Records were kept on five-by-eight file cards, with different dates of vaccination and blood tests marked in colored pencils. Salk did most of the vaccinations himself, and Lorraine Friedman kept the records in order. The experiment had its warm and human moments. If they had to gird themselves for the trip to Polk, they found an extended family at Watson. Lucile Cochran was the lady of the house, and all the patients were her children. They were all in love with Dr. Salk, who could quiet the most fearful child, listen patiently to the most tortured question, remember everybody's name, and joke with them about their birthdays and parties and their favorite movie stars. The staff idolized him, and the cook insisted on making strawberry pie for every visit when she found out Dr. Salk liked it. It was very serene, proselytizing among the converted.

Perhaps the most remarkable thing about the work done at the Virus Research Laboratory during the summer of 1952 was how very few people knew what they were up to. Harry Weaver knew, because he was supplying the money. Tom Rivers knew because he was the chairman of the Committee on Research and the person Weaver consulted when he wanted an opinion on the scientific value of a project. Basil O'Connor knew because he made sure he was kept informed about everything important that was coming down the National Foundation pike. Very few others, however, were aware how far Dr. Salk had progressed down the still suspect route of killed-virus vaccination. The Pittsburgh newspapers were silent on the subject, and so was the Public Relations Department of the University Medical School. The vast publicity machine of the National Foundation was busy promoting the tests being conducted in Utah and Texas by Dr. William McDowell Hammon, to see if a shot of gamma globulin would provide temporary immunity during epidemics. Nobody from the Pennsylvania State Department of Welfare issued a press release about the field trials at the Polk State School, and nobody gossiped about the interesting new vaccine their children were taking at the Watson Home—or if they did, nobody listened.

In October 1952, Salk went to New York to join the other leaders in polio research who had gathered to hear Hammon report on his gamma globulin field trials. Hammon had recently come to Pittsburgh from UCLA to be the professor of epidemiology at the Graduate School of Public Health—a position Salk felt quite strongly should have been offered to him. Hammon had also been one of the experts who had established procedures for poliovirus typing while politely refusing to do the work, and Salk was not at all happy about having someone in so closely related a field working across the street. He had been angry two years earlier when he thought Hammon was snooping around his laboratory, and he treated his colleague at Muncipal Hospital to the same cautious secrecy he maintained before most of his fellow scientists. To Salk's great satisfaction, Hammon had no idea that he had started vaccine trials that summer. Neither did Salk's old mentor from the University of Michigan, Thomas Francis, or his perennial rival, Albert Sabin. John Enders didn't know, though he had spurred Salk's competitive ingenuity when he had answered an early letter of inquiry with the news that he could get antibody test results in six days rather than six weeks by using tissue-culture samples. Tom Rivers couldn't resist jocular hints at a bombshell to come, but few people at the New York meeting had any idea what he was talking about.

They found out three months later, when Harry Weaver called a round-table conference of the National Foundation's Committee on Immunization, a standing group of twelve leading virologists and four representatives from the National Foundation that had been formed in the spring of 1951 to discuss the issues that would be involved in any eventual vaccination program.

The meeting was held in Hershey, Pennsylvania, a town most famous for the chocolate factory that was its central industry and reason for being. Hershey had been chosen because it was reasonably central to people coming from New York, Pennsylvania, Ohio, Michigan, Maryland, and points beyond, but not so close to any one particular lab that it would smack of favoritism. Four months after the end of a summer of terrible epidemics, when polio had been a daily feature on the front page of every newspaper, Hershey had the added advantage of being well outside the beat of journalists who might badger the participants into premature "leaks" about new developments on the very newsworthy polio scene.

Like all the places where the National Foundation held its committee meetings, the Hotel Hershey was a first-class establishment with good food, comfortable conference rooms, attractive grounds, and sufficient space in hall and lobby for the kind of informal caucuses that are an important feature of any professional gathering. There the members of the Committee on Immunization met on January 23 and 24, 1953, to discuss, among other things, Dr. Salk's work in polio immunization.

On his way from Cincinnati to the Hershey meeting, Albert Sabin stopped in Pittsburgh to visit Salk's lab. Not having taken part in the laboratory work of the virus-typing program, Sabin had not yet mastered the intricacies of Enders' tissue-culture methods, and he wanted to see what Salk was doing. Salk had already concluded that Sabin considered him a brash upstart who would benefit greatly from the close guidance of someone wiser and more experienced—someone like Albert Sabin, for example. At an early meeting of the virus-typing committee in 1948, Salk had asked for opinions of the different, somewhat unorthodox procedures he felt would allow the project to be finished in less time. Sabin cut his description short with a dismissive, "Dr. Salk! You should know better than to ask that question," seeming to imply that the proposal was too absurd even to consider.

The dismissal rankled, and encouraged Salk's already strong instinct for secrecy. After that, Salk determined to keep his own counsel about his work until the results were settled beyond the possibility of any such attack, raising questions only when he also had the answer to report. He also polished a natural genius for burying his intentions in a murky sea of verbiage—a process he thought of as being statesmanlike and diplomatic but others found evasive and just plain unclear. Still, professional courtesy demanded that Salk invite Sabin home to dinner when he came to Pittsburgh, and that they travel together on the train ride to Hershey the next day. As they rolled across Pennsylvania, Sabin tried to draw Salk out on how far he had progressed in his research. Salk talked about tissue cultures and influenza and watched the passing landscape, saving his real news for the conference itself, where he was scheduled to speak after Hammon presented his final, conclusively inconclusive report on the gamma globulin trials.

Other meetings had been held in Hershey, and as far as most of the participants were concerned, the conference in January would be like the ones before it: stimulating, rancorous, and almost completely hypothetical. Most of the scientists in attendance agreed that there was no chance of getting a usable vaccine soon, so the hard decisions could be postponed.

To just about everybody at the meeting, Jonas Salk was a very junior member of the polio establishment. Tom Rivers had been the expert analyst of the Brodie field trial while Salk was still in medical school. G. Foard McGinnes and Harry Weaver, now both on the National Foundation staff, had been getting foundation grants long before Salk—as had everyone else there. Bill Hammon had helped draft the directions for the virus-typing project. John Paul held National Foundation grant no. 1. They had worked together through ignorance and shortages and war, and they were hardly about to give the floor to a new arrival without very good reason. Their debates had the stately measure of the middle ages, and much of the sudden violence of that epoch, too. Nobody won a hearing here without having earned it. As they gathered after lunch on the first day, however, and Salk, in his calm, methodical way, began to outline his thinking about vaccines and the results of his trials, everyone realized that the time for decisions had arrived. Not, however, without debate. The children vaccinated at the Polk State School had all developed polio antibodies. The children at the Watson Home had all shown higher levels of antibody protection after their vaccinations. No one had been hurt. No one had come down with polio during the summer. The next step would be to test the vaccine on a much larger group of children, but for that Salk would need more than personal confidence in the virtues of his laboratory's work. He needed the approval of both the National Foundation and the public, and he hoped to start by winning the support of the Committee on Immunization.

The chief objections came from Albert Sabin. Salk and Sabin were seated as far apart as possible at the long, rectangular conference table at the Hotel Hershey. Harry Weaver sat at the head of the table, with Salk to his right. Basil O'Connor sat at the foot, flanked by Hart Van Riper, medical director of the National Foundation, and William Workman, who was head of the Laboratory of Biologics Control of the National Institutes of Health, the federal office that licensed the manufacture of biological drugs. Sabin sat to their right, facing Salk diagonally across a large expanse of green felt.

Albert Sabin's scientific brilliance was matched by his rhetorical agility and his relish for a nimble battle of words. His manner, when dealing with a challenge, was to condescend it to oblivion with a kind of courtly high-mindedness that could have an opponent halfway home before he realized how thoroughly he had been dismissed. Like other well-established polio researchers, Sabin had happily delegated the work of the virus-typing program to the lesser lights and more prosaic technicians of the laboratory world. When Sabin first encountered Salk in connection with the program, he regarded him as a newcomer to the polio field, a young man whose work, however promising, could hardly be compared to his own long-established position in the forefront of research.

In reality, the two men had much in common. Eight years older than Salk, Sabin had spent his childhood in Bialystok, Russia, before emigrating to the United States in 1920. His family had settled near relatives in the Jewish section of Paterson, New Jersey, where young Albert had quickly learned a new language and the old lesson of using his brains to get ahead in the world. As Salk would eight years later, Sabin had entered New York University Medical School but had decided against a medical practice as he had earlier rejected his family's choice of a career in dentistry.

Graduating from medical school in 1931, Sabin was deeply impressed by the polio epidemic that hit New York City that summer, and started in his long and celebrated career of polio research, first at the Rockefeller Institute and then for many years at the Children's Medical Center of the University of Cincinnati. Other researchers, fascinated by the intellectual conquest of the mysterious poliovirus, might be content to leave the tedious practicalities of vaccine production to someone else, but Sabin had long since determined that he was going to produce a safe, effective vaccine. When young Dr. Salk from Pittsburgh announced that he had already developed a preliminary vaccine and was ready to expand his tests in human subjects, Sabin was quick to challenge his colleague.

The irony of Salk's sense that Sabin treated him as an outsider lay in the unpleasant fact that both men were viewed by some as intruders in the medical establishment. At a time when anti-Semitism was an open feature of academic life and "ambitious" was a popular synonym for Jewish, both Sabin and Salk were widely regarded as very ambitious people. Tom Rivers, one of the great men of virology but also a bigot and a country hick, was incapable of mentioning Sabin without noting that he was a Russian Jew. Rivers took great relish in repeating his reaction when a very young Albert Sabin, just back from a year in England, had shown up in his office wearing tweeds and spats, smoking a pipe and carrying a cane. "God damn you, Sabin!" Rivers had bellowed. "You can't turn a cheap East Side Jew into an Englishman in one year! Don't you ever come to see me with spats on again. Don't you ever speak to me in that broad accent again." Retelling the story with obvious satisfaction, Rivers would add, "You know, by God, he went back to being an East Side Jew, and he's been all right ever since." It mattered not at all to Rivers that Sabin had never lived on Manhattan's Lower East Side, haven for Jewish immigrants of a previous generation, or that the accent the Russian native learned in New

Jersey was no more or less authentic, for a second language, than the accent he had picked up in England.

Fifteen years later, Rivers offered an apology of sorts. "I consider you one of my most famous protégés," he wrote Sabin, "and have always had the highest regard for your ability. At times I have gotten provoked with you but that is nothing unusual and even when I have been provoked, I have never lost faith in you. I suppose you will provoke me again before you and I die and that is no reason why we shouldn't be friends." In the meantime, though, Rivers kept telling his funny story about how he had to remind Albert Sabin to go back to being an East Side Jew. In Rivers' world, everyone was a boy of some sort—an old boy, a smart boy, a good old boy, or a Jewboy. To tell them apart, Rivers distinguished Sabin as "the smart Jew" while Salk was "the young Jew." No one has ever recorded any sympathy between Salk and Sabin based on their shared distinction, in the eyes of some others, as "the Jews."

At the Hershey meeting, Sabin's immediate reaction to Salk's report was to argue again that years of further study would be needed before Salk could pretend to have a usable, or even a testable, vaccine. First he dismissed the studies at the Watson Home, reminding the assembled doctors that vaccinations given to children who had recovered from polio could only be considered as boosters to immunity, with no indication of how the vaccine would act on people with no exposure. Then he explored the uncertain meaning of Salk's data on antibody levels in monkeys. Finally, he proposed a program of ten to fifteen years of additional research to find an ideal dose of a killed-virus vaccine. "It is always difficult when you have to try to carry [such data] over from an animal to what the human dose is," he noted, "which will, of course, bring up the next question as to whether or not the basic dosages required for the human vaccination may not have to be determined on the population of very young children with no detectable antibody for the three types in ten years, and when that is available then correlate it with an assay in mice or monkeys."

There were many other dangers Sabin saw in Salk's use of virus produced in tissue cultures, each accompanied by its own problems, which would "of course" require delays. Joseph Smadel, the excitable and often profane chief of virus research at the army's Walter Reed Hospital, could leap up and make his pungent demands for the start of a full-scale field trial, but Sabin, for his part, was quite sure that this enormously interesting project would require at least a decade of refinement before anybody could with good conscience talk about a safe vaccine.

Albert Sabin did not succeed in blocking the testing of the Salk vaccine, although he did cast a good many highly publicized doubts on the wisdom and safety of the 1954 field trials. Looking back on the debate, and on the long rivalry that has continued to exist between the two scientists, many people have dismissed Sabin's objections as the product of professional jealousy. Vivid reports of feuding personalities make it easy to forget that there are legitimate scientific principles in conflict here, along with very large egos. When people describe Salk's polio vaccine and the one later developed by Albert Sabin, they most often mark the difference as between an injected vaccine and one taken orally, in a sugar cube or as part of a sweet syrup. Since inoculation is the most ancient form of vaccination, most people assume that the Salk vaccine, which after all came first, is in some way more traditional.

In fact, the opposite is true. Salk's innovation was his claim that it was indeed possible to achieve lasting immunity to a disease without ever having an actual infection, and that the immunity gained from a killed-virus vaccine might even be more powerful than that achieved through infection. The Sabin vaccine, by contrast, follows classic principles of immunology by provoking an infection with a harmless strain of virus, thus protecting the patient from later exposure to more dangerous infections. As Jenner had used cowpox to conquer smallpox and Pasteur had used dried and weakened rabies virus to halt the progress of hydrophobia, so Sabin intended to use a weakened form of poliovirus to conquer the paralytic strains of the disease.

These were not empty distinctions. The choice to support the Salk vaccine or wait for a more traditional live-virus product raised very real questions in medicine, immunological theory, and public health administration. What was at stake was millions of dollars, careers, honor, political and professional futures, and, of course, human lives. Still, the official debate at Hershey was all conducted within the frame of reference of the profession of research virologists.

Outside the frame, there was a great clamor to do something about polio. Children and parents were terrified. Doctors and nurses were frantic. While the scientists met in Hershey, the National Foundation was in the midst of the annual January March of Dimes campaign, a time when people asked where their money was going. The fund-raisers wanted some progress to announce, the press wanted some progress to report, and the public wanted some progress to give it hope and courage as it began the new year, six months after the worst polio epidemic ever. Scientists use the word "noise" to describe the miscellaneous extra data that is not related to what they're studying, but the noise that rose in the early months of 1953 was too loud to be ignored.

WIDE-ANGLE

PARENTS and CHILDREN

In the summer and early fall, when most epidemics of infantile paralysis occur, parents naturally think of this disease whenever a child becomes sick.

—BENJAMIN SPOCK

Voices of America, 1953

"When I was growing up in Wisconsin, in Oshkosh, my mother would never let me go to the State Fair. I always wanted to go, but she'd say, 'Do you want to get polio and spend your life in an iron lung?' What a terrifying thing that was—the iron lung."

"Parents in Los Angeles were terrified of polio. There had been some very bad epidemics there. I remember riding my bicycle around and around the block, because I wasn't allowed to play with anybody."

"Polio? That was the big fear when I was young—especially growing up in the South. You didn't want to be anywhere near it. In 1952, we still didn't have TV in Shreveport. I remember going to Dallas and seeing television for the first time. In the news every day was a tally of the polio cases—like today they total up the car crashes on holiday weekends. Every day they would report 'another so many polio cases today.' That was my first sense of what news was."

"When I was a kid in Boston, my parents would never let us go to the movies in the summer or swim in pools. Of course the ocean was okay. You wouldn't get polio from the ocean. That had this faith in salt water."

"We were always very aware of polio, especially growing up in California, where the governor's daughter had polio. A big game was to play polio, to take turns pretending we had polio, that we were crippled. It sounds like a sick joke, but we did play that."

"Polio! I remember polio! Polio took a couple of years of Riverview out of my life, and now Chicago doesn't even have an amusement park any more. Polio sent me off to camp—or was that just the excuse for shipping a five-and-a-half-year-old out? That was the excuse you gave for a lot of things. God! Polio!"

"Polio! Oh, what a scare it was, every year. I lived out in the country, and my mother kept me very secluded—with the result that when I went to Baltimore, to college, I came down with everything."

"A little boy in our neighborhood in Texas told us (a group of children who had been laboriously extracting nectar from honeysuckle blooms) that this would give us polio. I just went home, sat on my bed, and waited for it to happen; prayed; regretted my misspent life. The image of the iron lung is an abiding terror."

"When I was a teenager in Oakland, California, my mother worried that I might catch polio from kissing. She was no prude, but she used to tell me, 'Don't kiss boys. You might end up with a crooked leg.' She wasn't an educated person, but she was worried, and that was her way of saying so."

"My cousin had polio when he was one year old, in Bowling Green, Ohio. We were together a good deal. We were very mobile, and his handicap didn't stop us, it just took longer to get places. I remember we were walking down Main Street together, on the sidewalk, and this car slowed down to stare at us. I remember being so angry, but he just went on."

"I had polio when I was six. We went on a trip to Canada, and I sat for hours in the waiting room at the train station with my mother—we figured I must have caught it there, because I

*was sick by the time we got home. They told my parents I would
die, and my mother always said the only reason I was alive was
because I was so stubborn. I got polio from going to Canada."*

*"I was so afraid of polio. I grew up in Brooklyn, and for
New York Jews, there was a lot of terror then. It was connected
with the Rosenbergs, I think—all of a sudden, one day, these
little children could be left without their parents. And the atom
bomb. Those were the two things I remember being afraid of
—polio and the bomb. We had drills in school. It all went
together. My parents were so afraid, there was no consciousness
of the risk of a vaccine. That just wasn't an issue."*

*"Just today, I was bending over to take a drink from a foun-
tain. The water wouldn't go up, there was just a trickle over
the spout, and I heard my mother's voice saying, 'Don't drink
that—you'll get polio.' It was just a flash from my childhood."*

•

At the start of 1953, the parents and children of America did
not know that the disease they feared the most—more than
cancer, more than smallpox, more than rheumatic fever—would
soon become a minor footnote in the records of the nation's
health. Nor did they really notice that the previous summer's
epidemics had reached from Alaska to Puerto Rico and covered
each of what were then the forty-eight states. What they knew
was that people in their neighborhood had been stricken. They
didn't see statistics. They saw friends in the hospital, cousins
on crutches, mothers in wheelchairs feeding babies in high
chairs. Everyone was sure that the epidemic had been particularly severe in his area, whether that was Minneapolis or Ho-
nolulu. When the figures were gathered and the news went out
that the summer of 1952 had been the latest peak in a steadily
rising chart of polio cases, there was every reason to assume
that the next year would be even worse, and the year after that
more terrible still. More and more adults were being paralyzed,
too. Soon no one would be safe from the Crippler.

Four decades later, it is almost impossible to imagine
hundreds of thousands of American parents volunteering their

children to act as test subjects for a new vaccine, but in 1953 and 1954, when many of today's parents were themselves children, they eagerly and proudly served in precisely that role. Amid the many debates that raged around the decision to extend the testing of the Salk polio vaccine, one question that was almost never asked was whether parents would cooperate. Everyone assumed, correctly, that they would. A generation later, it is important to remember why.

The parents of 1953 were terrified of polio, and with good cause. The first generation to spend their entire lives under the shadow of the epidemics, they needed no persuasion whatsoever to be convinced that the danger was real. When word began to spread that a doctor in Pittsburgh was working on a vaccine that might prevent polio, parents paid attention. So did grandparents, uncles, teachers, doctors, and anybody else who had ever had a brush with the ravaging effects of paralysis. In 1953, when few did not have some firsthand knowledge of polio, they followed the news of Salk's work with a close attention they rarely gave to foreign wars or distant explorations.

The terrors of polio were real, but they were also deepened by a number of other less tangible threats—simultaneous currents of fear and vulnerability that had little rational connection to epidemic disease but still exerted a strong emotional pull over the decisions people made for their children's well-being. In the early 1950s, the summer dread of paralysis was joined by the new and horrible possibility of nuclear holocaust and by the pervasive fear of Communist infiltration of the United States—threats that knew no season, and that added greatly to the sum total of parental anxiety.

For the virologists and immunologists working in laboratories sponsored by the National Foundation in 1953, there was absolutely no relation between their work and the new hydrogen bombs being tested in the Pacific. To the school and community leaders who would soon be asked to participate in the Salk vaccine field trial, to the volunteers from hospitals and civic organizations who would help run the vaccination clinics, and, most of all, to the parents who would allow their children to test this new product, the relationship was obvious. They were afraid of polio and of the bomb, and they tended to think of them in the same terms, as sudden forces that would attack without warning and destroy their own and their children's lives.

The association was hard to escape. The children who would take part in the first large-scale tests of the Salk vaccine had all been born between 1945 and 1947, either in the immediate wake of Hiroshima or in the following two years, when atomic fears rose steadily. In 1946 *New Yorker* writer E. B. White had mourned Bikini Lagoon, site of American bomb tests, saying, "It all seems unspeakably precious, like a lovely child stricken with a fatal disease." By 1953 there had been reports from Japan that bombs, like polio, could leave a generation of survivors who were tragically twisted and maimed. Soon newspapers would begin to report the first discoveries of something called fallout—a poisonous dust that came from nuclear explosions, a lethal cloud so light it could be wafted across the earth by a passing breeze. No one was safe from the dangers of nuclear war, any more than from the threat of polio, and least of all children.

For the elementary schoolchildren who would take part in the Salk vaccine field trial in 1954, the two dangers were even more closely identified, perhaps because they were both linked to going to school. The school buildings where children in Pittsburgh got their polio shots, and the other schools across the nation where the field-trial clinics would be held, were also where they learned to crouch under desks and in basement hallways, heads between knees, hands clasped behind their necks, to protect themselves against the fatal flash of falling bombs. The era of the Salk vaccine was also the era of "Duck and Cover" drills and bomb shelters; the elaborate precautions that children practiced in school convinced them that polio and nuclear bombs were parallel dangers that loomed larger than any other fears.

The helpless fear of nuclear contamination was reinforced by the growing sense of Communist menace, which made another war seem chillingly possible. The fear of communism, like the fear of nuclear war, had no rational connection to the effort to test and distribute a vaccine to protect against paralytic poliomyelitis, but, once again, it was an issue that grew up alongside the children of the postwar Baby Boom. In March 1946, as obstetricians and demographers alike were beginning to notice the unusually large number of babies arriving on the American scene, Winston Churchill first introduced the image of an iron curtain across Europe to describe the tense new separation of the Communist East from the democratic West. The year 1947, when the Polio Pioneers were infants and toddlers, was also the year the Federal Loyalty Review program was born. By 1953 the fear of world Communist dominion had been brought close to home by Senator Joseph McCarthy, the conservative Republican from Wisconsin whose scattershot accusations of disloyalty made it seem that the entire nation had been infiltrated by Communist subversives.

In the political vocabulary of the early fifties, communism was a contagion that threatened to become an epidemic of betrayal, a hidden enemy that attacked from within to paralyze the country. To fight against it there was a need for the same kind of social quarantine urged for polio, a need to stay away from crowds and strangers. Even for those who did not succumb to Senator McCarthy's increasingly shrill efforts to root out subversives, the polio vaccine program drew popular support from the atmosphere of mass vulnerability that marked the emerging era of Cold War politics.

At a time when many felt helpless before the threats of bombs, radiation, and Communist infiltration of American society, it was very comforting to find something positive that could be done to fight at least one of the many dangers that seemed to loom so large. Both public and private observers welcomed the appearance of a scientist whose discoveries had purely peaceful uses. Making a common comparison, one journalist wrote: "In the dawn hours, a citizen of Las Vegas, Nevada, may be awakened by the sound of rattling windows, or a quick, bright flash in the sky. This is how the shattering power of the atom bomb, exploding 60 miles away, intrudes itself upon him. . . . No windows rattle in Pittsburgh. There is no bright flash, followed by streaming black headlines proclaiming the event. Still, the scientist is at work there, too. In a different way, a quieter way."

The widespread epidemics of 1952 had strained the resources of the National Foundation, but they also had enhanced its reputation. Of the fifty-eight thousand new polio patients diagnosed that summer, forty thousand had received some financial assistance from the foundation. Alaska, Hawaii, Puerto Rico, and forty-seven of the forty-eight states had exhausted their treasuries and had to apply to National Headquarters for extra funds from emergency reserves. Iron lungs, the horror and salvation of so many polio patients, did not come cheap, and neither did the airplanes to fly them to epidemic areas where patients needed them faster than trucks or trains could arrive. Extra shifts of nurses had to be hired for the intensive care that polio patients required, and more doctors had to be trained to recognize the early symptoms that would allow treatment to start before it was too late.

As infantile paralysis became front-page news and reporters renamed the disease "polio" to fit their headlines, people began referring to "the Polio Foundation," and they volunteered in record numbers to help it in its efforts. Working for the National Foundation now meant more than just collecting change in movie theaters. Polio Emergency Volunteers trained to serve in hospital wards. Chapter chairmen went to educational meetings to learn about new progress in polio research. Mothers who marched door-to-door became known as the local authorities on poliomyelitis, and their reassurances would help many people decide that the new vaccine they would soon be hearing about was safe. Everybody who could spare a coin gave to the March of Dimes fund-raising campaign that began on January 1, 1953. They raised over $50 million that year, $10 million more than in 1952, and the money went to a growing range of victims, but it was still parents and children who were the at the heart of the polio crusade.

Parents clamored for an end to polio because they were afraid, and they seized upon the early news of Salk's vaccine because they trusted science and had confidence in the National Foundation. Nor were they as bothered by the prospect of mass vaccination clinics as conservative medical organizations liked to suppose. Even before they started producing babies in record numbers, this was a generation of parents unusually comfortable with the idea of mass enterprise of any sort. Most had learned their first lessons in politics from the big-government programs of the New Deal, already closely associated with the polio cause, and had graduated to the largest national program of all, World War II. The men who became the fathers of the Polio Pioneers had gone into the army and had let the government shave their heads, drape them with dog tags, dress them in uniforms that matched the color of the local dirt, and send them off to Sicily, Normandy, Okinawa, and Seoul. The women who would be their mothers had spent the war years working in offices and factories where they were introduced to mass production, and had lined up to buy queer gelatinous substances and mysterious powders that they were told to regard as valid substitutes for meat and butter and eggs.

In the years after the war, when the production of babies far outstripped the supply of pediatricians, as many parents were concerned about establishing a relationship between physician and patient as with violating it. Millions of them had bought a new book, *Baby and Child Care*, by Dr. Benjamin Spock, to help them cope when no doctor was at hand. Families that were entering lotteries for apartments in housing developments subsidized by the federal government or lining up to buy a cookie-cutter piece of paradise in Levittown were hardly offended by the prospect of vaccination clinics. People who had accepted the plausibility of Spam were not likely to doubt the safety of a polio vaccine sponsored by the National Foundation for Infantile Paralysis.

For many people, in fact, the new polio vaccine was something to be trusted precisely because it was new. After the privations of the Depression and the shortages of the war years, families of the 1950s embraced materialism as a long-lost friend. In the epoch of mass-produced luxuries of every sort, the Salk vaccine was a consumer product at its most desirable: it was a result of technological innovation, it was good for the children, and, in the buzzword of the day, it was NEW, NEW, NEW. In 1953, when *Consumer Reports* compared the Salk vaccine and gamma globulin in the same spirit it tested and ranked dishwashers and automobiles, the magazine's editors were simply recognizing that one person's medical breakthrough was another's market choice.

The parents who looked forward to early tests of Salk's vaccine, like those who took part in the initial studies Salk continued to conduct in Pittsburgh, paid little attention to the scientific debates. Caught between fear of disease and faith in progress, they were ready to seize the hem of the robe of any savior. Salk was honest and scrupulous, but to the parents of 1953 it wouldn't have mattered if he wasn't—or at least not until it was too late.

PART THREE

LINING UP
for the
PARADE

As in manufacturing, so in science—retooling is an extravagance to be reserved for the occasion that demands it. The significance of crises is the indication they provide that an occasion for retooling has arrived.

—THOMAS S. KUHN

New York, 1953

For every great enterprise there is a moment of truth, an instant you can point to and say, "That's when we knew it would happen. That's when the engine was started, the battle launched, the letter signed, the river crossed." But what went before that moment? How many hours of debate and revision? How many people who had to be consulted, how many others who couldn't make up their minds? Afterward, everyone remembers the radiant second of decision, when the proper course of action became so very clear. No one commemorates the long dark corridor of hesitation where the leaders gathered, nervous and uncertain, waiting for the last possible instant to say, "Yes. Now. Go."

How many meetings had Basil O'Connor sat through in the three decades since he and Roosevelt formed their partnership? Two thousand? Five thousand? Ten thousand? Meetings with clients who were nervous, angry, or bored. Meetings with other lawyers whose cases he would take before the appellate court. Meetings to negotiate the oil-lease agreements that had made him rich. Meetings to draft Roosevelt's speeches and plot his campaigns. Meetings at the American Red Cross, pushing to reorganize that slow-moving giant just when it was stretching its services to the widest reaches of a global war. Meetings at Hyde Park to break ground for the presidential library that was Roosevelt's dream, and then the last gathering there to lay FDR in his grave. Meetings at Warm Springs or Palm Springs, meet-

169

ings looking out over the rolling lawns of the Greenbrier or in the gilded conference rooms of the Waldorf-Astoria, all to discuss the National Foundation's programs. Meetings with national directors, regional directors, chapter chairmen, women's activities directors, March of Dimes leaders, Mothers' March coordinators, block captains and school captains and apartment captains and volunteer leaders in every state and major city of the country. Meetings to inspire. Meetings to plan. Meetings to listen. Meetings to instruct.

Sometimes he sat at the big banquet table at the front of the hall and rose after dinner to address the crowd. Sometimes he sat at a conference table ringed with experts and said very little, but his short, probing questions would bring the discussion out of whatever blind alley it had been stumbling through. For years he had attended the foundation's meetings of research scientists, preparing for the day when he would have to plan some action on the basis of their work. The members of the advisory committees knew a lot more about polio than Basil O'Connor ever would, but sometimes they needed him to remind them of why they were there. The purpose of the National Foundation for Infantile Paralysis was not simply to advance the sum total of human knowledge about poliomyelitis, but also to do something about it.

The last two years had pushed O'Connor hard. After half a lifetime of fighting polio, he had suddenly discovered he was as vulnerable as anyone else. His favorite daughter, Bettyann O'Connor Culver, had been paralyzed in the summer of 1950 —thirty years old, married, the mother of five children, and suddenly flat on her back on a stretcher on her way to Warm Springs for therapy, where as a child she'd gone to visit Roosevelt. "Daddy," she said when she called with the terrible news. "Daddy, I've got some of your polio." She'd improved since then, but she still wasn't fully recovered. At least she hadn't died, like Helen Hayes' daughter. The first lady of the American theater, they called her, but still she'd telephoned O'Connor in the middle of the night, begging for the respirator that wasn't enough to save her child.

This last summer, 1952, had been the worst epidemic season ever. Almost fifty-eight thousand cases of polio were reported *across the country; more children died of polio than any other communicable disease. Then in June the years of smoking and drinking and working too hard caught up with O'Connor: a heart attack kept him away from his desk and his meetings until October. The doctors had given him a clean bill of health, but he felt a new urgency to his longstanding pledge to "lick polio" in his lifetime. He was sixty-one years old. Victory was possible, and he wanted to be there to greet it.*

Different researchers kept bringing promising news, but nothing they were ready to agree on as really useful. William McDowell Hammon had spent the last two summers seeing what protection you could give with a shot of gamma globulin, the gooey serum full of antibodies that doctors had learned to extract from blood plasma during World War II. The stuff was scarce, it cost a fortune, and there wasn't enough in the world to protect a fraction of the people who needed it, but it proved that you could get at least temporary immunity to polio through antibodies in the blood. David Bodian of Johns Hopkins and Dorothy Millicent Horstmann of Yale had both jumped on the news, doing separate studies that finally proved poliovirus circulated in the blood before it attacked the nervous system. That meant a vaccine would work, if anybody could make one. John Enders had figured out how to produce virus in a test tube, but he wouldn't be pushed into making a vaccine. Bodian's colleague, Howard Howe, was working on a killed-virus vaccine, but he hadn't mastered the new tissue-culture methods he would need. John Paul had vaccinated a few infants near his laboratory in New Haven. Hilary Koprowski said he had made a vaccine at his laboratory at the Lederle company, but nobody knew how good it really was. Albert Sabin was working on attenuating virus strains in Cincinnati. They all were hopeful, but they all were slow. Then along came Jonas Salk, who said he had a vaccine that was almost ready. "Premature," his critics called it. "Untried." "Imperfect." However long he might have left to live, O'Connor suspected it wasn't long enough to wait for perfection.

O'Connor was already interested in Salk, this slight young man who combined nervous intensity with a cool willingness to forge ahead with experiments on a scale others were afraid to try. They had gotten to know each other on the way back from Copenhagen, after the second International Conference on Poliomyelitis in the fall of 1951. John Enders had been the hero of the meeting, reporting on his success in growing poliovirus in tissue culture, but Salk had done some excellent work in the typing project and Harry Weaver said he was someone to watch. When Weaver realized that Salk and Enders were returning to the United States on the same ship as the foundation president, he urged O'Connor to invite them to join his table.

First-class travel on the Queen Mary, with meals at Basil O'Connor's private table—that was something new for these laboratory types. Dinner meant jokes and cocktails and social banter, O'Connor at the center of his entourage. He had brought along Bettyann, too, hoping the trip would cheer her up about her slow recovery. At first he was bored at having to entertain these scientists. He began to needle Salk, and everyone was shocked when Salk answered in kind, but O'Connor's interest was raised. He was as much taken with Salk's ability to trade dinner-table barbs as with his comprehensive views of the role of medical research, and he was touched by the attentive, courteous way Salk talked to his daughter. He liked that combination of spunk and sympathy, the ability to stop in the middle of asking for a million-dollar budget to help you get a cinder from your eye. During the long days at sea, O'Connor walked the decks or lounged in the pool with Salk, talking about nothing and everything. O'Connor was a guarded man, wary of intimacy, more accustomed to command than to listen, but something about Salk drew him out. Over the last fifteen years, he had helped give out millions of dollars to doctors and researchers whose work he respected. Here was one he actually liked.

Maybe it was the echo of his own ambitions he was hearing. A generation later, here was another young man making the same journey from obscurity to achievement, overcoming the same obstacles that faced anybody who was not Anglo-Saxon, not Protestant, not the child of wealthy or educated parents. Salk was a scientist, not a lawyer, a Jew; not an Irish Catholic; but he was using the same tools that had served O'Connor so well: intelligence, efficiency, hard work, and the ability to see beyond the boundaries of his profession to make a place for his work in the great scheme of society.

O'Connor found the young doctor more than a bit naive in the ways of the world, but that was all right—he would come along. Salk, for his part, thought the older man was fascinatingly vulgar and pretentious, with his cigarette holder, his bouton- niere, his secretary in constant attendance, and his lavish tips to stewards and porters. O'Connor was a good deal flashier than Salk ever wanted to become, but it could be very appealing to travel with a man whose brilliant mind was matched with Broadway tastes. They traded jokes and shared social philoso- phy, and each man felt superior to the other in the ways that mattered most to his own self-esteem. Their manners couldn't have been more different, but they shared the same driving determination not to get trapped by traditional methods and ideas. Other people insisted those traditions were the wisdom of the ages, but maybe the time had come to see how dangerous it really was to break with the way things had always been done.

After the boat docked, the two men went their separate ways. Salk had kept pushing forward since then, working up a trial vaccine and testing it on children while everyone else was still wondering if they dared to move beyond monkeys. Now there were more meetings than ever. As O'Connor listened to the experts tear apart this person's research and praise that one's laboratory's results, dismiss one program as inadequate and worry that another was premature, he waited for the shift in direction that has to come if a meeting is going to matter—the point when every item on the agenda has been picked up, pulled apart, and put back together and it's time to turn to the hard decisions of where to put the money and the effort, when to wait and when to stake your reputation on a program, the moment when you have to decide what to do, really do, to- morrow. A lot of people like to talk at meetings, but not so many are able to get things settled; it takes a strong hand and sometimes a loud voice to make that happen.

Tom Rivers was good at pushing a group across that line from discussion to decision, and so was Harry Weaver. So was Basil O'Connor, though he tried to hold his famous temper and keep to the soft voice of sweetest reason. "I'm not a doctor," he would tell the people around the table. "I'm not a scientist, and I'm not trying to push anybody into anything. I'm just a lawyer. But these are the issues we have to face, and it would be a great help if you could put your minds to them for a moment. Yes, a great help indeed."

O'Connor wasn't afraid to make his own decisions, but he wanted the facts that would let him decide in an intelligent way. That was the way FDR had done things, back in the days when they were pulling together the Brain Trust before the election of 1932. O'Connor and Samuel Rosenman and Raymond Moley would scout out the interesting thinkers, the people with fresh new ideas about the economy, or agriculture, or any of the other areas a new president would need to know. Anybody promising they'd bring up to Albany to meet the governor, and Roosevelt would pour on the charm at dinner and then pump his visiting expert dry when the men retired to his study for coffee and brandy and cigars. First Roosevelt would ask a few general questions, and then more and more specific ones, and by the end of the evening he wouldn't be asking at all, but pronouncing his own opinions. Then he'd send them all back to New York on the midnight train, satisfied that he knew what he needed. You can listen to everybody, but in the end you still have to make up your mind for yourself. O'Connor liked and trusted Salk. The man was a careful, meticulous scientist. He was also a sharp guy, which in O'Connor's experience was a rarer quality.

The Committee on Immunization was as paralyzed by its expertise as polio patients were by their disease. They wanted to spend twenty years studying Salk's methods, but the public wanted protection now, and they were paying to get it. Still, it would be nice to have some expert endorsement before he put seven million dollars into a project. That was what a field trial of Salk's vaccine would cost. Seven million dollars and a lifetime of goodwill, and perhaps a lot of children's lives.

Seven million dollars. How long had it been since that had seemed like a lot of money to Basil O'Connor? He was out to lick polio, and the American people would give him whatever he needed to do it. They always had. This summer he would be spending almost that much on gamma globulin, for protection that wouldn't last more than six weeks. Five-and-a-half million dollars to buy up the national supply. The government classified it as a strategic material and controlled the supply *through the Office of Defense Mobilization, but he'd talked the Department of Defense into letting him buy it all, a million doses, and he planned to give it all away this summer.*

The Public Health Service sent some boys up from Atlanta to argue with him on that one. He gave them lunch in a private dining room at the Bankers' Club and heard them out, because you never know when you might learn something. It was bad epidemiology, they argued, and a waste of a strategic material. What really rankled, though, was his plan to have the local chapters of the National Foundation give it out in mass vaccination clinics. You can't bypass the health departments, they said. You can't turn your local fund-raisers into an amateur medical network. They won on that, and now the health officers would be distributing the gamma globulin he had bought and the American public had paid for. Distributing it to the wrong people, too, because they insisted on giving most of it to families of polio cases instead of to all children in epidemic areas.

At least the program was going forward. One million people would be getting some protection against polio. Millions more would be getting hope. Some doctor had gotten in the papers, complaining that the gamma globulin program was a waste of money. He had worked out the cost to $7,000 for every case of paralytic polio it prevented. That showed what he knew. It cost $40,000 to care for a single paralyzed child for the rest of his life, and that wasn't counting the cost of broken hearts. When you calculate it that way, gamma globulin was cheap.

Now it was the virologists complaining about steamroller tactics. Every year the epidemics got worse, and still they said it was wrong to hurry. Even those who conceded that a killed-virus vaccine was worth pursuing insisted that the proper way to test it was to study a small population of vaccinated people over a long period of time—say fifteen or twenty years. Ten at the minimum. While they argued, O'Connor calculated. Estimate fifty thousand cases of polio a year, 20 percent of them paralytic. Multiply that by twenty years, and you had a million cases of polio and two hundred thousand people paralyzed while the scientists worked to design the perfect vaccine tested in an unimpeachably traditional scientific study. A million people is a lot of sickness to endure in the name of scientific tradition.

Salk said his vaccine was safe. No one at the Watson Home had been hurt by it. No one at the Polk State School had been hurt. Salk was extending his trials to six hundred children from the Pittsburgh area who had never had polio, and there had been not a single bad reaction. Salk said his vaccine would prevent paralysis. He didn't know how well, or how long the protection would last, but he was sure it would do something, and that it was safe. If you could save a single child from disaster, how could you go too fast?

1

In January 1953, 161 people had been vaccinated with one or another of several experimental polio vaccines made in the Virus Research Laboratory at the University of Pittsburgh Medical School. Salk gave all the vaccinations himself. His secretary, Lorraine Friedman, kept the records and also kept track of the many blood samples brought back to the lab for further testing. As is customary in scientific research, the results of these first trials were announced in a formal paper, "Studies in Human Subjects on Active Immunization Against Poliomyelitis," which was published in the *Journal of the American Medical Association* on March 28, 1953. The paper was an elaboration of the report Salk had given at the scientific meeting in Hershey, Pennsylvania, in January.

Thirteen months after that first published report, on April 26, 1954, the first of over 650,000 children in 211 health districts of 44 states received injections in a national field trial designed to test the safety and efficacy of what was known by then as Salk polio vaccine. The vaccine was made from three different strains of poliovirus grown in tissue cultures at the Connaught Laboratories of the University of Toronto, Canada, and then shipped over the border to two of the largest pharmaceutical manufacturers in the United States: Parke, Davis and Company in Detroit and Eli Lilly and Company in Indianapolis. Both companies had built special facilities where they inactivated the virus strains, filtered them, and combined them into a single vaccine. Samples from each production batch of vaccine were tested for safety by the manufacturer, by the federal laboratories of the National Institutes of Health in Bethesda, Maryland, and by Salk's laboratory. School doctors and private physicians volunteered to give the vaccinations in the clinics held in public and private schools across the country. Twenty-eight laboratories stood ready to do further analyses of the forty thousand blood samples taken from 2 percent of the student subjects.

Detailed health records for each child who took part in the program, including the 1.2 million who were not vaccinated but served as an observed control group, were gathered at the Poliomyelitis Vaccine Evaluation Center established for that purpose at the University of Michigan in Ann Arbor. When, after a year of study, the evaluators declared the vaccine to be safe and effective, the news was first reported on NBC Television and quickly became the lead story on all radio and television stations and in newspapers and magazines around the world.

In little over a year, a small laboratory experiment had become a national event of a size and complexity never seen before. The testing of the Salk vaccine was the largest field trial ever held, the greatest peacetime mobilization of civilians in American history, and the most eagerly observed and heavily publicized scientific program until the space launches a decade later. Jonas Salk became an instant hero and an enduring celebrity, the idol and icon of his age. The announcement that his vaccine worked was a landmark in twentieth-century history, and one of the few events that burned itself into the consciousness of the world because the news was good.

Privately funded, privately organized and supervised, and quite publicly and conspicuously successful, the development and testing of the Salk vaccine was in many ways a crowning example of democratic self-help, the mass organization of individual citizens in a united effort for the public good. It was also an effort marred by bitter disputes over procedure, vicious struggles for power and prestige, a small but tragic residue of avoidable injury, and a complete failure to make an orderly transition from experimentation to implementation and from laboratory prototypes to large-scale commercial production. Almost forty years later, the only thing everyone agrees on is that it was something that could never be done again.

The conflicts that surrounded the Salk vaccine field trial were not between good and evil, right and wrong, but between different ideas about what constituted the good and the right. For over twenty years, several groups had been attacking the problems of polio along entirely separate lines. The National Foundation for Infantile Paralysis created a national network of concerned volunteers, community "experts" on polio who raised money for the care of the disease's victims at the same time that they raised awareness of the malady itself. Research scientists, many supported in whole or part by the National Foundation, studied problems in virology and immunology. Doctors learned to recognize the elusive symptoms of polio and prescribe ever better treatments and therapies. The Public Health Service charted epidemics and quarantined victims. The public worried, hoped, and waited.

In the early months of 1953, when reports began to appear that a polio vaccine might be at hand, each of these groups, and each individual within each group, was firmly in possession of a set of assumptions about how matters would proceed. Unfortunately, they were rarely the same assumptions. Everyone agreed that it would be a great thing to eliminate paralytic poliomyelitis. After that the consensus started to break down right away. Many of the principals involved in organizing the Salk vaccine field trial seemed to operate on the theory that if they moved ahead as fast as possible their own course of action would develop unstoppable momentum, enough to bring all opposition into line. This wasn't true, but for a time it led to the ragged spectacle of a program moving briskly in several directions at once, like an unruly parade in which each section has its own band and travels its own route, banging their several drums as loudly as possible along their separate ways. Through most of 1953 and much of 1954, the march against polio was accompanied by the loud clash of agendas, the shrill noise of shattering assumptions, and the bladdery whoosh of fond dreams punctured and expectations dashed.

When the Committee on Immunization met in Hershey, Pennsylvania, at the end of January 1953, Basil O'Connor sat at the foot of the conference table and said very little, but he took in a great deal. While Salk showed his charts of successful antibody formation and read his statistics on the long-term health of laboratory animals injected with his vaccine, O'Connor was thinking that if this was not *the* polio vaccine, it certainly sounded like *a* polio vaccine.

To O'Connor that was enough to start on. It was all very well to take the long view and say the foundation should wait for the best possible vaccine before moving ahead, but it sometimes amazed him that all these farsighted scientists couldn't see the nose in front of their faces when it came to serving the people who made their research possible. The public wanted something to tide them over until perfection arrived, and O'Connor saw it as his job to give it to them as soon as he could. An imperfectly effective vaccine, as long as it was safe, was preferable to no vaccine at all. On that basis, he concluded that Salk's vaccine was an idea worth backing, and henceforth he did. To the hilt. Over several people's dead bodies. To the end of his life, and to the bottom of the National Foundation's very deep pockets.

Jonas Salk, for his part, wanted the support and endorsement of the National Foundation. He was excited about the results of his early studies, which showed that it was possible to spur the immune system to produce antibodies to polio without causing an actual infection. He felt he had established an important principle of immunology, one that would advance his career while relieving the suffering of thousands. He wanted to get his vaccine proven—tested, refined, licensed, distributed, and used. He would have been a good deal happier if the expert advisors at the National Foundation looked on his vaccine as more than a promising stopgap, but he was willing to settle for the provisional support that would at least give the killed-virus vaccine a chance to be tried.

The alternative was to continue at Pittsburgh, chairman of a department that was still almost nonexistent, never quite inside the inner circle at professional meetings, watching rivals like Bill Hammon, the gamma globulin man, get all the glory while Salk's ideas were taken over and torn apart by other people— perhaps people neither as skillful nor as scrupulous as he. Faced with these options, it would have taken inner resources of immense depth to oppose the call for a speedy trial of his vaccine, and Salk didn't really oppose it at all. In fact, he had little choice. The juggernaut of public awareness had already begun to roll over the hesitations of scientific tradition.

The one who first started the parade moving was Harry Weaver, the National Foundation's aggressive, dynamic director of research. Weaver was no friend of the publicists—for years he had tried to bar Dorothy Ducas, the foundation's director of public information, from scientific meetings—but some news was too good not to share. For five years, Salk had been telling Weaver that a vaccine was inevitable after the end of the virus-typing project. Weaver had taken him at his word, and had started planning as soon as he learned the results of Salk's first tests at the Watson Home for Crippled Children. The Committee on Immunization met in Hershey on January 24, 1953. Two days later, Harry Weaver was at the Waldorf-Astoria, hinting to the National Foundation's Board of Trustees that great announcements were in the offing. The next morning, newspapers around the world carried the first stories of a new polio vaccine.

Salk had helped Weaver draft his speech, full of reminders that much work remained to be done, but the rumors of the meeting that soon started appearing focused far more on the fact of a vaccine than on the many tests still needed before it would become available. Somebody who had been at the Hershey meeting leaked further details to the press. With each re-telling, Salk's vaccine was reported to be closer to perfection and its mass distribution nearer at hand.

On February 9, *Time* magazine devoted most of its "Medicine" page to the prospects of a polio vaccine in the near future, featuring a large picture of Salk identified as "ready for the big attack" and predicting that "Dr. Salk's labs can probably make enough vaccine for Dr. Weaver's field test this year. But if the test succeeds, it will take at least another year to get mass production quantities of vaccine." By February 26, Dr. Herdis von Magnis, a Danish virologist and good friend of Salk's, was writing, "Of course you know that your work makes headlines all over the world by now, and I am certainly most impressed . . . I shall be studying your papers very hard, I assure you, and so will everybody else."

By the time he received this letter, Salk was very well aware of what he called "the repercussions from the cozy little conference at Hershey, Pennsylvania, attended by a mere handful of people." The same day Magnis wrote from Denmark, Salk had been in New York, addressing a very high-powered group Tom Rivers had called together to advise the National Foundation on how to deal with public reaction to these reports, and to the formal article that was soon to appear in the AMA *Journal*.

Meeting at the Waldorf-Astoria, Basil O'Connor's favorite site for such affairs, the gathering was less an advisory session than a testing of the waters. Despite the long and technical discussions of how the vaccine was made, the real agenda was to gather support—moral and professional—from the people whose cooperation was absolutely essential to any plan for wider testing. The president of the American Medical Association was there, along with the chancellor of the University of Pittsburgh, the assistant surgeon general of the United States Public Health Service, the vice president for medical affairs of the Rockefeller Foundation, and authorities from the world of pediatrics and public health. Joseph Smadel, the one member of the Committee on Immunization who had called for an immediate field trial, came up from the army's Walter Reed Hospital to lend his support. Max Theiler, developer of the yellow-fever vaccine, was there, and so was Margaret Hickey, the influential public affairs editor of the *Ladies' Home Journal*.

After Basil O'Connor had welcomed the guests and Tom Rivers had assured them that in his opinion Salk's vaccine was safe enough to warrant further testing, and after Salk gave a carefully detailed description of his work to date, Rivers cut to the heart of the issue in his characteristic blunt fashion. "Everybody and his brother is going to want the vaccine, just like everybody and his brother is going to want gamma globulin this coming summer," Rivers said. "There is a question here of what the National Foundation should do and what Dr. Salk should do. Dr. Salk is over a barrel. Terrific pressure is going to be put on him. Terrific pressure is going to be put on the foundation and there is always the danger of going too fast. There is also the danger of going too slow, because if you have something that is good, the public should have it as soon as possible."

Rivers wasn't really expecting an answer to the vague question of "what they should do," but he wanted the people gathered there to know what was coming. By virtue of the asking, the question of how and when to go forward with mass testing of Salk's vaccine had been taken outside the realm of virus research and into the more public arena of practicing physicians, medical administrators, opinion shapers, and the appointed guardians of the public health.

These were not the people to whom research scientists generally appealed for intellectual or moral support, and most of them were certainly not the people Salk's fellow virologists considered capable of deciding the merits of his work. The meeting at the Waldorf violated one of the first rules of scientific research, a rule so basic that it need never be stated, which is that the value of laboratory work can only be judged by other scientists active in the same areas of research.

Lest Salk forget this truism, his colleagues were quick to refresh his memory. John Paul, experimenting with a live-virus vaccine in his laboratory at the Yale Poliomyelitis Study Unit, was impressed with Salk's work and wrote to congratulate him, but he thought that an extended field trial was a very bad idea. Not that he said that in so many words, or at least not to Salk himself. What he said—over dinner, on the telephone, and in charmingly indirect letters—was that it would be a terrible pity if the brilliant work being done in Pittsburgh were ruined by allowing the National Foundation officials to take it over. Paul called Salk's studies "the first significant work in experimental vaccination done as yet," but cautioned: "You must not and no doubt will not be railroaded into doing anything that you yourself have not planned or desired." For the next fifteen months, he would continue to try to block a field trial of Salk's vaccine.

Next came a letter from Albert Sabin. Using the tone that Salk always found so infuriating, one of wise sympathy with the struggles of a naive young man, he composed a thinly veiled warning disguised as a letter of condolence. "Although it was nice to see your happy face in *Time*," Sabin wrote, "the stuff that went with it was awful—I knew you couldn't possibly have had anything to do with it, for if you did they would have gotten the story straight. Please don't let them push you to do anything prematurely. . . . John Paul talked to me over the phone today—and his reaction is pretty much like mine. Tommy Francis,

John and I expect to discuss it this Saturday when we're in Washington for a meeting. . . . The foundation has made unwarranted and premature promises before and there is nothing much we have been able to do about it. However, this is the first time they have made a public statement based on work which the investigator has not yet completed or had an opportunity to present at a scientific meeting or in a scientific journal. It is good to know that you will do the best possible job, regardless of what is said by others."

The message was clear. Salk could either be one of "us," the true scientists who discuss the issues at meetings in Washington and report their final conclusions in professional journals, or one of "them"—the spotlight seekers who put themselves at the beck and call of reckless publicists and fund-raisers, and get their picture in *Time* magazine. Like John Paul, but far more aggressively, Sabin tried for months to convince Salk to withdraw his vaccine from trial. When not lambasting Salk's work in public statements, Sabin appealed to him in private to abandon what he assured him would be an embarrassing failure. At a conference in Atlantic City, he even tried to enlist a psychologist on the University of Pittsburgh faculty to talk to Salk. As Salk later heard the story, Sabin had paced the boardwalk for two solid hours, explaining how terribly concerned he was about Salk's well-being. The field trial would be a hideous fiasco, he feared, like committing professional suicide. Was there nothing they could do to help their troubled colleague see the light?

It could have been very persuasive, if Salk had ever felt he had really become "one of us," but Jonas Salk never felt he had received a very warm welcome into the professional fellowship of expert researchers. He had been working independently and he would continue to work independently, managing the National Foundation with the same insistence on hard work and personal control that had already brought him such fast and positive results in his laboratory efforts. The tricky part would be to avoid promising more than he could deliver. He had to keep himself from being pushed into anything that would brand him a charlatan before the public or a laughingstock among his peers, but that was a challenge he was willing to face. As would soon become clear, this was far harder to do than Salk suspected.

II

In early march of 1953, jonas salk thought he had no greater adversary than the editors of the *Journal of the American Medical Association*, where the first formal scientific report of his polio vaccine experiments would soon be published, followed in the next issue by his report on the success of the influenza vaccine he had begun testing at Fort Dix, New Jersey, before he even began to work on polio. Instead of back-to-back triumphs, however, Salk feared that the articles would end by making him look like a fool. Proofs of the first article were so badly garbled that the headings to charts were switched around and the titles of works listed in the bibliography were rewritten. In the second article, the editors had changed "mineral oil" to "liquid petroleum," giving Salk's adjuvant the popular name for a common laxative. On March 16, Salk took the train to Chicago, where the American Medical Association has its headquarters, to deal with the offending editors directly. Certainly his complaints were justified, but the personal appearance was a typically Salkian touch that would be repeated many times over the coming year. To avoid any sense of wasted time, he brought along his new portable dictating machine, an object that was clearly the joy of his life, and spent the trip answering letters.

The editorial problems of professional journals soon paled before far more garish and embarrassing exposure in Earl Wilson's syndicated gossip column "On Broadway." The prospect of a polio vaccine in the near future was flashed across the country as a hot item in a venue better known for breaking the news about which nightclubs were in and which marriages were out. "New Polio Vaccine!" Wilson trumpeted, "Big Hopes Seen." Equally upset by the unorthodox release and by the way it stole the thunder from his carefully planned scientific publication, Salk took the train to New York to consult directly with Basil O'Connor. If Earl Wilson had made his work the subject of popular gossip, the only remedy he could imagine was to find an outlet even more public yet.

At that point, Basil O'Connor's regard for Jonas Salk had not yet developed into the protective affection he later felt, and he had other things on his mind besides Dr. Salk's reputation within the scientific community. Money was one of them. Medical care for polio victims, added to the cost of next summer's gamma globulin program, would almost deplete the foundation's resources. If a field trial of Salk's vaccine was to take place any time soon, it was essential that the foundation refill its empty treasury. When Salk arrived in his office with the suggestion that the National Foundation sponsor a radio broadcast in which he, personally, would explain the true status of his work, O'Connor was delighted with the idea. If Jonas Salk spoke on national radio to explain that he had a vaccine, but it needed work, people everywhere would reach into their pockets for that extra contribution that would speed him in his efforts.

If Salk really believed that such a broadcast would quiet the public demand for a vaccine right away, O'Connor apparently felt no special need to disabuse him. Many people doubted that the ambitious young scientist ever believed that for a moment, and they may have been right. He always insisted that was his motive, but what he wanted even more than quiet was control. It would have been nice to have both, but if recapturing control meant becoming a media figure, he may well have reasoned, so be it.

On March 26, 1953, at 10:45 P.M. Eastern Time, the CBS radio network carried the program "The Scientist Speaks for Himself." First Basil O'Connor reminded his listeners of the important role they, the American people, had as partners of the scientists who were working to eradicate disease. Then it was Salk's turn to address the nation. He spoke calmly and slowly, a patient teacher engaged in what amounted to a tutorial on the scientific method. Starting with the 1909 discovery that polio was a viral disease, he traced the progress of research through the many stages leading up to the good news that his vaccine had been able to cause immunity that lasted at least four or five months—the length of a polio season. Many people had contributed to this progress, Salk emphasized, and much work remained to be done. The public had been made fearful by premature experiments in the past, but new knowledge had brought new certainty to the enterprise of polio prevention.

"Although progress has been more rapid than we had any right to expect, there will be no vaccine available for widespread use for the next polio season," he cautioned. "Certain things cannot be hastened, since each new step cannot be made without establishing first the wisdom of the one before. We are now faced with facts and not merely with theories. With this new enlightenment we can now move forward more rapidly and with more confidence."

Few of the thousands of people who heard that broadcast, or the hundreds of thousands more who read about it in the next morning's papers, had more than the vaguest understanding of what Salk was saying. Nor did they know or care that Salk had committed a grave breach of professional etiquette in presenting his work directly to the public, before it had even been published. As far as the layman could tell, the general point was that there was a real polio vaccine in existence, but it would take a while to produce enough of it to go around.

The radio broadcast brought Salk a brief flurry of public attention and a lasting reputation in the scientific community as a publicity seeker, but it did seem to halt the rumors that a vaccine would be available that summer. Meanwhile, Salk continued to expand and supervise the ongoing experiments at the Virus Research Lab. Many technical questions remained before any of the various vaccine formulations coming from his laboratory would be ready for large-scale production and testing. Four weeks after Salk had made his first report at Hershey, Tom Rivers had suggested that he vaccinate twenty-five thousand people in the Pittsburgh area as the next test of his vaccine. Salk had protested that he was not yet sure which of the various vaccine formulations was the best or when his laboratory would be able to make enough vaccine to do such a project, but he agreed completely with the idea that testing should continue in his own laboratory, under his direct supervision. Ignoring the call for twenty-five thousand subjects, a number Rivers had plucked from the air to indicate how many he thought would be necessary for a full-scale field trial, Salk continued a steady but far more modest expansion of his studies. Not only did he intend to move at his own pace but also in his own way, which was quietly, covertly, and with strict personal supervision.

When Salk needed new volunteers for vaccination studies in the spring of 1953, he went back to the Watson Home for Crippled Children, the scene of his last success, and enlisted the help of Dr. Robert Nix, the staff pediatrician. Nix took care of the Watson children when they got sick—and polio patients are notoriously susceptible to respiratory ailments—but that was only part of a far-flung practice that included the nearby communities of Sewickley, Ambridge, Aliquippa, and Coraopolis. A young man, Nix combined the modern specialty of pediatrics with a somewhat old-fashioned country-doctor manner, and he gave what was called the "family trial" exactly the kind of low profile that Salk wanted.

Five hundred people? Nothing simpler. Nix handed the assignment over to his nurse-receptionist, the only other person who worked in the office he had set up on the second floor above his garage in Sewickley, and Betty just went through her patient list, calling to ask parents if they'd be willing to bring the children up to the Watson Home on the weekend for a series of polio shots. Then the word got out and other people called to see if they could be included. Even the people in the fancy estates up on the hill in Sewickley Heights were calling. "Hey, Bob," they'd say, "you think I could bring my grandkids in to take part in this thing?" Nix was the kind of doctor that people called by his first name, and the kind who would answer, "Sure." There was a number they could call at Watson to get on the list. Parents who were concerned about safety were reassured to learn that Salk had just vaccinated his own three sons. He brought the vaccine home from work and gave them their shots in the family kitchen. That's how simple it was.

The family trial in the spring of 1953 took its tone from the country setting and from Salk himself. In his mind there was no question as to whether or not the vaccine worked, but only which formulation would work best. Half the children received vaccine made with mineral-oil adjuvant. Half got vaccine made with a new water-based medium. Whole families trooped off to be vaccinated together, and many brought picnics and spent the rest of the day on the grounds of the Watson estate, enjoying the mild spring weather. Harry Weaver brought his children from New York to be vaccinated, and so did a few old friends of the Salk family. None of them talked much about what they were doing, and no reporters were on hand. It was serene, bucolic, secret, and secure.

It was also very hard work. Approximately six hundred people took part in the family trial before it was over, but it often seemed like many more. Each of them received two or three vaccinations, and each gave several more blood samples, needed to test how long their antibody levels remained high. Hundreds of children would be brought up every weekend, either to be vaccinated or to give blood. On Saturday morning, Salk would drive up in a station wagon carrying all the equipment and records, the rear fitted with special racks to hold the vials of blood samples. Lorraine Friedman had devised yet another system of index cards and colored tape to keep everything correctly sorted, and they'd be there fourteen to eighteen hours at a stretch, giving shots and taking blood samples and writing down everybody's name. At the end of the day, the equipment was repacked in the station wagon. Sunday the blood samples went to the cold room at the Virus Research Lab to be worked on Monday, and the next weekend they did it all over again with another group.

To measure the different effects of various vaccine formulations, Salk needed blood samples from every person who took part. Some children had to give blood every week, some every two weeks, every four weeks, or every eight weeks, right through the summer. Postcards would come reminding them of their day and time to reappear, and there was more than one child who watched the mail, hiding under the stairs when the day came or, more effectively, simply hiding the card.

Still, there was never any question that what these children were doing was serious and important. People showed up, sometimes cutting short vacations to be there. When a colony of families from Sewickley made their annual summer trip to the Jersey shore, the doctors in the group brought along test tubes and equipment to do the bleedings there. They drew the blood serum, stored it in glass tubes, wrapped the tubes in paper, packed them tight in cardboard boxes, and sent them back to Pittsburgh through the mail—and they kept quiet about what they were doing. Dr. Salk would not know how effective these shots were until the fall, and it was important not to raise great hopes. Everybody understood that—and also understood how very lucky they all were to be able to receive protection before the rest of the world.

The people who went to the Watson Home to take part in the family trial, like the people who watched the later vaccinations in the Pittsburgh schools, were always impressed by how Dr. Salk seemed to be doing everything himself. What they could not see were the great many other workers holding things together back at the lab. By 1953 the Virus Research Lab had become a substantial operation, less like a university laboratory than a mid-size industrial plant. Apart from the many temporary workers and volunteers who had come in for the local field trials, and the occasional graduate or postgraduate student who was passing through, there were twenty-five people on the full-time staff. Working under Salk were two assistant research professors, four research associates, two research fellows, eight research assistants, six technicians, a secretary, and an administrative assistant, as Lorraine Friedman was officially called. Visitors arrived at the lab two or three times a month to study tissue-culture and virus-inactivation techniques, to look at equipment, to bring back reports to their own government, their own lab, their own company, or simply to see where all the excitement was coming from. Even Sir Alexander Fleming, discoverer of penicillin, asked for a tour. It was a far cry from the total of four people who had greeted Salk when he started his career in Thomas Francis' laboratory in Ann Arbor.

Supplies were arriving in massive quantities, bringing with them a proportional rise in storage and shipping problems, wrong orders, and late arrivals. Carpenters came often, though never quite soon enough to keep up with the pace of expansion and renovation. The lab was buying 10,000 glass venules a month for blood samples, specially produced for them by the Scientific Glass Instrument Company. The hospital laundry provided over 200 lab coats a month, along with over 70 uniforms, 300 hand towels, 150 trousers and blouses, and an odd dozen or so of bath towels and bags—all of which had to be counted each month on a laundry list.

Then there was the sheer number of animals coming in and going out. The switch to tissue cultures had greatly reduced the number of monkeys needed to produce poliovirus but it had hardly eliminated them from the scene, and they were joined by several other animals used for a variety of tests for safety. Hens, chicks, and fertile eggs were supplied by nearby Shalom Farm, where Salk had arranged for his brother Herman to begin a business as a supplier of laboratory animals on a property owned by a Pittsburgh lawyer who had become a friend of the family. The Research Supply Company in Philadelphia was sending 1,000 white mice every week in January and February of 1953. Some experiments needed all gray mice, males weighing 15 to 20 grams; some needed white mice of either sex. All had to be picked up at the freight depot. Squirrel monkeys were bought from a supplier called Monkey Business, and shipped north from Florida. Okatie Farm, the National Foundation's monkey-conditioning center, started the year sending Salk fifty monkeys a week—fully half the animals Okatie had. These, too, had to be picked up at the depot, where the empty crates would later be returned. With the monkeys came a standing order for 2,400 pounds of monkey feed every two weeks.

None of this came cheap. In 1953, when you could buy a modest house in suburban New York for $15,000, the Virus Research Lab spent $63,000 on monkeys, $16,000 on chimpanzees, $18,000 on mice, $12,500 on animal feed—and another $30,000 on various "expendable supplies" like dry ice, glassware, postage, and chemicals. However much the public may have envisioned the romantic investigator devoting his midnight hours to solitary research, and however isolated Salk may have felt as he defended his work against more orthodox scientists, at his laboratory he was not alone.

III

WHILE JONAS SALK WAS COLLECTING BLOOD SAMPLES IN Pittsburgh and showing the latest innovations in bottle sealers to admiring colleagues from other laboratories, Basil O'Connor was acting on his own conviction that it was his privilege and his duty to protect the American people from the ravages of paralytic poliomyelitis in whatever way he could, and to do it as soon as possible. By March 1953, he was convinced there would never be any certainty sufficiently certain for the cautious, disputatious experts on the Committee on Immunization, and so he asked Tom Rivers to form yet another expert advisory group, this one made up of leaders in the practice of public health who had no personal stake in polio research. Rivers chose Dr. Thomas Murdock, a member of the American Medical Association Board of Trustees, who represented the practicing physicians; Dr. David Price, assistant surgeon general of the U.S. Public Health Service, and Dr. Joseph Smadel, chief of the Department of Virus and Rickettsial Diseases at the Army Medical Service Graduate School, representing two branches of government health service; and Dr. Ernest Stebbins, director of the School of Hygiene and Public Health at Johns Hopkins, Dr. Norman Topping, vice president of medical affairs at the University of Pennsylvania, and Dr. Thomas Turner, professor of microbiology at the Johns Hopkins School of Public Health, who represented the academic administrators. As Rivers later admitted, "Joe Smadel and I were the only ones who knew anything about viruses. The others were men of good judgement, and they could listen to an argument and make up their minds."

To emphasize the movement from theories of immunization to practical questions of vaccination, the new group was called the Vaccine Advisory Committee. Without ever coming to a formal vote, the issue of a national field trial of Salk's vaccine had changed from "if" to "how." The Committee on Immunization continued to meet, as it had in Hershey, but the march of progress had stepped right around its debates.

For several months, the members of the older group didn't realize what had happened. As the polio season approached, most of the news reports concerned the mass vaccinations of gamma globulin scheduled for that summer. William McDowell Hammon was the man of the hour, gamma globulin was the hope of the moment, and the question of Salk's vaccine seemed safely postponed. Albert Sabin spoke at the annual convention of the American Medical Association in June, and cautioned the 38,500 delegates and guests assembled in New York City not to believe the rumors of Salk's progress.

"Since there is an impression that a practicable vaccine for poliomyelitis is either at hand or immediately around the corner," he began his address, "it may be best to start this discussion with the statement that such a vaccine is not now at hand and that one can only guess as to what is around the corner." Like most of the virologists on the Committee on Immunization, Sabin knew perfectly well that Salk's vaccine was not too far away, but he assumed that no field trial would proceed without considerable further consultation.

The National Foundation, meanwhile, was going through its own identity crisis. For twenty years, it had been raising money to help the victims of the mysterious scourge of polio. For fourteen years, it has put roughly a quarter of that money into research. Now that it was time to put research into action, several different people assumed they would be in control.

Once again, the first to seize the baton was Harry Weaver. Weaver had arrived at the National Foundation in 1946 and proceeded to institute a number of brilliant programs that had speeded progress toward a polio vaccine much faster than anyone had imagined possible, but he had stepped on a lot of toes in the process. Weaver's great strength was his rare ability to look beyond present activities and make plans for future needs.

His weakness was his tendency to proceed on these plans without consulting anybody, making it plain he considered other people's opinions a needless drag on his own swift progress toward the best solution to any problem. In May 1953, a week before the first meeting of the Vaccine Advisory Committee, Weaver took it upon himself to circulate a document with the simple title "Plans for 1954" that was in fact a detailed outline for a national field trial of the vaccine Salk was still busy insisting he did not have.

According to Weaver's plan, one hundred communities were to take part in a field trial between November 11, 1953, and May 30, 1954. Approximately five thousand children in each community were to be vaccinated "on a volunteer basis by [a] local physician under the direction of persons associated with the study"—nine teams that would fan out across the country to conduct the field trial, with a two-week leave to go home for Christmas. Jonas Salk was to administer the program but would have no say in its evaluation. Trial results would be examined in a series of independent experiments by top virologists working around the country, and those evaluations would then be screened by a committee of public health experts headed, as ever, by Tom Rivers.

Despite its attractive sweep and apparently well-organized structure, there were a number of problems with this program. It assumed the consent and cooperation of the state and local health departments, which was not something that anyone could take for granted. It assumed a sufficient supply of vaccine would be ready by November, although little had been done to change from laboratory production to large-scale manufacture, or even to settle on a single vaccine formula. It also assumed the full cooperation of Jonas Salk, whom Weaver had not even informed when he drafted this memo.

The first Salk knew about this program was when Weaver mentioned it on a visit to Pittsburgh in June. As had happened during the virus-typing project, Salk was deeply insulted at being treated like a technician, capable enough at making a product but not worth consulting when it came time to decide the product's fate. His plan for a field trial was steadily to increase the scope of tests he was already doing in Pittsburgh and the surrounding area, halting vaccinations during the summer polio season when local epidemics might confuse results, and then resuming his studies on an expanded scale in the fall. Tom Rivers, speaking for the members of the Vaccine Advisory Committee and as one of the elder statesmen of the profession, had seemed to support that plan in a letter published in the *Journal of the American Medical Association* in April. Now Rivers had endorsed another program altogether, one that Harry Weaver hinted very strongly would proceed whether Salk liked it or not.

To Rivers and Weaver, it seemed obvious that they should be the ones to decide when Salk's vaccine would be ready for large-scale testing and commercial production and how any field trial was to be conducted. The fact that a bright young man from Pittsburgh had done some good work in the lab to develop a promising vaccine did not make him a giant in his field, or in public policy planning, or anywhere else, for that matter. Salk was smart and his vaccine had merit and he should certainly get another grant at the end of the year, but a smart idea on how to improve operations on the line, even a brilliant idea, does not make you head of the company.

For Salk, this was a hard truth to face. He could have expected this kind of dismissal from his critics, but it was a shock to hear it from the people he considered his allies. As Weaver told a later interviewer, "Jonas was indeed in an uncomfortable position. He felt that his baby was premature and was being torn from his arms. He did not like this. Yet it couldn't be any other way. He couldn't take responsibility for the field trials himself. He could not be architect, carpenter, and building inspector— or judge, jury, prosecutor, and defense attorney all at once."

As he had three months before, when news of his vaccine was appearing in gossip columns before it did in professional journals, Salk rushed to New York to meet with Basil O'Connor. Leaving aside the design of a field trial, whatever that might be, the first business was to convince the smartly tailored lawyer who led the National Foundation that there was no vaccine ready to test. There were principles to be explored, possibilities to be extended, but that was it. While Weaver was announcing a field trial to reporters in New York, the people at the Virus Research Lab in Pittsburgh were still experimenting with different forms of virus inactivation. They were thinking about eliminating the mineral-oil adjuvant. They were developing a new form of safety testing that allowed them to bypass some of the difficult and time-consuming animal tests. There were dozens of variables still to be settled before they could move to commercial production. Planning a field trial was so premature as to be ludicrous.

Confronted by a tense, angry researcher who was clearly ready to quit if he did not regain control of his own work, O'Connor made the only decision he could. He studied the charts and technical records that Salk had brought from Pittsburgh and accepted Salk's insistence that the vaccine was not ready for the tests Weaver had planned. More important, O'Connor assured Salk that nothing would be done with his vaccine that Salk did not want done. In return, he simply asked if it would be possible for Salk to settle all his variables in time for a field trial before the 1954 polio season. Yes, Salk agreed, that was possible. Not certain, but possible. He would try.

It was June 22, 1953, when Salk met with O'Connor. The next day he returned to Pittsburgh, relieved that his vaccine was not to be rushed into premature testing, newly committed to working as hard as possible to have it ready soon, and also flushed with a growing certainty that he and Basil O'Connor shared a rare bond of intellectual sympathy. Salk had taken to reading *The Prophet*, Kahlil Gibran's 1923 volume of mystic pronouncements whose message of spiritual and physical fulfillment was enjoying a revival at the time. A year before, he had sent an inscribed copy as a gift to John Enders in Boston. Now he began quoting passages in his letters to Basil O'Connor. Their meeting in New York, he said, "revealed to me so clearly what Gibran must have meant when he said, 'It is well to give when asked, but it is better to give unasked, through understanding; and to the open-handed the search for one who shall receive is joy greater than giving.' " More prosaically, as he later told writer Richard Carter, "We understood each other perfectly, as only a couple of crazy guys like us can. I felt much better when I returned to Pittsburgh."

Through the summer of 1953, a misleading calm settled over the field-trial debate. The National Foundation was busy promoting gamma globulin clinics, which also absorbed the immediate attention of the national and international press. At the Virus Research Laboratory in Pittsburgh, new vaccinations were suspended for the summer months, but the laboratory staff continued to analyze new blood samples from vaccinated children as part of the urgent business of determining how long the vaccine's protection would last. If they needed any prodding to hurry in their work, they had only to pass the four hundred new polio patients admitted to Municipal Hospital that summer. In other laboratories, other researchers continued their own work, confident that the weight of scientific opinion and the demands of ordinary prudence would keep O'Connor from pursing his rash announcements of a vaccine ready before the next polio season.

With the arrival of the fall, all the conflicts reappeared. Harry Weaver had been present at Salk's urgent meeting with O'Connor in June, and one thing that had not been discussed was Weaver's continuing assumption that he would be directing the field trial, whenever it took place. Salk was not the only one having a hard time with Weaver's unilateral decisions, however. Dr. Hart Van Riper, the medical director of the National Foundation, found Weaver particularly abrasive, and while Weaver was planning "his" field trial, Van Riper was planning to get rid of Harry Weaver.

Van Riper was an M.D., which in the pecking order of the 1950s put him ahead of a Ph.D. like Harry Weaver. He had been a pediatrician in Florida until his wife was paralyzed by polio, when he had moved to New York and joined the National Foundation. Tall, articulate, well-tailored, and rather vain, he looked like the Hollywood model of a distinguished physician. He was not an expert epidemiologist, but he made an excellent impression when he spoke before congressional committees and medical societies, and it was important for the foundation to have such a person on its staff. As a medical director, he was neither very bad nor very good, but he had been there longer than Harry Weaver, and he was supposed to be his boss.

During the summer of 1953, as Weaver pushed ahead with

his plans for a field trial starting the next fall, he simply ignored Van Riper. The man who was the foundation's chief link to the medical profession was not invited to meetings called to discuss the use of physicians in the field trial. Weaver's assistants were under orders not to speak to Van Riper. He was not allowed to see reports or memos, he complained to O'Connor. His position was intolerable.

O'Connor, too, was becoming increasingly annoyed with his brilliant but egocentric director of research. It was all very well to think you were smarter than everybody else, but it was just plain dumb to make them know you thought so, which was what Harry Weaver had been doing. Weaver had even taken to excluding O'Connor from his meetings, making sure to schedule them when he knew the foundation's president would be out of town. At the end of August, O'Connor left for Europe and told Hart Van Riper to handle the conflict as he saw best. On September 1, Weaver told Van Riper he would resign rather than suffer his interference, and Van Riper eagerly took him up on the offer.

With Harry Weaver gone, responsibility for planning different parts of the Salk vaccine field trial was divided among the staff of the National Foundation. Many of the people in charge were administrators O'Connor had lured from the American Red Cross. Ray Barrows had come to the National Foundation in 1951 to serve as executive director for the organization at its time of greatest growth. Melvin Glasser, who had been in charge of international programs at the American Red Cross when Basil O'Connor had been director, had come to the foundation in 1952 as deputy executive Director in charge of future planning; now, at O'Connor's urgent request, he became operational director of the field trial. Dr. G. Foard McGinnes, another Red Cross veteran with considerable experience as a public health physician, was to work with the pharmaceutical manufacturers.

Dr. Henry Kumm, an experienced researcher with little of Weaver's flash or arrogance, advanced from assistant director to director of research after Weaver left. Dr. Joseph Bell, one of the top epidemiologists at the Public Health Service, had already arrived from the NIH campus in Bethesda to be the scientific director of the field trial. Dr. Thomas Dublin had also come from the National Institutes of Health to advise on statistical procedures. What they still lacked, however, was an agreed-upon plan and the strong leader who could make it happen.

Throughout the fall, Basil O'Connor continued to assume that the field trial would be administered and evaluated by the National Foundation. They would get expert advice, as they always had, but the center of control would be 120 Broadway. That was where the war on polio had started, and that was where the decisive battle should be launched. The Public Health Service had seized control of the gamma globulin program and changed the plans for distribution in ways he was sure had lessened its protective force. O'Connor didn't want that to happen again.

In other quarters, however, it seemed just as obvious that the National Foundation was in no way qualified to evaluate a field trial of a product they sponsored and promoted. Dr. Alexander Langmuir, the ambitious new chief of the Epidemiology Branch of the Public Health Service's Communicable Disease Center (now the Centers for Disease Control), thought that his staff would be very well suited to administer a nationwide field trial. One of his objectives in insisting that they evaluate the gamma globulin trials in the summer of 1953 had been to establish a precedent for such a role. Other health officials simply stated that any evaluation that originated from the National Foundation would be, by definition, suspect.

Meanwhile, the foundation's scientific advisors on virus research thought that they were still in control, not only of the design of the trial, but of its very existence. The vast difference, in O'Connor's mind, between "advise" and "direct" did not become clear to these advisors until the Committee on Immunization reconvened in Detroit on October 24 to consult with the foundation directors about field-trial plans.

By this time, Albert Sabin had become the chief spokesman for those who opposed the National Foundation's plans for an immediate field trial of the Salk vaccine. Sabin, long a prominent figure in polio research, was also an excellent speaker, often asked to preside over meetings and address professional conferences. At ever opportunity, he reminded his listeners of the many things that had not yet been established—and might never be established—about the readiness of Salk's vaccine for human testing. On October 12, Sabin had testified before a congressional committee that "I, for one, would strongly oppose large-scale tests of tens of thousands and hundreds of thousands of children based on the work on any one investigator, however eminent, however great he may be, until that work has been reproduced by at least another laboratory and shown to be reproducible, and shown that it can be gotten every time."

Two weeks later, when the Committee on Immunization gathered in Detroit for a meeting with Basil O'Connor and Henry Kumm, the new director of research, few were aware of how far the foundation had gone in planning for just such a field trial. Sabin intended to report on his own work with an attenuated virus, hoping to delay any national program until his own vaccine was ready. Joseph Melnick, from Yale, had a similar report and a similar expectation of support. John Paul, who worked with Melnick and was also at the meeting, recalled that "when the question was asked whether a choice was going to be available as to the kind of immunization or the approach to be used against poliomyelitis, Mr. O'Connor remarked sharply: 'That's not the function of this Committee.' "

When the scientists realized that O'Connor was not interested in hearing their proposals for alternate experiments, they were furious. O'Connor had dismissed them as contentious laboratory drones, incapable of making policy decisions. Without meaning to, he had also created bitter enemies for himself, for the National Foundation, and by association, for Jonas Salk. For months various members of the committee considered ways to declare their independence from the National Foundation. They began to court Alex Langmuir at the Communicable Disease Center in Atlanta. They considered applying to the National Institutes of Health to take over funding of their research. They made speeches that amounted to resolutions of no confidence in the foundation's programs. To the degree that O'Connor was aware of these activities, he regretted them as a troublesome impediment to a speedy trial of Salk's vaccine. At no point did he think of changing his plans.

To understand the bitterness that the virus researchers felt, you have to keep in mind that intellectual pride was a central part of their professional identities. They were doctors, teachers, and laboratory scientists, men of discipline and reason who had built their careers on the careful pursuit of unimpeachable truths. In most respects, their expectations were very modest. A grand gesture was to bring a flask of whiskey when you went to meet a colleague at the airport on a freezing winter afternoon; a high time was to get to travel to a conference at somebody else's expense; glamour was being sent on an urgent assignment to an epidemic area, leaving overnight. They made none of the demands for special treatment or accommodations that equally eminent businessmen or lawyers or politicians might use to assert their importance; they would have been astonished to think of asking for a personal secretary at a conference or a better room at a hotel. But they held their reputations very dear, and what they would not tolerate was somebody trying to tell them how to do their work.

Basil O'Connor never lacked the courage of his convictions. Jonas Salk thought of him as an entrepreneur of health, attacking polio as the capitalist conquerors of the nineteenth century had attacked Wall Street. Mel Glasser called him an iconoclast and a pirate. If he had to ignore the members of the Committee on Immunization to get a field trial of Salk's vaccine, O'Connor was willing to do so—even though they were the nation's leading authorities in virus research. What he could not ignore, however, was the continuing confusion and disagreement over what kind of field trial should be held.

Like any other specialized endeavor, field trials have their own vocabulary. The title itself is something of a euphemism. Don't call it a test, and certainly don't call it an experiment—people will think they're dealing with Dr. Frankenstein. The product may be experimental, but the process of testing it is not. Trial sounds good, and a field trial is when you take a study out of the lab and into the great world—into the field.

However you phrase things, the purpose of a field trial is to see whether or not a new treatment or medication is safe and if it is effective. Those who take part in the field trial are known as the subjects, or the test population. The investigators watch them to see if they suffer any side effects and compare their health to that of other, similar people who have not received the substance under trial. The members of this comparison group are called the controls, or the control population.

When people in the control population know perfectly well that they haven't received any new treatment, they are called "observed controls." When all the people taking part in a field trial get a dose of something, but have no idea whether they are being given a potential lifesaver or a harmless, inert solution known as a placebo—a sugar pill, perhaps, or an injection of colored water—they are "blind controls." A "double blind" study is one in which even the people who are administering the field trial don't know who gets the real thing and who gets placebo, and won't know until after all the diagnoses have been gathered, counted, compared, and evaluated.

An observed-control field trial is much simpler to administer than a blind control. As a scientific proof, however, it has distinct drawbacks, particularly with a disease as difficult to diagnose as polio. Doctors who know that their patients have been vaccinated will react to every headache according to their own expectations about the vaccine; so will patients, who in the case of a polio vaccine might not report mild illnesses that they assume cannot possibly be polio or, alternately, might develop all the symptoms of paralysis simply because they think they should.

For some of the same reasons, a single-blind control is not the best kind of study when dealing with a fearful disease like polio. In a single-blind study, the subjects will pester the doctors to tell them what they got or didn't get, or will exert great pressure to get "the real stuff." Doctors have to live in their communities, and it's not very comfortable to spend the rest of your life in the same town with a family you've refused to protect from a crippling epidemic for statistical reasons. If it's your brother's family, or your own, it's not very comfortable to live that way even for a week.

In double-blind placebo-control studies, subjects and investigators alike are much less susceptible to the kind of pressure that throws statistical validity right out the window. Unfortunately, a double-blind field trial is considerably more compli-

cated to run. Twice as many people have to be treated to get
the same measure of results, and a look-alike placebo has to be
produced to give to half of them. Every dose of both trial medication and placebo has to be coded, and the codes have to be
cryptic enough not to be cracked by the ingenious minds of
people out to protect themselves or their families. Somebody
has to keep careful records of who got what, and they have to
keep those records secret until all the reports of everybody's
health or illness come in, at which time the reports have to be
matched against the codes. Only then can the investigators begin
to determine how well the treatment worked.

In most cases, it is worth making the extra effort. Statistical
recordkeeping is the heart's blood of epidemiology, the only
true way of telling where diseases wane and flourish and whether
human intervention has altered an epidemic's course. Without
this carefully gathered numerical record, all findings would be
suspect. Among professional biostatisticians, an observed-
control trial is considered to be about as scientifically valid as
asking the inventor's mother. Blind controls are the only thing
worth talking about, and a double-blind trial is absolutely required if you want your results to be above reproach.

For the Salk vaccine field trials, however, statisticians were
not the first people consulted. Early in the planning stages, long
before he became convinced that he really did have to listen to
dissenting opinions from time to time, Basil O'Connor had
committed himself to observed controls. Health officials in
thirty-three states had agreed to participate on the basis of an
observed-control trial in which all consenting second-graders
would be vaccinated with Salk vaccine. O'Connor had appealed
to them personally, and had appeared before state and local
chapters of the National Foundation making a great many
promises that he had no intention of breaking.

By the time he realized that many doctors and epidemiologists
would not respect the results of such a trial, O'Connor had to
deal with the fact that Jonas Salk also wanted an observed-
control trial of his vaccine. Convinced that the vaccine worked,
Salk insisted it was unethical not to give genuine vaccine to as
many children as possible. He also thought it was unworkable
to use any other plan. Half hoping and half fearing that he

would have to direct the trial himself, and suspecting that in any case it would be evaluated by the National Foundation, Salk felt that the whole affair was quite complicated enough without dealing with placebos. If the field trial was to take place before the start of the polio season in the spring of 1954, he was sure it would have to be an observed-control trial.

The members of the Vaccine Advisory Committee thought that this was absurd. Basil O'Connor had charged them with the responsibility of approving the safety and merit of any field-trial plan, and they saw little virtue in mounting so vast an effort in a way that would produce incomplete or unconvincing results. Salk wanted to vaccinate only second-graders, saying that was the age group most susceptible to polio, but if that were true, then the unvaccinated first- and third-graders he intended to study for comparison would be an inherently different population, and not a valid source of comparison. If he vaccinated all the children in the second grade who volunteered, using those who didn't as his control, the study would run into another kind of statistical bias. It was a well-known fact that people of higher income and higher levels of education were most likely to volunteer for such experiments; it was also well established that these same people were more susceptible to polio, having never been exposed to the mild natural infections of infancy that came with the crowded, less hygienic conditions known to the poor. Again, then, Salk was proposing a comparison of significantly different populations.

Joe Bell, the epidemiologist Harry Weaver had brought from the NIH to be scientific director of the field trial, was adamant about the need for a placebo-control field trial and had long since persuaded Harry Weaver of his view, but Weaver was gone now and the point still had not been settled. If Salk and O'Connor wanted anyone important in the world of science or public health to believe their vaccine studies, and thus make a meaningful step forward in polio prevention, Bell felt they had to have a double-blind field trial.

Bell had a number of other requirements for what he considered a properly run field trial, including elaborate safety tests that O'Connor feared would delay the trial for another year and technical changes in production that Salk thought would destroy the effectiveness of his vaccine. Where Harry Weaver had alienated people by moving ahead in secret, Joe Bell frustrated them by insisting on the most methodical, ponderous, slow-moving trial possible. Once more, O'Connor made it clear that the scientists were his advisors, not his directors. Delegates from the council of the Association of State and Territorial Health Officers visited O'Connor in New York to let him known they had no confidence in anything but a double-blind field trial, especially if evaluated by the National Foundation. Still, O'Connor thought that it would be best if the National Foundation ran the field trial itself and did it the way that Salk wanted, which was using an observed control. Furious, Joe Bell left the foundation in mid-October and returned to the NIH with some very bitter opinions of the autocratic Mr. O'Connor.

Bell's departure from the field trial confirmed Jonas Salk's growing conviction that the only way his vaccine would be tested was if he did everything himself. All that fall, as relations among the field-trial planners became more and more tense, Salk's schedule ranged from the merely punishing to the physically impossible. He seemed to be constantly on the road, constantly in the field, forever dictating letters and telegrams or placing long-distance telephone calls to people he could not see in person. Back in Pittsburgh, his wife Donna led the life of a single parent, his three young sons swallowed their resentment of their absentee father, and the people at the Virus Research Lab worked evenings and weekends, spurring each other on in the exhilaration of being so very near the goal.

On September 8, Salk had been in New York City, reporting to the Vaccine Advisory Committee on his results from the vaccinations done at the Watson Home the previous spring. On September 23, he was in Syracuse, New York, where he had addressed the New York State Department of Health and met privately with Basil O'Connor to discuss the foundation's plans for vaccine manufacture. On October 3, he was in West Virginia, at the Greenbrier, trying to persuade the Vaccine Advisory Committee to back an observed-control field trial. During the period October 7–11, he had addressed the national convention of the American Academy of Pediatrics in Miami, made promotional films and tapes for the National Foundation, and generated a great deal of publicity about what the public assumed was an orderly program for a well-planned field trial in the coming months. Reporting on the successes with more potent vaccines made without adjuvants, Salk ended his speech to the nation's pediatricians by warning, "Our problem is to select not only the fast lane but the one that is safest and most certain." The words were cautious, but the clear implication was that he was on the direct road to a national field trial.

On October 20, Salk had been in Canada to visit the Connaught Laboratories at the University of Toronto, where live virus was being grown in bulk for vaccine production. From there he had gone to Detroit for three days, delivering a paper at an international symposium and trying—unsuccessfully—to fend off the hostile reactions of the Committee on Immunization to the news that a field trial would take place whether or not they approved. On November 6, he had been in Washington, D.C., for the day; November 10–13 he was in New York City to meet with potential vaccine manufacturers and to address the National Foundation's annual Conference on Women's Activities (where, in his haste, he had different people make reservations for him at three different hotels); and on December 8 he was back in Detroit. This is not an unusual travel schedule for a salesman, a journalist, a political candidate, or a vaudeville performer, but Salk was none of these. He was a research scientist, and scientists do their work in labs.

IV

For Jonas Salk, already overextended, the physical and intellectual demands of his travels and his professional disputes were increased by the pressure from both the National Foundation and the public for him to serve as the spokesman and hero of the vaccine development story. Salk was the very model of the dedicated scientist—soft-spoken, hardworking, patient with the uninformed, hesitant to make great claims for his work but fierce in his insistence that it *would* be possible to end the reign of terror that polio had brought. The vaccine story had the drama of life and death, the charm of little children, the awesome spectacle of decades of obscure and difficult research, and the human interest of families and ordinary people involved in a great and selfless effort. There was no way on God's green earth that journalists weren't going to write about it.

Good press relations had always been an intrinsic, essential part of the fight against polio. Before Franklin Roosevelt was elected president or even governor, Louis Howe had raised money for Warm Springs by posing the physical therapists like bathing beauties and getting their pictures in the Sunday papers. Eleanor Roosevelt had danced with Hollywood's handsomest heroes at the President's Birthday Balls, smiling for the newsreel cameras. After Roosevelt's death in 1945, Basil O'Connor was the individual most closely associated with the fight to end polio, and he was quite used to having his speeches reported in the society features and gossip columns of the national papers rather than in the back pages reserved for scientific reports.

Jonas Salk was used to no such thing. He was accustomed to

working in the closed community of scientists and the isolation of the laboratory. Like many researchers, he put a high value on his achievements but was very cautious—an outsider would almost say furtive—about letting anybody know what he was up to before the results were in. He hated the idea of photographers in the lab and reporters hovering outside the building. He hated the requests for speeches and public appearances, the call for "just a few hours" with the foundation's publicists, the press releases that gave a timetable for results he had not yet achieved. He found his new role as a public figure awkward and unfamiliar, and he made it far more difficult than it might have been by his mistaken assumption that the rules of the laboratory would continue to apply as he conducted his work under the increasingly bright light of public interest.

The public relations staff at the National Foundation headquarters knew perfectly well that Dr. Salk was not going to preside over dance marathons or appear with Little League teams, but they thought it reasonable and appropriate to arrange a few dignified photo sessions, perhaps a speech or two or the promise of an exclusive interview in a very prominant journal. Promoters necessarily do a good part of their work before the results are in, creating a climate of acceptance for a product that is still in production—and they do this as much for miracle drugs as for miracle detergents. Salk was a personable man whose very presence inspired trust, and God knows a vaccine against polio would sell itself to a world just waiting to buy it, but the money that supported his lab had to come from somewhere, and the children who would test his vaccine weren't just standing on the corner, lined up with their left sleeves rolled and their right hands clutching consent forms. If the publicists couldn't be out there in advance, making people aware of the possibility of a polio vaccine in the future, keeping them confident that the National Foundation was full of good people who deserved financial support right now and moral support as soon as there was something to be tested, the Salk vaccine field trial would be a party to which nobody came.

Salk recognized this, at least to some degree, and whenever he showed signs of forgetting, Basil O'Connor or one of his assistants was on the phone to freshen his awareness. But he *hated* it. However much he may have dreamed of success, he was not prepared to deal with it in the highly public form in which it arrived. As early results indicated that the gamma globulin clinics had not been a great success in preventing polio, public interest turned to the renewed reports that Salk's vaccine might be available for the coming year. With every speech Salk made, and particularly after his widely reported address to the American Academy of Pediatrics in October, there was a new surge of attention to both the polio vaccine and the man identified with its development.

The requests for interviews came from all directions: from National Foundation headquarters and from the local chapter offices, from old friends, from local newsletters and mass circulation magazines. They came in the mail, addressed directly to the Virus Research Lab, or they were forwarded by the National Foundation or the University of Pittsburgh mailroom. They came by telephone and telegraph, and they came from places too prominent to ignore. *The New York Times* had already published a long article in its Sunday *Magazine* that compared the temporary protection of gamma globulin with the hope for a lasting cure from Salk's laboratory. The Public Affairs Division of CBS Television wanted to include Salk's lab in a series of twenty-six half-hour programs built around interesting research projects now going on in American Universities. *Life* magazine was ready to assign its science writer, Robert Coughlan, to do a story on the vaccine that the editors promised would be a model of thoroughness and accuracy. Reporters from *Time* and *Newsweek* were now vying with ones from the *Pittsburgh Press* and the *Post-Gazette*. Everyone, it seemed, wanted a piece of Dr. Salk.

Salk didn't like to say no to these requests, but he didn't want to say yes, either. Someone more experienced in dealing with the press would have prepared a few cordial answers for general distribution and a set policy for dealing with more substantial media requests, but Salk didn't do that. Instead, he vacillated —sometimes cooperating with the National Foundation, sometimes passing all requests to the Office of Public Information at the University of Pittsburgh, sometimes making his own decisions on whom to see or not to see, and sometimes hiding in his office in the hope that everybody would just go away and leave him alone. Reporters and photojournalists spent hours cooling their heels at the Virus Research Lab while Salk lay on the couch in his inner office and agonized over whether to co-operate on their stories. Photographers spent half the day arranging their lights and choosing their props, and the other half hoping Salk would appear before they had to take it all down again. When he had to make a decision on a publicity question, he was more likely to consult with his wife or his secretary than with the public relations professionals who could have given him a more accurate sense of what results his actions would bring. Wary of misrepresentation, he tried to control everything that was written about himself or his work. He revised the university press releases, editing out all specific details of the work being done at the Virus Research Lab, including the projects of his associates. He demanded substantial cuts in the story that appeared in *Life*. In the midst of his many other activities in the fall of 1953, he tried to rewrite the National Foundation press kits and sent the director of public relations detailed suggestions on how she should restructure their publicity campaigns, including the illustrations. He asked journalists to submit their articles for his approval before publication, and he confessed more than once that he would really rather write the articles himself.

No matter what they did, Salk found the results painful. When he began to feel too besieged by reporters or by the request for appearances from the National Foundation, he would turn for protection to a rival group that also felt a proprietary interest in his work, the public information staff of the University of Pittsburgh.

Despite the looming presence of the National Foundation, many people at the University of Pittsburgh persisted in the opinion that since Salk was a member of the university faculty and the Virus Research Laboratory was part of the Medical School, what came out of Salk's laboratory was a Pitt story before it was anything else—and a story they were obliged to shield from sensational or premature release. By 1953 the effort to transform the university into a medical powerhouse was starting to show results in other areas besides virus research, and

Francis Pray, the director of public information, was bringing in a good many new people to handle news from the health centers. One of these newcomers was Tom Coleman, fresh from the University of Nebraska, where he had developed considerable experience in what he described as "the medical writing trouble-shooting problem-solving whole public affairs area." Coleman's title was assistant to the vice chancellor for public information, with jurisdiction over all public affairs and public information for the health center, but it was clear from the first that his main occupation for the foreseeable future would be to handle Jonas Salk.

Coleman had grown up in Washington, D.C., when Roosevelt was in the White House, and had come of age as a reporter in the years when the March of Dimes was a publicity event without precedent or parallel. There was no question in his mind that the publicists of the National Foundation were slick, arrogant fear-mongers, raising money through a campaign of terror. He was also quite convinced that they were better at what they were doing than anybody else. To the best of his ability, for the next two years, he sought to shield Salk from the kinds of promotion that he felt would destroy his work as a scientist, while working to remind the world that the University of Pittsburgh had a large role in Salk's success. Coleman was outnumbered and outmaneuvered at every turn, but he tried.

A good many of Coleman's problems came from the fact that Salk was not an easy man to help. He would give special interviews and early information to people he liked. If he took a dislike to a journalist, he could be cold and uncooperative. In the world of academic research, where people carry on rancorous debates in the "Notes and Queries" columns of professional journals, it is common to respond to every misinterpretation or attack with a detailed rebuttal. When dealing with mass-media journalism, it is often better to ignore negative reports entirely, except for a firm "No comment," but this was a very difficult strategy for Salk to accept. The net effect of his many efforts to explain his position, unfortunately, was exactly the opposite of what he intended, since he often antagonized reporters while convincing his colleagues that he was seeking publicity. It was, they agreed, unbecoming to his professional dignity to give these interviews. It was unseemly to announce results that had not been confirmed by other laboratories. It was unprecedented, unwarranted, unethical, and unforgivable.

Worst of all, Salk could have added, it interfered with the progress of his work. On November 16, when the design, the timing, the size, and the very possibility of a vaccine field trial were all the subjects of bitter disputes both within the National Foundation and between the foundation and the separate spheres of research science and public health, Salk was shocked to learn that Basil O'Connor had just held a press conference in which he announced that the National Foundation would be ready to begin a national field trial by the first week in February. That afternoon Salk called O'Connor's office, collect, to dictate a statement he had drafted: "There are just so many hours in the day that my associates and I have at our disposal. Unless we can work in the way we see fit, uninterrupted by the many requests for material for newspaper and magazine stories, there will be insufficient time for the job that remains. There will be time enough, after the next phase of the work succeeds or fails, to inform the public of what has taken place. At the risk of being regarded as uncooperative I must ask that the laboratory and I be forgotten for the next six months. We make this request in the public interest since it is in this way that we and the press can be of greatest service."

On the bottom of his heavily revised draft of this statement, Salk crossed off the names of magazines whose interviews he had just canceled. He then telephoned the same statement to the director of public relations for the University of Pittsburgh Medical School.

The attitude of the people assigned to write about Salk's work was generally far less complicated or hostile than he imagined. They were onto a big story and they didn't want to miss a scoop, but most of them were less interested in sensationalism than in making sure they had the facts clear and the names right. The personal questions that Salk found so offensive were the journalists' attempts to give a human shape to the disembodied shadow that was all most people knew about the life of the working scientist. If their perspectives sometimes seemed in-appropriate or ill informed, it was perhaps because they were inventing the conventions and the rhetoric of science reporting as they went along.

Like so many other features of everyday life in the 1950s, science reporting, as a journalistic specialty, was a by-product of World War II. The dawn of the atomic age created a demand for writers who could follow what Einstein, Teller, and Oppenheimer were talking about and translate it into language the ordinary reader could comprehend. Several of the major newspapers had decided that they should have somebody to specialize in science writing the way they had a crime reporter, a labor reporter, or a business reporter, but in the years before Sputnik or the American space program, it was still a young, undeveloped field. Today there are at least two hundred papers in the United States with full-time science reporters, and a major journalistic enterprise like *The New York Times* will have half a dozen writers who deal with nothing but science. In the early 1950s, there were perhaps ten papers in the country that had regular reporters assigned to cover scientific developments, and probably fewer magazines, where stories were more likely to be commissioned from outside writers as the occasion arose. Radio news was limited to war, politics, and weather, with the occasional flash bulletin about great inventions or disasters. Television news was almost nonexistent.

The journalists who made a specialty of science reporting were a small fraternity, and they all knew each other. John Troan, then health science writer for the *Pittsburgh Press* and the man who did more reporting on the work at the Virus Research Lab than anybody else, could tick off the members of the newspaper club: "We had Al Blakeslee from the AP. We had Jack Geiger from International News Service, he's now professor of public health at the City University of New York—he went to medical school after he left newspaper writing. We had Earl Ubell from the *New York Herald Tribune*. We had Bill Laurence with *The New York Times*—he was the dean of the science writers. Pierre Fraley was with the *Philadelphia Bulletin*. We had some good ones on the West Coast, too. We had Silverman with the *San Francisco Chronicle*. We had Jack Allen, and George Dusheck

—they were in San Francisco, too. There was Chris Clausen at the *Los Angeles Herald Examiner*. They asked some good questions and were very knowledgeable."

Troan was one of the very few reporters with whom Salk would cooperate, and he became something of an authority on news from the laboratories at Pittsburgh's Municipal Hospital. Cynics noted that Troan wrote for the flagship paper of the Scripps-Howard wire service, so that his friendly reports of the vaccine work going on in Pittsburgh got national exposure, but Salk's willingness to talk to him dated from long before the days when he felt the need to defend his vaccine. When Salk had just arrived at the University of Pittsburgh, Troan interviewed him about the influenza vaccine he was testing at Fort Dix, and became the first of many journalists to confront the scientist's desire to review the story before it was published.

Good reporters always check their facts, but few of them, good or bad, ever let their subjects sit in judgment on their stories. Troan was the exception to that rule. When conflicting schedules made it impossible for him to submit his story in advance, Troan promised never to ask for another interview if Salk didn't like the article. Sunday morning an anxious Salk, working at Fort Dix, bought the Pittsburgh paper in Atlantic City and sent a telegram to Troan congratulating him on the good job. Of course, if he had known Salk was going to hit the polio jackpot, Troan later confessed, he never would have made that promise—but there it was. From then on, Troan had Salk's trust, and his home telephone number.

He also had a mole in the Virus Lab. Dr. L. James Lewis, a bacteriologist on the laboratory team, would call him when something important was happening. Troan would hang around the Bamboo Garden, a Chinese restaurant Salk favored for fast lunches, and he'd just happen to run into Salk a good deal. On one of those days, Salk was working on the wording of the letter to go out with permission forms for early vaccine trials in the Pittsburgh schools, and Troan helped him with his phrasing— and then asked in return that Salk schedule his press conference announcing the trial so that Troan could have a scoop for the first edition of the *Press* that day. When the public announcement came, Troan asked enough questions to cover the story he had already written, then telephoned the press room to run it. Bill Burns, the news anchor in Pittsburgh's radio station KDKA, came up to Troan later to tell him how impressed he'd been by how quickly he'd filed his report to get it into the early edition. "God," he said, "I never saw anybody who could dictate a story so fast!"

Other writers, frustrated by Salk's tendency to answer a question with another question, to talk about general principles instead of specific events, and to deal in abstractions that evaporated when you tried to put them into a story, would try to work through Troan to get their story. The Pittsburgh stringer for Luce publications was Bill Jacobs, who was also the assistant city editor for the *Pittsburgh Press* and Troan's boss. When Salk didn't want to grant *Life* a half-day to do photographs in the lab, the home office contacted Jacobs, who asked Troan to intervene. Salk relented and a photographer from *Life* arrived in Pittsburgh, along with the National Foundation's chief photographer, John Blecha. Troan was there, too, when the *Life* photographer asked Salk to pose holding a rack of the test tubes used to culture poliovirus. "Just a little higher," he asked, as Salk pretended to hold the cultures up to the light, "Just a little higher," until the test tubes fell from the rack and broke on the floor. Terrified that they were being exposed to polio, all three newsmen dashed for the door while Salk got a rag and doused the mess with formaldehyde. The *Life* man was so rattled he lost his film and had to borrow photographs from Blecha. Revealingly, one of Blecha's best shots showed Salk standing in the entry to his office, one arm crossed over his chest, the other stretched out to block the door.

When Gilbert Cant, *Time* magazine's medical editor, came to Pittsburgh to do an interview, Salk took an immediate dislike to the man and refused to talk to him. Again Bill Jacobs asked Troan to intervene, and again Salk relented. The problem, as Troan soon discovered, had been that the *Time* editor had not seemed completely convinced of the merits of Salk's work. Mimicking the hostile tone in which Cant had asked his questions, Salk complained about having to put up with treatment like that. He wasn't used to having to sell his work to people he considered his intellectual inferiors, and he didn't like it.

People who have known Salk for many years, or who knew him best in the years before the polio vaccine, often comment that the barrage of publicity surrounding the vaccine made him cautious and distrustful. "Jonas has changed," they will say. "He used to be so approachable." This is not entirely true. He may have lost some of the joking charm that softened the edges of his intensity, but he was always wary of self-revelation. Salk's natural caution was like a stutter, getting in the way of that which he most wanted to say, and the stutter was never more in evidence than during the months when the polio vaccine field trial was struggling to come into being.

The highly detailed record that scientists make of their laboratory procedures is called a protocol. When preparation of a new drug passes from laboratory to commercial manufacture, the protocols serve as the blueprint for operations. It is perfectly appropriate that a protocol is also the name of the signed document that lists the points of agreement for those negotiating a treaty, as well as the common name for the ritual forms and courtesies used by government and military officials. The effort to draft the protocols for commercial manufacture of the Salk vaccine required all the delicacy of diplomatic negotiations, and the struggle for agreement threatened all the hostility of war.

The process was complicated by the unusual circumstances under which the new vaccine would be produced. In the fall of 1953, Salk had inoculated approximately seven hundred people with some version or another of a killed-virus polio vaccine produced in his laboratory. This was a major expansion of the studies he had begun only the year before, but there was no way that the Virus Research Laboratory could make enough vaccine to conduct a field trial on the scale that everyone now expected. Indeed, one of the things being tested in the field trial would be the safety and ease with which Salk's laboratory procedures could be adapted to the very different circumstances of large-scale mass production.

Before he left the National Foundation on September 1, the farsighted Harry Weaver had anticipated this problem and taken steps to solve it. As early as the spring of 1953, he had ap-

proached Parke, Davis and Company, one of the leading pharmaceutical houses in the United States, to see if they would be
interested in manufacturing vaccine for a field trial. Parke, Davis
had experience in working with biological products and making
vaccines with adjuvants. The director of their Microbiological
Research Division, Dr. Fred Stimpert, had been working on
polio when Salk was still in medical school, and he was very
interested in the possibilities of a killed-virus vaccine. He was
also eager to convert his operations to the tissue-culture techniques that John Enders had developed and Jonas Salk had used
to produce large quantities of live poliovirus without large numbers of monkeys. Given the time pressures of the field-trial schedule, however, Parke, Davis was willing to enter into an unusual
agreement whereby they would purchase live virus from the
Connaught Laboratories of the University of Toronto—across
the Canadian border some two hundred miles east of their manufacturing plant in Detroit, where the imported virus would be
inactivated to make vaccine. The researchers at Connaught had
put in a great deal of work on culturing poliovirus, and had
developed the synthetic medium in which much of the virus was
now grown—named Medium 199 after the number of attempts
it had taken to get the formula right.

Long before negotiations reached that stage, several other
manufacturers had begun paying close attention to the news
coming out of Pittsburgh. In the beginning of February, the
director of tissue-culture research in the Biological Research
Division of Eli Lilly and Company had read about Salk's vaccine
in *Time* and had written at once to express his interest in helping
in its manufacture. Salk's reply, with a typically lengthy explanation of the many demands on his time of late, offered only
weak assurances. "You may be sure that when the time is proper
we will call upon you," he answered. "It is not our intention
to take the problem beyond a certain point and that point is
indeed short of mass production."

Six months later, Bettylee Hampil, director of virus research
at Sharp and Dohme, offered Salk $2,000 a year to be a con-
sultant to the company "on tissue culture methods and problems
connected with the possible (or should I say inevitable?) production of polio vaccines." The job would be simple, she prom-

ised, often entailing no more than an answer to a telephone query, and could easily be kept "highly confidential," but Salk turned it down, confessing "there are just so many things that I can attend to at once." Shortly after that, the president of Eli Lilly wrote to R. H. Fitzgerald, the chancellor of the University of Pittsburgh, to make sure his company wasn't excluded from any plans for commercial manufacture that the university might be making.

When questioned, Salk assured the chancellor that there had been no agreement signed with any manufacturer, and that his only commitment was to share the fruits of his research with "all those who are interested in helping solve the problem of poliomyelitis." What Salk had not known, and did not discover until September, was that Harry Weaver had an oral agreement with Parke, Davis to be sole manufacturers of vaccine for the field trial.

Salk had a troubled romance with Parke, Davis that dated back to the mid-1940s, when they had offered him a well-paid position as consultant on virus inactivation that Thomas Francis had insisted he refuse. While he was working in Francis' lab at the University of Michigan, Salk had helped his younger brother, Herman, get a job at Parke, Davis. After he moved to Pittsburgh, Salk *had* become a consultant to the Detroit company, working with them on vaccine adjuvants, but he had been incensed when Parke, Davis issued a press release in March 1953, the day after his first article appeared in the AMA *Journal*, implying that his laboratory and theirs were working together on the polio vaccine.

Over the next six months, the once-cordial relations between Salk and Parke, Davis deteriorated further. Fred Stimpert, put in charge of vaccine production at Parke, Davis, had his own ideas about how things were to be done. He also had trouble understanding Salk's specifications for making the new vaccine—partly because he and his staff were not used to dealing with such precise instructions, and partly because Salk considered the specifications an experimental document that he could change repeatedly as new results were obtained in his own lab.

Those who were eager to stage a field trial in the winter and spring of 1953–54 treated Salk's insistence that the vaccine was not finished as the sign of a man who was young and nervous, unwilling to relinquish authority or share control, never wanting to concede he was finished because a final product would demand a final judgment—of the creator as well as his creation. Basil O'Connor, counting on public pressure to create unity, continued to issue statements assuring the world that the field trial would begin soon. Tom Rivers talked in tones of irritation and resignation about the way Jonas just couldn't let go of his vaccine, wouldn't come up with specifications for the manufacturers, wouldn't stop fiddling with the adjuvants or the intervals of vaccination. In Rivers' opinion, it was time to stop tinkering and hit the road. "The first automobile was a far cry from today's cars," River later said, "but we did not go on walking while waiting for the 1954 models with all their improvements. So why let children continue to run the risk of polio when we have what might be the Model T of polio vaccines ready?"

This kind of statement seemed to Salk to ignore the real importance of his efforts. He felt he was trying, against enormous odds, to get out the best possible product in the shortest possible time, testing a satisfactory vaccine while continuing to work on improvements. He wanted to show not just that the killed-virus vaccine was better than nothing, but that it was better than anything—or at least would be, when he and his associates had finished working out the last wrinkles with adjuvants, vehicles, preservatives, and safety tests.

Like most pharmaceutical companies, Parke, Davis had less lofty goals. The people there assumed their object was to produce the best available vaccine, not to discover the best conceivable one. They were accustomed to working in secret and in competition, doing things in whatever way gave them the best results at the lowest cost. When they had trouble with the centrifuge used to concentrate virus particles, they decided to eliminate that step in the process. When their incubator failed to keep the virus samples at a constant temperature, they assumed the variation of a few degrees would make no difference. When they asked Salk why they were not achieving the expected results, he often dismayed them by suggesting an entirely different procedure. As Salk later said, "They couldn't wait to get rid of me and my damn research project." It took a long time and a great deal of effort to persuade them that Salk's protocols were not a series of suggested guidelines but a set of sacred and inviolable commandments, to be followed with an unquestioning devotion that was not to waver even when the ways of the maker seemed mysterious indeed.

Salk, meanwhile, suspected a subtle form of sabotage. He thought Parke, Davis was trying to discredit his inactivation process so the company could switch to a method of virus inactivation with ultraviolet radiation on which it held a patent. On September 24, three weeks after Harry Weaver left the National Foundation, Salk had traveled to Syracuse, New York, for a private meeting with Basil O'Connor. He insisted to O'Connor that the manufacture of vaccine for the field trial was too crucial and complicated a task to give to a single company. Too much could go wrong if Parke, Davis were given a monopoly on production. They had to call in some competition.

One result of Harry Weaver's departure from the National Foundation in the fall of 1953 was that Basil O'Connor began to take a much more active role in the work of organizing the field trial and dealing with the many parties involved. O'Connor was growing used to Salk's sudden appearances on urgent missions of damage control. The intense young doctor from Pittsburgh had wanted to get rid of Harry Weaver. He wanted to get rid of Joe Bell. Now he wanted to get rid of the manufacturer, too. Still, there was at least some justice in his fears. It would do no harm to canvas a few other companies and see who else might be able to come into the field trial, if needed.

The task was simplified by the fact that there would be no patent on the vaccine. Shortly after Salk's first article had appeared in the AMA *Journal* the previous March, Harry Weaver had set the foundation's lawyers to study the question and they had concluded that since neither the processes nor the materials Salk used were new discoveries, no patent was possible. The vaccine might bear Salk's name, but he would receive no direct profit from its production.

Neither would be pharmaceutical companies, at least at first, though their eventual rewards would be vast. The National Foundation's condition for inviting a manufacturer to participate in the field trial was that the foundation, which would pay the expenses of manufacture, would then receive the vaccine at cost. In return for this altruistic contribution to public health, the manufacturer would be in a position to produce and sell vaccine the moment it was licensed, should that ever happen, charging the usual 300 percent markup.

On November 11, 1953, O'Connor met in New York with top executives of most of America's leading pharmaceutical houses to acquaint them with the possibilities of working on the polio vaccine field trial. Apart from Parke, Davis, five other companies were both willing and able to join the effort: Eli Lilly and Company, the Pitman-Moore Company, Sharpe and Dohme, Wyeth Laboratories, and Cutter Laboratories.

These were all highly reputable organizations with their own research laboratories and their own reputations to protect. Nonetheless, they were still commercial enterprises. Pharmaceutical companies are at best benevolent opportunists, seeking to make a tidy profit by improving the quality (and quantity) of life. They want their products to work, because medical effectiveness is the key to lasting sales, and they want them to be safe, both for humane reasons and because one major lawsuit could be ruinous. If at all possible, they also want them to be simple to make.

Simplicity is difficult to achieve when you are dealing with living organisms, even ones as small as viruses. In the pharmaceutical world, the great division is between biologicals and chemicals—drugs that are made from living substances and drugs that are made from chemical compounds. Biologicals are tricky to produce, expensive to store, and easy to get wrong. Nobody enjoys working with monkeys, or worrying about mutant strains of microbes, or following the elaborate rules of isolation that are needed for any manufacture of living organisms. Drug companies produce the biologicals as a public service, and get out of the business whenever they can. They live off the chemicals. Chemicals let you sleep easy at night and wake up rich in the morning. When the public thinks of great medical breakthroughs, it tends to think of immunizing vaccines that prevent dreaded diseases like smallpox, typhus, or yellow fever. People in the pharmaceutical business think the greatest wonder drug of all is aspirin, a simple compound of carbon, hydrogen, and oxygen that occurs naturally as a by-product of coal tar and is also easy to synthesize.

From a manufacturing perspective, making the Salk vaccine was a project that required substantial outlays before any profit would be seen. Separate facilities would have to be built for culturing each of the three strains of poliovirus. Animal quarters would have to be enlarged to house the thousands of monkeys that each company would need on the premises at any given time. Animal handlers would have to be hired to care for the monkeys, and veterinarians to teach the handlers how best to do that. They would need very accurate incubators to grow the poliovirus, and vast numbers of the huge glass bottles in which the virus was inactivated. Company representatives suggested that the National Foundation should provide grants for them to build these new facilities, but Basil O'Connor had flatly refused.

Despite these difficulties, they were all very interested in making a polio vaccine, for reasons both humanitarian and commercial. Everyone could tell this would be a product that would sell itself. Without the customary protection of secret formulas and patented procedures, the manufacturers had to rely on speed and efficiency to give them a profitable share of the potential market. Participation in the field trial would give a company a significant lead in producing the huge supplies of vaccine that would be wanted if and when a license were granted. If the vaccine failed to prove safe and effective in the field trial, they would have worked for nothing, but they were willing to take that risk to reserve a piece of what promised to be a very large pie.

Still, no definite plans were made to enroll other companies in manufacturing the vaccine. The only agreement that existed was the one Weaver had reached with Parke, Davis; an agreement that Salk was trying, reluctantly, to keep. By the beginning of December, Salk was more frustrated than ever by what he considered the deliberate refusal by some at Parke, Davis to follow the particulars of his techniques. In a long, fervent memo to O'Connor that he rewrote several times before deciding not to send, Salk voiced his fear that the people at Parke, Davis were both incapable of doing the work that was needed and unwilling to do it in any case. "The entire program is being jeopardized by the attitude that prevails," he wrote, "and I would urge very strongly that we waste as little time as possible attempting to bring them into line or getting their cooperation, [and] that every effort be made to overcome the obstacle by making arrangements with Eli Lilly."

V

On October 28, 1953, when Jonas Salk celebrated his thirty-ninth birthday, Basil O'Connor sent a telegram full of punning wisdom to mark the day. "You Connaught know life until you are one year older," O'Connor assured him. "Until then you have to rely on the sage of 120 Broadway and Albert (not Einstein) to see you through this adolescent period. Twenty years from now this will be interesting but good history and you will be a man. . . . Best wishes from one who knows." By the end of November, O'Connor realized that patience and humor would not be enough to see any of them through.

In the space of ten weeks, the National Foundation had lost both its director of research and the scientific director of its field trial; had jeopardized the support of the state health officials whose cooperation would be essential in gathering information about polio cases after a field trial; had alienated the research scientists whose laboratories, carefully nurtured by foundation grants over the years, were the only places capable of doing the huge volume of sophisticated biological analysis the field trial would demand; and had reached a near-impasse with the company that was at present the only manufacturer of the polio vaccine. Meanwhile, Jonas Salk, their principal investigator and the man the public identified as the sole creator of the new vaccine, was being driven to distraction by what he saw as a constant need to stamp out the brush fires of opposition.

If the National Foundation was to salvage the hope for a field trial before the summer of 1954, O'Connor realized he would have to take decisive action to avoid the morass of problems in

224

which the entire effort threatened to sink. The most urgent business was to find a disinterested third party who would be able to turn the focus away from professional rivalries, power struggles, and theoretical disputes and back to the neglected question of whether or not Salk's vaccine worked. The person he turned to was Thomas Francis, Jr., who had introduced Salk to the making of killed-virus vaccines and who was still the director of the School of Public Health at the University of Michigan.

During the summer and fall of 1953, when the chances of actually conducting a polio vaccine field trial seemed to be going to hell in a handbasket, Francis had been traveling through Europe with his wife, enjoying the first and last sabbatical leave of his career. The National Foundation for Infantile Paralysis had paid for part of it, giving Francis $1,000 to attend a world conference on medical education in London in August and another $1,000 grant to take part in an international conference on microbiology in Rome in September. From there he and his wife went to Scandinavia, touring the countryside and the laboratories of Francis' colleagues. In late November, they returned to London, where Francis received a transatlantic call from Hart Van Riper asking if he would direct the field trial for Salk's vaccine.

There were many virtues to the choice. Francis was an active supporter of killed-virus vaccines who openly doubted that the short history of immunology had established a "tradition" of live-virus vaccination. He was very familiar with both the problems and the benefits of Salk's techniques, most of which were based on the work with influenza Salk had begun under Francis, and he respected Salk's skill while knowing how to guard against his desire for control. An admirer of Sabin's work but not his personality, Francis was unlikely to be moved by the latter's public pronouncements about the naive folly of moving forward with a killed-virus vaccine. Most important, everybody knew that when Tommy Francis talked about working up to a standard, it was one of unimpeachable thoroughness; even the most dedicated opponent of the new vaccine could never say a trial supervised by Francis was political, biased, or incomplete.

In 1953 transatlantic telephone calls were reserved for the

most urgent matters. The National Foundation—and the fight against polio—obviously needed him badly. After speaking to Hart Van Riper and consulting with colleagues in England who were familiar with the whole history of the foundation's programs, Francis cut short his sabbatical and returned to the United States. Reaching New York on December 5, he met Van Riper and O'Connor for breakfast and promptly got into an argument when he insisted on the need for a double-blind field trial.

Two weeks earlier, O'Connor had held a well-attended press conference to announce that a field trial of Salk's vaccine would begin in early February, using the observed-control plan that Harry Weaver had first outlined six months before. Now Thomas Francis insisted that O'Connor would have to retract that pledge. The next day, Francis spoke to Jonas Salk. Although Salk had been arguing for the last six months that an observed-control field trial was the only kind possible, he now agreed that if Francis were directing the evaluation, a double-blind trial would be perfectly fine. Officials at the National Foundation were astonished to learn of Salk's abrupt capitulation, and they began to feel new hope that the field trial might really take place.

Thomas Francis was far from sure, however, that he wanted to take on the job. Long after the field trial was over, Tom Rivers remembered a scene in his office at the Rockefeller Institute: "I can still see Tommy Francis pacing backwards and forwards, backwards and forwards, trying to make up his mind if he would do this job. That was characteristic of Tommy. He had a hell of a time making up his mind." Then, lest he be misunderstood, Rivers added, "He's a smart boy, Tommy. Smart man."

Rivers was right on both counts. Francis' ability to anticipate the possible ramifications of an issue—one of the talents that qualified him as a "smart boy"—made him a good person to run a complicated project like the polio vaccine field trial, but also made it terribly difficult for him to take the job, knowing from the first all the troubles it would bring. He was a worrier and a brooder, often critical of the people who worked for him but even more critical of himself. He walked the floor in the middle of the night, restlessly reviewing the things he had done or failed to do, the things he ought to do in the future, and the things others should be doing. Some said he was disorganized, but it was usually the disorganization of a man who was forever taking on more than he could possibly do—and generally doing it all exceptionally well. An avid reader, art collector, active member of professional organizations, and internationally respected epidemiologist whose studies ranged from the survey of infectious disease in nearby Tecumseh, Michigan, to work in Japan with the Atomic Bomb Casualty Commission of the United States' National Academy of Sciences, Thomas Francis had no illusions that the poliomyelitis field trial would be something he could squeeze in among his other interests and activities. He knew beyond any doubt that it would consume all his energy for several years while leaving him with no fame, no glory, and no advances in his own research. After a great deal of hesitation, he took the job.

Why? First of all because that was the sort of person he was. Heroes come in many guises. Some wear the marks of torture or battle, the badges of courage earned by working in difficult places against people who are not always kind. Then there are people like Thomas Francis, Jr., highly respected in his field and unknown outside it, the sort of person you would pass without a second thought if you ever noticed him in the first place. Francis looked like what he was: a hardworking academic administrator in a small midwestern city, middle-aged, middle-income, nicely dressed but slightly inclined to a paunch, sporting a mustache that had never inspired a single comparison to Clark Gable. Demanding, high-principled, sometimes whimsical, loyal to the comrades of his youth, he was closer to Judge Hardy than to Albert Einstein. Basil O'Connor asked him to direct the field trial because nobody would doubt the integrity of a report that came from Thomas Francis, Jr.'s desk. Francis did it because it was a job that needed to be done.

Francis was also predisposed to take the job because of the years of support he had received from the National Foundation, which had broken its longstanding policy of not supporting "bricks and mortar" grants when it funded the construction of Michigan's School of Public Health. The foundation continued to give Francis' laboratory grants of several hundred thousand dollars a year throughout the field-trial period, and Hart Van Riper made it clear that they were willing to commit another million dollars to the separate establishment of the Vaccine Evaluation Center. Without ever being a fervent supporter of either Salk or his vaccine, Francis was annoyed at the stubborn hostility of the opposition, and he felt a duty to help the National Foundation, his former assistant, and the cause of the killed-virus vaccine.

The key demand that Francis made—the nonnegotiable condition for his even thinking about taking on the job—was that he had to design the trial and he had to have complete control of the information that came in. Neither O'Connor nor Salk was to have anything to do with the evaluation. Apart from a very few people who were borrowed from the National Foundation's statistical division to help set up the tabulations, the foundation's staff was to be excluded from the evaluation process. They could recruit volunteers and exhort doctors, draft forms and produce filmstrips, purchase gross lots of lollipops, syringes, and adhesive labels, but when it came to the results, they would have to wait along with everybody else. When somebody called Salk, he had to be able to say without qualification that he knew nothing about the trial results. The same had to be true for O'Connor, and for everybody in the home office. That was Francis' starting condition, and he stuck to it.

The second nonnegotiable item was the use of a double-blind field trial, with half the children injected with an inert placebo as a control. On January 11, 1954, Francis was in New York, meeting the Advisory Group on Evaluation, explaining to them that an injected control was vital to the project—not just for his cooperation, but to have statistically respectable results to report. If O'Connor felt obligated to keep his pledge of an observed-control trial in some areas, Francis could live with that, but he wanted everyone to be clear that the results of these trials would be of secondary importance. If there was any question about rationing vaccine, these areas would be at the end of the line. Before the meeting, Francis wrote out his thoughts on a yellow legal pad. Jotting down notes in his tiny script, he asked himself:

will it clearly be free study or will B.O'C be on the path?

completely understood vacc. is safe (inactive) and warranted

completely understood vacc. is antigenic
~~or no desire to go~~ or *no* go.

An experienced administrator, used to anticipating betrayals from above, he also asked "What if [the] study can't proceed? What happens to our build up?"

Francis and O'Connor continued to argue and negotiate for several more weeks, using Hart Van Riper as their intermediary, until finally a compromise was reached. There would be two different field trials, run simultaneously. To honor the commitments O'Connor had already made in thirty-three states, all children in the second grade who requested to participate would be vaccinated with the Salk vaccine, and the observed infection rate of children in the first and third grades would be used for comparison. In eighty-six counties of eleven other states, children in first, second, and third grades would be given injections of either vaccine or of a harmless solution of pink water. Neither the children nor the doctors would have any idea which was which. The districts where the double-blind trial took place were fewer in number but included twice as many children, and Francis made it clear that they would be at the center of his evaluation.

On January 25, 1954, several months after Harry Weaver had planned to send his vaccination teams across the country and two weeks before the date Basil O'Connor had announced in November for the start of the trial, Thomas Francis put in writing all the terms by which he was agreeing to undertake the evaluation of the Salk vaccine. For the first time, there appeared to be an established plan. The next step was to see if it could possibly be put into action before the start of the next polio season.

VI

ORGANIZING THE LOGISTICAL DETAILS OF THE SALK VACCINE field trial was like teaching a large troupe of elephants to do the mambo. It was very hard work, it included a great many messy tasks that would only be noticed if they were left undone, and it carried the constant danger of being crushed under the sheer weight of the bodies one was trying to move. In other words, it was precisely the kind of program the National Foundation staff was used to mounting.

The people who worked at foundation headquarters had been grappling for months with the cumbersome job of organizing a national event which did not yet have a plan, a director, a schedule, or a firm commitment that it would even take place. The problems were easy to identify, but the solutions were a good deal harder to find. How do you line up hundreds of thousands of children and give them a shot in the arm? How do you persuade parents to let them take an experimental medication, or schools to take the time, or teachers and volunteers to handle the paperwork? Whom do you hire to give the vaccinations? How do you pay them? Where do you get a million needles, Band-Aids, and lollipops? How do you design forms so simple they can be filled out by untrained workers across the country, yet so sophisticated that no one will be able to crack the codes of the double-blind control study? How do you do it by next month? Any one of these questions is enough to send the ordinary person looking for a darkened room and a quiet couch on which to recline with a cold towel across the eyes. This is not fun work.

Nevertheless, it had to be done. During all the disputes about the shape of scientific inquiry, none of the feuding scientific advisors had discussed the practical questions of how to get things done on the scale they were contemplating. While Jonas Salk was exploring new principles of antibody formation and Thomas Francis was establishing new standards for epidemiological surveys, the people who worked for and with the National Foundation for Infantile Paralysis were creating their own landmark event in organizational administration. The Salk vaccine field trial would not only test a new vaccine, but also invent a new way to conduct those tests.

A few things were certain. One was that in order to have a statistically significant sample there would have to be a great many children involved. Despite the high epidemic toll of recent years, the field-trial planners had to prepare for the possibility of as few as ten thousand cases in the entire United States, as had happened as recently as 1947. To be fairly confident that they would run into an epidemic somewhere, they had to go to areas all around the country, since no one could predict with any certainty where epidemics would appear. At the same time, they had to vaccinate a lot of children in any place they went, to have a large enough sample to provide measurable results.

The job of choosing where the field trial would be held was given to Gabriel Stickle, a statistician who had been hired by the National Foundation in 1951 to keep track of what it was spending on patient care. With the help and instruction of Thomas Dublin, an outstanding epidemiologist from the NIH who had joined the foundation as an expert advisor to its special Field Trial Unit, Stickle turned from recording the past to planning the future.

The first step was to try to predict which areas would have relatively large numbers of polio cases the following year—a question that was complicated by contradictory studies, some of which suggested that polio incidence fell for several years after a heavy outbreak and others which suggested it rose. Taking on the daunting task of organizing the scattered data on the incidence of poliomyelitis over the past thirty years, Stickle and his associates decided that areas that had a high incidence of polio in a given year tended to continue to have a higher than average incidence for the following two or three years, and that sparsely populated areas tended to have higher polio incidence (though fewer cases in sheer numbers) than the more densely populated urban centers.

On the basis of that theory, which would prove to be correct, the foundation's Statistical Services Division listed all counties in the United States with high incidence of polio in 1952 and 1953, then eliminated counties with populations so small that there was no local health department and those so large that they would be unmanageable. What remained were counties with populations of between fifty thousand and two hundred thousand that had had major outbreaks of polio within the last two years. The next step was to determine which of these counties had health departments that could manage a placebo-controlled study. The list of several hundred counties was submitted to state health officers, who knew quite well which local health departments were run by people opposed to the field trial on principle and which were simply not capable of doing the job.

As some health districts were being eliminated for reasons that had nothing to do with statistical accuracy, others campaigned to be included even though they didn't really fit the statistical profile of choice. One of the striking exceptions to the county population ceiling of two hundred thousand were the five counties that make up New York City—an area where there was strong political and popular pressure to take part in the field trial as well as a superbly well-organized health department, capable of handling a sophisticated study on any scale. Six health districts from New York City were included in the trial.

The field-trial plan called for the participation of almost 2 million schoolchildren spread across 217 health districts in 44 states, which also meant there would have to be many thousands of adults helping to keep them in line. Since polio was indifferent to divisions of religion, race, or educational philosophy, it was vital to bridge the barriers that so often separated public, private, and parochial schools. The National Foundation had spent years establishing good relations with the National Congress of Parents and Teachers, better known as the PTA, and with such organizations as the National Council of Catholic Women, the National Council of Negro Women, and the National Council of Jewish Women; now they turned to them to help organize support within the various school systems and to rally the many volunteers who would be needed to manage the operations of the individual field-trial clinics.

The tasks were myriad. Someone would have to go to the airport and get the vaccine as it was flown in from the factory, and it had to be someone who had sufficient respect for the experiment not to tamper with the supplies. Someone would have to take charge of any vaccine not used, and return it to the evaluation center in Ann Arbor, Michigan. Someone would have to make sure all the forms got to the clinics in time. Parents were needed to hold the hands of frightened children, call their names, distribute lollipops, bandages, and pats on the head. Teachers were needed to bring the children from their class-rooms, keep them in line, take attendance, and answer the many questions that children have before, during, and after any event. Three thousand one hundred county chapters of the National Foundation were mobilized to act as information and recruit-ment centers; March of Dimes volunteers who had worked on fund-raising campaigns were now pressed into service to recruit other workers, run informational meetings, distribute literature, gather supplies, drive people to clinics, and provide hundreds of hours of unpaid clerical assistance.

There had been some thought at the beginning of trying to hire people to do this work, but Basil O'Connor insisted on using the National Foundation's local volunteers. They knew the community, they knew how to work, they didn't demand a salary, and they had a commitment to the cause that no amount of money could buy. Like the long-ago decision to recruit the local postmasters as the first chairmen of the Birthday Ball Com-mittees, the transformation of the National Foundation's local chapters from collection agencies to information centers pro-vided an instant national network of field-trial supporters who did not have to work to get the respect and attention of their neighbors. Their word was trusted when people might have been hesitant to believe a stranger, even one as worthy as Thomas Francis or Jonas Salk. It was an irresistible combination, and it

proved to be a very effective one. Areas that had active foundation chapters showed much higher participation in the field
trial than areas that did not.

After the health districts had agreed to participate, the schools
to host the clinics, and the children to come, doctors and nurses
had to be on hand to give the vaccinations. There was another
job, too, that would fall to them: taking blood samples before
the first of the three inoculations and again after the last, to see
what antibodies the children had to begin with, whether or not
the level of antibodies had been elevated by the course of vaccinations, how the antibody responses differed with different
lots of vaccines, and how they compared with the control group
of children who had not been vaccinated at all but still gave
blood. Only 2 percent of the children gave blood samples, but
that still meant forty thousand children at a time, each of whom
needed a bit of extra time and attention.

After the field trial was over, Thomas Francis' official tally
of volunteer workers came to 150,000. The National Congress
of Parents and Teachers estimated over twice as many people
had been involved: 20,000 doctors, 40,000 nurses, 14,000 principals, 50,000 teachers, and 200,000 lay volunteers. Even that
total was probably far too low. It didn't include the school
officials and community leaders who were crucial for public
acceptance of the program, and it didn't count the friends who
came along to help carry the cartons, the mothers who dropped
by to bring their children and stayed to pass out buttons, the
teachers who took it upon themselves to call up absentees, and
all the other people who performed those little, nameless, un-
remembered acts that kept the whole program moving along.

If the first logistical challenge of the field trial was its size,
the second was its need for consistency. Salk's vaccine trials in
the Pittsburgh area, like most trials, had really been an ongoing
study of a number of different products. As he examined the
results of his first vaccinations, he was able to change the formulations of later vaccines, or the intervals between vaccinations, or the dosage. When a new question arose, he started a
new study to find the answer. For the national trial, all the
questions had to be in place before they began, and they had
to be the same questions in each community. If there wasn't a

slot for a question on the reporting form, it would not be asked, and there would be no results to measure.

Finally, everything would have to be done very fast. Planners knew they had to complete the field-trial vaccinations before the polio season began, when natural epidemics would make it impossible to tell who was getting polio from the vaccine and who was getting polio in spite of it. Despite the intensity of the laboratory work, Salk's early tests in Pittsburgh had had a leisurely, almost social air—medical research masquerading as a covered-dish supper. The national field trial would be more like a huge military operation, calling for speed, coordination, clear lines of command, and vast movements of troops and supplies, all massed against the enemies of time, suspicion, ignorance, ineptitude, and fate.

During the months of preparation that preceded the field trial, the National Foundation offices at 120 Broadway were in a condition of sustained pandemonium. Called together by Mel Glasser, the operational director of the Field Trial Unit, and Ray Barrows, the administrative director of the National Foundation, various departments of the foundation staff had been meeting since early September to discuss their activities for the coming months. Responsibilities were divided to make best use of individual staff members' connections and talents. Steve Alex, the foundation's public relations man in Washington, dealt with pharmaceutical houses and with Congress. Elaine Whitelaw, director of clubs and organizations, recruited volunteer workers and speakers from the ranks of other national and community groups. Members of the foundation's Educational Division stumped the National Educational Association and all its branches. Virginia Blood concentrated on the nurses' associations, Hart Van Riper on the medical groups, Foard McGinnes on the National Institutes of Health, Dave Preston and Ed Stegen on other scientific groups and publications. In every community, they had to identify and seek out the special-interest groups that would persuade the school board and the board of health to participate. By the time the field trial began, there was enormous public support for the entire program, but much of that enthusiasm had been generated by the hard work of the National Foundation staff during the preceding months.

On the eleventh floor of 120 Broadway, the foundation's staff was continuing all its regular operations while also acting as the command post for field-trial mobilization. Mel Glasser, who had taken over the administration of the field trial on September 1, spent his days drafting and reviewing memos, attending meetings, and authorizing the purchase of massive quantities of everything from carbon paper to cynomolgus monkeys. At one point, when the constant interruptions and urgent telephone calls became too distracting, he suggested to O'Connor that he try working at home. O'Connor countered with the offer of an empty room in his law firm on another floor of the same building, and installed Glasser in Franklin Roosevelt's old office, still furnished with the big shabby desk Roosevelt had moved there when they formed their partnership thirty years before. As so often happened at the National Foundation, sentiment was put to the service of efficient progress, and both benefited from the union.

One of Glasser's biggest problems was obtaining medical supplies. Long after the field trial was over, he remembered one crisis in painful detail. "We would need one million two hundred thousand needles for the field trial," he said, "and it seemed like an insurmountable problem, because there just weren't that many around, and if you tried to use the existing supply, the whole business of trying to get appropriate sterilization equipment in [to] every school and then getting people whom you could trust to sterilize them—that was one of my major logistical problems. Getting the needles, getting them in the right place, and seeing they were sterile." The solution appeared only when Becton, Dickinson and Company, a surgical supply firm, agreed to speed up production of the new disposal syringe it was about to put on the market. When a strike at the factory halted production just weeks before the field trial, Glasser developed a stiff neck that left him immobilized until the day the strike was settled. Busy as he was, he was fascinated to see how closely he had identified his own well-being with the success of the field-trial operation.

Long before the syringes could be used, parents, children, and school officials had to be informed of what was happening. The Department of Public Information, as the publicity staff was called, was working at top speed to turn out press releases, informational releases, and all the varied literature demanded by the field trial itself. Dorothy Ducas, public information director for the foundation, made sure the field trial received the proper attention not only in newspapers, radio, and television, but also in the newsletters and bulletins of schools, churches, and clubs all over the country, including the many divisions of the National Foundation for Infantile Paralysis. There was a publication for chapter people and volunteers, a house organ for the headquarters staff, and a steady flow of news releases from the bottomless source on lower Broadway.

Parents were eager for an end to polio, but they still had to be reassured of the safety of the field trial, on which they heard so many conflicting reports. In this delicate process, success or failure might hinge on a single word. One of the simplest and most inspired touches in the campaign to recruit participants was the decision to have "request" forms rather than "consent" forms. Parents could either request to participate or refuse; the altered language changed their agreement from a risk to an honor. For the children, too, a turn of phrase changed what could have been a fearful mystery into an adventure that linked them to the heroic founders of their nation. Dave Preston, the resident expert in technical science writing, came up with the idea of calling the children Polio Pioneers, turning them all into proud trailblazers on the newest frontier of science.

The Radio and Film Department turned out a filmstrip, *Bob and Barbara*, explaining the field trial in terms a six-year-old could understand, and another for adults, and distributed one thousand copies of each for use in the classroom, at parents' meetings, and at information sessions of all sorts. Teachers received guides with suggestions for classroom programs and props that might help explain the vaccinations, answers to questions the children were most likely to ask, and questionnaires to be returned after the field trial, recording how the children had fared.

Because of the two different field-trial designs, every piece of information had to be written twice. Instructions for observed-control areas were printed on blue paper, with an initial order of 37,500 copies for the teachers' guides alone. Instructions for placebo-control areas were printed on yellow paper, with over 100,000 copies in the first printing. Then there were the purple pages that not many people got to see. Those were the instructions that would have been passed out if something had gone terribly wrong.

For the past ten years, the National Foundation's director of health education had issued pamphlets every spring telling parents how best to protect themselves and their children against polio, and how to respond if polio did strike their families. In the 1954 *Polio Pointers for Parents*, the material was expanded to describe the field trial and also the gamma globulin clinics that would be held in areas where the field trial did not take place. Twenty-five million pamphlets were distributed to parents across the country, in addition to the several million pieces of explanatory literature that went only to those whose children would be Polio Pioneers.

All of this was quite apart from the detailed instructions needed for those who would be working in the vaccination clinics, keeping the records, examining later cases of suspected polio in field-trial areas, and filing reports of all this information with the Vaccine Evaluation Center. Most of the school volunteers were women, and it fell to the Women's Division to draft their instruction. They did it in one intense session. Elaine Whitelaw, her assistant Virginia Blood, a formidable woman who was capable of sending seasoned staffers hiding under their desks to escape her wrath, and Bea Wright, a volunteer coordinator who was herself a polio survivor, closeted themselves in a hotel room to gather their thoughts on procedures. The session lasted all night, as Whitelaw walked through the procedures, Wright suggested changes, and Blood scribbled their ideas on everything from how to stage informational meetings to how to shepherd the children from classroom to registration table to vaccination station and back.

These instructions eventually became part of the fifty-eight-page *Manual of Suggested Procedures*, a detailed briefing book on how to prepare and manage every aspect of a field-trial clinic. The National Foundation also issued a book of *Operational*

Memoranda, drafted in consultation with Thomas Francis and his staff, which consisted of seventeen different sets of instructions for each category of people responsible for different aspects of field-trial operations, from state health officers to school volunteer committee chairmen. Details left out of the original instructions were included in later notices. By June 8, 1954, the instructions ranged from Bulletin no. 1, the National Foundation for Infantile Paralysis *Manual of Suggested Procedures*, to Bulletin no. 11, *Follow-up and Evaluation—Notification of Deaths and Untoward Reactions*. Most of the bulletins spawned little subbulletins detailing modifications, corrections, and special cases. The bulletin on vaccine safety, for example, had a subbulletin on possible ill effects on children allergic to penicillin. Bulletin no. 1, the *Manual of Suggested Procedures* that was the basic bible of field-trial operations, had prompted seven separate commentaries that corrected or expanded the original text.

By the end of the field-trial clinics, there were at least eighteen of these bulletins—no. 18 dealt with the procedures for distributing Polio Pioneer cards and buttons. Sometimes the planners got carried away by their desire to anticipate all problems. Bulletin no. 1.42, *Filing and Routing of Class Registration Schedules and Individual Vaccination Records*, explained precisely how to separate the forms: "It is suggested that the person who is to do this work grasp the stub of the form with one hand and the bottom margins below the carbon with the other, then pull firmly to detach. As a result, the carbon should be in one hand and three copies of the form in the other hand. The carbon should be discarded while separate stacks should be made of the original, duplicate and triplicate copies."

A few local health departments stopped reading the bulletins, complaining there were too many of them, but it was far more common to get telegrams begging for an additional shipment. The people who had so often been accused of overzealous promotion had become the prophets of order and clarity in an unprecedented experiment that could easily have become a legendary example of chaotic mismanagement.

VII

By the time that thomas francis agreed to direct the field-trial evaluation, Jonas Salk was more than happy to relinquish control and return to what he still insisted were the most urgent questions of vaccine formulation. Unfortunately, the forces of disruption continued to camp outside his door. Often he had to stop all work to give detailed tours of his facilities to representatives of manufacturers, visitors from the NIH's Laboratory of Biologics Control, or, worst of all, reporters. At the end of November, the Salks moved from suburban Wexford to a larger house in downtown Pittsburgh, and Salk proudly wrote to friends that he was now living only seven minutes from the lab—but that didn't necessarily mean he spent any more time at home. Less time commuting meant more time at work, where there were not only blood tests and vaccine preparations to oversee, but also medical-school lectures, students, and all the memos and meetings and political jockeying that are part of academic life—things that Salk avoided as much as possible, but that still required precious time.

Then there was the mail, which had started to mount as soon as features on the new vaccine began to appear in popular magazines. Old acquaintances wrote, asking if this was the same Jonas Salk they had met at Rockaway Beach thirty years before, or in high school, or at a family wedding in Bayonne, New Jersey. Former staff members wrote, begging to be caught up on all the gossip or asking if Jonas could speak to their husband's chapter of the Elks. Relatives asked for help in getting their children into medical school; journals from *Current Biography* to the *Lithuanian Daily Friend* requested biographical information.

A member of the air force wrote about the cure for polio to be found in "the juice of the gourd." One man sent several letters explaining how polio could be prevented by eating "slightly radioactive" breakfast cereal, which would destroy the virus as it entered the body; another intrepid crackpot had worked out elaborate equations showing that polio incidence was tied to levels of nuclear radiation and could be predicted by studying the volume of beans harvested each spring in the Midwest. A former vitamin salesman in Coral Gables, Florida, who had appointed himself president, corresponding secretary, and general messiah of an organization he called Polio Prevention, Inc., sent inflammatory pamphlets designed to reveal, among other things, that the National Foundation was in league with the cola manufacturers to increase polio incidence by encouraging malnutrition.

Most of these letters received individual answers, some of them composed by the secretaries but many dictated personally by Salk. There were elaborate answers for just about all Salk's mail, in fact, from a request for information on technical developments in virus inactivation to a letter to the editor of *Who's Who in World Jewry* explaining precisely why he had not answered their request for biographical information. These in turn prompted a subgenre of replies in which people felt compelled to remark on their surprise at his lengthy analysis of why he was too busy to answer their letters.

The same spirit that prompted these letters inspired Salk to supervise the most minute operations of his laboratory. Indeed, the more minute, the better; while some research associates grumbled that Salk never had time to review their papers or support them in their plans for independent research, he went over the carpenter's bills, inspected the animal quarters, arranged for a new air-conditioning system, and vetoed a plan to repaint storage closets in the hospital basement.

The details of monkey feeds and test-tube stopper supplies, petty as they might be, were probably a refreshingly simple change from the dangers and uncertainties of human subject testing and vaccine production. Designing human trials, and charting all the variables to be tested before coming up with a manufacturing protocol, was in turn an engrossing escape from the politics of committee meetings and the secrecy of the manufacturer's agendas. Three days in the warm room for tissue cultures? Gamma globulin shots before vaccination? Saline solution or adjuvant? Monkey kidneys or monkey testes? One cc of vaccine? A booster after two weeks? Two months? Two years? The technical problems to be solved were vast but finite—if you worked hard enough and long enough, there could be answers. No amount of effort would make Salk understand why colleagues rejected his findings or insisted on delaying the tests of his work. There was no laboratory technique to discover why Parke, Davis would not follow his procedures. These were questions beyond the ken of science.

Salk felt his vaccine would prevent paralysis and save lives. His wife had confidence in him. His secretary trusted him. The staff at Watson Home revered him. The director at the Polk State School thought he should get the Nobel Prize. Science columnist David Dietz called his work the top achievement in the world of science in 1953, above the development of the hydrogen bomb, and he, too, predicted a Nobel Prize for Dr. Salk. Old friends sent mushy letters; total strangers sent pictures and rosaries. Why didn't the scientific community help?

Part of the problem was competition and jealousy, part was lingering doubt about the safety and usefulness of Salk's vaccine. In the world of research scientists, a corollary to the need to publish one's findings in a scholarly journal is the insistence that new discoveries are not judged true until they have been duplicated by others. The catch was that while many people criticized Salk's work, few tried to duplicate it. Those who did seemed not to have understood what he was doing. In August, when Salk had spent a great deal of time drafting an evasive reply to outside inquiries about the current status of his vaccine, he had appended a joking footnote to Harry Weaver: "I think this should qualify us for the Third and Fourth Assistant Janitorships in the State Department." Three months later, he no longer saw any humor whatsoever in questions raised about the vaccine.

On November 10, 1953, while Salk had been in New York

with Basil O'Connor and the pharmaceutical company executives, and Thomas Francis, Jr., was still touring Europe with his wife, the American Public Health Association heard Doctors Albert Milzer, Sidney Levinson, and Howard J. Shaughnessy report on their inability to inactivate poliovirus as Salk had done. Milzer, Levinson, and Shaughnessy, who worked together at Michael Reese Hospital in Chicago, favored ultraviolet radiation as a means of killing viruses, and claimed "for reasons not clear to us" to have been unable to duplicate Salk's results with formalin.

When Salk heard about their report, which received ample coverage in the daily press, he mounted an immediate campaign to discredit their methods. He called Levinson in Chicago and grilled him on his experiments. In a letter to the editor of the *American Journal of Public Health*, where their paper was to be published in January, Salk wrote that it was clear that the doctors had not followed his procedures. What was worse, he said, "these investigators have, without justification, impugned experiments that were carefully conducted and they have aroused fear and doubt by their irresponsible remarks in a scientific paper in which evidence rather than opinion should stand out."

On December 10, Levinson agreed to change the report before publication, but by then new dragons loomed. A few days later, Salk received a letter from Dr. Aims C. McGuinness, chairman of the Committee on the Control of Infectious Diseases of the American Academy of Pediatrics, asking for his comments on a proposal that the academy reconsider its resolution to support the vaccine field trial, which has passed triumphantly when Salk addressed the academy at its annual meeting in October. The proposal, which McGuinness enclosed, came from Dr. Henry Kempe of the University of California Medical Center in San Francisco. Reading Kempe's letter to McGuinness, which repeated every objection that had ever been raised—and answered—about the safety of a killed-virus vaccine, including the demand that "leading virologists" be surveyed on their willingness to let their own children take the vaccine, Salk became more and more furious. This was not a simple inquiry, he was sure, but a concerted plot by an antivaccination clique.

Over the next three weeks, he spent a great deal of time drafting and revising answers to Kempe's letter, some to go out over his own name and some to be issued as a statement from the foundation's Vaccine Advisory Committee. Salk saved his hottest ire for Aims McGuinness, who he felt was trying to stir up opposition by circulating Kempe's letter. Starting with the ironic understatement that he was "rather amused by some things in your letter," Salk quickly revealed how deeply and personally he had been insulted.

"I think the whole situation is most unfortunate," he wrote in one of the many replies he drafted but never mailed, "and although I am unaware of anything that I have done in the past that should merit the degree of distrust that is implied by the great concern that so many people have in spite of the statements that I have made very clearly in publication and in spite of the fact that nothing has been done, nor will be done, until the proper time is ready, as I see it . . .

"The obvious implication," Salk continued, "is that Salk is not to be trusted and, furthermore, that questions raised by Kempe have been raised for the very first time. Has it not occurred to you and to others who share Kempe's view that all of these questions have been considered and may have been answered to the satisfaction of the principal investigator concerned. Is it necessary for me to have a character testimony and by what right does one go forth casting aspersions and for these aspersions to parade as facts without what one might call the accused being faced by his accuser."

Even for a rough draft, this was unusually incoherent; not for several weeks was Salk composed enough to draft the letter he finally sent. On January 7, he wrote McGuinness, "I would like to be able to write a full and detailed reply to Kempe but if I allowed myself to answer all of the questions raised in letters of this kind it would seriously curtail my already limited time." What he did not mention was how often he had drafted precisely that kind of letter, and how much it had indeed kept him from more productive work.

The interruption was all the more maddening—and therefore all the more time-consuming—because Kempe's letter had also been sent to several other leading virologists for their comments.

Thomas Francis answered by objecting to an essentially political document disguised as a letter of scientific inquiry. Joseph Melnick equivocated. Albert Sabin, who wrote that "I completely agree with [Kempe's] conclusion 'that the formalin-inactivated vaccine is insufficiently tested for mass trial, potentially unsafe, of undetermined potency, and of undetermined stability,' " sent a copy of his letter to Salk with the following note: "Dear Jonas, This is for your information—so that you'll know what I am saying behind your back. This incidentally is also the opinion of many others whose judgment you respect. 'Love and Kisses' are being saved up. Albert."

Within Salk's own laboratory at Pittsburgh, the atmosphere was also growing strained. When he was first organizing his lab and doing the initial work on virus typing, Salk had shown a remarkable concern for the sensibilities of his fellow workers. When he dictated the weekly memos that were his instructions to the laboratory staff, he avoided the terse style typical of such directives and adopted a vocabulary of almost antique delicacy. "I would like to propose" that you use thirty monkeys for the following test, he would say, or "I would like to suggest" the following rotation of staff. When the scientific papers that had come out of the typing program were gathered for a privately printed volume distributed by the National Foundation in 1951, Salk had insisted on putting his assistants' names before his own in the list of authors, even though they had not been members of the Typing Committee or taken part in its discussions.

Two years later, everything was suddenly Salk, Salk, Salk. Nobody from *Time* wanted to talk to Julie Youngner about what he ate for breakfast, although the color scale he developed to measure the concentration of virus in a tissue culture is a procedure of elegant simplicity still prized for its aesthetic appeal as well as its efficiency. Nobody wanted to interview Val Bazeley about how he had come from Australia to show the lab team how to boost its production of virus. It was not Salk's fault that the journalists relegated his lab team to a side note and put the boss' picture on the cover, but it was not pleasant for the people who worked ninety-hour weeks and saw their names virtually forgotten in the published record of their labors. Salk and all his associates were doing heroic work to get the vaccine ready in time, but the effort was taking a toll on everyone's temper.

The disputes with Milzer and with Aims McGuinness had distracted Salk from his dissatisfaction with Parke, Davis, but the problems with manufacture had not grown less over time. Eager to press forward with an early trial, Basil O'Connor still planned to have Parke, Davis supply all vaccine for the spring of 1954, treating his meeting with the other companies as a way of starting them on production for vaccine supplies for 1955.

On December 8, 1953, an extremely reluctant Jonas Salk signed a formal agreement appointing Parke, Davis the exclusive manufacturer of polio vaccine for the 1954 field trial. Still, the conflicts continued. Writing to G. Foard McGinnes, in charge of vaccine procurement for the National Foundation, Salk complained that while Fred Stimpert at Parke, Davis claimed to be confident that certain results would occur in a consistent manner using procedures Salk had not approved, "there has been too much confidence and not enough fact in the experience to date." In that same letter, Salk referred to the specifications as "the thing we signed in Detroit on 8 December." When McGinnes forwarded Salk's complaints to Parke, Davis, Stimpert felt constrained to point out that "this 'thing' (as you call it) is, of course, the basis of our contract with the foundation and must include any changes, deletions, or additions suggested by you or required by our experiences in the course of processing."

In February 1954, six months after they had tried to begin production and only two months before the start of the polio season in the United States, the National Foundation for Infantile Paralysis abandoned its exclusive contract with Parke, Davis and opened the production of Salk vaccine to several other companies. They might not have acceptable quantities of vaccine ready in time for the field trial (in the end, only Parke, Davis and Eli Lilly did), but at least the monopoly had been broken. Competing against each other for the vast market a successful vaccine would create, the different companies would be forced to follow a single set of specifications, ones approved by Jonas Salk.

To increase the incentive to go into vaccine production, and to ensure that there would be enough companies prepared to make vaccine if it were licensed in 1955, Basil O'Connor made another of his famous gambles. If all six companies agreed to enter immediately into the production of Salk polio vaccine, the National Foundation would buy their entire first year's output, whether or not the product was ever licensed. If the field trial showed that the vaccine prevented paralytic polio, the foundation would use its purchase to vaccinate the most vulnerable age groups the following summer, free of charge. If the field trial showed that the vaccine was harmful or ineffective, the foundation would have spent $9 million on a product no one could use, in addition to the $7 million they had put into mounting the trial itself. Even to Basil O'Connor, this was beginning to sound like real money.

By this time at least the problem of drafting protocols had been settled. After months of badgering from Tom Rivers, from William Workman of the Laboratory of Biologics Control, and from Joseph Smadel of Walter Reed Hospital, Salk had accepted Smadel's offer to write the protocols if Salk would provide the necessary information. Salk was happy to be rid of the job, though he still spent weeks revising Smadel's text, followed by more weeks of conferences and changes before the manufacturers accepted the protocols as directions they could both understand and hope to follow.

At this point, the sleeping giant of the federal government began to rouse itself and consider what position it should occupy in the line of march.

VIII

ON APRIL 11, 1953, PRESIDENT DWIGHT EISENHOWER, THE first Republican elected to the White House in twenty years, expanded the New Deal's Federal Security Agency and renamed it the Department of Health, Education and Welfare, with Mrs. Oveta Culp Hobby as its first secretary. Like the Secretary of Defense or the Secretary of State, Hobby was a member of the president's Cabinet, charged with broad responsibilities. Among the many social-service programs that were now gathered under her office was the Public Health Service, which in turn included the National Institutes of Health. One of those institutes was the National Institute of Microbiology, which had jurisdiction over what was then called the Laboratory of Biologics Control. Under regulations first established in the Pure Food and Drug Act of 1902, this laboratory would have to rule on the question of whether or not the Salk vaccine could be licensed for commercial manufacture, should the field trial show that it was a safe and effective biological product.

For an organization founded by the president of the United States, the National Foundation for Infantile Paralysis had been paying remarkably little attention to Washington—a policy decision that came directly from the foundation's president, Basil O'Connor. O'Connor had a deep contempt for federal bureaucracy, an attitude rooted in his immense confidence in his own capacities and nourished by his extensive experience with the back-room deals and last-minute adjustments by which national policy is often shaped. He had no interest in obtaining federal funds for polio research, just as he had no interest in joining in the United Way, the Community Chest, or any other form of group fund-raising. Cooperation meant loss of identity, loss of control, and loss of revenue. Government help meant government regulation, delays, and the danger of being stuck in other people's pork barrels. There had never been any question in O'Connor's mind that he could find a way to control polio by himself, without any help—or interference—from anybody in Washington.

The federal government, for its part, was quite happy to let the National Foundation keep its independence. Secretary Hobby, who had been the director of the Women's Army Corps in World War II and had no background in either health or education, was convinced that both medical care and drug development were areas of private enterprise that functioned best without undue government interference. As for federal support of research, Dr. Victor Haas, founding director of the National Microbiological Institute of the National Institutes of Health, put the position very clearly in his testimony before a congressional committee in the fall of 1953: "We have felt for many years that the National Foundation for Infantile Paralysis supports research on such a scale that it would not be wise for us to direct our resources away from other important fields which are not so well covered to this one which is." To prove that they had acted on this feeling, he had only to compare the research budgets of the two organizations: the NIH had spent $72,000 on polio research in 1953, the National Foundation had spent almost $2 million.

The Salk vaccine field trial was a new departure, however, and it demanded new alliances. One of them, O'Connor realized, would have to be with Washington. Although the vaccine field trial was privately planned, funded, administered, and evaluated, it still depended on the cooperation of many different people employed in various aspects of public health. Their duties were as different as their degrees of enthusiasm about the project, but their cooperation on all levels was vital to the success of the trial.

In drawing the Public Health Service into the earliest stages of field-trial planning, O'Connor was trying to diminish the effect of what he knew was a guiding principle shared by both government and industry, which is that the responsibility for any failures must be shunted onto someone else. Unless the federal government took part in the planning of the field-trial program, any problems that came up during or after licensing would be blamed on the National Foundation. Unless the foundation knew from the start what information and standards would be required for licensing by the Laboratory of Biologics Control, the entire field trial might be a wasted effort. O'Connor's opinion of government officials was no higher than it had ever been, but if there were any problems in producing the polio vaccine, he wanted the authorities to know about them sooner rather than later.

In any case, the National Foundation's freedom from government interference had always depended in part on the fact that it was reaping so little return on its investment in polio research. The NIH administrators were happy to let the foundation sponsor basic research in virology, which allowed them to distribute their own funds in other areas. The Social Security Administration was perfectly willing to have the National Foundation pay for hospital costs and rehabilitation programs that allowed polio paralytics and their families to become self-sufficient. State and city universities had long since overcome their early qualms about letting scientists on their faculties accept National Foundation grants, and now counted on the indirect costs they would receive from those grants when calculating their operating budgets. Once the National Foundation moved from giving out money to giving out medicine, however, everything changed.

This had become evident during the summer of 1953, when the mass distribution of gamma globulin became a rehearsal for the polio vaccine field trials expected for the following year. The National Foundation had developed valuable experience in mass purchasing and distribution, the public had been introduced to the idea that you cured polio by lining up for injections at schools or other public areas—and the administrators of the Public Health Service had realized that they had to step in or let Basil O'Connor create what was in effect a shadow network of health services.

Still angry about the last-minute changes in distribution that had been forced on him in the gamma globulin program, O'Connor was determined to have the polio vaccine field trial approved from the beginning so there would be no arguments over its structure at the end. Officially, he was relying on the Vaccine Advisory Committee to make the final decision on when or if the field trial could take place. Unofficially, he wanted the Public Health Service to give its blessings to the effort before it began.

It was not a responsibility that anybody in power in the government really wanted to take. Strictly speaking, it was not their job. The Laboratory of Biologics Control had the power to approve or deny licenses to commercial products, but it was neither obliged nor equipped to take part in what amounted to a feasibility study in an early stage of product development. Many individuals who worked for the new Department of Health, Education and Welfare were interested in the Salk vaccine and eager to have a say in its production and testing, but they were hampered by their own ignorance about polio, their lack of experience in conducting field trials on the scale the National Foundation proposed, and an even more crucial absence of the strong administrative support that can only come from above. Tom Rivers, always candid, put it squarely: "The Public Health Service would eventually have to license the vaccine," he said, "and nobody in the Public Health Service knew anything about polio. So we got them tangled up in this mess, and we had an awful time teaching them about polio."

The educational process took many forms. William Workman, director of the Laboratory of Biologics Control, had been invited to the Hershey meeting when Salk first presented his results on the original vaccinations at the Watson Home and the Polk State School. Six months later, in July 1953, Workman agreed to go to Toronto to study the procedures used to grow poliovirus in tissue culture at the Connaught Laboratories. Dr. Roderick Murray, acting director of the Laboratory of Biologics Control, met with manufacturers at Salk's laboratory in Pittsburgh in November 1953. In December, William Workman and Joseph Smadel drew up what would be the first of several "Specifications and Minimum Requirements" to be used by the manufacturers in producing a vaccine for the field trial. In January

1954, Dr. Bernice Eddy, a microbiologist on the Laboratory of Biologics Control staff, visited Pittsburgh to learn about safety tests in tissue cultures; later she had to borrow equipment from Salk's laboratory to duplicate his procedures in Bethesda. Dr. David Price, the assistant surgeon general of the Public Health Service, was a member of the Vaccine Advisory Committee— one of the five out of six whom Rivers had characterized as having vast experience in public health administration and little specific knowledge of poliomyelitis.

Other branches of the federal government were involved as a matter of routine necessity. To import live virus from Connaught required a permit from the Division of Foreign Quarantine of HEW. The health records that would provide the statistical basis for the vaccine evaluation would have to come from state and local health officials—always the keepers of vital statistics. The House Committee on Interstate Commerce was keeping its eye on vaccine developments, since pharmaceutical products were considered an object of interstate trade and therefore under its jurisdiction.

In January 1954, and again in March, foundation executives met with leaders of the Association of State and Territorial Health Officers—the group that had originally demanded a placebo-controlled field trial and whose members would do much of the reporting of polio incidence in the summer after the field trial. Turning to yet another branch of the federal government, Thomas Francis had sought help from the only organization in the country used to dealing in statistical information in the volume he would be handling, and Robert Voight, a statistician from the Census Bureau, had already moved to Ann Arbor to help him prepare for the deluge of information that would soon begin to arrive. Other statisticians and tabulators from the Census Bureau would join them in the coming months.

It was much easier to borrow manpower than to inspire faith. Meeting with scientific advisors to discuss polio vaccine developments, the federal officials who would have the ultimate responsibility for vaccine safety found it very disheartening to see the discord among people who had devoted their lives to polio research. The debates that raged over the conference table often had more to do with professional power struggles than with virology, but the disturbing impression was that the expert advisors could not agree on their advice.

The Laboratory of Biologics Control's uncertainty about the real safety of Salk's vaccine wasn't eased in the early months of 1954 when different manufacturers kept forgetting this step or that one in the protocols, and turning out batches of contaminated vaccine. Cutter Laboratories left out the Type II virus from the vaccine for reasons that were doubtless clear to someone, and they were cut from the field trial. Parke, Davis halted the formalin treatment in some batches before all the virus was inactivated. Eli Lilly, which had the best record of any of the manufacturers, forgot to filter some of the virus before the formalin inactivation, leaving clumps that contained live virus. When Lilly finally produced trial lots of vaccine that seemed to have followed all the rules, some of the monkeys injected with it developed mysterious lesions on their spinal cords.

By this time, the starting date of the proposed field trial had been postponed several times. In November, Basil O'Connor had announced that the trial would begin no later than the first week in February. By February they were hoping for early March. After March 11, a tentative day of April 19 was set. Two weeks later, William Workman declared the field trial should be postponed until the cause of the monkeys' lesions was discovered and new specifications were prepared and tested, which meant postponing it until the following year, since the polio season was fast arriving.

Responding to this latest crisis, Jonas Salk and G. Foard McGinnes hurried out to the NIH campus in Bethesda and summoned David Bodian from Johns Hopkins to meet them there. Bodian was a great expert on the pathology of polio, and he took his reputation with him out to NIH. Arriving from Baltimore, an hour north, Bodian looked at the lesions, presented in cross sections, and compared them to all the cross sections of tissue from infected monkeys he had examined over his years of polio work. Finally, he declared, "That's not polio."

James Shannon, then assistant director of the NIH and later one of its most powerful directors, was unconvinced. He wanted each batch of vaccine tested on upward of three hundred monkeys—a number that would have been impossible to procure, impossible to pay for, and inhumane to even contemplate. He settled for a change in the testing techniques. The vaccine used in the field trial was already given three separate tests for safety—by the manufacturing laboratory, by the Laboratory of Biologics Control, and by the Virus Research Lab at the University of Pittsburgh. Any evidence of any live virus in even one of those tests, and the entire production lot was discarded. Now another requirement was added. No vaccine would be approved unless eleven consecutive lots had passed the safety tests. Manufacturers would not be able to discard bad lots and present only their successes for further testing. The manufacturers had to face rigid standards of production, and the NIH administrators had to face the chance that there would be a field trial this year.

Before he would give the final go-ahead for the national field trial, William Workman made Salk vaccinate another five thousand children with commercially prepared vaccine, on the reasonable premise that vaccine produced in an industrial plant might act differently from the home-brew. When it became clear that this additional test, coupled with continuing snarls in vaccine production, would delay the start of the field trial past the date when the polio season began in the South, where the warmer climate sometimes brought earlier cases of poliomyelitis, O'Connor proposed that the extra trials be done in the southern states. He was overruled, however, and Georgia, Arizona, Maryland, and the District of Columbia all had to be dropped from the program. To fill the ranks, forty-six health districts in Canada were added, and two small areas in Finland.

The final safety test of the commercial vaccine was done in Pittsburgh and surrounding areas of Allegheny County at the end of March. The vaccine they were using was Parke, Davis lot no. 503. On March 29, Salk sent a jocular telegram to Basil O'Connor: "In your honor Saint Basil School was first to receive 503. This should provide that extra margin of safety. Jonas."

By this time, Salk was getting very good at running vaccination clinics. Dr. Robert Korns, an energetic and accomplished young epidemiologist from the New York State Department of

Health who had worked on the 1953 gamma globulin evaluation, had been released from his regular duties to serve as
Thomas Francis' assistant director in the vaccine evaluation
program. One of his tasks was to inspect the sites of vaccination
clinics, and one of the first places he went was Pittsburgh, to
observe Salk's trial.

No one had ever reported any ill effects during any of the
trials in the Pittsburgh area, but the fact remained that so far
Salk had made most of the vaccine he tested, done all the vaccinations, kept all the records, and interpreted all the results—a
situation that demanded at least a disinterested second opinion.
Francis had instructed Korns to watch for adverse reactions Salk
might not be noting and to observe how Salk reported on subsequent illnesses in the children who made up the study population. Korns was impressed with Salk's ability to give ten
vaccinations per minute, but dubious about his cooperation in
the field trial to come. On his return to Ann Arbor, he "quoted
Dr. Salk as saying that he had no great sympathy with our
concern over the control study."

Meanwhile, the journalistic blitz was on. *The New York
Times Magazine* had featured Salk in January as the star of "A
Stirring Medical Drama." *Life* had made the vaccine its cover
story on February 22. *Time* featured a portrait of a haunted-
looking Salk surrounded by disembodied crutches, leg braces,
and syringes on the cover of its March 29 issue, with the headline, "Polio Fighter Salk: Is This the Year?" In the two months
before the field trial began, *Collier's, Consumer Reports, Popular Mechanics, School Life,* and *U.S. News and World Report*
all had feature articles on the vaccine trials to come. *Time,
Newsweek,* and *Science News Letter* gave weekly updates on
the latest developments in their regular medical pages. *Better
Homes and Gardens,* victim of an early deadline and a trusting
editor, featured a story in its March issue that "described" field-
trial vaccination clinics as though the trial had actually started
in February, complete with fabricated quotations from children
who insisted the shots were "just a little 'ol mosquito bite."

As a public event, the field trial was also an open season for
settling old scores. Albert Sabin had seized many opportunities
to make public statements about the unwarranted speed of the

National Foundation. Representatives of the American Medical Association objected to the prospect of mass vaccination clinics, which seemed a step closer to the dreaded specter of socialized medicine. In the end, however, it was a long-departed advisor, Paul de Kruif, who did the most concrete damage.

De Kruif had never forgiven Basil O'Connor for refusing to fund several research projects he had supported when he worked at the National Foundation. After he left the foundation and returned to Michigan in 1941, he attacked both the organization and O'Connor personally in several of his books. Now he began planting rumors that the Salk vaccine was a lethal product. Through the biomedical grapevine, he had learned about the bad batches of vaccine that had paralyzed monkeys in the NIH tests. First he consulted with his good friends at the Michigan State Health Service, urging them to demand that the National Foundation provide insurance policies for all doctors and health officials who might be liable for injuries caused by the field trial. This was a passing headache for Mel Glasser, who consulted with various attorneys before assuring the nervous doctors that there was no such insurance available, but that in any case the foundation, as the official "investigator" in the field trial, would be the entity liable to lawsuit. Then, apparently, de Kruif went outside the medical circle entirely, and took his case to Walter Winchell.

In the years when Franklin Roosevelt was president, Walter Winchell had been one of the nation's most popular newspaper columnists. He had elevated Broadway gossip to a subject of national concern and circulated his widely imitated blend of scandal, politics, and bizarre punctuation to over one thousand newspapers in the early 1940s. By 1954, however, his career was in decline, and the bitterness that had always lurked beneath his gossip had turned to venomous attacks on many of the people and institutions he had once championed—including his favorite president's favorite charity, the National Foundation for Infantile Paralysis.

On April 4, just two weeks before the latest of the many dates when the field trial had been scheduled to begin, Winchell opened his still popular Sunday night radio program with his familiar greeting, "Good evening, Mr. and Mrs. America, and

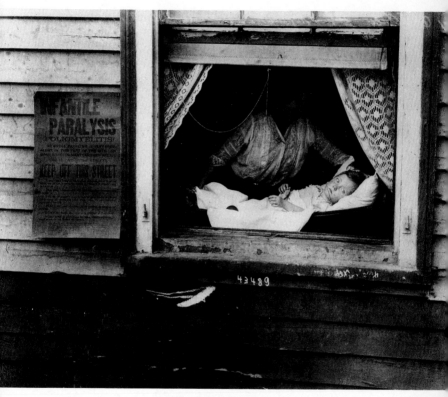

*Mother and child quarantined during the 1916 polio epidemic,
Brooklyn, New York*

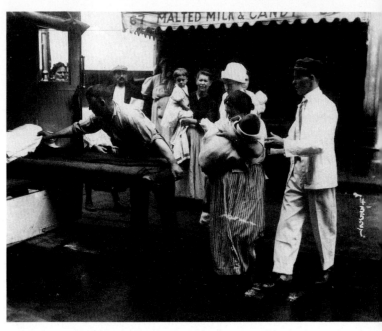

New York epidemic, 1916:
a health worker waits for a mother to release her stricken child to the hospital

The new image of the cheerful convalescent:
Franklin Roosevelt with paralyzed children at Warm Springs, Georgia

FDR, braced against a sturdy chair, waves a giant check representing proceeds from the first President's Birthday Ball fund-raiser.

November 1928: FDR, propped and posed to hide his paralysis, visits Warm Springs with the fashionably dressed Basil O'Connor.

Politics, show business, and charity: Lucille Ball, Red Skelton, and other Hollywood stars join Eleanor Roosevelt, cutting cake at the annual President's Birthday Ball.

Counting dimes at the White House: Basil O'Connor poised to report to Franklin Roosevelt on the proceeds of the March of Dimes. Note the radio microphone before them.

Terrified parents rushing their daughter to the doctor, North Carolina, 1948

Twin brothers Larry and Jerry Clay comfort each other in their shared hospital room, Tyler, Texas, 1954.

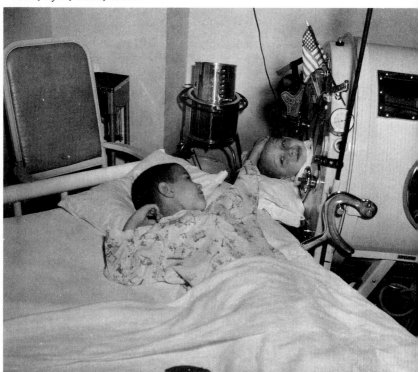

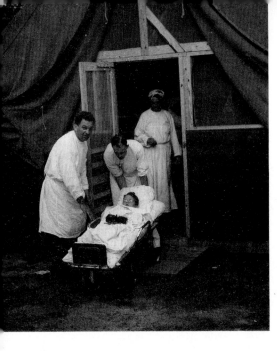

Hickory, North Carolina, 1948: emergency medical crews, brought from Chicago and Philadelphia by the National Foundation, work in tents set up because there were no contagious hospitals for polio victims.

1952, the worst epidemic year in history: polio patients in iron lungs and rocking beds at Rancho Los Amigos Medical Center, Downey, California

Howdy Doody supports the March of Dimes in January 1955: the popular television puppet was created in 1947, making him the exact contemporary of the Polio Pioneers who watched his daily program.

A volunteer, wearing an armband, collects from a commuter during the January March of Dimes campaign in Lexington, Kentucky, 1952.

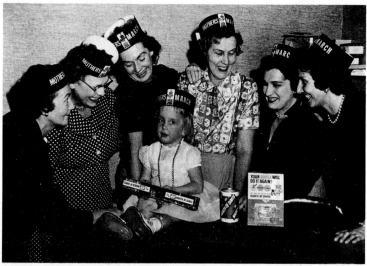

Volunteers for the Mothers' March on Polio, a one-night door-to-door collection for the March of Dimes.

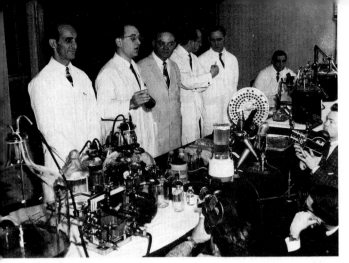

The Virus Research Laboratory Team, University of Pittsburgh. Standing left to right: Dr. L. James Lewis, Dr. Julius S. Youngner, Major Byron L. Bennett, Dr. Jonas Salk, Dr. Percival Bazeley.

Jonas Salk checks preparation of roller tubes used for cultures of poliovirus. The ability to grow the virus in tissue cultures made possible the large-scale production of vaccine.

Monkeys being inspected at La Guardia Airport before shipment to Okatie Farms conditioning center. Even using the new tissue-culture techniques, the vaccine program required vast numbers of laboratory animals, four thousand a month in 1954.

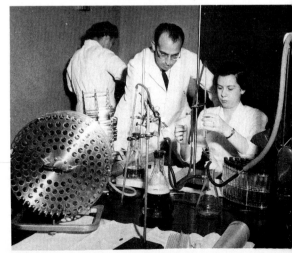

Donald Anderson,
the first March of Dimes poster child, 1946

March of Dimes poster child, 1948:
Terry Tullos

March of Dimes poster child, 1949:
Linda Brown

March of Dimes poster child, 1950:
Wanda Wiley

March of Dimes poster child, 1952:
Larry Jim Gross against the
backdrop of the Korean War

March of Dimes poster children, 1953:
Pam and Pat O'Neil

March of Dimes poster child, 1954:
Delbert Dains

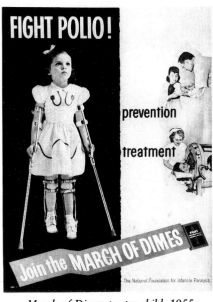

March of Dimes poster child, 1955:
Mary Kosloski

Jonas Salk, chief creator of the Salk polio vaccine

Dr. Albert Sabin, who developed the oral polio vaccine introduced in the United States in 1961

Dr. John Enders won the Nobel Prize, with Dr. Thomas H. Weller and Dr. Frederick C. Robbins, in 1954 for his discovery of how to culture poliovirus in non-nervous tissue.

The National Foundation's Vaccine Advisory Committee, studying one of the "little pink bottles" of Salk vaccine. Seated, left to right: Doctors Ernest Stebbins, Thomas M. Rivers, and Thomas B. Turner. Standing: Doctors Joseph E. Smadel, Norman H. Topping, and David E. Price.

Dr. Thomas Francis, Jr., at the
Vaccine Evaluation Center,
University of Michigan, 1955

Basil O'Connor, president of
the National Foundation for
Infantile Paralysis, 1938–1972

1953 family trial at the D. T. Watson Home for Crippled Children: Jonathan Salk being vaccinated by his father while his mother, Donna, comforts him

1954 Salk Vaccine National Field Trial, Sally B. Reynolds School, Jackson, Mississippi

1954 Polio Pioneers, Provo, Utah. This souvenir button went to all children who received all three shots.

Center, left to right: *Thomas Francis, Basil O'Connor, and Jonas Salk surrounded by photographers on the day of the announcement that polio vaccine was safe and effective, Rackham Hall, University of Michigan, April 12, 1955*

Press report of field trial results being delivered under guard, April 12, 1955

Rackham Hall, April 12, 1955

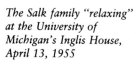

The Salk family "relaxing" at the University of Michigan's Inglis House, April 13, 1955

Jonas Salk receives a citation from President Dwight Eisenhower in the White House Rose Garden, April 23, 1955. Front row, left to right: Basil O'Connor, Peter Salk, Jonas Salk, President Eisenhower, Secretary of Health, Education and Welfare Oveta Culp Hobby. Back row: Surgeon General Leonard Scheele, Dr. Chester Keefer, Donna Salk.

A Herblock cartoon in The Washington Post *captures public dismay at the lack of federal planning for vaccine distribution, May 13, 1955.*

"Rush" shipment of Salk vaccine

By 1956, new campaigns were needed to get people to take the vaccine they had worked so hard to finance. Here, Elvis Presley gets vaccinated by Dr. Harold Fuerst while New York City Commissioner of Health Dr. Leona Baumgartner looks on.

*As classrooms became laboratories for testing the Salk vaccine,
children were transformed into scientific pioneers.*

*Jonas Salk and Randy Kerr,
the official "first polio pioneer," meet for the first time on
the twenty-fifth anniversary of the Francis Report, April 12, 1980.*

all the ships at sea." Speaking in the confident, rapid-fire growl that he had made the standard for broadcast urgency, he then announced, "Attention everyone! In a few moments I will report on a new polio vaccine—it may be a killer!" After the commercial, Winchell continued with his shocker: "Attention all doctors and families: the National Foundation for Infantile Paralysis plans to inoculate one million children with a new vaccine this month. . . . The U.S. Public Health Service tested ten batches of this new vaccine. . . . They found (I am told) that seven of the ten contained Live (not dead) polio virus. . . . That it killed several monkeys. . . . The name of the vaccine is the Salk Vaccine, named for Dr. Jonas Salk of the University of Pittsburgh."

Anybody who missed the initial broadcast could read all about it in Winchell's syndicated newspaper column the next morning. Although his column was now carried by only 150 papers, that was still a substantial circulation, and it included papers in New York and Washington, where most of the field-trial planners were sure to see it. Since polio was still big news even if Winchell was not, the broadcast was noted on the news pages of many other papers around the country. In a follow-up broadcast the next Sunday, Winchell went on to claim that the National Foundation for Infantile Paralysis was stockpiling little white coffins in depots around the country, so they would be ready for the children who were killed during the field trial. His source, he said, was a "famous name temporarily withheld by request."

Walter Winchell had long been a friend of the National Foundation, happy to publicize its fund-raising events and its therapeutic programs. A rumor had reached foundation headquarters the day before that Winchell was planning an attack, but the reality still came as a shocking surprise. Many of the top staff of the National Foundation were at a scientific meeting at the Homestead, in Hot Springs, Virginia, when Winchell went on the air. Dorothy Ducas sprang into action immediately, rushing to get the foundation's rebuttal out to the wire services and into the newsrooms of America in time for it to be included in the same newspaper editions that reported on Winchell's attack. Hurriedly drafting a response to the charges, she took it to the meeting's scientists for their approval and then telephoned it to her staff in New York, where they were able to get it out to the Associated Press, United Press International, and the major news sources of the country.

After the Winchell broadcasts, several state medical societies tried to withdraw their districts from the field trial—only to find that the public was furious at the possibility of being denied a chance to take part. By this time, the start of the field trial had been postponed yet again, to April 26. On April 19, only days before the first vaccinations were to start, Fairfax County, Virginia; Winnebago County, Illinois; the state of North Carolina; and the city of Summit, Ohio, all asked to be reinstated because of public pressure. National Foundation representatives and local leaders called meetings in field-trial communities, health departments issued letters and statements, and worried parents were reassured. Although a few withdrew from the trial, most remained.

To those who were making the decision, it still seemed possible that the entire trial might be postponed another year. There was little anybody could learn in another year that they didn't know already—little they could ever learn without the very field trial they were debating—but they were all made nervous by the accelerating rush of events. Up until the very last moment, the members of the Vaccine Advisory Committee still couldn't quite bring themselves to say the trial vaccine was safe to use. Neither could the director of the Laboratory of Biologics Control. The children were ready, the photographers had their flashbulbs in the sockets, the lollipops were waiting, the polio season was edging north, but the people making the decisions were scared. They were scared by Walter Winchell's little white coffins. They were scared by the virulent strains of virus Salk insisted on using in his vaccine. They were scared by Albert Sabin's eternal "what ifs." What if they gave the go-ahead and children started keeling over across the country? It was absolutely terrifying.

On Friday, April 23, 1954, Thomas Francis flew to Washington for the final meetings that would decide whether or not to proceed with the field trial. The next morning, he went out to the NIH campus in Bethesda, Maryland. Assembled there were six of the seven members of the Vaccine Advisory Committee, representatives of the manufacturers, and officials from the National Institutes of Health. Jonas Salk had come in from Pittsburgh. Basil O'Connor and Tom Rivers had come from New York. David Bodian, who had no official position in the proceedings, had once again come down from Baltimore to lend the weight of his expert advice. Reporters, photographers, and publicists waited in the corridors, smoking and gossiping and hoping there would be something to report.

Inside the meeting room, they discussed the successful safety tests of the latest commercial vaccine lots, and the manufacturers assured everyone that they were producing consistently acceptable vaccine. They reviewed the results of the most recent trials in Pittsburgh, where no one had taken sick from commercially produced vaccine, and discussed the current health of the Watson Home children, who continued to show higher levels of antibody protection than they had before vaccination. William Workman showed movies of mice that had been paralyzed, but David Bodian insisted that whatever ailed them, it was not polio. They reviewed everything there was to say and think about the safety of the field trial, but still they waited to make a formal decision.

A much smaller group met the next day at the Carlton Hotel in Washington, and the people there really didn't know what they were going to do. The assistant surgeon general was there, ready to follow the recommendation of the Vaccine Advisory Committee. Jonas Salk sat out in the corridor, barred from the meeting but making himself available if anybody wanted to consult. Thomas Francis, too, was asked to stay outside while the committee met.

They had heard all about the virtues of longer trials on more test populations, about more monkeys, more safety tests, more time. They had changed the safety-screening procedures, and watched five thousand additional children get vaccinated in the Pittsburgh area over the last month. They had been reminded yet again by Basil O'Connor of how many children would be paralyzed for each year that they postponed their decision. They did not need to be reminded that delay would tell them nothing about the real safety of the vaccine; that could only be discovered through a field trial.

They had been wrangling for weeks. The month before, Tom Rivers had told Jim Shannon, assistant director of the NIH, to take his statistics and shove them up his ass, and Basil O'Connor had sent him back to New York to cool off. At other meetings, Rivers had screamed and cursed his Vaccine Advisory Committee for what he called its cowardice. Now he was restrained, formal, gracious. A vote was taken, and the Vaccine Advisory Committee recommended that the field trial begin.

After all the doubt, delay, and division, they voted unanimously. Fully aware of the significance of the moment, they asked if they could each have duplicate copies of their official resolution, to keep as mementos. Basil O'Connor had drafted it, carefully removing all the lawyerlike *whereases* that Dorothy Ducas always told him made it impossible for ordinary people to understand his meaning, but the grand occasion seemed to demand an elevated level of rhetoric. The committee asked for the formal language to be put back in. When the document had been retyped, they signed it. William Sebrell, director of the NIH, brought a written statement from the Public Health Service granting approval for the field trial, and Leonard Scheele, the surgeon general, arrived to confirm that the statement was satisfactory. Exhausted and relieved, O'Connor joked that the only way to make it better would be to pin it to a thousand-dollar bill.

Out in the hallways, the reporters and photographers began to appear from the pressroom the National Foundation had set up at the Statler Hotel. Thomas Francis slipped away, leaving Robert Korns to make a statement in his stead. Jonas Salk and Basil O'Connor prepared for a second installment of "The Scientist Speaks for Himself," to be broadcast that evening. Telegrams went out to the 211 health departments where the field trial would be held, telling them they could start the clinics as soon as possible. Steve Alex, at the Washington office of the National Foundation, began lining up media coverage for the nearby school in suburban Virginia that had been chosen to begin the national trial.

The next morning, the first children were vaccinated. The Polio Pioneers were on the march.

WIDE-ANGLE

POLIO
PIONEERS

It was too quick, said medical colleagues nationwide: Salk had gone public without first publishing everything in the journals. He rushed out a killed-virus serum without waiting for a safe live-virus one, which would be better. Doctors walked out of professional meetings; some quit the foundation that funded the testing. Salk was after personal glory, they said. Salk was after money, they said. Salk was after big prizes.

Salk tested the serum on five thousand Pittsburgh schoolchildren, of whom I was three, because I kept changing elementary schools. Our parents, like ninety-five percent of all Pittsburgh parents, signed the consent forms. Did the other mothers then bend over the desk in relief and sob? I don't know. But I don't suppose any of them gave much of a damn what Salk had been after.

—ANNIE DILLARD

Everybody in the public health field knows that when you reach the point where you can begin to inoculate an agent into millions of children, your problems have only just begun.

—ALBERT SABIN

The children who took part in the Salk vaccine field trial had no interest in the relative merits of observed controls and placebo controls or in any of the other debates that had tied the scientific advisors into knots for so many months. They were unaware of the production problems that had delayed the field trial and were quite indifferent to the delicate balance between the autonomy of private industry and the authority of the federal government. If they had heard that the vaccine might be dangerous, they had been reassured by parents and teachers who reminded them of the even greater dangers of polio.

Suddenly transformed from commonplace elementary school students to Polio Pioneers, they were excited by the attention they were receiving and by the interruption of the ordinary school routine, but they accepted the field trial itself as it was presented to them, in whatever form and on whatever day that might be. Conducting a scientific experiment in the nation's schools, and using the youngest students as the subjects, seemed no more remarkable to them than any of the other arbitrary rituals adults were always expecting them to observe. Line up in size place for recess. Put the stamp on the upper right corner of the envelope. Pledge allegiance to the flag. Steal second base but not first. Eat your dinner before dessert. Go to the gym to get your polio shot. By the time you were finished with first grade, you knew these were not issues one discussed. This was the way things were.

The children's concerns were far more basic. Where will they stick the needle? Will it hurt? Will I cry? Will I get the real stuff? Can I go swimming this summer? Does a booster shot mean they use a bigger needle? Does this mean I won't ever have to walk with crutches?

Across the country, teachers explained the field trial in terms a child of six or seven could understand. The vaccine had been developed by very careful scientists who wanted to help the children stay healthy. It was pink, and it came in little bottles. The shot would feel like a tiny prick, no more than a mosquito bite, and would only hurt for a moment. No one would know how well it worked until next year. They were pioneers. Pioneers are special people who go first. They were very lucky to be able to get vaccine.

In the eleven states that took part in the double-blind placebo trials, the explanations went further. Doctors needed to measure how well the vaccine worked, the children were told. To do that, they had to compare children who got vaccine to children who didn't. Nobody could know who got which, or the experiment would not come out right. Next year they would each find out what they had received. No one would know how well it worked until next year. They were all pioneers. Pioneers are special people who go first. They were all very lucky.

Teachers showed the filmstrip or read the cartoon storybook the National Foundation had provided, reminded the children of the lollipop reward waiting at the end for those who kept up their courage—and then they moved on to the next lesson of the day. Some used the field trial as an exercise in penmanship as well as science. "Dear Dr. Salk," the teacher would write on the board in clear, careful print. "Dear Dr. Salk," the children would copy, clutching their pencils in fingers that were still much more comfortable with crayons and blocks. "Thank you for making the polio vaccine. I hope it works. I hope nobody ever gets polio again." Then they signed their names, as the teacher told them to, and added whatever else came to mind—their age, their grade, their house number, a picture of a rainbow, an airplane, an ecstatically radiant sun. The teacher collected all the papers and sent them off to Pittsburgh in a fat brown envelope, the start of a pile that would grow much higher the following year.

•

Finally, the field trial had begun. In McLean, Virginia, outside Washington, six-year-old Randy Kerr became the officially designated "first" child to be vaccinated. Smiling for the reporters and photographers that the National Foundation publicists had dragged out to the suburbs far too early on a Monday morning, he announced it hurt less than a penicillin shot. Did he suspect that he would repeat the performance at anniversary celebrations for decades to come, long after his Polio Pioneer button had rusted under the edges and he towered over Dr. Salk? He was willing. It was fun to be a Polio Pioneer. It was fun to have your picture taken.

The photographers were always there. They were there in Palm Beach, Florida, and in Missoula, Montana, in the tenement districts of Manhattan and the farm towns of Iowa. Whether the clinics were set up in the auditorium, classroom, gym, or on the open lawn, the photographers took the same pictures: the line of children waiting to get their shots; the wide-eyed little cowboy sandwiched between a nurse who held his shoulders and a doctor who pricked his arm; the brave little girl who grinned at the needle; and then the group of proud survivors, broad smiles stretching the cheeks that still glistened with tears, each right hand pointing to the left upper arm to show where the magic shot had been given.

Each community had its heroes, its martyrs, and its treats. In Glen Ellyn, Illinois, first-grader Linda Lou Anderson counted to twenty so she wouldn't notice the needle. In New York's suburban Westchester County, Joshua Smith asked his little brother in which arm he had gotten the shot, and then punched him there, hard. In Lexington, Kentucky, the parent leader at Christ the King parochial school had to tell her daughter she could not be one of the children giving a blood sample, because too many others had volunteered. In Cliffside Park, New Jersey, the children grabbed jelly beans and rushed for the schoolroom where a television had been set up to amuse them while they waited for their classmates to finish. Children well enough to be vaccinated but too sick to be in school came to the door of the field-trial clinics and got their shots there. Some came early, so as not to spread their colds to others, and earned a special status among their friends because they had been the first, the very first to get the new polio vaccine.

The children were not just pioneers. They were also pint-size epidemiologists, absorbing a powerful lesson in scientific

method even before they received their dose of vaccine or placebo. All across the country, selected schools had been transformed into laboratories. Dr. Leona Baumgartner, New York
City's commissioner of health, was amazed and delighted to see
how well the children had accepted the rigors and responsibilities of their role as laboratory assistants. She and Basil
O'Connor, accompanied by the inevitable horde of journalists,
had arranged to meet at P.S. 61 in Manhattan's Lower East Side
Health District, chosen as the city's demonstration school.

"I went down early," Baumgartner recalled, "because I was
interested to see what the kids knew about this ... and you
would have thought all those youngsters were going to Christmas or something, they were so polished up and dressed up. I
walked into a classroom where they were all standing around,
and I said, 'What's going on here, anyway?' They were so excited
about it, and they told me about it. They told me that part of
the kids were going to get the real stuff, and some part of them
weren't going to get the real stuff, and nobody was going to
know who got what. And all of the information would go out
to Ann Arbor, and out there they would know which stuff
they got.

"So I said, 'Gee, that sounds kind of dumb to me. Why do
they give you stuff that isn't any good?' They were shocked,
they had to correct me. And those youngsters [gave] as good a
description of a controlled experiment as I've ever heard. I was
very excited, because it seemed to me that if you could teach a
generation of kids about what a controlled experiment was, and
about what science really was, this was a plus value regardless
of whether the vaccine was any good or not."

Parents sometimes had more trouble accepting the strictures
of the scientific method. Some were hostile to the National
Foundation or to any medical interference in their family's life.
Some preferred the risk of an epidemic summer to the possible
hazards of an untried vaccine and decided to wait until the
results were in. In observed-control areas, it was hard to convince parents that their children had to give blood samples even
though they would not be receiving vaccine—it seemed so un-
fair. Most, however, were happy to cooperate and eager to take
part. Statisticians had predicted a participation rate of 50 per-

cent, but it was never that low, not even in Michigan, where the state medical society had campaigned against the vaccine. In some health districts, as many as 90 percent of the eligible children brought back the letters requesting participation. Ninety-six percent of the children who started the program completed their shots, despite the fact that the vaccinations began so late in the year that the third shot was given after school had recessed for the summer.

It was hard work finding those children and setting up a clinic after school was over. It was difficult from the beginning to figure out the forms, and to keep the codes straight in the placebo areas so that everybody got consistent doses of the same thing. The volunteers who worked in the vaccination clinics had attended training sessions and held rehearsals, and they gratefully followed the instruction manuals the National Foundation had provided. Films and booklets often arrived late, however, and sometimes they had to rehearse without their props. The foundation had planned to send out dummy boxes of vaccine to use in practice sessions, but even the boxes weren't ready until the moment of the field trial. As best they could, the volunteers in each community managed with what they had and what they knew, determined to show that they could rise to the challenge they had been given.

For the older brothers and sisters of the Polio Pioneers, and for their parents and grandparents and all the adults who followed the polio story so avidly in the newspapers and magazines that seemed, for a time, to write of little else, the field trial of 1954 had an additional significance. As soon as it became known that a vaccine was available, and that it would be used first on children in the first three grades of elementary school, it was treated as one more proof that the howling surge of infants who had begun to appear in 1946 marked the beginning of a new and very different generation. Born in peacetime and growing up in an era of rising prosperity, these first beneficiaries of new schools, new subdivisions, new highways, and new shopping centers were now the first to receive a new medicine, the first to be protected against a nightmare that had haunted the past two generations. No effort, it seemed, was too great to improve the lives of these special children.

Individual school districts tried to involve the older children in the field trial. In Lexington, Kentucky, where parents had raised enough money to build a new hospital wing for polio patients in 1948, children were given "Polio Volunteer" armbands and allowed to help in the work of transforming the school gym into a temporary clinic. In Quincy, Massachusetts, where children in the first three grades of public school were being vaccinated, fourth-grade classes made identification tags for all the children and volunteers. The fifth-graders mowed the lawn in front of the school. The sixth-graders washed the windows. It was a new way of being in school, and a new way of receiving medicine. It was a great adventure.

Not everything went perfectly. In several placebo-control areas, the cartons full of identical little pink bottles got scrambled. Some children received alternate doses of vaccine and placebo instead of three doses of one or the other, and the Vaccine Evaluation Center had to throw out their reports. In Arlington, Massachusetts, volunteers were furious when they discovered that a doctor had dumped all the bottles out of their cartons, losing the careful codes that would tell the evaluators who got placebo and who received vaccine. Determined that their children would not be deprived of vaccinations because of the error of a public health official, they convinced Thomas Francis to send a shipment of new vials in time for their district to take part. To be dropped from the field trial was a blow to local honor as well as to health.

There was a degree of pilferage, though not as much as had been feared. Some of the doctors who gave the shots in the clinics used the opportunity to take home vaccine to use on their own children, and their friends' children, and so on. Several hundred such cases were reported, but they did not affect the trial. Parents were often more scrupulous in their recordkeeping than the local health officials—mothers who had moved out of their field-trial area wrote directly to Ann Arbor asking where they should bring their children to get the third shot—and included the code number of vaccine the child had received in the earlier clinics.

Each part of the country provided its own unique problems. To keep the clinics moving smoothly and to cut the mistakes and abuses, the National Foundation sent staff members fanning out across the continent. They divided up the map, just as they had done on the fund-raising tours, and they took their suitcases, their enthusiasm, and their iron digestions on the road once more. Years later they would still remember the names of hotels in Halifax, Nova Scotia, and Elkhart, Indiana, and how strange it was to go outside of Salk Lake City and be the only person there who wasn't a Mormon. Elaine Whitelaw spent a week in Lexington, Kentucky, with Margaret Hickey, who was picking up local color for a long article on the field trial for the *Ladies' Home Journal.* Then it was north to Boston, where she thought she would spend a day or two and ended up staying two weeks. In Massachusetts, each child had to be provided with a new syringe. Twenty-one separate towns had to be covered, each with its own health officer, and local officials insisted on calling a town meeting in every area where the field trial was held, so that everyone could discuss it. After the first weekend, she called her colleague, Virginia Blood, who was working the clinics in Hartford, Connecticut. "You'd better get up here," she said. "All the ground rules in Massachusetts are different. And bring me a change of clothes."

Helen Hayes, who had become a dedicated fund-raiser for the National Foundation after her daughter died of polio, was there in Massachusetts with Whitelaw, drumming up coverage with the enormous press entourage that followed her every-where. One of their stops was at a large Catholic school that was acting as a vaccination center for other sectarian private schools that were too small to justify a separate clinic. Watching the orderly march of uniformed children going for their shots, Whitelaw suddenly realized that something crucial was missing. Gingerly, she asked when they were going to begin taking blood samples from 2 percent of the children, as the rules of the field trial required. "Oh, yes," answered the mother superior se-renely, "that will be taken care of. We're waiting for the little Lutherans. They will give all the blood." At that moment, a small yellow bus pulled up with eight little Protestant sacrificial lambs. Helen Hayes, Irish herself, had to go outside and sit on the steps of the school so she could laugh without offending the mother superior.

The staff of the Vaccine Evaluation Center was making its own tours, exhorting the health officials to keep accurate records and reminding the doctors of the need to call in the physical therapists trained to assess the degree of paralysis if any field-trial subject should get polio in the months ahead. Robert Voight gave pep talks on the importance of statistics. Robert Korns, who described himself as Dr. Francis' eyes and ears out in the field, took off on a zigzag tour of America. The son of a missionary, Korns had spent his childhood in China and had never seen much of the United States, and he enjoyed the whistle-stop excitement of his travels. It was interesting to arrive in a town he had never heard of and be met at the station by the health commissioner. It was fun to assemble all the local doctors and have them hang on his words. That didn't make his work any less important, or his message any less serious, but it added a bit of spice to the drudgery. Sometimes he would cross paths with Elaine Whitelaw and they would have lunch and trade stories about the strange and comic situations they had encountered in their travels. Then they would move on, going their separate ways. It was exhausting, exhilarating, sometimes infuriating, and often inspiring to see how different communities rose to the new responsibilities the field trial thrust upon them.

All through May, the Vaccine Evaluation Center in Ann Arbor was receiving urgent telegrams and telephone calls about forms that had not yet been delivered. State departments of public health would wire: send us fifty copies of form FT-9, one hundred copies of FT-10. Laboratories that were to study the blood samples were late in getting directions on their paperwork. By the time the forms arrived, the workers had lost some of their momentum and had to be prodded back into action.

Sometimes they needed no cajoling. Denver, Colorado, had the highest level of participation of eligible children of any city in the nation, but the people who had made out the registration records had done them completely wrong. Looking at the enormous sheets of meaningless figures that arrived in Ann Arbor, Thomas Francis assumed that the entire city was going to have to be dropped from the evaluation, but he had not reckoned on the power of civic pride. Denver was not about to be dropped. Teachers gave up their summer vacations to reconstruct the registration records in time for the fall, and they kept their title as the premier field-trial city.

As much as the Salk vaccine field trial established a new model for voluntary mobilization for public health, it also reflected the prevailing realities of American society. When Bea Wright was sent from National Foundation headquarters to Montgomery, Alabama, to speak to a group of black parents about field-trial participation, the superintendent of schools called her to task for addressing the woman who chaired the meeting by her last name. Blacks were to be called by their first names only, he told her. Black children in Montgomery received their vaccinations out on the lawn, because they were not allowed inside the white schools where the vaccination clinics were all held. That was why Wright was there—to work out the special instructions for this special situation—and she always remembered it as one of the most horrible experiences of her life. If the black children had to go to the bathroom, they had to find a way themselves, because they were not allowed into the big school where the white children spent their time. On May 17, between the second and third vaccinations of the field trial, the United States Supreme Court issued the landmark decision, in *Brown* v. *Board of Education*, that racial segregation in public schools was unconstitutional, but it would take more than a court ruling to get the little children off the lawn and into the building.

"I continued to speak to the black people separately, entirely separately," Wright recalled. "They didn't seem to be affronted by it. They expected it. This was the thing that was terrible. They just thought this is how it had to be for them. But they were as interested in having their children protected, and they did a very great deal in the community, the mothers of those children, to see that the community found out about how the black children were being affected as well as the white children. And they did everything they could to help. I was very grateful to them but it was a very harrowing experience for me, because I wanted to cooperate and coming from the Foundation I knew I had better cooperate or there would be trouble, but I found it extremely difficult."

While the Supreme Court was mandating equality in the nation's schools, another national event of the spring of 1954 underlined the pervasive fear and suspicion of the time, the dark background against which the hope and cooperation of the Salk vaccine field trial stood out so brightly. In the weeks that the field-trial notices were going out to parents, Senator Joseph McCarthy was taking on his largest adversary, the United States Army, charging that a Communist spy ring operated at the U.S. Army Signal Corps installation at Fort Monmouth, New Jersey. The prosecution of this case lasted from April 22 to June 17, 1954, almost precisely the period of the polio vaccination clinics, and the Army-McCarthy hearings were broadcast on national television. National Foundation staff members, sent out across the country to help supervise the vaccinations, would return to their hotel rooms from a day of mass immunization against contagious disease and watch the replay of how the country was or wasn't succumbing to the dread contagion of communism; the children and parents, hearing the same language in their homes, could feel doubly protected.

By the end of June, the last of the vaccinations had been given. The blood samples had been sent to the laboratories, the children had received their pins and cards, the parents and the volunteers had gotten letters of thanks and certificates of merit from the local health departments and foundation chapters. Copies of Field Trial form no. 3, the records of the classroom rosters, began to arrive in Ann Arbor in the middle of July, the first of the many that would keep over one hundred tabulators busy for the next nine months. Eventually, there would be forty-six little boxes of microfilmed registers, records of every class and every child who had taken part in this largest field trial ever held. Box no. 1 held the records from Montgomery County, Alabama, through Pulaski County, Arkansas. Box no. 46 was Alberta, Canada, through Helsinki, Finland. Everything was there. Now somebody would have to decide what it meant.

PART FOUR

PROOF
by
NUMBERS

Between scientists and chaos, there is nothing but a wall of archives, labels, protocol books, figures, and papers.

—BRUNO LATOUR AND STEVE WOOLGAR

Ann Arbor, 1954–55

Many scientists like to describe their work in the language of exploration. They compare themselves to heroic navigators who travel beyond the boundaries of existing knowledge, and talk about the need to extend the frontiers of understanding. Some will also claim a fellowship with artists—in conversation, they often reveal an aesthete's fondness for "elegant" theories and "pretty" solutions, and gossip about each other's laboratory techniques like ballet dancers sizing each other up along the barre.

The secret that every scientist knows, but few discuss, is how much of their time they spend as clerks. The more candid will admit that a scientific paper published in a reputable journal is their most important means of professional advancement, but almost none are willing to go beyond that, to acknowledge the immense quantities of paper that are essential to an active laboratory—scribbled memos and laboratory notations, formal and informal letters to enemies and friends, correspondence regarding supplies, subscriptions, and recommendations, grant applications, evaluations, progress reports, final reports, and all the other kinds of writing that clog the files and crowd the days of every research center.

In the iconography of research, a scientist is a figure in a laboratory jacket who spends his life in the company of elaborate and somewhat mysterious pieces of equipment: squinting into a microscope, gazing at a test tube held before him at arm's length, or staring solemnly yet proudly at a grand machine that will split atoms, shake serum, insert balloons in arteries, or boost

279

monkeys into space. If the machinery is small enough, he holds it aloft, like a connoisseur admiring the color of the claret. If it is too various or sprawling for this, he arranges it on tables and shelves, tier on glistening tier of tools that allow the scientist to pursue the narrow path of progress. For very large items like atom accelerators, it's common for the scientist to be photographed inside the machine he controls. If the investigator happens to be a woman, convention demands that she hide the fact as far as possible behind a laboratory coat. In any case, the iconography is the same—brilliant scientist peering at enigmatic equipment, seeing secrets only he or she can discern.

For the polio story, it was glassware that everybody loved to see. Beakers, retorts, graduated cylinders, square bottles, round bottles, thin-necked flasks the size of beer barrels, and especially ranks of test tubes resting in wire cages, spinning on perforated wheels, or evoking satisfied smiles from unidentified lab assistants who could tell at a glance that the anonymous sludge inside the tube was a thriving virus colony and not, say, Jell-O. It was no wonder that Owens-Illinois, a major supplier of laboratory glassware, sent photographers to take pictures of prominent researchers in their laboratories. Cups and plates and windowpanes might keep the company in business, but honor and prestige lay in the fragile, pellucid mystery of scientific vessels.

Such tableaux were never seen at the Vaccine Evaluation Center that Thomas Francis established in Ann Arbor. Starting in the early months of 1954, when he had agreed to direct the field-trial evaluation, he had been preparing a sorting house for all the data that the field trial would produce, the mountain of tiny and irreducible facts that would combine to answer the vital questions of how well Salk's polio vaccine had protected the children who received it. It would take a year of grueling labor to part the sea of memos and punch cards, opening a path to the promised land of health.

The University of Michigan School of Public Health was far too crowded and public for the confidential work that needed to be done. Instead, Francis took over the old red brick maternity hospital around the corner on Catherine Street. When Jonas Salk was just starting his career in research, he had paced the floors of this building, nervously waiting the arrivals of his first

*two sons. Now babies were born at a new hospital, and this
was just an abandoned bit of campus real estate. In a few years,
the small, two-story building would be torn down to make room
for a parking lot, but from 1954 to 1959 it became the Special
Projects Research Building, exclusive domain of the Poliomyelitis Vaccine Evaluation Center.*

*The offices that Thomas Francis established there combined
the secrecy of a war room, in which the fates of nations are
decided by a few people bending over a map in the small hours
of the night, with the disheveled charm that often attaches itself
to the ad hoc research centers of any university. They borrowed
what furnishings and equipment they needed. The University of
Michigan painted the old building, put up walls, provided lights
and desks and window shades. The Census Bureau loaned sur-
plus calculators, typewriters, posture chairs, collators, and file
cabinets. A few people flew in from the National Foundation
headquarters to help design forms, but they never stayed long
and they never had anything to do with the evaluation itself.
Neither did anybody from the Michigan School of Public
Health, where Francis had asked Dr. Gordon Brown to take
over the direction of his lab for the duration. When the University of Michigan News Service assigned Louis Graff, their
health sciences reporter, to cover the evaluation, Francis let him
sit at a desk in the corner of the large meeting room, but he
never told him anything. Very politely and very firmly, he made
it clear that no news would be available for quite some time.*

*Nobody who worked at the Evaluation Center had been in-
volved in any of the prior stages of the field trial. Rensis Likert
and Angus Campbell came over from the Institute for Social
Research, just across the campus, and advised Francis on designing forms and asking the right questions to find out what
you needed to know. Others arrived from farther afield. Robert
Voight had left the Census Bureau to run the statistical operations, and Eva Tolchinsky also soon followed from Washington to work on tabulations. Robert Korns took a leave of
absence from the New York State Department of Health, left
his wife and five children in their house in the woods outside
Albany, and moved to Ann Arbor to be Francis' deputy director.
They stayed for over a year, living in rented rooms and devoting*

themselves to the messy and often frustrating task of gathering and interpreting the information that would reveal how well the new vaccine had worked.

Others made shorter detours from their regular jobs, but the work they did was no less vital. Herbert Wenner was a good lab man, part of the original virus-typing program, and he took off a month from his own lab in Kansas to tour the other laboratories and show them how to set up for the work ahead. Morton Boisen came to be Robert Voight's assistant, helping to supervise the hundred graduate students, hired for the tabulations, who worked in the small building behind the Evaluation Center. John Napier was supervisor of statistical procedures, and Fay Hemphill was technical advisor.

It wasn't a chummy business they were doing, but they worked well together. Thomas Francis, always polished and precise, had a dry humor when you got to know him. Bob Korns was a calmer kind of fellow, tall and mild and efficient without seeming nervous about it, and he had no trouble handling the place when Francis was away meeting with his many committees. Still, it would have been hard to persuade the casual observer that their labors had much to do with science. The picture was all wrong for the role.

1

THOMAS FRANCIS KNEW THAT THE WORK HE WAS DOING WAS completely unglamorous, and he considered it his job to keep it that way. While families cowered at home for fear of polio, scientists quarreled about the virtues and dangers of each other's work, and Basil O'Connor threw thrift and caution to the winds in his drive to end the disease, Francis dedicated himself and his staff to the dogged, repetitive, frustrating task of gathering detailed reports on the health or illness of 1.8 million children. The information gathered in Ann Arbor was as vital to the success of the polio vaccine as the navigator's log to the settlement of the newly discovered island or the pirate's map to the unearthing of the treasure, but there was nothing of the picturesque in the stacks of telegrams, laboratory reports, and punch cards that soon started to pile up in his new office. If the world was seeking a hero or waiting for the flash of a shooting star, it would have to look elsewhere.

The difficult part of the field-trial evaluation was not interpreting the information, but getting it. The reports Francis needed traveled a slow route from volunteer clerks at each of several thousand field-trial clinics, to volunteer district coordinators, to overworked and sometimes unenthusiastic state and local health departments, to individual doctors and hospitals charged with the extra task of reporting on their patients while also caring for them, to research laboratories asked to master new and difficult techniques of virus analysis for a temporary project guaranteed to bring them no credit whatsoever.

Most of these people discharged their duties faithfully and

well. The remainder kept the directors of the Evaluation Center busy through the summer as they struggled to gather reports from the sloppy as well as the precise, the laggard as well as the prompt. By midsummer Francis, Korns, and Voight had all become eloquent speakers on the avoidable anguish of having to go back and find out information that should have been included in the first place, but there was no evidence that the lectures improved the process. They may have made Francis feel better, though his history of ulcers suggests not. The last of the delinquent reports did not arrive until March 9, 1955, almost a full year after the field trial had begun.

Soon after he agreed to direct the evaluation program, Francis began dictating a "Daily Memo" which was in effect a diary of his travels, meetings, and telephone conversations—and a record of the immense variety of problems that came to his ear every hour of every day. Francis suffered fools, but not gladly. In his own laboratory, he felt free to tear apart a colleague's unsatisfactory work. When confronted with annoying people or policies elsewhere, he expressed his scorn only to close friends and in private moments. What he did not say in person he often recorded in private notes that formed the bulk of his Daily Memo. Here he could complain that National Foundation officials were being obtuse or uncooperative, and could remark on an "alleged filmstrip" that never seemed to be ready. Here he could observe to himself that Salk was a good man who needed to be reminded of the impossibility of getting others to accept laboratory results of which they have not seen the proof. Various other people were judged lazy, self-interested, or vicious—but that was for Francis to know and not to broadcast. Praise was something you said out loud; criticism was for the private memo.

When the pressures became too great, Francis found some escape in whimsy. In June 1954, as the avalanche of field-trial data was beginning to blanket the Vaccine Evaluation Center, Francis wrote a letter to Basil O'Connor applying for a grant, "at the conclusion of this present evaluation program," to sit and think. "I don't want to have to think all the time and for a given period," he admitted. "What I would like to have are funds that when thinking is necessary I could afford to take off a period for a place where it could be carried out."

In the meantime, however, there were papers to sort and policy statements to issue. Basil O'Connor had a favorite speech he gave in many different versions, saying that the battle against polio proved the wonderful things that could be accomplished by free citizens working together in a democracy. During the summer of 1954, however, many people chose to exercise their democratic option by doing whatever they felt like, acting on that other popular adage, "It's a free country." After the excitement of the vaccination clinics, there was a definite drop in everybody's energy level, from the lowliest health clerk to the most prestigious laboratory director. As the slow and quiet days of summer passed, many people had trouble focusing on the fact that the main component of the field trial—the evaluation—couldn't begin until the people doing the evaluating had all the necessary reports. When Robert Korns got to Kansas on one of his many tours of the field-trial territory, he discovered the health officers there regarded the field-trial regulations as "suggestions" and didn't feel they had to fill out forms if they didn't want to. On Monday, August 16, Francis noted the receipt of a typical letter "from health officer of Fond-du-lac, Wisconsin, stating that Foundation representatives were too busy to be bothered about Registration Schedules." As Francis added ruefully, "This appears to be a widespread attitude."

Meanwhile, a small but significant number of parents who had volunteered their children for the field trial thought a shot of gamma globulin would be the perfect insurance while waiting to see if the Salk vaccine worked, and Francis found himself drafting many letters and memos urging them not to do so. If they had been vaccinated in the field trial, it would be impossible to know what was protecting them—vaccine or gamma globulin. If they were in an observed control, the gamma globulin might lower the general incidence of polio and make the vaccine seem less effective. Few of these parents, determined to use every chance to protect their children, gave a hoot about statistical validity.

Not everybody was uncooperative. At the Communicable Disease Center in Atlanta, chief epidemiologist Dr. Alexander Langmuir still saw the polio vaccine field trial as an important opportunity to enhance the power of his agency. The people at the National Institutes of Health could talk all they wanted about the primacy of research, but he would show them what active government service was all about. The Communicable Disease Center had not been given charge of the field-trial evaluation, but it could still find some way to take part in the most significant epidemiological experiment of the century.

One of Langmuir's many inspirations for boosting the size and influence of his department had been the formation of something called the Epidemic Intelligence Service, a field staff of epidemiologists that had seen a surge in enlistment when active duty with the Public Health Service became an alternative to the medical draft during the Korean War. Recruitment remained high after the troops returned from Korea in 1953, and the next year Langmuir made it known that he would be happy to assign a few officers from his corps to help the Vaccine Evaluation Center. They were all accustomed to travel, trained in polio work, and experienced in dealing with the various strengths and foibles of state and local health departments. Robert Korns, in a memo to Francis, noted "[Langmuir] insists he is not looking for the glory of the CDC, but obviously feels out of the picture and wants to be on the inside." Rather than being put off by any such ulterior motives, Francis was quite able to benefit from them, and readily accepted the offer. Twenty-two Epidemic Intelligence Officers, nurses and physicians worked with state health departments and participating laboratories during the evaluation of the trial, and three assisted at the Vaccine Evaluation Center.

Extra epidemiologists could speed the collection of health records and the processing of blood samples, and they could remind flagging local officials of the importance of the enterprise in which they had all been joined. They could not do anything, however, about the daily reports on the number of children stricken with polio around the country, or the heartbreaking mail from people around the world who wanted Thomas Francis to tell them how the vaccine could cure their children already paralyzed. Whenever a child got sick that summer, people worried that the vaccine had caused it, and passed the burden of their fears to Thomas Francis. Parents took their children to the hospital and blamed their headaches and fevers on the vaccine.

Children died of meningitis and chickenpox, but doctors worried that it might have been brought on by the vaccine.

People who were cheerful and cooperative in April got testy about their ignorance by July, and it seemed at times that all of them called the Evaluation Center to get some extra information that would confirm or soothe their fears. As the health officers in Davenport, Iowa, explained when they called Ann Arbor, everyone would be relieved if Francis would break the code and tell them if the dead child had had vaccine or placebo. "If it were placebo, there would be no further question; if it were vaccine there would be considerable suspicion." This was just the sort of bias that Francis had foreseen when he insisted on the double-blind control, but it was much harder to argue for statistical integrity when real children were really sick. The atmosphere at the Vaccine Evaluation Center was one of busy camaraderie, but there was no question that the weight of responsibility, and the bulk of the work, fell on the director.

Thomas Francis also bore the main burden of fending off all the reporters who wanted a story, or a comment on a story, or a chart, or a photo, or a hint, or anything at all that would give their readers some news, and some hope, as another polio season took its toll. They were fated to go unsatisfied. On July 12, as Francis was preparing for the only press conference he would agree to give until just before his final announcement, his wife Dorothy was in a car crash that left her in the hospital for the next six months, and Francis abandoned his plans to meet the press. Faced with immense public responsibility and now personal tragedy, Francis sent his son to Scotland to spend the summer and arranged for a family friend to take his daughter east for her freshman year at Wellesley, but for the rest of the year he interrupted his work three times a day to visit Dorothy in the hospital.

On June 1, the National Foundation pulled much of its staff off the polio vaccination program. Mel Glasser went back to planning the foundation's future. Elaine Whitelaw and Dorothy Ducas turned their energy to the formidable task of gathering volunteers for the Emergency March of Dimes to be held that August to raise the extra $20 million in expenses that hadn't been covered by the original fund drive in January. Tom Dublin, the epidemiologist from the NIH, and Hart Van Riper, the foundation's liaison to doctors, were now the only foundation staff with official reason to be in touch with the Vaccine Evaluation Center.

Unofficial fishing expeditions for advance results were, of course, another question. By the middle of August, someone was calling at least once a week, trying to worm out some clue as to the results—while Francis was grappling with the fact that several laboratories (including John Enders') had not even begun to do the studies he needed for his evaluation. O'Connor had promised not to interfere in the evaluation, but that did not keep him from delegating other people to ask any number of questions, all of which came down to the central one: How was the vaccine working?

There were many ways of asking. Had there been polio cases in vaccinated children? When would it be convenient for Francis to have a series of interviews about the progress of the work? Could he make some statement for the August Emergency March of Dimes? We hear the Canadian government has ordered enough vaccine for four hundred thousand children—what does Francis think of that? Henry Kumm went to Pittsburgh to ask the same questions of Salk, who referred him back to Francis —who referred him back to the statements issued periodically assuring the press, and through them, the public, that the study was to be trusted because it was completely free of interference from the National Foundation.

Basil O'Connor's curiosity was understandable. He had staked his reputation and his influence on this vaccine, spent $7 million on the field trial, and pledged $9 million more to buy vaccine supplies if the manufacturers would continue production while waiting for the results. It would have been a great comfort to know if he had made the right decision.

O'Connor was hardly the only person trying to guess how the field-trial results were shaping up. Foreign governments were very eager to know how vigorously they should try to duplicate Salk's procedures, and they sent a number of queries through official and unofficial channels to try to discover Francis' opinion. The United States Army, which had supported so much of Francis' work on influenza, felt it was only reasonable that he should give the surgeon generals of the armed forces advance notice of what measures were worth taking to protect their personnel overseas in epidemic areas. Private individuals, both physicians and laymen, called and wrote often with detailed explanations of why they were particularly in need of vaccine for personal use.

Bothersome as these intrusions were, they were still simpler to handle than the continuing assumption from 120 Broadway that Thomas Francis was in some way working for the National Foundation and bound to cooperate in its promotional campaigns. When a publicist from the foundation appeared with a sample of the press release they were planning for the Emergency March of Dimes, featuring a personality profile of the Vaccine Evaluation Center's director, Francis was appalled. Salk, confronted by a similar cartoon-illustrated biography ten months before, had written Dorothy Ducas a letter of several pages explaining precisely how he thought it should be altered to avoid embarrassment and misrepresentation. Francis took the more direct route of telling the publicist to leave his office and never return.

His attitude must have maddened and mystified the people in New York. They had spent millions of dollars to fund the field trial, many of those dollars on expensive changes like the placebo-injected control that Francis had insisted was essential, and yet Francis seemed to be unable to make the connection between these higher costs and the urgent need to raise more money. The National Foundation was $20 million in debt, and Thomas Francis wouldn't deign to pose for pictures to be used for fund-raising? From what particular part of heaven did he think the pennies came?

For Jonas Salk, the summer and fall of 1954 had not been nearly as peaceful or productive as he had hoped. After the frenzy of preparing for the field trial, he had looked forward to a time when he could relax, answer the mail, finish up the many papers he had been promising to write, give some of the interviews he had told so many journalists last winter he would have time for "in six months," and perhaps even say hello to his family. Instead, he spent most of his time plugging holes in leaking dikes.

Some of the problems were ones he brought upon himself. While everyone else thought the field trial was testing a specific vaccine he had developed, Salk still believed it was his general theories of immunization that were on trial and the vaccine specifications were open to revision. Long before the field-trial results were known, Salk wanted to improve the vaccine. As early as May 1954, while the vaccination clinics were in progress, he was arguing for changing the specifications for future production. He had a new, faster method for producing virus by dissolving the monkey kidneys in trypsin, an enzyme that broke down the walls between the cells and allowed a greater volume of virus growth, and he was eager to put it into use. He wanted to change the inactivation period, and the interval between injections. Perhaps in response to Tom Rivers' condescending comparison of his vaccine to a Model T car, Salk wrote to Basil O'Connor, "I would be reluctant to await the decision as to whether this year's model is adequate before deciding upon the use of a better one for which we have not only the blueprint, but we have even more experience than was available when the present year's model was put on the road."

Some of the changes Salk wanted to make were vital to the success of the field trial. At the very moment when children were receiving their vaccinations across the country, tests at the Pittsburgh lab had shown that some production lots of vaccine were considerably less potent than others. Three shots of this weak vaccine might not protect children at all, and if a bad epidemic happened to hit an area with bad vaccine, all of Salk's work would be discredited. Hastily reporting his results to Thomas Francis, Salk persuaded him to send different production lots of vaccine for the second and third inoculations of areas that had received weak vaccine at first. What Francis would not reveal, however, was which areas had received the weak vaccine, so Salk was in suspense for the rest of the summer, wondering if stronger epidemics had indeed coincided with inferior vaccine.

Salk hoped that an enterprising reporter would undertake an informal survey of field-trial areas and discover this information for him, and he was rather disappointed when no one did. In the meantime, he was kept busy supervising the blood tests that his laboratory was doing as part of the field-trial analysis, rechecking the laboratory work for areas that were having trouble processing their blood samples, providing Medium 199 and horse serum to labs that were setting up their tissue-culture work, testing unused samples of vaccine that had been returned from field-trial clinics, and preparing a paper he was to deliver at the Third International Conference on Poliomyelitis, to be held in Rome during the first week of September.

As the summer advanced, all these distractions kept Salk from publishing the articles his colleagues relied on for technical information, and frayed his temper as well. Albert Sabin, who had as much reason as anybody to be eager for news of the field-trial results while he worked on his own attenuated-virus vaccine, continued to cite Salk's failure to publish his findings as a sign of the "prematurity" of a nationwide field trial. On July 12, Thomas Francis noted in his Daily Memo: "Dr. Salk telephoned. He states that the charts of the potency tests with the different lots of vaccine are being drawn up to send to us. This has been a long-continued promise. In fact, Dr. Salk has sent us very little information." Meanwhile, the editors of the *Journal of the American Medical Association*, with whom Salk had long had difficulties, rejected several articles Salk did submit, claiming they were too technical for their readers—the very doctors whose letters were crowding Salk's mailbags with technical questions about the new vaccine. Even Herdis von Magnis, the Danish virologist who was one of the few colleagues with whom Salk had consistently cordial dealings, took to writing letters begging for technical details of procedures she hoped to use in her lab but could not find described in the professional literature—requests Salk would answer with a promise of full publication of the details "soon."

"Soon" generally meant later or not at all, since no amount ·of energy or dedication will enable a person to do as much as Salk wanted and promised to do. He could not be out personally vaccinating half the children in Pittsburgh and at the same time write up his results, especially when he was also traveling to New York, Washington, Detroit, and Rome. He could not concentrate on scientific papers when he was dictating endless letters about precisely how to seal the venules for blood samples, or volunteering to redo the laboratory work for several of the other labs providing results for the field-trial evaluation. The success of the vaccine trial was more important than the length of his bibliography, but in the anxious months of waiting for Francis' report, Salk's failure to publish his results brought him many problems with people who were unwilling to concede the merits of his work until they had seen it spelled out in black and white.

At the same time that Thomas Francis was annoyed by Salk's continued promises of much-delayed papers, Salk thought Francis was being unreasonably close about the information that was coming in to the Evaluation Center. Salk felt aggrieved that he, who developed the trial vaccine, knew so little about how the field trial was going—and astonished that Basil O'Connor was equally ignorant. Disregarding Francis' repeated statements that the National Foundation would have no information before he was ready with his final report, Salk seems to have assumed the wall of silence was a facade erected for public display while couriers made their runs between the friendly bases of the powers allied behind the polio cause.

Instead, he was beginning to realize, the Evaluation Center was a fortified camp. As Francis noted after one of their many telephone conversations: "Salk said that the Center was in a remarkably strong position; he had asked Mr. O'Connor if he knew what was happening. Mr. O'Connor said that he did not, that the Center did. Salk expressed surprise that he did not know at least what was happening in the test areas."

As the summer drew to a close, a new problem arose in Pittsburgh. Testing unused vaccine that had been prepared for the field trial, Salk began to notice serious deterioration, especially against the highly dangerous Type I poliovirus. He suspected, correctly, that Merthiolate, a preservative William Workman had persuaded him to add as an extra safety precaution, was destroying the protective force of the inactivated virus. Since all his vaccine samples were identified by code, Salk appealed to Francis to tell him what manufacturers and what production lots he was testing. Francis sent Robert Voight from the Vaccine Evaluation Center to Pittsburgh rather than send codes through the mail, in yet another of the scrupulous delays that were so maddening when your own work was under fire.

On August 26, two months after the first child had been inoculated in the national field trial of his vaccine, Jonas Salk sailed for Rome on the SS *Independence*. Once again he was sailing with John Enders and Basil O'Connor, but this time with a great deal more fanfare. Photographers captured them together on the deck before sailing, the three heroes of the battle against polio. Although they did not know it at the time, Enders was about to win the Nobel Prize, Salk to be elevated to rarefied heights of international celebrity, and Basil O'Connor to achieve the completion of his fondest dream, the conquest of polio within his lifetime.

None of them could have triumphed over paralysis without the very different talents of the other two, and each looked as though nothing less than the tragic threat of epidemic disease could have ever brought them together. Enders, the tall Yankee in his bow tie and rumpled seersucker suit from Brooks Brothers, seemed tired and even more withdrawn than usual. O'Connor, his dark suit tailored to the latest fashion, his signature carnation firmly planted in his lapel, looked more ready for a Tammany banquet than an ocean voyage. Jonas Salk, his eyes wary, his collar pinned and his tie clipped to guard against wayward breezes, seemed to travel in his own cloud of nervous anticipation. The Rome conference would be both a well-earned vacation and, Salk hoped, an overdue opportunity to explain to his colleagues and peers the principles behind a killed-virus vaccine.

Certainly his friends from Pittsburgh thought so. Lucile Cochran and Jessie Wright sent a basket of fruit to see him on his journey with sweet memories of his friends at the Watson Home. Ben Braseley, a local lawyer who had become a great admirer of the Salk family, sent a telegram wishing Salk the rest and relaxation he deserved, and "the realization of your fondest expectations." Salk's wife, more simply, wished him "Good sailing good trip good time much love from the children and me—Donna."

Everybody in virus research from Europe and America was at the conference, many of them as guests of the National Foundation. The top laboratory directors were there from Paris,

Stockholm, Cambridge, and London. Even Thomas Francis left his work and his hospitalized wife to come to Rome. Free of the need to simplify things for reporters or to answer complicated questions in the brief and unsatisfying format of the press conference, Salk would be able to present proof that a killed-virus vaccine was capable of causing immunity without natural infection and also to suggest that his vaccine could provide lifetime immunity to poliomyelitis without the need for yearly boosters. There was no real way of proving the latter, since the earliest vaccinations had been done little more than two years before, but he believed that the high levels of antibodies already recorded could be sustained indefinitely. Certainly no one could dispute that his vaccine had raised antibody levels.

In Rome, however, that was exactly what they did. Albert Sabin once again questioned the safety of repeated vaccinations with material made from monkey kidneys, and he insisted that repeated vaccinations would be needed for any killed-virus vaccine. Sven Gard of Sweden claimed that Salk's methods of virus inactivation didn't work and asserted there was dangerous live virus remaining in his vaccine. Hilary Koprowski said that people who had received his live-virus vaccine four years ago still showed immunity, and he flatly declared that they were living in the era of live-virus vaccines. Thomas Francis and David Bodian rose to dispute all these premises, and Salk defended his own work while issuing his first public speech on the dangers of live-virus vaccines. Long before the end of the conference, however, Salk had realized that the weight of professional opinion still leaned heavily toward a live-virus vaccine. When he returned from the conference, it was with a growing sense of estrangement from many of his colleagues in the world of virus research. Over the next twelve months, as experience lent substance to at least some of their objections, the gulf would widen.

Meanwhile, the problem of Merthiolate, the preservative that caused the vaccine to lose its potency, was yet to be settled. In November 1954, after all the field-trial vaccine had been administered and the registration cards filled in, after all the people who did get polio were evaluated and the results were gathered in Ann Arbor for the final reading, the National Foundation called a joint meeting of the original Committee on Immunization and the newer Vaccine Advisory Committee.

It was to be a gathering of all the expert advisors, and perhaps a reconciliation as well. Almost two years before, Basil O'Connor had asked for the Vaccine Advisory Committee to be formed of people not involved in polio research, and he had pledged himself to follow their decision on whether or not to conduct the field trial. Now he wanted those advisors to hear from the virologists, and he wanted the virologists to listen to the people who had had to make the choice.

If O'Connor hoped for union, Salk saw a massing of the opposition. On November 8, he telegraphed O'Connor at the Waldorf Towers: "I WILL NOT SUBJECT MYSELF NOR MY WORK NOR MY PRINCIPLES TO A COMBINE SUCH AS THE SO-CALLED COMMITTEES ON VACCINE AND IMMUNIZATION. I CAN NOT ATTEND THE PROPOSED MEETING OF 18–29 DECEMBER. J.E.S." Four hours later, he sent another telegram, detailing how specific amounts of Merthiolate, added to vaccine, reduced its effectiveness, and ended, "IT IS SAID TO AWAIT CERTAINTY IS TO AWAIT ETERNITY. J.E.S."

Salk was outraged that the leaders of the National Foundation still thought other people should be called in to advise him and examine his conclusions. Salk's plan for 1955 was to have another field trial, one that would confirm his latest findings on vaccination intervals and duration of immunity and at the same time postpone the disputes he foresaw over licensing and distribution. His proper role was to advise the National Foundation for Infantile Paralysis of what to do in relation to vaccine development, and to keep them informed of his own progress. That was the direction in which instruction was to flow. It was galling to have them put things the other way around.

In the end, Salk *was* at the December meeting, but before that happened, there was another meeting, this one at his laboratory in Pittsburgh, to discuss problems of future production. Representatives from all the manufacturers were there, along with Robert Korns of the Vaccine Evaluation Center, William Workman, and, of course, Basil O'Connor. By then, everybody agreed that the Merthiolate problem was real—and then began to squabble about whose fault it was. On November 30, Thomas Francis recorded Hart Van Riper's account of his "terrible" conversation with James Shannon. "Sebrell says I said merthiolate might have a part in inactivation for safety." Francis noted.

"This is not the case for I argued that the safety tests were done before merthiolate was added. He doubted the sufficiency of the safety tests. I said I thought 54 monkeys & the tissue cultures was pretty good."

James Shannon was the assistant director of the National Institutes of Health. William Sebrell was the director. Both had been present at almost all the meetings where various members of the NIH staff, and particularly William Workman, the director of the NIH's Laboratory of Biologics Control, had insisted Merthiolate was needed to prevent bacterial contamination of the vaccine. The manufacturers reminded each other that they were merely following the protocols provided, which had been drafted by the NIH's William Workman and Joseph Smadel. Smadel resigned from the Vaccine Advisory Committee. Workman insisted the protocols had been approved by Jonas Salk.

The "you said that I said that you said" debate continued at this adolescent level for some time. After everybody was through insisting that the addition of Merthiolate had been somebody else's idea, there was still the question of what to do about the weakened lots of vaccine. To Salk the most important issue was the need to tell people that the newly formulated vaccine was more effective than the product used in the field trial. To the directors of the NIH, the problem was that the safety of vaccine without Merthiolate had never been proven. If the field trial was a success, they would be asked to license a product that would not be the same as the one that had undergone such extensive tests.

To be sure that this new vaccine was safe, Workman returned to the plan he had proposed the year before—an additional trial of several thousand children to test the new commercial formula. Then the question arose of where to do the tests. In New York, where they had good health officials but sometimes uncooperative parents? In Georgia, where communities had been forced to drop out of the field trial when polio cases appeared before the program was ready to begin? In the end, Salk returned to the area where the people knew him best, Pittsburgh and its suburbs. He would vaccinate five thousand children in Allegheny County in the early months of 1955. There would be no specific mention of the Merthiolate problem—the new vaccinations would be presented as an extra test needed to gather further information about the vaccine. There was nothing to be gained by discrediting the field-trial vaccine before the results were in.

On December 10, three weeks after his meeting with manufacturers in Pittsburgh, Jonas Salk was in New York presenting a paper on "The Present Status of the Poliomyelitis Problem" at the annual meeting of the Association for Research in Nervous and Mental Disease. That same day, Dorothy Ducas had scheduled a press conference at Manhattan's Roosevelt Hotel. Ducas had sent Salk a copy of the notice that went out to all the newspapers, wire services, and radio and television networks, and he had provided the text of his paper to be distributed to the press the night before. Three weeks before the start of the annual March of Dimes campaign and only six months after the August emergency fund drive, the publicists were eager to give the public some word of encouragement from the man who seemed to many to hold the promise of salvation from the terrifying threat of paralysis.

At the conference, however, Salk told the assembled reporters, photographers, and newsreel and television cameramen that while he would answer questions, he would not allow them to quote or broadcast his remarks. When Basil O'Connor forwarded to him a letter of protest he soon received from the American Broadcasting Company, Salk replied that "for me to make a direct statement on radio or television was equivalent, on this particular occasion, to my writing the news item under my byline."

The incident, small in itself, was a sharp reminder of the very different standards and expectations attached to the polio vaccine story by the general public and the community of research scientists. In the coming months, as Salk was more and more often accused of pandering to the publicists, the curious gesture of standing before the press but refusing to make a statement would become emblematic of his divided allegiances, torn between his gratitude to the individual people and the public organization whose contributions had made possible his work, but still instinctively loyal to the standards of his profession. As Dorothy Ducas remarked, looking back on her years with the

National Foundation, "I liked most of these scientists. I think they were extraordinary people. But scientists have one weak spot, and that is their suspicion of anybody who is not a scientist. They just don't trust anybody but themselves."

One week later, Jonas Salk returned to New York for the meeting he had at first refused to attend. In the joint session of the Vaccine Advisory Committee and the Committee on Immunization, Salk was the only outside guest and Basil O'Connor the only person who was not a scientist. For the better part of two days, the group discussed technical and philosophical problems of polio vaccine research. They heard reports on live-virus vaccines being tested by Sabin and others. They heard Salk's report on the Merthiolate problems and his newest work on the spacing of vaccinations. Tom Rivers scolded his fellow virologists, saying there had been too many doubts raised about Salk's work and too few offers to help with the research needed to answer those questions. It made him angry, having to deal with these people who felt so free to criticize and so reluctant to help, and when Rivers got angry he fell back to the language of his childhood in Georgia. Every time there was a problem, he thundered, poor Jonas had to root hog or die, and he was getting tired!

By then it was the second day of the meeting, and they had been talking for hours about the proper powers of committees in directing the course of research. It was the question of control that had caused so much bad feeling a year before in Detroit, when the Committee on Immunization realized that Basil O'Connor was going ahead with the field trial no matter what they advised, and it was not about to be resolved by bringing in twice as many people to discuss the issue. Late in the afternoon, when people were beginning to think about their travel connections home, O'Connor forced one of those turns in the conversation for which he was justly famous.

O'Connor had devoted much of his life to combating polio. He had raised himself by his bootstraps to become a rich and respected lawyer, the confidant of the most powerful president in American history, and a formidable leader of health and welfare organizations. There was little he had ever reached for that he hadn't achieved, but there was nothing he wanted more than this last great triumph. While the scientists around the table had been debating the future course of polio research, O'Connor had kept his eye on the big picture, which in his view would always be framed by politics and business. The question they should be discussing, he felt, was not who should have authority over research funding, but what role would be left for research if the public demanded immediate access to a polio vaccine of imperfect quality, the federal overseers bowed to that demand, and the commercial manufacturers devoted themselves to producing and marketing a highly profitable but not very effective vaccine.

Thomas Francis was at this meeting, and he had already made it clear that he really and sincerely did not yet know what the final results of the field trial would be. He had also said that his evaluation would be finished in March or April. The question on O'Connor's mind was what the National Foundation for Infantile Paralysis should do if Francis concluded that the Salk vaccine was, say, 35 percent effective.

From a business perspective, that would be quite acceptable. A product that would protect only thirty-five out of every hundred people exposed to paralytic polio wasn't nearly as good as everybody gathered at the meeting knew it could be, but it was about twice as good as the manufacturers felt would justify full-scale commercial production. "If we get a thirty-five percent effective vaccine the commercial houses will bring it out," O'Connor informed the scientists gathered at the Waldorf. "They have told me they will bring out a twenty-five percent effective vaccine. They have indicated rather clearly that they will bring one out even if it is fifteen percent effective, and I am not at all sure that they will not bring one out that wasn't effective at all provided it is safe. Now these are the facts of life to face."

Another fact to face was that the Laboratory of Biologics Control would license such a product, and do it fast. At the meeting with manufacturers at Salk's lab in Pittsburgh, William Workman had given the impression that he would accept extremely low levels of effectiveness, as long as the product was safe, and had said he could get the license granted within a week—a remarkably short time for a process that often stretched over many months.

More than almost anybody in the room, perhaps even more than Jonas Salk, O'Connor hoped the field trial would prove the vaccine a great success. If it wasn't, however, then he hoped it would be a great failure. It was the middle ground that had him worried. A vaccine that was 35 percent effective, or 25 percent, or whatever figure they came out with, was not going to "lick polio." O'Connor felt a personal determination and a moral responsibility to push for a much better vaccine for the public that had supported the National Foundation for so many years, but he also had a clear premonition that the public would stop supporting them once a vaccine, any vaccine, was out. After that, people would say it was up to the commercial houses to pay for research. O'Connor put it in terms that would quickly bring anybody out of an ivory tower and down to earth. "If we get a vaccine that seems to be effective," he said, "they can run away with the whole field on you, and frankly, you may never get a chance to get the public to support it with regard to further work on the vaccine."

These were all very smart people O'Connor was talking to, but he still had to spell it out in very small words. The extraordinary expenses of the last two years had stripped the foundation's treasuries. The January 1954 March of Dimes campaign hadn't raised enough money to pay for the field trial and the costs of the gamma globulin program, on top of the vast expenses of patient care the recent epidemics had brought. Contributions were still high, but not high enough, and the reason, O'Connor felt, was "the public just got the idea that the fight against polio was over." The National Foundation had had to suspend payments to hospitals in May and mount the Emergency March of Dimes in August to cover their costs for the year, and the $12 million they collected had still not been enough. They had had to borrow $17 million from bankers to buy gamma globulin for the summer of 1954, and the only collateral they had to present was the good name of the National Foundation for Infantile Paralysis. Mel Glasser, the foundation's executive vice president, had been horrified by the idea of taking on such a debt, but O'Connor had told him "the year the American people decide they don't want to give us what we need in order to do the job, we've got to close our doors! That's how democracy works!"

Now it seemed as though that moment might be approaching, and it was something O'Connor wanted his scientists to know. The public might stop giving money if it appeared the polio problem was solved. Even though a better vaccine might be developed, they might stop giving money. Even though lots of people still got polio, they might stop giving money. And if the money stopped, the research would stop, too, and that would be the end of the game.

Most of the people at the meeting had invested their careers in polio research, and none of them was happy at the idea of abandoning the field—not when they knew that there were real problems in the control of polio that were still to be solved. Tom Rivers insisted the public would continue to contribute, but O'Connor reminded him that collections had already dropped, even before the field-trial results were known. Howard Howe, up from Johns Hopkins, couldn't believe the public would be so shortsighted, but O'Connor kept on telling him it was so. It was not something he expected them to act on right there and then, but he wanted them to think about it, and see if they had any good ideas for how the National Foundation should respond.

Albert Sabin was at this meeting, listening to Basil O'Connor warn against precisely what he had predicted—the channeling of all the National Foundation's money and goodwill toward the distribution of what might be only an interim product that would mislead people into thinking the war against polio was over. It must have been cold comfort indeed to hear his worst fears announced as real possibilities before he had completed work on the vaccine he and many others expected would provide a permanent solution to the polio threat. One week later, Sabin would begin his own trial of an attenuated live-virus polio vaccine on less than a dozen inmates in Chillicothe Federal Prison in Ohio. For years after, he would accuse Basil O'Connor of favoritism in promoting Salk's vaccine over his own, despite the fact that both were supported by National Foundation grants. For the time being, he and everybody else waited for the field-trial results.

II

With the start of the new year, the national foundation began to plan in earnest for the formal announcement of Thomas Francis' results—whatever they might be. The staff at the Vaccine Evaluation Center had been tabulating data from the field trial since the end of October, but Francis now did not expect to be able to begin analyzing it until the second week of March 1955, and he wanted as much time as possible to prepare his report. After so much work and such an elaborate effort to design a field trial that set new heights for epidemiological accuracy, he had no intention of doing a sloppy or incomplete analysis.

At the same time, if the report was favorable and the vaccine was licensed, it would be important for any vaccination program to take place before the end of June, when natural infection might interfere with the effect of the vaccine. The field trial had been delayed by concerns about safety. It would be a tragic irony if the licensing were delayed by demands of protocol. The second week in April was the latest possible date for Francis to make his report and still hope to vaccinate children that same spring.

Between them, these conflicting needs for time and haste made it impossible to follow the traditional approach for such an announcement: publication in a professional journal preceded by a summary "report" given at a major meeting of a prestigious professional society. The announcement of the results of what many called the Francis Field Trial would have to be a separate event, standing on its own without any support from established conferences or organizations.

302

Today, when most major hospitals have a pressroom and celebrity doctors appear on the evening news, it seems commonplace to plan a special conference to report the results of a nationwide medical experiment that had already received several years of intense media attention. As in so many other respects, however, the 1954 polio vaccine field trial was the example that set the precedent. Jonas Salk had combined existing theories and techniques to develop a new product that protected against paralytic poliomyelitis. Thomas Francis had combined basic principles of epidemiology with unparalleled public interest to develop a new standard for the size, speed, and rigor of field trials. Now the National Foundation was trying to combine scientific courtesy with the public's right to know the results of an experiment to which millions of people had contributed their time, their money, and their children. Although no one quite realized it yet, a new era of scientific publicity was about to begin.

In truth, it began some months before Francis' announcement, when Salk made an exception to his policy of not granting individual interviews and appeared on television in February as the featured guest on Edward R. Murrow's half-hour program *See It Now*. Murrow was an intense and elegant reporter with a reputation for high intellectual standards, and to appear with him on *See It Now* must have seemed very different to Salk from allowing a photo spread on his domestic life in *Look* magazine. In recent months, Murrow had interviewed poet Carl Sandburg and nuclear physicist J. Robert Oppenheimer. The week before his broadcast from Pittsburgh, he would interview Indian Prime Minister Jawaharlal Nehru. His wartime broadcasts from Europe and probing investigations of postwar America had given the stamp of journalistic integrity to radio and television news.

Murrow was also a man who knew about the ravages of polio. Ida Anderson, the beloved high-school teacher who had first recognized his powerful presence as a speaker, had been cruelly twisted by paralytic polio as a child. Chet Williams, the college friend who had helped Murrow find his first job in New York, mounted the stairs to their shared apartment with a limp that was a daily reminder of what even a mild case of the disease could do. When Fred Friendly, Murrow's producer at CBS, proposed an interview with Salk, Murrow quickly agreed.

Friendly had first gone to Basil O'Connor with the idea, and then he and Murrow had taken the night train out to Pittsburgh to win over the sometimes prickly scientist. Murrow was in awe of Salk's achievement, and Salk was impressed by Murrow's intelligence and stature. The man who had broadcast from the rooftops of London during the worst bombings of World War II wanted to come to Pittsburgh to interview Jonas Salk. For Salk it was a very flattering acknowledgment of the seriousness of the war on polio, and an irresistible opportunity to present his own views of how that war was progressing. When Tom Coleman, the University of Pittsburgh publicist who handled Salk's press relations, tried to stop the filming, he soon discovered, he said, that "Ed Murrow was the only person for whom Jonas had stars in his eyes."

On Tuesday night, February 22, *See It Now* gave the nation what Murrow called an interim report on the polio vaccine. It was, he assured his listeners, "a polio program without any appeal for funds." Salk, worried that Merthiolate problems would create misleadingly poor results in the field trial, was eager to use the chance to tell people how much the vaccine had been improved in the year since the field trial began. Describing the massive field trial of the previous spring as a "little spur," a "little offshoot," and a "little side test" within the larger progress of research, he pointed to his further studies that would combine with the field-trial results to "provide an indication of a trend." Personally, Salk confessed, the results of the field trial would be an anticlimax. The moment of triumph had come when he first realized that he could provoke immunity with a small quantity of killed polio virus. "What has been happening over the past two and a half years has been drudgery. It's just been hard work. But the exaltation was at that time." Whatever the results of the field trial, he insisted, the real year of victory would be the year when there was little or no paralytic polio.

For much of the rest of the program, Salk described the basic principles of virology upon which his vaccine was based, including an on-camera demonstration of how a monkey kidney is ground up in a Waring blender before being suspended in nutrients to provide the tissue culture on which the poliovirus would be grown. It was a gracious performance, modest and informative, praising the people who had channeled their fear of polio into productive contributions to the March of Dimes. Calling for further progress in preventive medicine, Salk insisted that this was not the "Salk" vaccine but the culmination of the work of many people. It was, however, the Salk program, and many viewers probably agreed with Murrow's vision of a successful field trial transforming Salk into "a minor god."

In the meantime, however, neither this prospective divinity nor anyone else outside Ann Arbor knew how well the vaccine had worked. Like the arrangements for the field trial a year before, the plans for the announcement of Francis' results were hedged with qualifications. The National Foundation planned to print ten thousand copies of the report, but they would not know what it said until the day of his announcement. Eli Lilly and Company had offered to produce a closed-circuit telecast shown in hotels and movie theaters in sixty-one cities on the night of the announcement, to an invited audience of fifty-four thousand doctors, in the hopes that the hour-long broadcast would be devoted to introducing the new product they all would be using, and buying, soon. Preparing their springtime flurry of informational pamphlets for parents, the National Foundation writers worked every possible variation into the reminder that the free vaccination program plans for the schoolchildren who had not received vaccine in the field trial would take place *if, and only if*, the vaccine was licensed.

Whatever the results, Francis' announcement would be a dramatic moment, the culmination of years of effort and millions of dollars invested in the polio wars. When the Wright brothers first flew at Kitty Hawk, they had been alone. When Alexander Graham Bell first spoke over the telephone, he had called his assistant from the next room. Louis Pasteur had conducted the first human trial of his rabies vaccine at an unplanned moment when a frantic father brought his dying son to Paris, but the test of the Salk polio vaccine had been far too public to expect any such privacy in announcing the results. If the vaccine had worked, the whole world was ready to join in the rejoicing. If it had failed to protect the children, it would be one of the most public and conspicuous failures on record. Not until the space launches of the next decade would so many people be assembled to witness the results of a scientific project whose outcome was still unknown.

The first question was where to hold the conference. Basil O'Connor joked that Thomas Francis could give his report in the men's room and the reporters would all turn out to cover the story, but he wanted the reality of the announcement to be as dignified as possible. Jonas Salk envisioned a meeting of the National Academy of Sciences in Washington, the august body established by Abraham Lincoln to advise the United States government on scientific matters. Salk was not a member of the National Academy, where election was an honor bestowed on distinguished researchers as a mark of the respect of their peers, but he hoped to become one, and he was ecstatic when it seemed for a time that Francis would give his report before that group. Thomas Francis, who *was* a member of the National Academy, proposed a private report to the National Foundation's Board of Trustees and the Vaccine Advisory Committee, with printed copies for general distribution, but that was dismissed as impossibly exclusive. The University of Pittsburgh was eager to host the meeting, but Francis balked at taking his Michigan work and presenting it at another university. Officials at the University of Michigan had no strong opinion about where the announcement should take place, as long as their school figured strongly. Groping to establish a shape for an event without precedent, all of the principals were uncertain of almost everything except that they each wanted to be in control.

On Monday, March 7, when the site of the announcement was still undecided, Thomas Francis joined Arthur Brandon and Lou Graff from the University News Service for a meeting with Harlan Hatcher, president of the University of Michigan. Hatcher had not been paying close attention to the Vaccine Evaluation Center, a quiet establishment that had the virtue of not requiring any funding or faculty hiring by the university, but he was now made aware that the announcement of the Francis field-trial report would be a major public event. The next day, Art Brandon called the Evaluation Center office on

Catherine Street to say that Hatcher wanted very much to have the announcement in Ann Arbor.

Pressing to meet the deadline for his report, Francis was eager to be rid of the endless negotiations over where that report was to be given. He had other work to do. The IBM punch cards holding all the field-trial data were only now ready. The University Tabulating Service would begin work on them on Thursday, March 10. If all went well, they could begin the statistical analysis by the last week of March. In the meantime, Francis had to decide how to organize the results, whatever they might be. Should he present the data by area, or by degree of injury? When reporting on the observed-control trial, should he combine the first and third grades, as the control group, or separate them as two different age groups, both used as controls? How should he describe the control of vaccinated versus unvaccinated second-graders? What should he make of the incomplete reports from Canada and Finland? Who should he hire to draw the charts and graphs?

Wherever the announcement took place, Francis insisted, it was to be a scientific session, not a press conference or public relations event. As the evaluation reached its final days, however, it became harder and harder to maintain the dignity and secrecy he had preserved for so long. Already people were saying that the conference was a promotional charade, claiming that the National Foundation would not stage such an event if the news were not good. On Friday, March 4, Francis had called New York to protest an unauthorized press release describing the Eli Lilly broadcast, which he felt made it seem that licensing was inevitable. Talking to Hart Van Riper, whose usually high level of diplomacy was no match for Francis' outrage, he demanded that the National Foundation stop treating the members of the Vaccine Evaluation Center "as flunkies." Taking notes on his conversation, Francis crossed out "asked" and recorded that he had "insisted" on being consulted before any further releases were issued. As a measure of his indifference to the publicists' work, Francis had never learned to spell either Lou Graff's or Dorothy Ducas' name. To him they would always be "Graf" and "Dukas," and the farther away they stayed, the more comfortable he felt.

On Monday, March 21, it was settled that the announcement

would be in Ann Arbor. The National Academy of Sciences had declined to host the meeting. Both Basil O'Connor and Hart Van Riper were eager to accommodate Thomas Francis and assumed, probably rightly, that he would be most comfortable giving his report on his home ground. The University News Service was contemplating the biggest Michigan story ever—a highly parochial perspective that made the National Foundation publicists cringe, but with which they would have to live. Discussing the plans with Hart Van Riper, Thomas Francis made a private note: "Tell Brandon and Graf: don't let anybody push you around—or take too much for granted."

As for the journalists who acted as the first source of information for the general public, there was no question that they would all be there, ready to give their readers, listeners, and viewers the earliest possible news. Fred Friendly had already started plans to have another *See It Now* program broadcast from Ann Arbor on the evening of the announcement—a pioneer venture into live broadcasting outside a television studio. He had cleared it with Salk and with Alan Gregg of the Rockefeller Foundation, who would be moderating the scientific meeting, and then with Thomas Francis and the University of Michigan. Years afterward, Friendly called the program "one of the greatest exclusives of all time," and speculated that the idea was so novel that no other program had thought to ask. NBC was planning its own television coverage, and foreign news services were already inquiring where and when the announcement would be held, so they could be sure their representatives were there.

Once the location was chosen, the next decision was the day. The University News Service wanted the announcement on a Tuesday, so they would have Monday to set up the rooms. Eli Lilly also preferred a Tuesday night, when they would be able to get clear lines for their closed-circuit broadcast. Edward R. Murrow also had to have the report on Tuesday, if it was to be the subject of his live broadcast of *See It Now*. Thomas Francis needed every second to finish his report. The date they settled on was Tuesday, April 12, the tenth anniversary of the death of Franklin Roosevelt. Basil O'Connor groaned, knowing that Republicans would claim that he had planned it that way, but there was nothing to be done. April 12 was also thirteen years to the day since Jonas Salk had first arrived in Ann Arbor, fresh from his medical internship and ready to begin his career in laboratory work, but nobody noticed.

Dorothy Ducas, director of public relations for the National Foundation, was just plain mad when she realized that Basil O'Connor had given the University of Michigan full control over news coverage of the announcement. It was wrong of him to do that, after all the work that she and her staff had put into telling the polio story. He always thought he knew better than anybody else, she fumed, but this time he had made a big mistake. Her staff deserved the privilege of writing the big story, the first information most reporters would have on the field-trial results. The people at Michigan didn't know anything about it. They hadn't worked for years, first making people aware of the need to do something about polio, and then assuring them that much was being done. They hadn't been in on the field trial. They didn't know about the parents and grandparents around the country, the aunts and uncles and brothers and sisters who had collected money for the March of Dimes and were waiting so eagerly to hear the results of the trial. Ducas had been covering polio since the first President's Birthday Ball, and now the story she had waited years to write was going to someone else.

The press release was important because it would be distributed shortly before Francis gave his report, making it the first news most reporters had of the field-trial results.

Lou Graff was a nice enough fellow, she supposed, but he was young and new to the business, just as green as grass. Three years ago, he had been an instructor in the philosophy department. What did he know about managing a huge event like this? What did he know about polio, for that matter? This wasn't a Michigan story. This was a story for the world.

Lou Graff knew that he was new to the business of public relations and new to science, too, but he was determined to write this story himself. The Vaccine Evaluation Center was at Michigan and Thomas Francis was at Michigan and no matter what anybody in New York might think, this was his story. He had worked hard all year to get Francis to trust him. He had stood as a buffer between Francis and the National Foundation, and had at least convinced the scientist that he had no intention of slipping a photographer into the tabulating room or scheduling a press conference behind his back. Graff had been a great help, in fact, when reporters came fishing for early information, and Francis could send him to make a statement about how there was not anything to say. Still, he had never been privy to a single secret of what was going on inside the Evaluation Center. He had been embarrassed by the few releases that had come out of New York, embarrassed to see that Francis gave the people there more information than he was getting. As a matter of pride and policy, he would handle the release from Ann Arbor without any help from the National Foundation.

Meanwhile, the news that everyone was gathering to hear had yet to be put into words. Thomas Francis wrote the final report himself, a single man putting pen to paper to make sense and substance of the frantic activity that had occupied so many people for so many months. Overworked, distracted by the elaborate negotiations over where and when to give his report, pulled at for months by competing groups that demanded his attention and claimed his allegiance, he was determined that his report should be a model of integrity, clarity, and thoroughness. The vaccine had worked well, and the glory, he knew, would go to Jonas Salk, but the responsibility for finishing the field trial by the same high standards it had begun belonged to him, Thomas Francis.

He had begun writing at the beginning of March, working on the background description of the field trial's organization and analytic methods while waiting for the numbers that would give him its results. On April 1, when the hubbub of the Evaluation Center became too distracting, he packed up his papers to work in his study at home. Even there the telephone rarely stopped ringing. Every time a reporter speculated in print or on the air about the results of the trial, another called Francis to ask for his comments. If the reporters had such unimpeachable sources, he answered, they should go back to them for statements. They would get none from him.

In the early hours of the morning on Friday, April 8, Francis finished the final draft of the summary report, *An Evaluation of the 1954 Poliomyelitis Vaccine Trials*. There would be fifty pages of text, and an even longer appendix of charts and tables. For over a year, he and his staff had fit together little pieces of information, a mass of details that added up to a broad declarative statement that the new vaccine had helped protect the nation's children against paralytic polio. In a scientific experiment marked by almost unmanageable quantities of paperwork, he had finished the literary monument to their work. No author was listed, but the title page indicated that it came from the Poliomyelitis Vaccine Evaluation Center of the University of Michigan, sponsored by the National Foundation for Infantile Paralysis. Immediately following came ten pages listing all the people who had been in charge of different aspects of the evaluation, and the organizations that had lent their staff and services. Some of the data was still incomplete, and there would have to be another, fuller report issued later, but Francis knew that this was the version that most of the world would see, and he wanted to be sure that everyone was properly thanked.

Over the weekend, Francis had the report retyped, changing many of the final figures and incorporating all the corrections he had inserted in the margins. On Monday, April 11, the day before the formal announcement of his results, he finally allowed Lou Graff to see the report. Graff had to come back three or four times before Francis approved his press release, and it was already evening by the time he went to the University Administration Building, where the assistant director of the News Service was waiting to help him type, stencil, and collate what would be for many people the first authoritative information about the real value of the Salk polio vaccine. While he was there, he called the National Foundation's press temporary headquarters on the Michigan campus and said they could send one person to check the release for accuracy.

Dorothy Ducas dispatched Dave Preston, her science editor, to see what Lou Graff had made of the most anticipated medical news in memory. Preston's elation at the confirmation that the vaccine worked was eclipsed by his disappointment at the way the story had been handled. "Well, they've written a release," he told her, "and I can't say it's wrong, but it isn't the way we would have written it." "Did you tell them that?" Ducas demanded. "Yes," Preston answered, "but they didn't pay much attention."

The press release, the backbone of many reporters' stories for the following day, was exactly three pages long, and began with the terse statement, "The vaccine works. It is safe, effective, and potent." Safe and effective were the words of the federal requirements for licensing. Potent was Graff's own addition, and he was proud of it. He had worked a long time on his lead and finally decided that simplicity would carry the greatest weight. In the following paragraphs, he introduced Dr. Thomas Francis, Jr., as the "University of Michigan Director of the Poliomyelitis Vaccine Evaluation Center," and summarized the statistical findings of the report. Terming the vaccine "incredibly safe," Graff ended where Ducas would have begun: "The field trials and the evaluation were made possible by grants totaling $7,500,000 in March of Dimes Funds from the National Foundation for Infantile Paralysis."

When Preston left, Graff burned the many drafts he had gone through during the day. As a final security measure, he locked up the stencils. Dr. Francis had approved his story, which was far more important than what the flaks from the National Foundation thought. It was three o'clock Tuesday morning. In six hours, the show would begin.

III

THE SITE FOR ANNOUNCING THE MOMENTOUS NEWS WAS neither the small, dilapidated Vaccine Evaluation Center nor Thomas Francis' School of Public Health, a spare and functional red brick box of a building. Five hundred distinguished guests had received engraved invitations "to hear a report of the evaluation of the efficacy of the poliomyelitis vaccine used in a field study sponsored by the National Foundation for Infantile Paralysis in the spring of 1954," and the place they assembled had to be of a grandeur commensurate with the occasion.

Rackham Hall, chosen for the announcement, was close to the center of the main campus of the University of Michigan. It had a large auditorium on the main floor and a smaller one upstairs that would be suitable for press conferences after the scientific meeting. It had elevators, a street-level parking entrance, and a large library on the third floor that was easily converted to a pressroom.

Perhaps even more important, Rackham Hall was elegant. Built in the early 1930s, its design spoke of a belief in progress, modernism, and the need for oversized settings for the pursuit of higher truths. Everything in Rackham, from the door handles to the light fixtures and on to the rooms themselves, was significantly larger than it needed to be. The hallways seemed like grand reception chambers, the bathrooms were marble palaces each large enough for a debutante tea dance, the ashtrays were tall ceramic urns that could conceal a small child in perfect comfort, and the windows could not possibly be opened except by giants.

The main auditorium, where Francis would give his report and other speakers, including Jonas Salk, would address the audience, combined classicism with futurism, terracotta columns and stenciled decorations of antique design with planets etched into the frosted glass of the light fixtures and star bursts on the doors. Painted in shades of salmon, gold, and midnight blue, it looked like a Minoan palace refurbished for Flash Gordon, making it well suited to the combination of ancient awe and technological triumph that marked most people's attitude toward the polio vaccine.

Chairs for the speakers had been set up on the curving apron of the stage, where a lectern with a large University of Michigan seal was banked with masses of ferns and chrysanthemums. Howard London, who produced many of the National Foundation's movies and radio programs, had set up a master control in the auditorium's projection booth so that two microphones on the stage provided all the sound for newsreel, radio, and television. The last two rows of seats had been covered by an eight-foot-wide platform built to serve as a stand for sixteen television and newsreel cameras. There would be no photographs during the reading of the scientific papers, but nothing could shield the assembled scientists from the shock of having to pass the buzz and whir of movie cameras as they came to their seats.

On the third floor of Rackham Hall, where the Gothic tradition of academic architecture reasserted itself in a profusion of stained-glass windows and carved-oak panels, the University News Service staff had been working overtime to stock what was known as the Assembly Hall with nine long tables, forty-one telephones, six Western Union teletype machines, fifteen typewriters, and a substantial supply of copy paper, carbon paper, and sharpened pencils. Here the fourth estate set up its camp for the day of the announcement, plunking typewriters on the tables, sending clouds of cigarette smoke up to the coffered ceilings, and drinking endless Dixie cups of coffee from the kitchen across the hall.

Many of the reporters had arrived the night before, grumbling about the secrecy and the lack of time they had to prepare their stories, and also about how much had been leaked already. John

Troan, from the *Pittsburgh Press*, got on the train in Pennsylvania and found Bill Laurence from *The New York Times* already aboard. "Hey, Bill," he asked. "You all set for the story?" "What story?" Laurence growled. "Jesus Christ, there ain't even any meat left on the bone." The *New York World-Telegram* had carried a front-page story two weeks before, claiming that the vaccine was 100 percent effective, which took some of the air out of the final announcement even though everybody with half a brain knew it couldn't possibly be true. A week before, though, William Workman had spent the day in Pittsburgh, closeted with Salk as they went over the final version of the specifications for manufacture—Jim Lewis, Troan's secret informant in Salk's lab, had been very excited when he called with that news. It still didn't mean the vaccine was a success, since they might have been playing the same game of "just in case" that everyone had been practicing since the field trial began, but it was certainly encouraging. Troan had taken a gamble and written that the vaccine would be licensed within ten days, and he was proud to see his story copyrighted and reprinted in papers around the country. Now he would find out if it were actually true.

When the train arrived in Ann Arbor, Troan saw Ed Stegen, the National Foundation's chief publicist for the field-trial story, and took him out drinking, in the vain hope that he would get a few details in advance. In fact, Stegan knew no more than anybody else. Troan still reasoned that they wouldn't have invited them all out to Ann Arbor to announce a failure, and he stayed up much of the night writing the bottom half of his articles—the background material that he already knew, that he would bolster with the facts and statistics when he got them the next morning. Then he went back to the room in the Michigan Union he was sharing with Albert Bloom, the medical writer for the *Pittsburgh Post-Gazette*. Bloom, an Orthodox Jew, had come to Ann Arbor with a suitcase full of kosher food with which to celebrate a solitary Passover, but without a place to stay, and Troan had taken him in.

A lot of people from Pittsburgh came to Ann Arbor. They had been convinced of the vaccine's merits from the earliest trials in 1952, and they had no expectations of a negative report.

All the top staff from the Virus Research Lab was there, their expenses paid by the National Foundation. Lucile Cochran and Jessie Wright were invited from the Watson Home, and the chancellor, the vice chancellor, and the dean of the Medical School from the University of Pittsburgh. Mr. and Mrs. Alan Scaife, whose foundation had so often helped finance Salk's laboratory expansion, were invited to see his anticipated triumph.

Salk's family was there as well, the people who had lived with him while he devoted so much of his time, hope, energy, and pride to the pursuit of this vaccine, and the people who had known best the keen hurt of his disappointments along the way. Donna had been surprised when her husband suggested it, and at first she was reluctant to travel to a professional meeting with three unpredictable young boys, but Jonas assured her it would be something special. Nothing would replace the years of absence and inattention, the relentless schedule of hours in the laboratory and at meetings, but at least the boys would be able to see how really important the work had been that had so often called their father away. Besides, it would be pleasant to revisit Ann Arbor after eight years and see old friends; so much time had passed since they had gone on picnics with Tommy and Dot Francis and their children, who must by now be almost grown. It would be a thrill for the boys to see their father on the stage, and even worth having to put up with scratchy pants, tight neckties, and all the other paraphernalia of respectability. Lee Salk, Jonas' younger brother, came to share the excitement of the day; their parents remained in New York, planning to watch the closed-circuit broadcast that night.

Ann Arbor was a very small city in 1955, and there were problems accommodating all these people. The one hotel was soon full. The Salk family was invited to stay at Inglis House, a private estate in residential Ann Arbor that the university owned and used to house official guests. Most of the visitors got rooms in the Michigan Union, on campus. Women were not allowed to stay there, however; Lorraine Friedman stayed at the Michigan League, the campus women's center, and so did Fred Friendly's assistant. Latecomers had to go as far as Ypsilanti, twenty miles away, to find a room.

At eight-thirty Tuesday morning, Lou Graff picked up three hundred copies of the press release he had prepared in the early hours of the morning, an equal number of copies of Thomas Francis' speech, and of a medical abstract prepared by Robert Korns. The National Foundation's press corps had spent time Monday assembling their own packet of the speeches Basil O'Connor, Alan Gregg, Hart Van Riper, Tom Rivers, and David Bodian would be giving, both at the morning meeting and during the closed-circuit broadcast at six that night. At the front of the package was a note reminding reporters that the contents of the Francis Report might force the speakers to abandon their prepared texts, though most of the speeches were general enough to suit almost any results. Tom Coleman had arrived from Pittsburgh with copies of the scientific paper Salk would read. Robert Voight, who had served as security director for the Evaluation Center as well as chief of statistical operations, joined Graff and the Ann Arbor policeman who had been hired to guard the precious texts. They loaded everything into a truck and drove across the campus to the back entrance of Rackham Hall, where they transferred the press packets onto a handcart and proceeded up the elevator to the third floor.

Well over a hundred reporters had converged on Ann Arbor from all over North America, and many of them were trying to meet deadlines for afternoon papers. Canadian television had sent a camera crew. Foreign reporters had come from as far away as France, Denmark, and Israel. They had been told they would receive the report at nine-ten in the morning, Eastern Time, with a release time of ten-twenty. This was precious little time to get out a story they had been waiting weeks, months, and, in some cases, years to write.

The plan had been to avoid crowding by dividing the press releases into five piles, one for each of the five long tables set up at the far end of the pressrooms. What nobody at the University News Service had considered was how they were to cross from the elevator to the tables with their stacks of documents. Downstairs at the freight entrance, it took Graff and Voight longer than they had expected to load the reports onto the cart.

When nobody appeared by nine-fifteen, the reporters began to watch the elevator. When the doors opened a minute later, an astonished Graff was overwhelmed by a shoving mob of reporters grabbing papers off his cart. Suddenly, people were leaping and climbing over each other to get a copy. Blocked by the crowd, Graff climbed on a table to distribute press packets from the hall. A reporter called, "Hey, Lou, throw me a copy," and the photographers snapped a besieged young publicist tossing out copies of the report to the rabid newshounds gathered about him.

"It works! It works!" reporters were shouting to each other. The writers from Pittsburgh, who had been covering Salk's work from the beginning, had been sure of that. What they wanted to know was how well it worked. Albert Bloom had no urgent deadline, since the *Post-Gazette* was a morning paper, but he held a telephone line open while John Troan dived in with the others and got them two copies of the report. Scanning the text, Troan dictated his story back to Pittsburgh, for yet another front-page feature on Dr. Salk. Art Snider of the *Chicago Daily News* pulled his telephone through the window and out onto the comparative quiet of the roof. "VICTORY OVER POLIO! POLIO VACCINE WORKS!" would be the two-inch headline run over the front-page masthead of that afternoon's paper, alongside a life-size photograph of a bottle of vaccine. Throughout the room, other reporters were filing their own stories. Later, many of them would criticize the chaotic scene in Rackham Hall, but for the moment they were intent on getting the details out. For one day, at least, hydrogen bomb tests and Supreme Court hearings on school desegregation were not the top of the news.

Looking back, Lou Graff admitted that the people handling the program at Ann Arbor were unprepared for the drive of the reporters—unprepared for their very professionalism in scrambling to get their story. Even in retrospect, though, he found it hard to see how they could have avoided the last-minute crush, given the restrictions imposed by Thomas Francis and the timetable in which they had to work. If he had it to do over again, Graff decided, he would not have given out the reports to the pressroom first, because few newspeople actually attended the conference. Perhaps it was just as well. Downstairs, all was solemn and scientific, while pandemonium reigned in the press-room above.

Wire-service copies of the report's opening page had been sent to leading radio and television stations, with strict notice that the news was not to be released before 10:20 A.M., when Thomas Francis was to begin reading his report. Many people watched the announcement on television. KTTV Los Angeles had arranged to broadcast the entire proceedings, which they fed to four other California stations. NBC television had a mobile camera unit parked outside Rackham Hall, doing live pickups from the steps and lobby of the building. Dave Garroway, the host of NBC's *Today* show, was unwilling to wait, and so the flash report that the field trial had been a success first reached the public on an early-morning program that was more entertainment than news, from a man who had J. Fred Muggs, a chimpanzee dressed up as a child, as his regular studio companion.

All over the country, people turned to their radios at ten o'clock to hear the full details. In Europe they tuned to the *Voice of America* broadcast. Judges suspended trials so that everyone in the courtroom could hear; department stores set up radio loudspeakers so shoppers could follow the news. Flushed by the first report that the vaccine worked, exuberant citizens rushed to ring church bells and fire sirens, shouted, clapped, sang, and made every kind of joyous noise they could. City councils and state legislatures postponed their regular business to draft resolutions congratulating Dr. Salk for his wonderful achievement.

The celebrities who had worked for the March of Dimes waited for the news from Ann Arbor as eagerly as the rest of the world. Eddie Cantor, who had invented the "March of Dimes" slogan for the National Foundation in 1938, proudly watched the announcement on television from his home in Los Angeles. Helen Hayes, whose daughter had died of polio, took the morning off from the rehearsals for her new play so she could hear the announcement. No sooner had Francis started to speak than her telephone rang; Marlene Dietrich, whose daughter had survived the disease, had woken early to hear the news and called Hayes immediately from Los Angeles to share it. Dietrich, the international film star famous for the roles in which she drove men mad with desire, had written Salk in Pittsburgh begging for vaccine for her grandchildren. Now she need no longer worry that the next generation might suffer the same terror she had felt.

The uproar in the pressroom at Rackham Hall had started forty minutes before the scientific meeting downstairs, but most of the guests had already arrived, and few were aware of the global storm of attention that was gathering around them. Like Lindbergh flying over the English Channel, so near his destination but for a few last moments still swaddled in the noise of his engines and the isolation of the clouds, Jonas Salk sat on the stage with little idea of the life-changing celebrity waiting for him. He had come to Rackham with Thomas Francis and Basil O'Connor, arriving just as Lou Graff was driving up with his press releases. They had breakfasted together at Inglis House, along with Tom Rivers, Hart Van Riper, and Alan Gregg, and Francis had finally told them all that his report would be favorable. It had been a wonderful moment—joy and relief and the pure pleasure of work well done—and the grueling schedule of the rest of the day now held no terrors. Grinning broadly, they had gone to the auditorium to pose for photographers before the meeting, with no inkling of the chaos upstairs. It was all too artificial to seem real. Salk had ended the photo session on an amiable note by going down into the audience to greet his family. Then he had gone back up to his own seat on the stage, ready to hear the other speeches and to give his own.

Inside the oval sweep of Rackham Auditorium, it was a far more dignified morning than many scientists later recalled, their memories full of the crush of photographers in the hallways and the foul scent of publicity that they said later had pervaded the entire day. John Enders, who often avoided meetings, had declined to come, but almost all the other virologists supported by the National Foundation were there, including Albert Sabin. So was William Workman, who had sent telegrams to fifteen polio experts inviting them to meet with him after the announcement to advise the government on licensing the vaccine.

Members of the Executive Board of the American Medical Association were there, and representatives from most of the nation's leading medical schools and schools of public health. The presidents of the six companies that had been producing polio vaccine in anticipation of this moment had come, bringing along their heads of production and testing, and the National Foundation staff was there in force. They had worked longer than anybody to make this day happen, and none of them wanted to miss it. Harry Weaver had come, too, to see the finale of the program he had hoped to lead.

The list went on. Everybody from Thomas Francis' laboratory at the School of Public Health trooped in to hear the announcement. For the University of Michigan graduate assistants who had spent so much time processing blood samples and stool specimens over the past nine months, April 12 was a glamorous reward for all their work. Hanging up their laboratory coats, they served as ushers and had an exhilarating taste of what bigtime science would be like in the future. Robert Voight was ready to explain statistics at a press conference scheduled immediately after the papers in the smaller auditorium upstairs. Robert Korns, Francis' deputy director, had no official part in the proceedings. There had been a plan for him to appear on the *Today* show, but Francis had vetoed the idea. Korns did not own a television and had never heard of Dave Garroway, so he was just as happy to remain inside and watch.

At ten o'clock, the meeting started. Hart Van Riper welcomed the guests on behalf of the National Foundation, reminding them that the epoch-making event they were witnessing had really taken place in laboratories across the nation, in the halls of government in Washington, in health departments across the land, in the classrooms of a thousand schools, and in millions of American homes. Then Thomas Francis presented his findings. He spoke for one hour and thirty-eight minutes, using an overhead projector to display the charts and graphs that made up the bulk of his report. His voice was quiet, his tone unemotional, but his message was clear. Beyond any possibility of doubt, the Salk vaccine had protected the children who had taken it. The effect varied between different manufacturers' production lots and between the three different strains of the virus, but in all cases the protection had been real and substantial. In placebo-control areas, where the vaccinated and unvaccinated populations had been identical, the vaccine had been 60 to 70 percent effective against Type I paralysis, and over 90 percent effective against Type II and Type III. Against bulbar polio, the relatively rare but dreaded paralysis that affected breathing, the vaccine had been 94 percent effective. In all cases, it had proved remarkably safe.

There was restrained applause when Francis finished, and a louder reception for the next speaker, Jonas Salk. Later many of his fellow scientists would insist that anyone could have made the killed-virus vaccine, but on April 12, at least, they acknowledged that it was Salk who had in fact done it, and done it faster than anybody else had thought possible. One could never do more than estimate the number of people saved from crippling or death by the early introduction of a polio vaccine, but no one who had lived through the epidemics of the last ten years could doubt that it was a glorious day when the world heard the first scientifically verified proof that hope and protection were at hand.

In preparing his paper, Salk had not known what Francis' results would be. He was fairly certain the vaccine was effective enough to be licensed, but beyond that, he had been braced for far worse showings than the ones that he had just heard. Throughout the field trial, he had devoted his energy to improving and defending the vaccine he had developed. The problems with Merthiolate and the advantages of his new method of growing virus convinced him that the field trial was only part of the refining process by which he and his associates would come up with a vastly improved product in the near future. His latest studies also showed it would be better to delay the third vaccination until seven months after the first two, instead of the four-week interval that had been used in the field trial. These were the subjects on which he was prepared to speak.

In the "Introductory Remarks" with which he prefaced his paper, Salk thanked everybody on earth—except the people from the Virus Research Lab. He thanked the staff at the Watson Home and the patients there. He thanked Basil O'Connor, Harry Weaver, Tom Rivers, Hart Van Riper, Foard McGinnes,

Henry Kumm, Dr. Boyd, and the members of the Vaccine Advisory Committee. He thanked the administrators and trustees of the University of Pittsburgh. He thanked the press for its restraint and for the accuracy with which reporters had informed the public about difficult technical developments.

Toward the end, Salk bowed to his associates in Pittsburgh. "This opportunity would have no meaning," he said, "if it were not for the devotion with which each of the many of the group that comprises our laboratory contributed and shared in that which needed to be done. I can speak of what they have done and repeat that they, as I have said of Mr. O'Connor, can enjoy 'the reward of a thing well done,' not only having done it but, I hope, their reward will come, too, from being able to do more."

Lorraine Friedman, the administrative force behind the smooth operation of the Virus Research Lab, never wavered in her devotion to her boss, but many of the others were disappointed and disillusioned by the vague and fleeting credit Salk had given to their work. They had been expecting at least a crumb of personal recognition to come their way. Salk was the man who had run the lab, made the big decisions, rallied the troops behind the right flags, and inspired the public confidence without which there could have been no field trials and no triumph. But what about all the people who had put in their hours in the cold room and the warm room and at the laboratory bench? What about people like Julie Youngner, who had first interested Salk in John Enders' tissue-culture work and who had spent so many hours peering at microscopic slides that he had had his eyeglass prescription changed twice in the course of the work, and then heard not a word of thanks or credit? What about Byron Bennett, the self-educated chief technician who lacked a graduate degree and depended on Salk's good comments for his professional future? How exquisitely subtle to distribute a paper "From the Virus Research Laboratory, School of Medicine, University of Pittsburgh." How elevating to say their satisfaction would come from further work. How humiliating to come all this way and not have your name mentioned even once.

If the people from Pittsburgh were bitter about Salk's scanty acknowledgment of their dedicated work, Thomas Francis and

Tom Rivers were both furious about the scientific paper that followed. In his anxiety that the report might make his vaccine seem worse than it was, Salk had forgotten the professional courtesy and scientific caution on which his reputation depended. By explaining at such length how the new vaccine was different from the one Francis evaluated and how the shots should be given at longer intervals, Salk seemed to be dismissing the importance of all that Francis had done. When he went on to claim that his new improved formula might reach 100 percent effectiveness, Francis' personal outrage turned to professional fury. "What the hell did you have to say that for?" he demanded after the formal announcement was over. "You're in no position to claim one hundred percent effectiveness. What's the matter with you?"

The rest of the speeches were short and fulsome. Alan Gregg, vice president of the Rockefeller Foundation, described the report they had just heard as the harvest of the seeds of hope sown the previous spring. Where Francis had been sober and statistical, Gregg was lyric. He invoked the "exquisite fitness" of hearing the Francis report on the anniversary of Roosevelt's death, the "selfless rejoicing" of those who had already been paralyzed by polio, the relief of parents and grandparents spared the anguish and fear of polio epidemics, the future generations in whose safety "dwells the delight of preventive medicine," the thousands of school and health professionals and National Foundation workers who had contributed to the field trial or cared for the prior victims of epidemics, the "myriads of faithful crusaders" who had raised money for the March of Dimes, and most of all, the loyalty, courage, steadfastness, and intelligence of the parents and children who had volunteered as Polio Pioneers. Ending with a flourish of oratory, he concluded, "It is as though music that began in the minor key, befitting bewildered suffering and dogged patience, now strikes the major chords of relief and exultation, modest but not doubtful, cautious but justifiably eager."

When Basil O'Connor rose to speak, he turned the focus back to where Hart Van Riper had put it in his welcoming remarks—on that huge, various, imaginary being whose actions had such real effects, the public. Speaking of the hurry and frustration of modern life, O'Connor described the crusade against polio as an expression of man's innate need to be part of a community and to engage in meaningful action. Public participation was the transcendence of the individual, O'Connor announced, the essence of democracy, and the force that makes possible great events like the triumph over poliomyelitis.

At two o'clock, the scientific meeting was over, and the five speakers adjourned to the press conference scheduled upstairs. Elaine Whitelaw had gone straight to a telephone to relay the details of the Francis report to Virginia Blood in New York; they were determined that the newsletter they sent to volunteer leaders would go out immediately, so the people who had worked so hard to get the vaccine tested would have their own personal record of the results. Meanwhile, most of the guests were enjoying a late, convivial lunch in a private dining room at the Michigan Union. Alex Langmuir, who had come to Ann Arbor from the Communicable Disease Center in Atlanta, saw that some of the most notable virologists had disappeared from the gathering—David Bodian, Karl Habel, William Hammon, Albert Sabin, Joseph Smadel, Thomas Turner. Where were they? he wondered. They had left to advise the government on what to do with the new vaccine that had just been so thoroughly and so successfully tested.

Leonard Scheele, the surgeon general of the United States, had dispatched William Workman to Ann Arbor to smooth the way for immediate licensing of the vaccine, along with Victor Haas, director of the National Institute of Microbiology, and David Price, the assistant surgeon general who had been on several of the National Foundation's advisory committees. Oveta Culp Hobby, the secretary of Health, Education and Welfare, was holding a telephone line open to Ann Arbor for the experts to call in their approval. The vaccine had been subjected to the most rigorous evaluation of any pharmaceutical product known. Its manufacture had already been tested and revised and tested again, not only by the individual companies but by the Laboratory of Biologics Control. There was no reason to delay.

The assembled scientists were given copies of Francis' report and of the six manufacturers' production reports on forty lots of vaccine, and were asked for an immediate recommendation on whether or not the product should be licensed. Expecting an instant decision, Hobby had scheduled a 4 P.M. press conference in Washington so all the media could witness her signing the historic documents. To Workman's dismay and Hobby's chagrin, the scientists insisted on reading the papers put before them. By the time they gave their approval, the Washington press had left, and Hobby was furious that she had to sign the momentous licenses for manufacture without the all-important recording witnesses of the news. She still issued the statement she had prepared: "It's a great day. It's a wonderful day for the whole world. It's a history-making day." That evening the crates marked "Polio Vaccine: RUSH" began to leave the warehouses for airports and shipping depots around the country.

By the time Hobby signed the licensing papers, many of the reporters covering the story in Ann Arbor had also decamped. Some had been on the telephone for five hours, first filing their leads on the details of the Francis report, then their second stories on intervals of vaccination and prospects for 1955 vaccine supplies, then the human-interest story about Dr. Francis or Dr. Salk or whomever they had chosen to make humanely interesting, and then the follow-up story on trial results in their local area, and finally the statistical breakdown for the inner pages. Other reporters, back in their respective offices around the country, had written about local supplies and described how various state medical societies planned to handle the first clinics. Photographers had gone out to the local airports to catch the first shipments of vaccine as they arrived. Stringers went to get a statement from Eleanor Roosevelt, laying a wreath of lilies on her husband's grave in Hyde Park, and from the little girl who was this year's poster child for the March of Dimes. Feature writers had prepared their stories on all the famous athletes, actors, and politicians who had overcome polio, and the cartoonists had drawn their graphic responses.

In the course of the day, camera crews in Ann Arbor had shot thirty-three reels of movie film, reporters had filed almost fifty thousand words with Western Union, and everyone had used every available telephone nonstop since nine-twenty in the morning. Wayne De Neff, science writer for the *Ann Arbor News*, had had the luxury of walking back to the quiet of his own office after getting his copy of the Francis Report and listening to the early part of the speeches. Covering the Salk vaccine evaluation announcement, he wrote, was like covering a major war campaign. Many of the scientists who left for the railroad station or the airport were surprised by the number of reporters that had been on hand. As public adulation of Salk grew over the next several weeks, their dismay would grow more intense as well.

No special celebration had been arranged for the people from Pittsburgh, and they, too, began to scatter soon after the announcement. Lorraine Friedman left for a long-delayed vacation, visiting friends in Illinois. Julie Youngner took a plane to California, and got good and drunk on the way. Byron Bennett rode the train back to Pittsburgh with Jim Lewis, who had so excitedly called John Troan to leak the latest developments in the lab. Bennett, an emotional man, was still hurt by Salk's failure to acknowledge his work more openly, and he cried during most of the trip.

At six o'clock that night, there was the special closed-circuit telecast produced by Eli Lilly for the benefit of physicians: a digest of the Francis Report so they would be ready immediately to answer their patients' questions and to start using the new vaccine. Speaking from a studio in Ann Arbor, Thomas Francis explained the tests and the structure of the field trial. Jonas Salk gave information on clinical applications. Tom Rivers assured the listening doctors that the vaccine had no harmful side effects. David Bodian discussed the nature and pathology of poliovirus. Hart Van Riper, the foundation's chief spokesman to the medical profession for several years, declared that the studies would continue, because this was only the beginning of the end of polio. Then the doctors saw films of the manufacturing process and of Jonas Salk demonstrating how to inoculate children with his vaccine. Daniel and Dora Salk, proud but not a bit surprised by their son's triumph or his fame, sat in the ballroom of the Waldorf-Astoria with a group of two thousand New York doctors who had assembled to watch the broadcast.

Lilly's broadcast, as much as Hobby's licensing, signaled the switch from scientific investigation to commercial production of vaccine. Until five-thirty that afternoon, the vaccine had been an experimental product, the subject of debate among research scientists and epidemiologists. After five-thirty it was a pharmaceutical product that individual physicians would buy and give to their patients, who would pay for the privilege. When the first rumors of Salk's vaccine began to appear in 1953, Parke, Davis had rushed into print to remind the world that they had worked with him for years, and they had scrambled to be the first company to deliver trial vaccine to the National Foundation headquarters. Now Eli Lilly was using the still novel medium of television to show that it, too, was in the vanguard of polio vaccine production. In 1953, Lilly products had accounted for almost 13 percent of the U.S. pharmaceutical market while Parke, Davis had held less than 8 percent, and Mr. Lilly was very interested in seeing that his company retained its market lead.

The Lilly program ended at seven o'clock, after which there was a dinner for the more distinguished guests who had gathered in Ann Arbor. At ten-thirty that night, there was to be the live broadcast of *See It Now*, shot in the large conference room on the first floor of the Vaccine Evaluation Center. Then, thirteen hours after it had started, the long day of good news would be over.

The Evaluation Center was filled with cameramen for the late-evening show, some from CBS and some from the University Broadcasting Network, as well as a still photographer from *Life* magazine. There were producers and directors, coffee fetchers and light-bulb changers all on hand. What the viewers saw, however, was a large, Spartan room full of unmatched file cabinets and stacks of papers. In the center was a battered conference table, around which were seated Edward R. Murrow, Jonas Salk, Thomas Francis, and Alan Gregg.

That morning, John Troan had slipped into the press section of the auditorium to hear the end of the speeches. He sat next to Ed Murrow, who smoked incessantly, and Troan was fascinated to see this man, so polished and calm on camera, looking very nervous as he faced the prospect of a live interview with a group of undramatic people discussing a subject that was very far from anything he understood. By the time of the broadcast, Murrow had settled on the tone of respect and celebration with which he would present the news.

"The sun was warm," Murrow said in his opening, "the earth coming alive; there was hope and promise in the air. The occasion called for banners in the breeze and trumpets in the distance." The reality of Rackham Hall, he continued, had been hot and still, the atmosphere somewhere between a clinic and a church, but perhaps that had been better for the true import of the day. "At a time when the media of modern communications are overly inclined to persuade, astonish, frighten, or amuse, and are tempted to exaggeration and prematurity in each of these gainful activities, there can be a lasting advantage in sobriety of statement."

After praising the unseen, unknown masses of private people, adults and children, who had contributed to the triumphs of the day, Murrow then turned to the three men seated beside him to discuss what the field-trial success meant. Recalling the frustrations of the past months, Thomas Francis first explained that the greatest difficulty of the field trial had been simply amassing the information he needed. Once gathered, the data had shown clearly that the vaccine was both effective and safe; not a single negative reaction had been traced to its use. Alan Gregg spoke of two new areas of work he hoped people would now be inspired to explore: the end of the common cold and the improvement of medical education. He warned, too, of the dangers of bootlegging, cheating, quarreling, and hoarding of vaccine supplies. Then Murrow turned to Jonas Salk.

Disputing Francis, Salk still thought the vaccine might be made 100 percent effective, and took the opportunity to say so. As for the current vaccine, he hoped that everyone would be able to benefit from its protection as soon as possible. Tests for prior immunity would not be really useful, he said; the best hope for control of epidemics was widespread vaccination. Using the kitchen metaphors he often favored, he talked about wider intervals between vaccinations as "the possibility of giving everyone some hamburger, instead of sirloin steak to a few."

Of the people around the table, Salk was by far the most

relaxed. He spoke eagerly, smiling, the only man whose face was not surrounded by swirling clouds of cigarette smoke. Alan Gregg looked down at his notes and Thomas Francis searched the ceiling for the words he wanted, but Salk looked at Murrow and out at the audience and seemed to be enjoying the contact. After years of effort and months of anxiety, his work—and his principles—had been vindicated. He did not boast or crow, but, perhaps for the first night in a long time, he did not fret, either. At the end of the half-hour, Murrow thanked his guests and, as he always did, wished them and his viewers "Good night and good luck."

PART FIVE

POLITICAL SCIENCE

Because I have this dream and, on occasion, surrender to its appalling precision of detail—I can, in my *beta* mind literally *hear* the crinkle of the envelope as I open the telegram from Stockholm, I can *smell* the leather and velvet scent of the blue box in which the Nobel medal lies—because I am no more than I am and less than I hope to be, I think hard, long of those who are the real thing, whose names will last in the household glory of the mind. I read about them, avidly. I imagine myself in their skin of glory—because that is what it is, a skin inside which their lives have changed and become luminous.

—F.R.S.

Stockholm, 1954

December 10 is not the day most foreigners choose to visit Sweden. Twilight comes early in the afternoon, darkness lasts until the middle of the morning, and the varied celebrations of Christmas have not yet begun to pierce the winter gloom. For John Enders, Thomas Weller, and Frederick Robbins, however, their journey there in 1954 was bright enough without the lure of summer sun. They were coming to Stockholm to receive the Nobel Prize in medicine, awarded for their 1949 discovery of how to culture poliovirus in nonnervous tissue. Linus Pauling, another grantee of the National Foundation, was there to receive the Nobel Prize in chemistry. Max Theiler had received the prize in 1951 for his development of the vaccine against yellow fever. What could be more natural than for the developer of the first successful polio vaccine to be the next to join this cavalcade of laboratory heros?

Honor and fame among research scientists is accorded on aesthetic grounds more often than most people outside the field would think. It is the elegance of method and the novelty of means, not the utility of results, that wins the laurel wreath— which is to say, for scientists, the grant, the prize, the endowed chair, the coveted membership in the exclusive professional society.

The biggest prize of all is the Nobel Prize, awarded annually in physics, chemistry, and physiology or medicine, as well as literature, world peace, and, since 1969, economics. Unlike

335

many other professional awards which garner little attention outside their immediate field, the Nobel Prize carries healthy amounts of both fame and fortune. Even more significant, however, is its effect on the standing of one's work. For scientists, to win the Nobel Prize is to receive the ultimate confirmation of your laboratory results.

Chronic yearning for the Nobel Prize, an ailment that afflicts many scientists, can have strange side effects. At the California Institute of Technology, where there are several Nobel laureates on the faculty and many more who aspire to that rank, pranksters have been known to telephone these hopefuls in the middle of the night and say they are calling from Stockholm with wonderful news. Groggy, stripped of their defenses by the lateness of the hour and by the very strength of their desire, the victims provide great comedy as their sleep-drugged minds deal first with the dazzling realization that this call is not a dream, and then with the growing, bitter awareness that it is not for real, either.

It is a cruel joke, but that is not unusual; cruelty is the foundation of more humor than many of us would like to admit. What shocks us here is both the lowness of the comedy—great minds stooping to childish tricks—and the even more disturbing exposure of ambition so naked, so simple, and so well known that it can be mocked with a phony Swedish accent that wouldn't pass muster at any hour if it were not the echo of so many months and years of hopeful calling into the void.

Jonas Salk wanted to be awarded the Nobel Prize, and a number of people thought he ought to have it. Unfortunately for his hopes, few of those people were the ones who mattered in the choice. Philip Hench, who won the Nobel Prize in 1950 for his work on the use of cortisone and ACTH for treating rheumatic disease, sought Salk out on a visit to Pittsburgh and declared his intention to nominate him for the Nobel Prize, but the call from Stockholm never came. Nor did Salk receive the lesser honors that would mark his stature among his peers and colleagues. He was never elected to the National Academy of Sciences, although Thomas Francis had felt so certain he would be that for several years he lobbied for other candidates on the assumption that Salk's nomination would need no support. Joseph Smadel was elected to the National Academy in 1957, David Bodian in 1958. Albert Sabin had been a member since 1951. Salk was not elected to the American Philosophical Society, either, whose ranks have included the nation's leading medical investigators since its founding by the great experimenter Benjamin Franklin. It made him angry and also a bit sad to feel the scorn of his fellow scientists. It was the result of jealousy and competition, he said, the dark spots of human nature, and what he suffered was the inevitable isolation of the pioneer. Those who did not like him said Salk was never honored because he was aggressive and ungenerous, because he was not a creative genius but merely a good manager, and because he had demeaned himself by seeking after fame.

According to at least some of Salk's fellow scientists, the blot on his professional reputation was not the unseemly cloud of celebrity that had engulfed him on April 12, 1955, never to disperse, or even the dangerous flaws in commercial testing that would for a time cast a shadow on his vaccine's safety. The problem, they insisted, was a lack of originality. "A lot of people wonder why Salk has not got the Nobel Prize," Tom Rivers once told an interviewer. "Well, it's just because the Nobel Prize is supposed to be given for original work. . . . Many a man is a great man, but that does not mean he gets the Nobel Prize. I think that Salk did a damn big job, but we have to realize that it is not original work."

Others echoed this view, often in almost exactly the same words. According to Albert Sabin, the excitement after the Francis announcement amounted to a terrible distortion of the facts. Years later, he could still barely contain his dismay at the popular reception of the news. " 'Polio is conquered!' " he repeated. "Everywhere, Ed Murrow, 'Polio has been conquered!' It was not conquered. And there was no evidence to say it was conquered, and it was no breakthrough, because what it took to make this vaccine was to grow the virus—that was the breakthrough—in large quantities. But its inactivation was as old as the hills. There was no new science in that vaccine. There had to be a hell of a lot of new science in the oral vaccine. There was no new science in the killed vaccine. No new science. No breakthrough." Alexander Langmuir said the same thing in *slightly gentler terms. "Why did Jonas never get the Nobel Prize?" he asked, and quickly answered his own question: "His contribution was largely developmental. The basic break-through was made by John Enders and his colleagues."*

"He was just a technician," others would say dismissively, with the strong implication that technical skill is incompatible with the kind of creative genius that leads to major break-throughs—to the discovery of an elusive structure, to the cre-ation of a new paradigm, to something NEW. They said it belligerently and tolerantly, in tones ranging from satisfaction to pity, but they always said the same thing. Salk's work on the killed-virus polio vaccine wasn't worth a prize because it wasn't new.

Looked at another way, this was the same reason it couldn't be patented. On the night after the announcement that the vac-cine was safe, effective, and potent, Edward R. Murrow asked on national television who owned the patent. Salk smiled be-nignly and answered, "Well, the people, I would say. There is no patent. Could you patent the sun?"

It was a noble and generous answer, reflecting the National Foundation's stated position that a vaccine developed with money from public donations should not be privately held, but it omitted the fact that the National Foundation's lawyers had studied the question before concluding that this particular star was already well charted and therefore in the public domain. Formaldehyde inactivation was a well-known process. The use of adjuvants to boost vaccine potency was a well-known pro-cess. The growth of virus on tissue culture was a well-known process. The creative combination of these well-known pro-cesses to make the first safe and effective means of protecting against paralytic poliomyelitis was irrelevant. In other words, what had he done that was new?

Should one then assume that the Nobel Prize committees are in fact a distinguished sort of patent court, awarding their hon-ors on terms of novelty alone, with no regard for useful or possible application? Since Alfred Nobel established the awards that bear his name for contributions to "the good of humanity," and stipulated that there be a separate Nobel Prize for the year's best efforts at the hackneyed and utilitarian goal of peace, this seems to be a misstatement of the idea. Nonetheless, it expresses very well the stance that many of his colleagues took toward Salk's vaccine.

On December 10, 1962, James Watson was in Stockholm, with Francis Crick and Maurice Wilkins, to receive the Nobel Prize in medicine. Watson had been in Cambridge on a postgraduate fellowship from the National Foundation when they had established the structure of DNA in 1953. How could Salk not have imagined this for himself?

I

ON APRIL 12, 1955, SOME SIX MONTHS AFTER HIS FORTIETH
birthday, Jonas Edward Salk stopped being a promising young
scientist and took the first steps toward becoming an international hero and a suspect creature in the ranks of his profession.
It was not by any means a conscious decision or a welcome
change, and it didn't happen overnight, but a radical transformation in the identity of Dr. Salk was, it seemed, a necessary
by-product of the launching of the polio vaccine he had developed. It was many years before Salk recognized that fact. He
would never accept it.

It began with the first flash of television news and gathered
force as the afternoon papers hit the street on April 12. "Salk's
Vaccine Does the Job Against Polio," announced the *Chicago
Daily News*. "Polio Threat Conquered By Salk Vaccine," read
that afternoon's *Arkansas Democrat*. "Salk Polio Vaccine
Proves Success; Millions Will Be Immunized Soon" reported
The New York Times the next morning, devoting half the front
page and all of three inside pages to the news. The *Boston Globe*
reported on April 14 that one doctor had already received 850
calls from parents who wanted their children vaccinated. The
Cincinnati Post photographed a grinning five-year-old perched
on the crates of vaccine that had already arrived at the Greater
Cincinnati Airport, and announced that ninety-four "shooting
centers" were being readied around the city. Everywhere there
were photographs of a smiling Dr. Salk. People were swept up
in a mood of national and then global celebration. It was only
human for them to ignore the qualifications: the vaccine varied

in effectiveness; against the dreaded Type I virus, it was only 70 percent effective; it did not prevent infection, only paralysis. What mattered was the simple conclusion: it works!

The Salks had planned to stay an extra night in Ann Arbor, since Jonas would be making his broadcast with Ed Murrow too late to return to Pittsburgh. They were looking forward to relaxing and visiting with old friends, but they had only packed clothes for two days, and they had things to do at home. Tom Coleman, the University of Pittsburgh publicist who had accompanied Salk to Ann Arbor, tried to warn them that relaxation was not necessarily on the bill, but he was dismissed with blithe assurances that he shouldn't worry, they could take care of themselves, and he should get on back to Pittsburgh.

Coleman wasn't the only one who recognized that sudden fame was about to descend on Jonas Salk. At breakfast that morning, Alan Gregg had warned Salk he would now have to decide between the celebrity lecture circuit and the laboratory, but Salk didn't quite grasp what he was saying. Edward R. Murrow took him aside and told him that a great tragedy had just befallen him: he had lost his anonymity. By then the telephones were ringing and the telegrams arriving, but still Salk didn't understand. A tidal wave of attention was breaking over his head, but he thought that he would somehow stand tall and simply let the waters pass.

Elva Minuse, a laboratory technician who had taught Salk when he was a medical student first working in Thomas Francis' lab in New York, had come out to Ann Arbor with Francis. By the next morning, the first sack of mail for the new hero had arrived at the University of Michigan, and Minuse offered to bring it up to Inglis House when she went to visit her old friends. She and Donna and Jonas opened it together, and discovered that many of the envelopes contained checks and money, most of it simply addressed to Dr. Salk. "Oh, my God," cried Donna. "How are we going to pay the taxes!"

That was just the beginning. For the rest of the week, the phone kept ringing, the telegrams kept arriving, the mail poured in, the unsolicited donations piled up, and the Salks stayed in Ann Arbor, hoping to exhaust the publicity before they returned home. From five in the morning to ten at night, the telephone never stopped ringing. People were calling from Europe and South America, from Australia and even from behind the Iron Curtain, where parts of the announcement had been broadcast on Voice of America. Every time Donna and Jonas looked up, it seemed, another car was arriving with another sack of mail.

For five long days they stayed in Ann Arbor. The phone rang, the boys whined about going home, Donna kept on wearing her good suit with the peplum jacket, and Jonas gave out increasingly harassed statements on how he really didn't know yet what he would do with the money but it would not be used for personal gain but for the benefit of mankind and maybe he would look at cancer or mental illness but it was hard to tell right now because he couldn't even seem to get out of the University of Michigan guesthouse, much less back to his lab.

It was a very nice house, however, and that may have helped in the adjustment to his strange new role in life. In fairy tales, when the goose girl or the miller's son is suddenly transported to the castle and placed upon a throne, the lucky recipient of fortune's favor adapts immediately to the placid business of living happily ever after. The details of transition are left unrecorded, perhaps because the mere proximity of courtyards and turrets is considered enough to effect the magic transformation from commoner to royalty. If so, Inglis House must have been a very good place to start getting used to fame.

It was not on the campus at all. To get there, you had to drive through residential Ann Arbor, navigate several winding roads, go up a long driveway, and pass behind a tall stone wall. The house itself, built in 1928, was designed with a small number of bedrooms and great quantities of stone walls, slate roofs, cast-iron vines on which real wisteria had been trained to grow, and French doors that led, variously, to the arboretum, the terrace, and the formal garden where four bronze turtles held aloft the shallow basin of a fountain.

Pictures taken there on April 12 were intended to show the happy family relaxing together, enjoying the serenity that follows work well done. In one photograph, they sit together on a sofa, eleven-year-old Peter Salk as intent on the magazine his father is reading as is five-year-old Jonathan. In another the three boys, all in suits, huddle around their father, also dressed for business, as he crouches on the patio assembling an Atomic Rocket kite. As the men of the family prepare to blast off to the new age of nuclear power, Mother keeps both feet firmly planted in domesticity, with only her head and shoulders leaning out through the French doors from the dining room. That is enough, however, to show the beaming smile with which she encourages the project.

The photographs were public relations fantasies, stagey poses that had no relation to the frantic celebrity that was already beginning to change their lives. If the photographer was seeking an image of Dr. Salk the family man, it would have been far more accurate to show a rowdy lunch at the kitchen table, though even that would have been a rarity for a father who had been working fifteen-hour days for the last two years. The boys were uncomfortable wearing those fancy clothes. They wanted to play baseball with their friends at home. The kite was a farce, never flown, never assembled past the point shown in the photo. There were some better toys inside, including a memorable rig with marbles sliding down ramps that kept them busy for hours, but the whole trip was hardly worth the trouble. The announcement had been long and confusing, sitting for hours in the hot auditorium, though it had been interesting to watch their father pose for all those pictures. Their mother said she was planning to change her name to Smith if that would get the phone to stop ringing, but that was one of those strange jokes that adults were always making. The children had their jokes, too, like trying to imitate Mr. Coleman's funny new voice.

Tom Coleman's voice was funny because he had lost it after hours of talking on the phone. No sooner had he stepped off the plane from Michigan than he heard himself being paged: "Mr. Thomas Coleman. Mr. Thomas Coleman. Please call Dr. Jonas Salk right away." It's hell here, Salk told him. Get back as fast as you can. By that time, the good news about the vaccine was all over Pittsburgh, and the people at United Airlines were so impressed that Jonas Salk had called that they bumped an elderly lady from her seat and put Coleman on the next flight back to the Willow Run Airport at Ypsilanti.

That same day Coleman was back at Inglis House, answering the telephone; by the second day he had lost his voice and had to send to Pittsburgh for an assistant to come out and relieve him. She would talk to people and pass their questions to Coleman, and he would whisper the answer for her to relay back. For a week, he operated like that, a voiceless publicist sitting on the hottest property in the world.

Apart from Coleman and his assistant, Salk was almost alone in facing the deluge. Thomas Francis had left Ann Arbor for Boston, where he was scheduled to make a speech, and he stayed an extra day to visit his daughter at Wellesley and spend some time with John Enders. Nobody from the National Foundation had remained in Ann Arbor. Basil O'Connor had left for New York the night of April 12. The foundation staff that had come out for the announcement had also returned, disappointed by what they saw as a lack of planning in Michigan and particularly by the undignified scramble for the press reports. It wasn't that they meant to abandon Salk. Even the most foresightful of people cannot anticipate everything. After years of feeding the public's fear of polio, none of them had realized quite how passionately that public would react when given a hero with whom to identify their relief. In his televised address on April 12, Tom Rivers had said, "The development of a vaccine awaited the brilliance and perseverance of a Salk, and America came up with a Salk." Now America was demanding a piece of its creation.

Thomas Francis did share some of the glory. A radio officer from the Holland-America Line cabled his blessings to Dr. Francis, and his thanks for "the opportunity [God] gave me to put my hard earned money [in] the glass jar for the March of Dimes." Harry Weaver, who was well aware of the scale of Francis' task in bringing both structure and scientific legitimacy to the field trial, wrote a graceful letter of appreciation. So did dozens of old friends and professional comrades. Albert Sabin had made a gracious statement of admiring praise for Francis' achievement. The lecture bureau that represented Countess Alexandra Tolstoy and Alistair Cooke hoped Dr. Francis would consider the pleasant and profitable role of a public speaker. Blanche Knopf called on April 15 to say that she and her husband Alfred would like to talk about publishing a book. But, as Francis had predicted, it was Salk who was the hero of the day, the year, and the rest of the century. Statisticians and epidemiologists spoke in reverent tones about the elegant precision of the Francis field trial, but few could hear them while the world was shouting about the miracle that Dr. Salk had wrought.

When the Salks came home from Ann Arbor, they found a welcoming throng at the airport and a police guard at the front door of their home. They had to arrange for an answering service to intercept the telephone calls and get a new, unlisted number for personal use. They also had to make some fast decisions about the awards and money that were still arriving with every mail. When Lorraine Friedman came back to work that Monday, she found her tiny office filled with mail. "There were just thousands and thousands of letters," she said. "All of it had to be sorted and responded to, except a few, which I thought Dr. Salk might want to respond to personally. But that was wholly unexpected, the extent of the public outpouring of feeling. All kinds of money, and offers, and what have you. We had boxes and boxes of April 12 material."

For Tom Coleman, the siege of Ann Arbor was only a training exercise for what was to follow. Coleman had four assistants who helped him cover the medical centers of the University of Pittsburgh, but even with extra staff borrowed from the main university public relations office he was still averaging eighteen hours a day, seven days a week for several months, just struggling to keep up with the letters, telegrams, and telephone calls that came for Jonas Salk.

Apart from all the requests for stories, interviews, medical advice and information, there was another very large category of mail, which got filed under fan letters. At their teachers' well-intentioned bidding, elementary-school classes around the country sharpened their pencils and mailed off their "thank you" letters. Most of them were copied from the blackboard, but many were distinguished by crayon drawings, prayer cards, or individual messages from children who signed themselves "Your obedient guinea pig" and hoped that now they would get the "real stuff" instead of the sugar water they had received as Polio

Pioneers. The children of Altoona, Pennsylvania, sent a hand-made scroll with all their signatures. A class in Argentina sent a leather album of letters. On April 23, Paul Winchell, the popular ventriloquist who had overcome polio as a child, urged the little viewers of his Saturday morning television show to send money to Doctor Salk in Pittsburgh, and many did.

There were fan letters from adults, too—tearful, thankful, grateful, or deranged, typed on company letterhead or scratched on lined foolscap. The people of Saskatoon, Saskatchewan, sent a telegram of thanks, signed with each resident's name, that was 108 feet 10 inches long and arrived rolled in a cardboard tube. The people of Amarillo, Texas, sent a car, which was sold so the proceeds could go back to Texas to buy vaccine. Another community sent a silver plow. Paintings arrived, and medallions, and keys to various cities. Most of all, there was money, contributions to a fund nobody had the time to set up. Seventeen years before, people had sent dimes to the White House to conquer polio; now they sent dollars to Pittsburgh, for Dr. Salk to use as he thought best. A trust fund for his sons? A magic new machine that would help him conquer cancer? A well-earned vacation? The donors didn't really care. Most just wanted to express their gratitude. Contributions came from Havana and Tokyo, and from thirty-three of the forty-eight states.

Not all the letters were pure congratulations. People wrote to advise Salk on matters technical and mystical, from how to use linear programming to plan vaccine distribution to how to predict polio epidemics from sightings of flying saucers. Hospitals and schools offered to name a wing after the doctor if he would help in their fund-raising. Grossinger's Hotel, a popular resort in New York's Catskill Mountains, offered a free vacation if the Salk family would be good enough to favor them with a visit. A law firm in New York wrote on behalf of a client who wanted to market children's clothes and novelties marked "Thank you, Dr. Salk," with a share of the profits to go to the National Foundation. Public relations agencies offered to handle his endorsement contracts and provided lists of clients already willing to sign with Salk. Charities and civic groups felt sure that Dr. Salk would be honored to become the leader of their latest fund drive. An invitation to be a guest of the Liberian embassy in Washington raised fears of international repercussions if Salk failed to accept, until Coleman discovered that the sponsors were really a local school that had rented the embassy for the evening, and so could be safely refused. Dozens of colleges and universities wanted to give Dr. Salk an honorary degree at commencement that spring, and many hoped he would also make a speech.

Hollywood called, often. Warner Brothers and Columbia Pictures were both interested in doing a movie. So was Twentieth Century Fox, whose public relations director, Frank McCarthy, hoped "to build a film around Dr. Salk, a really impressive humanitarian film of Dr. Salk as the central character . . . [a film that would] increase understanding of the medical profession and the problems of medical research." Fox had already produced *The Story of Pasteur*, starring Paul Muni, and the analogy was almost irresistible. Marlon Brando was said to be interested in playing Jonas Salk.

Warner Brothers called Thomas Francis, too, and he thought a film might be a good thing if done properly, but Salk demurred. First he tried to stand on his professional dignity, issuing the terse statement: "I am a scientist, and much remains to be done in scientific research. I do not feel that such a picture would add anything to the understanding of the fight against polio." Then he turned to humor: "I believe that such pictures are most appropriately made after the scientist is dead. I am willing to await my chances of such attention at that time." If that didn't work, the university PR people had prepared an additional statement, to be used if needed: "I do not intend to have the story of my life or the story of the development of the polio vaccine portrayed by motion pictures. If such is done, it will be without my knowledge or participation, and surely without authorization from me."

Undaunted, people came from Hollywood to try direct persuasion, and when Salk would not talk to them they turned to Coleman, asking him to use his influence over the reluctant doctor. "Only to let us do a script, to let us talk with him, let us do a script to bring back for his approval," the agents would say, and they also offered commissions, sometimes as high as five thousand dollars, if Coleman could get Salk to agree to sign with them. One producer followed Coleman to the American Medical Association convention in Atlantic City in June and shoved his way into his cab to try to buy the movie rights to Salk's life.

Sometimes Coleman would suggest there was no harm in a good script, tastefully done, but Salk, with strong agreement from his wife, continued to dismiss the idea. He could imagine the kind of movie Hollywood would make. There would be a fiery young doctor walking along an impossibly clean Manhattan esplanade overlooking the East River, gazing across the water and vowing to conquer polio, then turning to embrace the clear-eyed, dedicated social worker who would join him in his crusade when she became his wife. If they can come up with a legitimate story, he said, the total profits of which will go to research, then I will consider it. On those terms, the film never materialized, and a relieved Jonas Salk was left with only the actual drama of his life, not the Hollywood version.

To preserve sanity and dignity, he consulted with Tom Coleman and established some ground rules: he would only give papers before two or three major medical groups, and only make public appearances at places like the state legislature or his own medical school. For the other worthy organizations that asked him to appear, Coleman set up a program called Salk Soldiers, and enlisted some of the children from the Watson Home to make public appearances and receive awards on Salk's behalf. The children were ready to make little speeches of acceptance, and Tom Coleman took the responsibility for occasions requiring more extensive remarks. In the year after the vaccine was licensed, he made something like eighty speeches.

In Pittsburgh there were many reactions to Salk's new fame. Those who had taken part in the early vaccine trials were overjoyed at the national confirmation of the success of their efforts. People in other branches of research were sometimes jealous and felt that their specialties were being neglected in the continued excitement over the conquest of a comparatively minor ailment. A few people on his own lab team resented the treatment they had been given in Ann Arbor, and decided that Jonas wanted all the glory for himself. And everywhere, across the country, doctors and researchers looked at Jonas Salk, barely forty and already the sage and savior of humankind, and wondered what he had done that they couldn't—or hadn't—matched.

When his first efforts to get the vaccine called simply *the* polio vaccine had failed, Salk had tried to refer to it as the Pitt vaccine, and had persuaded John Troan to adopt that usage for the *Pittsburgh Press*. It never caught on, though, and around the world it was the Salk vaccine that people were talking about. The more publicity Salk received, the more his fellow scientists grew skeptical of his achievements, and in the spring of 1955 Jonas Salk received a great deal of publicity.

II

When Oveta Culp Hobby licensed the Salk vaccine on April 12, the director of the Laboratory of Biologics Control made his own statement to the press. "I consider it an honor and a privilege," William Workman said in Ann Arbor, "to help commemorate the progress which has been reported today in the conquest of poliomyelitis." "Honor," "privilege," "commemorate"—this is the language you use to dedicate a war memorial, not to mark your active participation in a continuing battle. Although a few small tasks remained to be completed, among them actually getting the vaccine to 150 million people in forty-eight states stretching from sea to shining sea, it seemed the war on polio was as good as over.

In fact, the federal battles had just begun. Despite polio's perennial association with Franklin Roosevelt and federal health-care programs with the Democratic Party, it was not until Dwight Eisenhower brought in the first Republican administration in twenty years that polio became a government issue, forcing the administration into the very sort of "liberal" policies concerning social welfare that conservatives saw as Eisenhower's betrayal of his party.

Until April 12, 1955, the question or whether or not the vaccine worked overshadowed all others. Thomas Francis' insistence on total secrecy made it easy to postpone planning for a future whose shape was not yet known. After April 12, however, the practical applications of the Francis Report sprang into new prominence. The most basic and immediate questions were how much the vaccine should cost, who should pay for it, and

350

who should have first priority for the limited supply. Although the National Foundation had already bought up most of the available vaccine (the $9 million guaranteed purchase Basil O'Connor had used to persuade the manufacturers to continue production during the field-trial evaluation), the six manufacturers felt production was going so well that they would soon have vaccine ready for the general market.

In late March, the New York State Commissioner of Health said Salk polio vaccine would cost $4.20 for each of the three shots needed for immunity. The day after the Ann Arbor announcement, newspapers were quoting a price of $3.50 a shot. Parke, Davis and Company set a price of $6.00 for the three-shot series, to be sold to doctors through druggists. None of these figures included the fee for the doctor who would administer the shots. The question quickly arose as to what the states or the federal government would do for those people who could not afford to immunize their children. Was this to be the vaccine of the rich? Would states with healthy budgets be the only ones to protect all their citizens? Were companies to allocate their shipments on the basis of need, or by the ability of their customers to pay? Should doctors support vaccination clinics managed by the local health departments, or should they protest this infringement on their own market?

To most of the leaders in Washington, Democratic as well as Republican, the question of government support for vaccination was to be decided on purely political grounds. Republicans feared that federal programs to pay for vaccine would outrage their conservative supporters, but also worried that inaction would allow the Democrats to claim the glory of the new vaccine for themselves by sponsoring popular legislation for mass distribution. Senators and representatives from both parties introduced bills to guarantee various levels of federal financing for vaccination. Hobby was dubious about the capacity of the Public Health Service to supervise a nationwide distribution program and felt that the individual states would demand control.

During his campaign for president, Eisenhower had opposed socialized medicine, but now he told the press that no child would be deprived of vaccine because of inability to pay. Protecting children was the most important thing, he insisted—a

characteristically simple approach that may have meant he was
not aware of the complexities of the situation but may also have
shown the grasp of fundamental priorities that marks a leader.
Privately, he said at one of his regular Legislative Leadership
Meetings that he would be willing to use his disaster-relief fund
to buy vaccine to prevent black marketing of scarce supplies.

"We could afford to put forty or fifty million into this and
distribute [vaccine] to states as long as they agree to our priorities," Eisenhower said. Vaccination clinics were not exactly
disaster relief, but "after this job," the president joked, "jail has
no terrors for me." Surgeon General Leonard Scheele agreed
that this would undercut the black market, and Eisenhower,
warming to the plan, said that it might violate his philosophy,
but he considered this a real emergency. Hobby begged for a
bit more patience and assured Eisenhower the question was very
complicated. Before rushing out and spending $50 million, she
said, he should at least wait and see what the states set up, then
fill in the gaps.

The ambivalence in Washington found its public expression
in the kind of contradictory statements for which governments
have long been famous. "Eisenhower Orders Voluntary Allocation System," a headline blared on April 15, with no suggestion as to how such a logical impossibility was to be achieved.
No one would be denied the vaccine because of financial need,
later reports continued, yet no one would be embarrassed by
having to submit to a means test; somehow health administrators would simply know who could and could not pay. The call
for a distribution program foundered on questions of jurisdiction: vaccine production and sale, as interstate commerce, were
subject to federal regulation, but vaccine distribution was a local
question and any federal inquiry would violate the intimate
privacy of the doctor-patient relationship. Herblock, the editorial cartoonist of the *Washington Post*, seized upon the con-
tradictions in the federal position of supporting a system of
allocation but making no provision to enforce one; on May 13,
at the high point of federal uncertainty about how to manage
vaccine distribution, *Post* readers opened their papers to see a
bewildered father and his children being told by a bloated figure
labeled "Administration," "Rest assured that if we catch one
polio germ crossing a state line . . ."

In the confusion of the weeks following the April 12 announcement, many people would remark on the contrast between Secretary Hobby's eagerness to license the new polio vaccine and her failure to prepare in any way for the urgent questions of inspection and distribution that would follow. Two years after taking office, she seemed to be oblivious to the problems that would arise from her lack of action. Her much quoted, much derided testimony of May 19, 1955—"No one could have foreseen the public demand for the Salk vaccine"—made her seem like a birdbrain in a tailored suit. The first woman in a Republican cabinet, given responsibility for the age-old female concerns of health, hearth, and the education of little children, appeared to have gotten flustered.

No one who had any personal acquaintance with Secretary Hobby believed this for a minute. Arriving in Washington from her home state of Texas, she had quickly established her reputation as one of the toughest administrators in Eisenhower's Cabinet, famed for her ability to get her way both with Congress and with private groups like the American Medical Association. Although she made no pretense to having medical or scientific training, the limitations of her background were more than balanced by her administrative experience as head of the Women's Army Corp and publisher of the *Houston Post*, where her husband, a former governor of Texas, was editor. An internal White House analysis of May 1953, noted that "at Cabinet meetings there was a tendency to suggest that Mrs. Hobby be called in whenever a matter arose which might incur rough going on Capitol Hill."

Even if Hobby had been an inexperienced incompetent, which she was not, that would not have been sufficient explanation for the failure of HEW to prepare for the problems of production supervision, allocation, and distribution that followed immediately after the licensing of the vaccine. Hobby's special consultant for medical affairs, the man she listened to far more carefully than she did to the surgeon general of the United States, was Dr. Chester Keefer, a well-known and well-respected professor at the Boston University School of Medicine. Keefer had been in charge of the national allocation of penicillin when it was first placed in commercial production in the United States in 1941—at a time when quantities were scarce, military and civilian demand was high, and people everywhere were under-standably hysterical in their desire for a substance that was often their only chance of survival against a variety of deadly infec-tions. He had then gone on to do similar work with allocations of streptomycin, cortisone, and gamma globulin, and while the experience may have turned him against the idea of government-controlled allocation, it cannot have failed to alert him to the fact that some federal policy on distribution might well be needed if another medical miracle were suddenly to appear. If anybody could be expected to know the clamor that would follow the announcement of a vaccine against polio, it was Keefer, and part of his job was to share that knowledge with Hobby.

Nonetheless, nothing was done. The failure of the Department of Health, Education and Welfare to make any plans for allo-cating the limited supplies of polio vaccine or to discuss any measures for paying for the vaccination of those unable to afford them, seems to have been not an oversight but an ideological decision. The only argument for government control of drug allocations that Hobby accepted was the need to avoid a threat to national defense, which did not seem at all relevant to polio. Far more comfortable seeking appropriations for civil-defense training in the schools and medical training in the case of nuclear attack, she apparently saw the polio vaccine program as a rou-tine matter of manufacture and commerce, best handled by the private sector. She also felt that the Public Health Service, which inspected drugs and guarded against epidemics, had no place in the delivery of medical care.

During the months when he was waiting for Thomas Francis to make his report, Basil O'Connor had tried personally to persuade Hobby to plan some sort of federal policy on vaccine allocation. O'Connor was accustomed to easy access to the power centers of Washington, and used to putting his message plainly once he arrived. His visit to Hobby was no exception. He told her that it was his personal judgment that the vaccine was going to work, and that if it worked the question of dis-tributing a limited supply of vaccine to a clamoring world would be a major public health problem. Furthermore, he continued firmly, it was a problem the National Foundation couldn't and shouldn't handle, because public health was her responsibility, not theirs. Hobby's reply, in essence, was that the marketplace would control supply and demand, and that her responsibilities ended with licensing. As O'Connor was wont to say, he had gotten exactly nowhere.

The questions of domestic allocation were complicated by the fact that polio was an international concern. Development and testing of the Salk vaccine had been almost entirely an American project, paid for with contributions from the people of the United States, and there was a certain assumption on the part of those people that American children would have top priority for vaccinations. But while both Jonas Salk and the National Foundation had already shared the information needed for foreign governments to make their own vaccine, few other nations had laboratories ready to do so, and many officials in the United States feared the foreign-policy repercussions of any claims of American hoarding.

On April 13, the day after licensing, Secretary of State John Foster Dulles, Eisenhower's powerful White House assistant Sherman Adams, and Special Assistant Nelson Rockefeller were all conferring on statements to prepare about sharing what they called "seed vaccine" with "friendly" nations. On April 21, the acting secretary of commerce wrote a memo to the president explaining why he felt it was important to establish at least token exports of Salk vaccine to foreign nations. Noting that rhesus monkeys were essential to both the production of the vaccine and the safety tests that followed, the secretary continued, "The case for export is based on humanitarian considerations, the monkey supply problem and the psychological and propaganda advantages that might accrue to the U.S. from a 'sharing' of the supply."

By May 6, Secretary of State Dulles was writing directly to Hobby urging export of the vaccine. "The whole effect of our declared intention of sharing this development with the rest of the world will be lost," Dulles claimed, "if we proceed on the assumption that children of other countries must wait until ours are fully taken care of. A greater amount of good will toward the United States will result from some small shipments now when it is a sacrifice to send them rather than later when supplies will also be available from other exporting countries as well as the United States."

The monkeys needed to make the vaccine on a commercial scale constituted a foreign-policy issue in themselves. The numbers were truly vast: while large university medical schools might need 500 monkeys a year, the laboratories making polio vaccine had asked for over 200,000, with orders ranging from 5,200 monkeys for Cutter Laboratories in Berkeley to a high of 69,800 from Eli Lilly in Indianapolis. Shipment of monkeys from India was a recurrent topic of diplomatic wrangling during the Eisenhower administration, as Indian Prime Minister Nehru made them one of the levers he used to pry additional aid and support from the United States. In March 1955, just when many people were looking forward to the public licensing and full production of the Salk vaccine, the Indian government had declared an embargo on monkey exports.

Two days after the announcement in Ann Arbor, Sherman Adams had received a confidential memo that anticipated most of these concerns and offered at least one easy solution:

> In view of the International and National publicity given to Dr. Salk and his wonderful polio vaccine, wouldn't it be excellent public relations for the President to receive him and make an appropriate award to him? This would show the citizens of the United States and the world
> 1.) that the President is interested in encouraging scientific efforts
> 2.) that he is just as interested as Franklin D. Roosevelt in Polio, and take away the perennial F.D.R. thunder over polio
> The presentation of the award could possibly be coordinated with either the inoculation of some children or delivery of some vaccine to a foreign country representative, such as India. This would tend to take the world's attention of [sic] the atomic and hydrogen bombs sabre rattling and show Nehru and his followers our real intentions.

In the margin Adams scribbled, "this is already being set up."

The special citation from President Eisenhower, presented at the White House on April 22, just ten days after the licensing of his vaccine, was one of the few awards that Jonas Salk accepted in person. Oveta Culp Hobby had called him in Pittsburgh to make it clear that this was a command performance. Once again, he had been asked to bring his wife and children, and once again Donna and the boys put on the suits they had worn in Ann Arbor. Tom Coleman came too, staying in a room registered in Salk's name, to protect the family from kidnappers, autograph seekers, and relentless telephone calls, and he was furious the next morning when Basil O'Connor removed him from the line of people taking limousines to the White House. "Coleman," he said, "you can get a cab." Coleman did just that, and reached the White House in time to see the president give the Salk boys commemorative pocketknives and listen patiently to eight-year-old Darrell Salk's comparison of his school art project and Eisenhower's paintings.

The reporters and photographers had turned out in massive numbers to record the historic details of Mrs. Salk's lilac suit and the president's tearful gratitude. What they did not record was the jockeying at the White House to make sure the publicity value of the moment went to Dwight Eisenhower and not to Jonas Salk. On the plane down to Washington, Salk had written a statement he wanted to make after Eisenhower presented his citation. Before going out on the terrace where all the reporters and photographers were waiting, White House press secretary James Hagerty announced that Mrs. Hobby would introduce the president, who would make a speech and give Salk his citation, after which Salk was to say "Thank you, Mr. President," and then bow out.

Hagerty had no intention of letting Eisenhower be upstaged by the man who was, at the moment, the most famous person in the world, but Salk was upset at not being able to make his little speech. He conferred with Basil O'Connor, who suggested going along with what the president wanted. Tom Coleman, still smarting from O'Connor's rudeness, urged Salk to forgo the ceremony and return to his hotel, if the White House was so worried about what he might say in public. Salk played along, threatening to leave if he wasn't allowed to make his statement, until Hagerty reluctantly let him get the last word of thanks for the occasion.

Salk's speech was hardly a bombshell. Saying once again, as

he had to Ed Murrow, that his own reward had come on that long-ago day when he first realized he could create immunity to paralytic polio, Salk concluded, "If I were to say that I'm honored on this occasion, I would not be telling the whole truth. I say, rather, that on behalf of all the people, in laboratories, in the field and those behind the lines, I gladly accept this recognition of what each of us has contributed, and I hope that we may have the opportunity to see, again in our lifetime, the beginning of the end of other fears that plague mankind."

Two days later, when a few of the children who were supposed to be protected from this terrible scourge began to be paralyzed from their polio vaccinations, the people in Washington realized that the battle had just shifted to another front, and they were in the trenches.

III

On April 26, four days after Jonas Salk and his family had stood in the Rose Garden of the White House watching the president of the United States express the gratitude of parents and grandparents everywhere who would now be spared the agonizing fears of polio, Dr. Mahlon Bierly was conducting antibody tests on Salk polio vaccine made by his employer, Wyeth Laboratories. He had traveled from the company headquarters in suburban Philadelphia to the manufacturing plant in Marietta, Pennsylvania, seventy miles west, something he did often, bringing blood samples for them to test there. At around four-thirty in the afternoon, he stopped in to say good-bye to the plant director.

As he entered the office, Dr. Fritz was just putting down the telephone receiver, and Bierly was afraid his colleague was having a heart attack right there at his desk. Fritz was pale, he was shaking, he could barely speak beyond a stammer. "What the hell is the matter?" Bierly demanded. "I just finished talking to Dr. Workman," Fritz answered. "Cutter vaccine is causing cases of polio in Idaho."

In the weeks just before the 1954 field trial, when Walter Winchell had raised fears about the safety of the Salk vaccine, most virologists conceded that some live virus might remain in some batches of vaccine, but not enough to be dangerous. In the formal response to Winchell's accusations issued by the University of Pittsburgh the following morning, Jonas Salk stated, "Massive safety tests in three separate laboratories guarantee that any live virus will be discovered and the whole batch destroyed. *That is the purpose of the tests.*"

In all the arguments about arranging those safety tests, however, no one had addressed the looming problem of quality control after the field trial. If the vaccine proved half as good as everyone hoped it would be, there would be an immediate demand for commercial mass production—and there was no practical way that these kinds of laborious tests could be continued on a commercial scale. In 1955 William Workman had arranged to release production lots of vaccine on the basis of review of manufacturers' protocols, with no outside laboratory testing. The demand for eleven consecutive batches of good vaccine had also been dropped.

There had been changes in production techniques as well as in safety procedures. As Salk had hoped and Workman had feared, the vaccine that went into mass distribution on April 13 was not the same vaccine tested the previous spring. In some ways it was better—potency had been improved with the elimination of Merthiolate. In some ways, however, it was a more problematic product. New methods of virus production and inactivation had been introduced that had not been tested outside Salk's lab—where the batches were small and rarely left to stand for any length of time—and they were being used by companies that had not taken part in the rigorous safety procedures of the field trial.

On April 25, health authorities in Chicago reported that a child had been paralyzed after receiving vaccine. It was an inconclusive incident, but it was soon followed by five more reports the next day, all in different parts of California. In each case the child had been vaccinated less than eleven days before, and in each case paralysis had begun in the arm or leg where the vaccine was injected. Next came reports of paralysis in Idaho, and the death from polio of a man there whose children had recently received their shots. All the children had received vaccine manufactured by Cutter Laboratories, located in Berkeley, California.

The responses to the Cutter incident, as it came to be called, were predictable and unedifying. Without exception, everybody blamed somebody else. Basil O'Connor pointed out that there had been no problems during the field trial, when the National Foundation was managing the vaccine program, and blamed the federal government for not telling the public the facts as they emerged. Thomas Francis said that he had been in charge of evaluation, not later production. The Public Health Service denied that its responsibility went beyond the act of licensing; the American Medical Association claimed that it was so far from being responsible that its advice had not even been sought; the manufacturers insisted that they had followed the protocols approved by the Laboratory of Biologics Control and already tested in the largest field trial ever staged for an experimental medication. Jonas Salk insisted that the manufacturers could not have been following his procedures properly.

For Salk, the Cutter incident was a tragedy of many parts. Faulty vaccine had caused needless injury and death. Fear and confusion were keeping many children from receiving the protection of good vaccine, leaving them vulnerable to the dangers of yet another polio season. Caught in a crossfire of questions and accusations about the vaccine he had fought so hard to introduce, Salk also faced the possibility that another casualty of the crisis would be the special trust the public had given him, personally. For the past five years, his days had been divided between the technical and experimental labors of developing the killed-virus polio vaccine, and the strategic effort of promoting his findings and defending his principles to his colleagues, his financial supporters, and the world at large. The laboratory work had been grindingly difficult and the infighting had often been corrosively bitter, but in the darkest moments of anger or frustration, he could always have found comfort in the knowledge that parents and children trusted and revered him, and that those who would benefit most from his vaccine were very, very grateful.

Time after time, Salk had put himself and his work directly before the public, going himself to the Watson Home to give vaccinations, making radio broadcasts like "The Scientist Speaks for Himself," using the mass intimacy of television to give people a glimpse of his laboratory and a chance to see and hear the man responsible for the vaccine they hoped would bring them the protection they craved. However the scientists and the bureaucrats might try to twist his motives or mangle his procedures, the real people would recognize what he was trying to do.

Was that trust to be lost? Until now, no one had ever been hurt by either Salk's work or his words. Not all the vaccines his laboratory made had been effective, but none had ever caused anybody any physical harm. The most hostile of his letters, the most frantic of his speeches denouncing this or that opponent, never wounded more than egos or destroyed more than professional schemes, and even in that disembodied world of paper battles he had been far less damaging than he had sometimes hoped. Salk's ambition had always been tempered with altruism, his precision softened with the kind of gentleness that led him to cut his son's hair in the family kitchen because the boy was afraid of barbers. Now, for the first time, innocent people were being seriously hurt by a vaccine that the world insisted should bear his name.

Salk had not been the first person called as the Cutter crisis was emerging, but he was one of the first that others turned to when the news hit. Tom Coleman, still scarcely able to talk after his laryngitis in Ann Arbor, was on the telephone for twenty-four hours straight, handling the frightened calls that came in to the University of Pittsburgh. Most of them, he noticed, were from physicians. "They were scared to death," he said, "because they had unfortunately given this vaccine to Aunt Nellie or Sister Jane or Cousin Joe. The vaccine was supposed to be limited to children ages five to eight and pregnant women, but they had given it to their family and friends, and all of a sudden the vaccine was bad." On April 12, Cutter had announced a special program in which it would provide polio vaccine to all of its workers and stockholders; those who had taken advantage of the offer were terrified, too. The only answer Coleman had for them at that time was to get a shot of gamma globulin, because that had a chance of tempering the effect if they had indeed been exposed to live poliovirus. Walter Winchell seized the opportunity to threaten an "exposé" of the contributions that had been coming in to Pittsburgh, but Salk was far too busy trying to deal with the tragic news from Washington to care about predatory gossip.

For parents the murky reports that appeared in the news created appalling anxiety and confusion. Two weeks earlier, they had celebrated their deliverance from polio and the fear of paralysis. Now they faced a danger that was even more terrifying than natural epidemics: the chance that their own best efforts to protect their family would paralyze their children. Those whose children had already been vaccinated waited in horror to see if they would become sick, and wavered in excruciating indecision over whether to complete the series of injections. Other parents sought advice from their equally confused doctors. Nobody could decide what to do.

The news coming from Washington frightened the six companies making Salk vaccine as much as it did the families who had received vaccine and the physicians who had inoculated them. Cutter Laboratories was one of the four manufacturers that had not participated in the field trial. As far as anyone knew, however, their procedures were the same as all the other companies. They had all worked with the same protocols, making the same product. What had happened to Cutter could have happened to Parke, Davis, Eli Lilly, Sharpe and Dohme, or Pitman-Moore. It could have happened to Wyeth. It might yet. They were terrified.

The person charged with sorting out the problem was Leonard Scheele, the surgeon general of the United States. Scheele was rarely consulted by Hobby on questions of policy, and he only became involved in the ongoing debates about the polio vaccine when he began receiving the first disturbing reports about vaccine-associated paralysis. His background was in laboratory research, and he didn't really have much experience with either poliomyelitis or pharmaceutical manufacture. People who worked with him praised him as a compromiser, but in the current incident he seemed to be trying to reconcile too many different points of view.

Over the next weeks and then months, Scheele followed several different courses, some dictated by the political realities of his own position, some by the very different suggestions of his various advisers, and some by what seems to have been a sense that a certain degree of official double-speak buys you the time to find out what you should be saying straight. At ten in the morning on April 27, only hours after learning of the new polio cases, he called Cutter headquarters and asked them to pull all their vaccine off the market, which they immediately did, but he did not make any statement declaring Cutter's vaccine unsafe at the press conference he held at one that afternoon. Following the recommendation of his advisors in the Public Health Service, who felt sure there was a local problem with Cutter production and not with the vaccine itself, he then urged that the vaccination program continue. On May 7, after learning that all the manufacturers had had at least some problems with virus inactivation, Scheele suspended the entire vaccination program pending further investigation. The next day, he told people not to panic, assured them the Salk vaccine was a magnificent achievement, and said the halt in vaccinations was merely a precaution. On May 13, eleven lots of Parke, Davis vaccine, newly and most carefully inspected, were cleared for use, and the vaccination program was resumed. For the rest of the summer, supplies from different companies would be released on a piecemeal basis, following individual inspection, but the push for nationwide immunization would never regain its original momentum.

The delays, the doubts, and the need for further testing all slowed production of vaccine. Far from the surpluses they had anticipated a month before, manufacturers in May were reporting shortages for the indefinite future. Rightly or wrongly, the public concluded that the problems were limited to Cutter vaccine, and parents renewed their demand for protection. The call from congressmen for various forms of rationing grew louder as supplies shrank. Former President Harry Truman attacked Eisenhower for trying to undermine the social welfare programs of his Democratic predecessors. Basil O'Connor used the very public forum of a speech at the American Public Health Association's annual Albert Lasker Awards for medical research and public health administration to berate the surgeon general for inaction, and circulated his telegram to Scheele demanding frank disclosure of precisely what was going on. Health officials attacked O'Connor and Salk for the haste with which they had introduced the vaccine, Hobby blamed the press for sensationalism, and reporters complained about the circus conditions under which they had been given their information about the new vaccine. In all accounts, "mess" was the word most often used.

The evidence that the vaccine was causing the illnesses seems far clearer in retrospect than it did at the time. Thomas Francis had just finished a year of study that concluded the Salk vaccine was sometimes no more than 60 percent effective against some strains of poliovirus, and while that was cause for rejoicing, it also meant at least some children would not be protected by their vaccinations. The polio season was beginning, and although there were no major epidemics in the communities where the stricken children lived, it had to be expected that a few cases would appear even among those getting their vaccinations. Some epidemiologists were convinced from the beginning that they were dealing with a classic example of vaccine-associated paralysis, but the officials who had to worry about the response of the manufacturers and the outcry of the frightened public waited for clearer confirmation before taking definite action. By that time, the course of indecision had been set.

On April 27, a newly created Poliomyelitis Surveillance Unit of the Communicable Disease Center went to California to investigate production procedures at the Cutter Laboratories. Meanwhile from the end of April through the rest of the summer of 1955, the Washington offices of the Department of Health, Education and Welfare and the Bethesda conference rooms of the National Institutes of Health were the scene of nearly constant meetings concerning the Cutter incident. Public Health Service officials consulted with NIH researchers; virologists conferred and issued white papers; manufacturers met with Hobby, who defended their right to keep their manufacturing processes secret, and then with the directors of the NIH, who interviewed representatives of each company separately to see what problems each was having in making safe vaccine.

All the regulars were on call—Bodian, Enders, Francis, Smadel—convening often and unhappily in Washington to discuss their opinions and recommendations. Jonas Salk was with them, though some objected that it was too much to expect him to be objective about the problems with which they had to deal.

On May 23, after Salk had stormed back to Pittsburgh, refusing to attend any more meetings of committees without power, Scheele appointed an official Technical Committee, made up of Bodian, Salk, Smadel, Richard Shope of the Rockefeller Institute, and NIH officials James Shannon, Roderick Murray, and William Workman, to recommend new safety regulations for the production of polio vaccine.

In what was becoming the weary tradition for such sessions, the committee met all night. By two-thirty in the morning, they had the first new standards for vaccine manufacture and testing. Additional safety tests would be conducted by both the manufacturers and the NIH's laboratories. The inactivation process would last longer. A few weeks later, bowing to the objections Albert Sabin and John Enders had raised from the first, the committee also recommended that the manufacturers use a less virulent substitute for the Mahoney strain of Type I poliovirus. It would take several months more to decide to require an extra filtration procedure before and during the process of inactivating virus, to guard against the "clumping" that might have shielded live virus from the effects of formalin. On June 7, Surgeon General Scheele scheduled a television broadcast as part of what he termed an urgent effort to restore confidence in the vaccine. A Gallup poll taken that week showed that only 36 percent of the people surveyed planned to be vaccinated when supplies were available.

It took months to reach even partial agreement on what had happened in Berkeley, and years to settle the lawsuits filed by the victims. Between April 12 and April 27, 1955, some 400,000 children had received vaccine manufactured by Cutter Laboratories. According to the authoritative report prepared in 1963 by Neal Nathanson of the Johns Hopkins School of Medicine and Alexander Langmuir of the Communicable Disease Center, there had been a final total of 204 cases of poliomyelitis associated with Cutter vaccine reported in the summer of 1955. Seventy-nine of these cases were vaccinated children, 105 their family contacts, and twenty what are called community contacts—primarily playmates of the vaccinated children. Three quarters of these people were paralyzed. Eleven died.

These people and their families would suffer for the rest of their lives. An equal victim, however, was the vast public that lost its enthusiasm for the vaccination program. That summer almost four thousand cases of polio were reported in an epidemic in Boston, Massachusetts. In Chicago, where people were enduring a record-breaking heat wave, parents once again agonized over the safety of taking their children to the beach. In a statement prepared to answer queries from foreign governments and private citizens about export of the Salk vaccine, Oveta Culp Hobby reached a new height of government euphemism. "The availability of the vaccine," she reported, "had been temporarily sharply reduced as a result of experience gained with large-scale production of the vaccine in the weeks following the announcement of the successful field trial."

Jonas Salk remained adamant that the problems had come from a failure to follow the safety procedures he had proposed, and he later cooperated with Melvin Belli when the famed litigator was suing Cutter on behalf of the paralyzed victims and their families. Others felt that the blame was neither so specific nor so limited. Perhaps if O'Connor had moved more slowly, there would have been time to catch safety problems before people were hurt. Perhaps if Salk's switch to the trypsin method of virus culture had been more thoroughly tested in commercial laboratories, the value of additional filtration would have emerged sooner. Perhaps the Laboratory of Biologics Control should have been more aggressive in demanding more elaborate safety screenings. Perhaps the Cutter company should not have been so confident in releasing vaccine that had not, as it turned out, been completely inactivated. The court ordered Cutter to compensate the 1955 victims, under the principle of implied warranty, but did not find that the company had knowingly produced a faulty product. Many people were characters in the tragedy that started in Berkeley, but there were no clear villains to blame.

IV

THE SWIFTEST RESPONSE TO THE CUTTER INCIDENT WAS NOT to change the regulations governing the production of the Salk polio vaccine, but to replace the people and agencies that had overseen those regulations. On July 13, 1955, Oveta Culp Hobby resigned as secretary of Health, Education and Welfare, effective August 1. She said she needed to spend more time with her ailing husband in Houston, but many believed her departure was hurried by the widespread opinion that her office had bungled the polio vaccine program. On July 27, Chester Keefer, her special assistant, also resigned. On July 31, William Sebrell retired as director of the National Institutes of Health. He was succeeded by the far more aggressive James Shannon, an early opponent of the Salk vaccine who guided the government research center through a period of enormous expansion, at least some of it supported by the newly perceived need for greater government involvement in the production and regulation of biological products.

The Laboratory of Biologics Control, which had been founded in the wake of a 1902 tragedy in which children died from contaminated diphtheria antitoxin, was reorganized in the wake of the tragic problems with polio vaccine. On July 15, 1955, it was renamed the Bureau of Biologics, with the promise of a greatly expanded staff and newly enlarged facilities for vaccine testing, and in December it was detached from the National Institute of Microbiology and raised to the status of a division within the NIH, under a new director. By 1956 over one hundred people worked in the polio division, testing vaccines.

For the epidemiologists of the Communicable Disease Center, the Cutter incident was the crisis that made their reputation. Later renamed the Centers for Disease Control, this branch of the Public Health Service tracks outbreaks of rabies, plague, and leprosy as well as chickenpox, influenza, and other common communicable diseases. Much of the CDC's stature comes from its excellent record in gathering information about emerging epidemics and, equally important, publishing the information it gathers—a talent that was developed during the summer of 1955. One of Surgeon General Scheele's first acts after the early reports of problems with Cutter vaccine was to establish a program of national surveillance, with all states reporting cases of poliomyelitis directly to the CDC in Atlanta. Daily reports on polio incidence were distributed to two hundred health officials, vaccine manufacturers, and members of the various advisory councils, often as their only source of detailed information, and they helped establish that the cases of vaccine-associated paralysis were almost entirely limited to Cutter Laboratories. On the strength of these daily memos, other companies continued vaccine production, confident their vaccine would be cleared for sale when the vaccination program was continued. Eli Lilly went on to make a profit of approximately $30 million on the Salk vaccine, and later treated Alexander Langmuir to a splendid luncheon at corporate headquarters in gratitude for the surveillance reports that had saved the company from ruinous delays.

The testing of the Salk polio vaccine, the largest field trial ever conducted, was also in all likelihood the last such trial that could ever be managed in its entirety by a private organization. Spurred by the kinds of problems that brought on the Cutter incident, the federal government has since assumed a much more active role in regulating the production of biomedical products, while the success of the National Foundation's efforts encouraged the massive growth of federal health and research programs during the 1960s. Public funding and oversight of scientific programs has become so important, in fact, that many who remember the 1954 polio field trial assume it was administered by the federal government. It is a mistake that outrages the people who worked themselves silly at the National Foundation without any outside help, but it reveals the changing public expectations of what the government can and should do to protect the health of its citizens.

While the power of the government was growing, that of the National Foundation was shrinking. For the individuals who had devoted their lives to ending the threat of polio, the successful development of the Salk vaccine meant the end of one stage of their quest and the start of a long search for new directions.

Many people expected the National Foundation to put itself out of business after the Salk vaccine was approved. In the habitual military language with which we describe disease, they thought that once the war on polio had been fought and the enemy conquered, it was time to turn in the weapons and send the soldiers home. Demobilization wasn't that simple, however. Old soldiers don't like to fade away, and the cheering mobs that line the route of the victory parade urge them on to new conquests and greater heights of glory. The first response to the report of the Salk vaccine success was a loud public call for the National Foundation to rally its seasoned forces behind another needy cause—arthritis, mental illness, birth defects, and cancer were a few of the possibilities proposed. Later, when the foundation tried to enter these fields, it was rebuffed by many of the same people and organizations that had called for help, but this was hard to foresee through the flush of triumph that enveloped them in the spring of 1955.

In any case, there were still many polio battles to be fought: people who had not yet been vaccinated; past victims who still required medical care and financial help; new research, including Albert Sabin's live-virus polio vaccine, to be supported. The work was not so easy now, however. The momentum that had kept polio at the forefront of the national consciousness from the record epidemic of 1953 through the triumphs and panics of 1955, uniting much of the nation in a mass movement of fellowship and fear, could not be sustained forever. "We thought we could leap from peak to peak," Elaine Whitelaw said later, "but we discovered we would have to spend a long time down in the valleys."

For one thing, donations were down, while expenses remained as high as ever. After 1955 each year's March of Dimes fund-raising drive took more effort and brought in fewer dollars. The Cutter fiasco didn't help at all, but there was more to the public resistance than disillusionment with tainted vaccine. Somehow, polio had ceased to be a vital concern. Patient care had always been the largest expense in the National Foundation budget, but now it seemed that the public expected the past victims of polio to rise up and walk away, cured by a miracle of federal licensing. Once lionized as heroic examples of human fortitude, the thousands of polio survivors who continued to need medical and financial help were suddenly ignored as embarrassing em-blems of their own poor timing, clumsy enough to get polio before the vaccine that could have protected them was found. As veterans of other wars would continue to discover, the same civilians who pray for them in the heat of battle don't like to be reminded of the wounded and the dead after the war is over.

For the scientists, doctors, and fund-raisers who had spent their careers helping polio victims and searching for ways to conquer the disease, the most frustrating adjustment to the post-vaccine era was the realization that people were neglecting to get their shots of Salk vaccine, now that it was available. The communal sigh of relief that had greeted the approval of the vaccine was followed by a curious but widespread state of mind by whose illogical reasoning many people felt safe simply be-cause the chance of protection existed, whether or not they themselves had received it.

Fewer than 450,000 children had received vaccine during the field trial, and few outside a narrow age group could be vac-cinated in 1955, given the limitations of production. It didn't matter. By 1957, when vaccine supplies were ample, the Na-tional Foundation found it had to mount elaborate advertising campaigns to get people to use the vaccine they had so impa-tiently awaited. The foundation's publicists in Washington set up a film studio in the Capitol to record senators urging their constituents to get their shots of Salk vaccine. After much per-suasion and several telephone calls to his mother, Elvis Presley agreed to be vaccinated in public, to set an example to his teenage fans. Joe Palooka, the cartoon boxer, was used in pam-phlets urging people to give polio a knockout punch by getting vaccinated. Once again, science and showmanship were working together to overcome polio.

Even among the people who had a professional commitment to polio research, there was a feeling of exhaustion. David Bodian, whom many close observers credited with knowing the most about the disease of polio and maintaining the most dignified stance through all the debates that had swirled around both Salk's and Sabin's vaccines, went to Europe in 1956 and investigated the procedures for vaccine production at various laboratories there. Not one of the virus researchers to whom he sent his report ever acknowledged it in any way. They were simply tired of the whole subject, he was forced to conclude.

Tired or not, Thomas Francis continued to work on the final report of the 1954 Field Trial Evaluation, the full version of the summary he had presented on April 12, 1955. It was a thankless and solitary job, much interrupted by urgent calls to meetings in Washington to discuss the fate of that same vaccine he had announced safe and effective amid such joyful company in Ann Arbor. On April 10, 1957, almost precisely two years after his historic announcement, he wrote in his datebook: "3:15 P.M. The last phase and acknowledgement of Final Report is typed. To go to printer today. The terminal stages were awful—*Selah*."

Basil O'Connor, the fierce and compassionate autocrat who had masterminded the war on polio, continued to fight its battles for the rest of his life. His wife Elvira had died suddenly in the harried summer of 1955, and in 1957 O'Connor married Hazel Royale, a physical therapist from Warm Springs, who then accompanied him to the many foundation meetings he continued to attend. His daughter Bettyann died in 1961, and his daughter Sheelagh in 1966, but Basil O'Connor carried on. Working to promote the use of the Salk vaccine and, later, the oral vaccine developed by Albert Sabin, he was determined at the same time to steer the foundation through the often rocky transition from an organization created to fight infantile paralysis to one devoted to preventing birth defects. As ever, he made many enemies along the way, and received many honors. He died in 1972, two months past his eightieth birthday, on a trip to Phoenix to attend a meeting of scientific advisors to the National Foundation. Revered and reviled, loved by a few and respected and feared by many, he had "licked polio" in his lifetime.

For Jonas Salk, a much younger man, it was harder to accept the success of his polio vaccine as the greatest triumph of his life. The vaccine whose development had been an exhilarating stage in the upward climb of his scientific career became, after its licensing, a distracting detour that threatened to take Salk ever further from the high road of biomedical research. First there was the real horror of the Cutter incident and the bitter, weary months of wrangling over new production standards and inspection policies. Next there was the continuing job of testing to find how long immunity created by the vaccinations would last, a question complicated by the clear and accurate premonition that Albert Sabin would soon be introducing a live-virus vaccine that, if taken by the same people, would make it impossible to know how lasting the immunity created by Salk's vaccine could really be.

And always, background and foreground, there were the unanticipated privileges and burdens of sudden fame—the introductions to fascinating people and invitations to boring banquets, the new encounters that inspired great plans and the new obligations that wasted precious time that could have been devoted to science. His fellows in the small world of virus research noted that Salk was not delivering the continuing series of breakthrough advances that he had seemed to promise in the heady days just after Ann Arbor, and many concluded that he was spending too much time in the conference room and on the banquet circuit to accomplish much in the lab.

In fact, Salk was combing the horizon for a new route to follow for the rest of his career. When he had come to Pittsburgh, it had been with the modest dream of directing his own laboratory. Forced to be philosophical about the many unexpected changes that had come to his life since then, he began to think of himself as a philosopher-scientist, and cast about for ways to ally himself with others who shared his new interest in art, philosophy, and the sources of creativity.

Almost as soon as the polio vaccine was licensed, long before the Cutter incident was settled or Thomas Francis had finished his final report, Salk began talking to Robert Oppenheimer, the controversial director of the Princeton Institute of Advanced

Studies who had directed the Los Alamos laboratory when the atom bomb was being built, only to be accused later of disloyalty and denied a security clearance, and to Leo Szilard, the visionary physicist who had helped develop the atom bomb and then campaigned against its use. They encouraged him to establish an independent intellectual center, a place without the strictures of academic departments and disciplines, free of the rivalries and limitations of university life. Basil O'Connor, eager to bring Salk the honor and ease he could not find in his own laboratory, and perhaps searching for a new cause that would be a fitting monument to all his dedicated labors, pledged the National Foundation's support to help realize Salk's vision.

The University of Pittsburgh, in the meantime, had brought Edward Litchfield, former chairman of the board of Smith-Corona, to be its new chancellor, and Litchfield had no intention of allowing an independent research center to be established under his jurisdiction but not under his control. When Litchfield's representative unfolded the university's table of organization at an early meeting to discuss the plan, Salk knew there was no place for him there. He had had many offers from other universities, and from other communities that were eager to adopt the famous doctor as a new citizen. If his vision was too broad for the steep hills and narrow ravines of Allegheny County, he would take it elsewhere. For over a year, Salk toured the country with Basil O'Connor and O'Connor's second wife, looking for what he later described as "a very special place, [whose] ambience should evoke and inspire creativity." After a time, they settled on a stretch of undeveloped California coast within the city of San Diego, in the small, exclusive enclave of La Jolla.

Salk was hoping to create a utopian intellectual community, a scientific center like the Max Planck Institute or the Pasteur Institute made even more stimulating by having artists and other humanists in residence. Even before it was built, however, reality intruded in the usual number of ugly ways, and the place that was supposed to enable philosopher-scientists to explore biological and medical research while considering what Salk called "the conditions conducive to the fulfillment of man's potential," instead became another trap of endless administrative details and professional rivalries.

Basil O'Connor, a master at being both supportive and demanding, insisted on putting Salk's name on the institute, and made it clear that the scientist had a moral obligation to put on a suit and eat creamed chicken at donors' banquets if that would help raise the money for his dream. The mayor of San Diego, himself crippled by polio, had promised to donate a beautiful stretch of coastal land along Torrey Pines Mesa, but the people of La Jolla mounted a great campaign to keep the institute from being built there. It was historic ground, an ancient home of coastal Indians, they said, and the entire area would be threatened by infected animals spreading rare and deadly diseases. The public airing of what some National Foundation staff dubbed "mad scientist" concerns was reinforced by more private local anxieties about being invaded by Jews, easterners, intellectuals, and other unfamiliar types. When Salk went to address a meeting at a school auditorium, prepared to deliver a high-minded speech on "Man's Reach," he was greeted by demonstrators screaming and holding up placards that said "Don't Kill Dogs in the Night." Salk left without ever being heard.

Sometimes it was hard to tell which was more humiliating, having to bear the insults of his opponents or the affection of his supporters. Charles Dail, the mayor of San Diego, had been disgusted by the opposition to Salk. When the referendum to let the institute use the land finally passed, Salk and Steve Alex, the National Foundation's publicist, had to hunt the mayor down on Shelter Island, a resort area of San Diego where he had taken his staff for their annual party, to have him sign papers that needed to be filed that same day. When they found him, drunk and disheveled, Dail embraced a livid Salk, calling him "Salkie Baby" and telling him how much he loved him. Salk left abruptly, and so was not there when Dail started ranting about how horrible the voters had been, threw his crutch through the window, and urinated on the documents he had just signed. Alex had to dry the papers off in the sun, through the broken window, to get them to City Hall by the 4:30 P.M. deadline. The dark side of the institute's freedom from academic restraints was that Salk now had no larger organization to shield him from such contacts. He could have gone anywhere, at that point, but this was where he had chosen to be, and so he put up with O'Connor's publicity and Dail's vulgarity, and was profoundly uncomfortable.

Salk's departure from the University of Pittsburgh was a fairly ordinary event in academic circles, where a gypsy life is often seen as a sign of prestige and advancement, but it was a great blow to local pride. After several years of rumors, the announcement in March 1960 that Salk was leaving was front-page news in the city's papers, and it demanded extraordinary apologies from the man who was, for a time at least, Pittsburgh's most famous citizen. "This is not an offer," Salk explained earnestly to reporters. "It is a man's dream."

When the dream institute was finally completed, a futuristic structure of free-flowing laboratories and quiet studies designed by Louis Kahn with numerous suggestions and revisions by Jonas Salk, it became yet another source of misery and distraction. The great minds that Salk invited there turned out to have great egos to match; soon the host found himself dismissed as a "mere technician" by the scientists he had gathered around him, who then added insult to injury by remodeling the laboratory spaces he had worked so hard to design.

"Let someone else do the administration," his wife would tell him. "Get back to the lab. That's where you're happy." But by then Salk had spent almost ten years away from the daily work of the laboratory bench—first dealing with the backwash of polio vaccine problems, and then seeking out a site for the institute, working to gain local support, raising money, going over architectural plans, and not least dealing with all the disruptions in his personal life that the two moves—into the public eye, and then to California—had caused. In that interval, there had been many new developments in biomedical research, and Jonas Salk was at a time of life when it's more appropriate to be a sage than a student.

"You don't have to marry these people," his wife would insist, but it was a bitter disappointment that the institute had not created the intellectual community Salk sought, and meanwhile his own marriage was falling apart. Donna Salk had no interest in the world of fancy dinners or fund-raisers, and she recoiled at the idea of supervising servants or selecting luncheon favors for the Ladies' Guild. She liked being asked to sit on the board of Tuskegee Institute and invited to make speeches about fair employment practices, and she knew perfectly well that she was given these opportunities because of her husband's fame, but she hated the other appurtenances of fame almost as much as she hated the ostentation of traveling with Basil O'Connor. In 1968 the Salks were divorced, and two years later Jonas married Françoise Gilot, a painter who was most famous as the former mistress of Pablo Picasso.

Salk no longer directs the institute that bears his name. The rooms that were to be occupied by philosophers and historians are largely empty, the separate building that was to house them remains unbuilt, and the city of San Diego has taken back some of the land it once promised to the institute. Salk maintains a large suite of offices there, however, his views of the Pacific interrupted only by the hang gliders who fly off the nearby bluffs, and he still hopes to establish a community of creative intellectuals, perhaps at the University of California campus down the road. Over the years he has written several philosophical books that ponder the elusive conditions of human fulfillment, and has continued to work on the refinement of his polio vaccine and to participate in conferences on virology. Lorraine Friedman is still his secretary. Donna Salk lives in La Jolla, too, and has resumed her career as a social worker. One by one, with detours and rebellions, Salk's three sons have followed him into medicine, into the laboratory, into the fierce defense of their father's work, his principles, his vaccine, and his reputation.

Salk returns to Pittsburgh from time to time, and he appears at the ceremonies marking all the significant anniversaries of the field trial and the Ann Arbor announcement of its successful results. Ten years after, then twenty, twenty-five, thirty years later and more, he returned to pose with the aging pioneers, many of them now older than Salk was when he went to the Watson Home to give the first injections of his secret new vaccine. Still active at seventy-five, he has spent his recent years working to develop a vaccine to help those suffering from AIDS. As ever, though, he is approaching this most dreaded disease from a direction other scientists have not explored, trying a vaccine that would be given to people who are already infected, to rob the virus of its virulence. With polio, he had argued that it didn't matter if you never had the disease, you could still be called immunized if you produced antibodies. With AIDS, he argues that it doesn't matter if you have the disease, as long as it can be controlled. Hostile virologists scoff at his principles, friendly ones fear his announcements are premature. The public applauds, and investors throw money at his feet. Times haven't changed. . . .

CLOSE-UP

THE HEALTHIEST GENERATION in HISTORY

It was a terrible feeling, like the kind of feeling you get when you're having a nightmare and you're running and your feet become like lead, it was that kind of sensation.

—BRIAN MAY

There are today some three hundred thousand polio survivors in the United States, victims of a nightmare that does not end on waking. Many of them are now suffering from what is called post-polio syndrome, or the late effects of polio—crippling degeneration that strikes decades after the first illness, often creating symptoms worse than those of the initial bout of disease. No one knows for sure why they are suffering, though some suspect it was the rigors of their rehabilitation that caused an early onset of arthritis and other degenerative diseases. The very toughness on which the "polios" prided themselves, and on which they built their recovery, is now sending them back to the braces, wheelchairs, and respirators they struggled so energetically to discard.

In other parts of the world, polio is still very much in evidence—in the withered legs of beggars, the twisted arms of women unable to marry because they are not strong enough to work, and in the continuing campaigns to provide vaccinations for children. In even the most troubled nations of South America and Central America, civil wars and revolutions stop each year for Vaccination Day. Rotary clubs in Africa organize emergency motor pools to distribute vaccine before it loses its potency for lack of refrigeration. Propped up against storefronts in Israel are life-size cardboard photographs of a child on crutches, a real cup attached to his outstretched hand. "Give to the Vaccination Program," the signs say in Hebrew and English. The World Health Organization holds periodic conferences to discuss vaccination programs and consider again the relative merits of the Salk and Sabin vaccines.

*The question of which vaccine is better has been a matter of
dispute for the last thirty years, in a debate that fades at times
to the murmur of a few zealots only to swell once more in volume
as the issues rise again to the front of public awareness and
social concern. To Sabin, the great difference between their
vaccines is that Salk's protects against polio, but his controls
the disease by spreading the immunity to others. To Salk, the
great difference is that Sabin's causes a steady and predictable
number of cases of paralysis, while his is safe. Some students
of public health argue for sequential use of both vaccines—first
the Salk vaccine to provoke an immune response without the
danger of paralysis, and then the Sabin vaccine for the longer-
lasting immunity believed to come with actual infection. The
truth that is sometimes buried in the acrimonious debates is that
both vaccines are powerful agents for personal and public
health, and that either may bring about the long-anticipated
global eradication of paralytic poliomyelitis—if not in this century, then in the new millennium that is so fast approaching.*

•

For the last twenty-five years, the Salk polio vaccine, still used
in Canada and in several countries in northern Europe, has been
almost unavailable in the United States and other parts of the
world. In 1961 the Public Health Service licensed the commercial production of an attenuated-virus oral polio vaccine developed by Albert Sabin. Because of the difficulty of finding a
suitable population in the United States that had not received
Salk vaccine, Sabin had conducted his field trials in the Soviet
Union in 1959. Some health officials in the United States were
skeptical of the scrupulousness or accuracy of the data collected
by their Russian counterparts, but there was little doubt that
the Sabin vaccine was worthy of both licensing and distribution.
In little more than five years, it completely supplanted the Salk
vaccine for common use within the United States. Foreign manufacturers of enhanced potency killed-virus vaccines plan to
introduce their product to the United States in 1990, claiming
that early market surveys show the public will be eager to switch
to a vaccine that promises complete safety and that is now no
more expensive than the live-virus vaccine, but only time will
confirm the accuracy of these predictions.

The great convenience and economy of not having to deal with needles has made the Sabin vaccine very attractive to health officials in parts of the world where neither sterilizers nor disposable syringes are readily available. Although the Sabin vaccine sometimes fails to immunize people in tropical and subtropical climates, where other endemic viral diseases apparently interfere with its effect, the live-virus vaccine's capacity to spread immunity through contact is still prized by epidemiologists who hope to achieve the greatest protection for an entire society in the shortest time and with the least effort. Whatever its advantages, however, it is true that the live-virus polio vaccine carries a small but real danger of causing the very disease it is designed to prevent. For every 4 million doses of oral polio vaccine, one will contain a virus that has reverted to its virulent state—contagious and paralytic. People with immune-deficiency diseases or those who take medication that suppresses their immune responses are particularly susceptible. Adults, usually the caretakers of infants who have been vaccinated, are stricken at least as often as children.

The current ascendancy of the Sabin vaccine in the United States is a result of politics as well as medical principle. After Sabin's Soviet Union field trial was completed, American congressmen, steeped in the rhetoric of Cold War competition, fumed about a Soviet-American "polio gap" on the analogy of the so-called missile gap, and proposed widespread use of the new vaccine. Sabin campaigned hard to have his vaccine adopted, and Salk campaigned hard to keep it from being used, at least in part because he knew that widespread inoculation with oral polio vaccine would make it difficult or impossible to prove the lifetime immunity he hoped to claim for his own vaccine.

Although the record of manufacture shows no difficulty in finding producers for the live-virus vaccine, Sabin maintained that he had to struggle to have his vaccine made. "There was no rush of pharmaceutical companies to make it," he insisted some years later. "They were all making killed-virus vaccine, and making a very good profit out of it, and the Public Health Service was not very dispassionate in this whole thing, and displayed no initiative in undertaking any change."

Basil O'Connor had supported Albert Sabin's research with

hundreds of thousands of dollars in National Foundation grants, but it is true that he argued for continuing with the proven successes of the Salk vaccine. The American Medical Association, however, advised physicians to use the oral vaccine, starting a trend that in less than a decade made the oral polio vaccine the treatment of preference in the United States and many other parts of the world. When President Nixon awarded Sabin the National Medal of Science in 1970, the scientist was very gratified to see that he was honored "for numerous fundamental contributions to the understanding of viruses and viral diseases, culminating in the development of the vaccine which has eliminated poliomyelitis as a major threat to human health." "Not *a* vaccine," he would later say with pride, "but *the* vaccine."

Ironically, it seems likely that the widespread acceptance of Sabin's vaccine was made much easier because of the earlier introduction of Salk's. Cautious physicians were reassured by the American Medical Association reminder that most of their patients had already received Salk vaccine and so would not be harmed by the live-virus vaccine, which they could consider a long-lasting booster. The public, newly accustomed to the idea that vaccines were introduced through highly publicized programs of mass inoculation, willingly showed up for a series of "Sabin on Sunday" clinics staged at schools, churches, and even in shopping-center parking lots.

Even before the Sabin vaccine was introduced, polio incidence in the United States had fallen from an average rate of 135 cases of paralysis per million people to a rate of 26 per million. After May 1955, there have been no cases of poliomyelitis associated with the Salk vaccine. The current annual rate of polio paralysis in the United States is 4 per million, almost all associated with the Sabin vaccine.

Vanquished as a menace in North America and Europe, polio has retained its place in the shared communal memory, a kind of Atlantis of terror that lingers in legend long after it has sunk out of sight. And, like many terrors of the past, the years have added power to the story while leading a younger generation to doubt that there was ever any reality behind the tale. *Children banned from beaches?* they ask in wonder. *Parents afraid of movie theaters? Medical experiments sponsored by a private organization and conducted in the public schools? You've got to be kidding! How terrifying!*

By the same transformation of shared mythology, Jonas Salk's stature as a scientific hero has risen over the years even as his real influence has waned. At a time when conservative intellectuals have made careers of bewailing the loss of what used to be called common knowledge, both Jonas Salk and his polio vaccine remain part of the shrinking stock of names and achievements that can be invoked in any number of contexts with fair certainty that they will be recognized and rightly valued. Historians of the Baby Boom humorously cite the three great doctors of that generation—Dr. Salk, Dr. Spock, and Dr. Seuss—but it is only the first they treat as the defining example of the scientific genius.

Still best known for the polio vaccine that he developed, Salk is one of a very small company of people whose very names evoke instant and unquestioning trust. When Michael Dukakis, campaigning for president in 1988, was asked about his personal heroes, he cited several broad categories like Olympic athletes and police officers, and one individual: Jonas Salk. Lobbyists bemoaning the high cost of liability insurance cite Salk's vaccine as a miracle that could not have happened in the litigious atmosphere of today. According to a recent front-page story in the *Wall Street Journal*, "when New York deal maker Morton Davis sought private financing for a new AIDS vaccine company built around Dr. Salk's work, money rained down from the heavens. 'We had to send back checks,' " Mr. Davis reported. Reporters seeking an authoritative statement on any new development in biomedicine will try to get a comment from Jonas Salk. Modest people who seek to emphasize the smallness of their own achievements will say, "Hey, I'm no Jonas Salk."

In the same way that people who have never seen a horse speak of "reining in" someone who has become too frisky, people who never think of polio when they stumble on the stairs still invoke it as the shining example of a danger overcome through the combined powers of science, commerce, and public action. In October 1986, President Ronald Reagan invoked the polio vaccine in a short list of "American" triumphs that was an accurate description of cultural commonplaces, if not of historical fact. "The history of these United States is one of individual achievement," Reagan said. "It was their hard work that built our cities and farmed our prairies; their genius that pushed beyond the boundaries of existing knowledge, reshaping our world with the steam engine, polio vaccine, and the silicon chip." The MacArthur Foundation, justifying the high fees it pays directors, says organizations need to spend that kind of money to get individuals of the caliber of Jonas Salk. Defending the cost of special schools for science education, Dr. Leon Lederman, winner of the 1988 Nobel Prize in physics, said, "If one of these kids makes a breakthrough like Jonas Salk, you pay for the school for a hundred years." A vanity press, offering to write and publish a limited edition of anyone's biography for little more than the cost of a world cruise, cites Salk's discovery of the polio vaccine, along with the end of World War II and the successful landing of human beings on the moon, as the epoch-making events that framed its potential clients' lives. In January 1987, *The New York Times* published an editorial essay comparing the danger of breathing other people's smoke to that of catching polio. "Failing to eliminate smoke from our children's environment," the author concluded, "is very much like forgetting to get them their polio shots—things might turn out all right, but then again, they might not." Not to have your children immunized against polio is the contemporary equivalent of not teaching them to say their prayers a century ago. It happens, but it is a sure sign of parental neglect.

The irony of these reverent invocations is that it would be almost impossible to repeat the events that led to the swift and successful introduction of the Salk polio vaccine. Even during the worst of epidemics, paralytic polio was a relatively rare disease, its incidence limited and its effects often mild. The private forces commanded by the National Foundation for Infantile Paralysis, immense and impressive as they were, could never have hoped to address far more difficult health problems like cancer, drug addiction, or alcohol abuse. To contemporary immunologists, battling the complexities of AIDS as well as the continuing enigmas of influenza and the common cold, polio is an enviably simple disease. The virus takes only three forms, which do not seem to mutate. The virus does not lie latent for extended periods or hide within the core of cells. Eighty years ago, people responded to polio like the terrified and bewildered natives of a remote country first confronted with the cannons and muskets of a foreign army. The devastation was dreadful, but now that we have repelled the invader only to find the island threatened by guerrilla warriors, turncoats, and spies, we have come to appreciate the simplicity of a straightforward attack.

But while we can't turn to the records of polio for solutions to AIDS or any other ailment lurking in the viral or microbial jungle, we can look to the past to understand why we react the way we do to the problems of the present. The strongest effect of the Salk vaccine program was felt not in the official chambers of Washington or the laboratories of medical research centers, but in the opinions and assumptions of the millions of children who participated in the 1954 field trial and the millions more who benefited from its effects.

Until very recently, it was common for disease to disrupt the predictable timetable of everybody's life. We think of people dying young, but death was only part of it. How ordinary it was for someone to miss a year of school while recovering from a debilitating disease, to postpone a marriage while nursing a near-relation through some final illness or other, to abandon home and work for a season or two in the mountains fighting off tuberculosis. The routine ear infections of childhood, still a major concern of any pediatrician, used to equally routinely deafen people for life, while the commonplace malady of strep throats was once a signal for the onset of rheumatic fever, which left its survivors with scarred and weakened hearts. Historians of art and culture often cite the late-nineteenth-century preoccupation with disease as a sign of the decadence of *fin-de-siècle* society, but to the people who really did have tuberculosis, to take one example, the alternating bouts of lassitude and fever were not a symptom of social malaise but a clinical manifestation of a deadly disease. Poets and artists may have found something romantic and attractive in their disability, but most people regarded the compromises of limited health as one of the painful but sometimes unavoidable demands of life.

Today, for the first time in human history, there exists a generation of adults that has never experienced epidemic disease. For today's concerned parents in the medically advanced nations of the western world, there is no such thing as an acceptable risk, at least when it comes to the treatment they will allow others to give their children. Whether the disease is polio, diphtheria, or any of the other ailments that once made childhood such a perilous time, they want a cure that is 100 percent safe, 100 percent effective, and that lasts as long as their children live. Anything less is considered intolerably inadequate.

In the years when polio epidemics raged, not so very long ago, expectations were a good deal lower. People were grateful for anything that would take them safely from June to September. Parents brought their children for a series of very painful shots of gamma globulin because there was a possibility that it would boost their natural resistance for a few weeks. Leading experts in the polio field had dreams that were equally modest. In 1951 both Howard Howe of Johns Hopkins and Thomas Turner of the University of Pennsylvania spoke of the wonderful day when a killed-virus vaccine might protect children over the first two to four years of life.

Today's American parents expect much more, and assume their expectations will be met. The biggest generation of babies the United States has ever known have all become adults, and one of the great lessons they retain from their youth is that if there is something bad out there, they just have to wait for an announcement telling them the moment when they are to line up to get their shots or pills, to be coated anew with whatever invisible shield has been invented this week for their greater protection against the assaults of time, decay, and fate.

The Salk vaccine was only one of the many medical discoveries that made the children of the 1940s and 1950s a uniquely healthy generation, shielded from the diseases that had threatened their parents but not yet exposed to the full dangers, either of drug-resistant viruses or of increasingly widespread environmental hazards, that would loom for their own offspring. Raised with the conviction that science could find a cure for any ills to which the body might be prey, many of today's adults have retained what may be highly unrealistic assumptions about what it means to be healthy—assumptions that will continue to tax the medical system with possibly unrealizable demands until well into the next century. Polio was not by any means the greatest danger facing the children of the 1950s, but it was one of the most feared, and both the intensity of that fear and the swiftness of its end help explain both the great expectations and the overwhelming doubts that dog that same generation in its middle years.

Thomas Francis died in 1969, shortly after his retirement from the University of Michigan School of Public Health. His papers were given to the Bentley Historical Library in Ann Arbor, just up the road from the Gerald Ford Presidential Library, where they repose in benign obscurity with the other documents stored along this boulevard of buried records. There, amid a lifetime of papers to and from funding agencies, monkey dealers, payroll inspectors, laboratory assistants, people requesting or consenting to give memorial addresses, notices of board meetings attended or missed, and all the other detritus of a distinguished academic career, is a single carton containing microfilm copies of all the field-trial results. I found myself in Box no. 28, sheet no. 47855, student no. 21, vaccination record 35/35/35/00, right after Jonathan Schindelheim, whose name evokes no memory at all. If you were a Polio Pioneer, you can look it up.

ACKNOWLEDGMENTS

I AM NOT A SCIENTIST, A DOCTOR, A POLITICIAN, A PUBLICIST, a philanthropist, or a member of any branch of government. In studying the many groups that participated in the introduction of the first successful polio vaccine, I have tried to understand their inner workings while keeping sight of how each appeared to all the others. To whatever degree I have succeeded in achieving accuracy without losing perspective, I am indebted to many people. Whatever factual errors remain are, of course, entirely my own.

When I first began thinking about polio, the officers of the March of Dimes Birth Defects Foundation very generously allowed me free access to their library and their historical files. Steve Alex, Virginia Blood, Dorothy Ducas, Melvin Glasser, Charles Massey, John O'Connor, Gabriel Stickle, and Elaine Whitelaw patiently endured many hours of questions; I thank them for their many contributions to my understanding of the National Foundation for Infantile Paralysis and its work. John Blecha, chief photographer of the March of Dimes, provided graphic images and recollections in equal measure; Mrs. Hazel O'Connor Dillmeier graciously shared her memories of her late husband. Dorothy Davis helped me reach all these people, and Nancy Cassatta solved many small and large mysteries. I am also grateful to Kenneth Cramer of the Dartmouth College Archives, to the Alumni Records staff of Vassar College, and to the archivists of the Franklin D. Roosevelt Presidential Library for help in finding information about Basil O'Connor, Franklin

Roosevelt, and the early years of what became the National Foundation for Infantile Paralysis.

I am particularly grateful to Dr. Jonas Salk for his cooperation in repeated interviews extending over several years, and also for his kind permission to use the vast collection of papers he has put on deposit at the Mandeville Department of Special Collections of the University Library at the University of California, San Diego. Geoffrey Wexler, manuscripts archivist, guided me through this collection while still cataloging its contents. Lorraine Friedman, who, as Dr. Salk's executive secretary for forty years, had the initial and long-lasting responsibility for assembling and maintaining this collection, was also kind enough to allow me to interview her about her work. Donna Salk and Peter Salk generously provided the kind of recollections that create a human context for the progress of science.

I am very grateful to the scientists and public health officials who had central roles in the polio vaccine drama, and who kindly granted lengthy interviews to discuss their work. Doctors Leona Baumgartner, David Bodian, Robert Korns, Alexander Langmuir, Albert Sabin, and Leonard Scheele were all unfailingly generous in answering my inexpert questions on scientific matters, and provided many insights into the business and politics of science. Dr. Clyde Culbertson and Dr. Mahlon Bierly kindly clarified some of the mysteries of commercial production of vaccines.

Jonathon Erlen, curator of the History of Medicine Collection, Falk Library, and Gloria Acklin Kreps of the University of Pittsburgh Health Sciences News Bureau, were extremely helpful in locating material at the University of Pittsburgh. Dr. Julius Youngner graciously shared his recollections of the early work at the Virus Research Laboratory, while Dr. Maurice Shapiro, Dr. and Mrs. Harry Margolis, and Mr. Alexander Lowenthal provided many insights into the growth of Pittsburgh during the early 1950s. Special thanks go to Thomas Coleman, who retains vivid memories of the unique pressures and opportunities that arose from the vast public interest in the success of the Salk vaccine, and to John Troan, who both recorded and recalled the polio years in Pittsburgh with a keen reporter's eye. For information on what is now the D. T. Watson Rehabilitation

Center, I am very grateful to Katheryn Kelley, JoAnne Pasquinelli, and John Righetti; Dr. Robert Nix contributed many spirited memories of both the Watson Home vaccine trials and the practice of pediatric medicine during the polio epidemic years, as did his assistant, Betty Alshouse Gundelfinger.

The staff of the Bentley Historical Library at the University of Michigan, and particularly Nancy Bartlett, provided much help in finding material in the Thomas Francis Collection. In addition to their generosity in making this collection available to scholars, Mrs. Thomas Francis, Jr., and her daughter, Dr. Mary Jane Francis, very kindly consented to several interviews and gave me access to family papers. Marion Brown, Wayne De Neff, Louis Graff, Dr. H. F. Maassab, and Elva Minuse, all opened important windows onto the operations of Dr. Francis' laboratory in Michigan, the Vaccine Evaluation Center, and the press coverage of the April 12 announcement of the Francis Field Trial results. Fred Friendly shared many stories of *See It Now* coverage of the vaccine story, and of his friendship with Jonas Salk; his assistant, Natalie Payne, was a great help in locating other material.

For help in obtaining government records relating to the licensing and regulation of vaccines, as well as to specific questions of politics and policies raised by the Salk vaccine, I would like to thank Elaine Baldwin of the National Institute of Allergies and Infectious Disease and Thomas Flavin of the National Institutes of Health, as well as Dwight Strandberg and other archivists at the Dwight D. Eisenhower Presidential Library in Abilene, Kansas. Richard and Barbara Greenberg kindly shared their recollections of the NIH during the tumultuous period of licensing the Salk vaccine. Martha Brown, Susan Gundlach, Judy Raymond, and Roberta Simon introduced me to the diverse world of "polio-experienced people." Richard Carter made many generous and insightful contributions to my research and kindly allowed me to use original source materials in his possession. I would also like to thank Terry Austin, director of Special Collections of the American Medical Association Library; Wilma Benjamin, librarian of the National Association of Parents and Teachers; Kay Salz, deputy archivist of the CBS News Archives; the staff of P.S. 61 in Manhattan, Victor Cohn,

Pauline Konove, and Florence Shulman for their many contributions. I would like to thank the National Endowment for the Humanities Travel to Collections Program for their support of my research.

I began this book while a visiting scholar at the Northwestern University Program on Women and completed it as a visiting scholar at the Northwestern University Center for Urban Affairs and Policy Research; I am very grateful to both those centers for their support, and particularly to Susan Hirsch, Margaret Gordon, and Hervey Juris. The staff of the Northwestern Library was at all times vital to the success of my research; special thanks go to Rolf Erickson, Russell Maylone, and to the staffs of the Reference Collection and the Government Publications for their patient unraveling of my endless tangled queries. Howard Becker and Dr. Jan Zeller made many helpful suggestions at different stages of this project. Susan Leon and William Reiss kept me working through their continuing enthusiasm and encouragement. To the members of my family, staunch supporters and best critics, endless thanks.

Notes

EPIGRAPHS:

PAGE

13 Who owns . . . patent the sun: Edward R. Murrow and Fred W. Friendly, eds., *See It Now* (New York: Simon & Schuster, 1955), p. 159.

17 The things that never . . . the dead: Thomas H. Johnson, ed., *The Complete Poems of Emily Dickinson* (Boston: Little, Brown, 1960), p. 635.

PART ONE: Paralysis, Politics, and Money

29 Contact . . . magic power: Susan Sontag, *Illness as Metaphor* (New York: Vintage Books, 1977), p. 6.

33 "Why, we will . . . dread disease": *New Rochelle Standard*, August 18, 1916.

39 "undue prevalence": *The New York Times*, October 19, 1930.

50 "a figure tall . . . civilized man": Will Durant, *New York World*, June 28, 1929.

51 "had somehow overcome . . . possessed": Colonel Edmund Starling as told to Thomas Sugrue, *Starling of the White House* (New York: Simon & Schuster, 1946), p. 307.

51 "Franklin Roosevelt underwent . . . in trouble": Francis Perkins, *The Roosevelt I Knew* (New York: Viking, 1946) p. 29.

51 "His thoughts expanded . . . day by day": Nathan Miller, *FDR: An Intimate History* (Garden City, N.Y.: Doubleday, 1983), p. 197.

51 "I am glad . . . of mankind": Joseph Lash, *Eleanor and Franklin* (New York: Norton, 1971), p. 424.

54 "O'Connor's brother John": John J. O'Connor was the classic Tammany pol on the federal level, representing the 16th District in Manhattan. By 1938 he and FDR had had a falling-out sufficient to make him the only member of Congress on the White House list of people to be "purged" in the next election, but he was standing at Basil's side at the Democratic National Convention in Chicago when FDR was nominated for president in 1932.

54 "I was looking . . . he liked it": Tex McCrary and Jinx Falkenburg, "New York Close-Up," *New York Herald Tribune*, January 15, 1951.

PAGE

55 **"my name . . . as it now is"**: Franklin D. Roosevelt to Van-Lear Black, September 24, 1924, Franklin D. Roosevelt Presidential Library, Hyde Park, New York.

56 **"Dear Franklin . . . money. DBO'C"**: Basil O'Connor to Franklin D. Roosevelt, no date, Franklin D. Roosevelt Presidential Library.

61 **"I thought . . . liked it"**: Richard Carter, *Breakthrough: The Saga of Jonas Salk* (New York: Trident Press, 1966), p. 12.

66 **"Committees are . . . get a new one"**: Alexander Langmuir, personal interview, August 19, 1986.

74 **"The government . . . on a dime"**: Ira T. Smith with Joe Alex Morris, *"Dear Mr. President . . ."* (New York: Julian Messner, 1949), pp. 158–59.

75 **"the sudden appearance . . . publicity"**: John Paul, *A History of Poliomyelitis* (New Haven: Yale University Press, 1971), p. 311.

87 **"They thought . . . majority stockholder"**: Elaine Whitelaw, personal interview, January 28, 1985.

PART TWO: Laboratory Life

91 **"Bacteria . . . in our love"**: Hans Zinsser, *Rats, Lice, and History* (Boston: Little, Brown, 1935), pp. 13–14.

91 **"What every scientist knows . . . football"**: Richard C. Lewontin, " 'Honest Jim' Watson's Big Thriller About DNA," *Chicago Sunday Sun-Times*, February 25, 1968.

106 **"that academic work . . . activities did"**: Thomas Francis, Jr., "Memo: Concerning Doctor Salk and Parke, Davis & Company," September 1, 1945, Thomas Francis Collection, Michigan Historical Collections, Bentley Historical Library, University of Michigan (hereafter, Thomas Francis Collection).

115 **"He was . . . bright"**: Basil O'Connor, interview with Richard Carter, no date, collection of Richard Carter.

117 **"It's still here . . . all myself"**: Jonas Salk, in conversation with Gloria Acklin, University of Pittsburgh Medical Center, 1986.

120 **First there was the problem of supply**: Some things never change. In 1928, when philanthropist Jeremiah Milbank established an international committee for polio research, the committee found that the greatest impediment to progress was the scarcity and cost of monkeys needed for laboratory experiments. In 1988 Dr. Robert C. Gallo, director of the Laboratory of Tumor Cell Biology at the National Cancer Institute, called the shortage of chimpanzees the leading bottleneck to AIDS research, followed by the mysterious nature of the AIDS virus. "It is conceivable that we may already have an effective vaccine," he said, "but we will never know unless we can get the chimps to fine-tune different dosages of different compounds" (Dennis L. Breo, "AIDS Enemy," *Chicago Tribune*, January 3, 1988, sec. 5).

121 **as many as fifty thousand monkeys:** By comparison, the U.S. Department of Agriculture estimated there was a total of approximately sixty thousand monkeys, chimpanzees, and other primates used in medical schools and laboratories across the country in 1983.

123 **"for each ... extra-hazardous work":** Jonas Salk to Harry Weaver, March 10, 1949, Carter, *Breakthrough*, p. 75.

132 **"He was going ... down there,"** Dr. Maurice Shapiro, personal interview, August 26, 1986.

133 **"further studies ... of man":** Jonas Salk to Harry Weaver, June 16, 1950, Jonas Salk Papers, MSS 1, University Library, Mandeville Department of Special Collections, University of California, San Diego (hereafter, Jonas Salk Papers).

133 **"Without much further ... becomes stabilized":** ibid.

134 **"I think ... in man":** ibid.

136 **"I look ... unto yourself":** *Wall Street Journal*, March 19, 1987.

147 **"God damn ... ever since":** Thomas Rivers, undated recorded interview, collection of Richard Carter.

148 **"I consider you ... be friends":** Thomas Rivers to Albert Sabin, December 2, 1946, Thomas Rivers Collection, American Philosophical Society, Philadelphia.

148 **"It is always ... or monkeys":** Albert Sabin, minutes, meeting of the Committee on Immunization, National Foundation for Infantile Paralysis, January, 23, 1953, p. 134.

WIDE-ANGLE: Parents and Children

153 **"In the summer ... sick":** Benjamin Spock, "Polio," *Baby and Child Care* (New York: Duell Sloan and Pearce, 1946), p. 419.

159 **"It all ... fatal disease":** E. B. White, "Notes and Comments," *New Yorker*, March 6, 1946, p. 13.

160 **"In the dawn ... quieter way":** "Scientist at Work," *Lansing State Journal*, April 11, 1953, p. 3.

PART THREE:: Lining Up for the Parade

167 **As in manufacturing ... has arrived:** Thomas Kuhn, *The Structure of Scientific Revolutions*, 2nd ed., vol. 2, no. 2, of the *International Encyclopedia of Unified Science* (Chicago: University of Chicago Press, 1970), p. 76.

181 **"Dr. Salk's labs ... of vaccine":** *Time*, February 9, 1953, p. 43.

181 **"Of course ... everybody else":** Herdis von Magnis to Jonas Salk, February 26, 1953, Jonas Salk Papers.

181 **"the repercussions ... handful of people":** Jonas Salk to Herdis von Magnis, March 16, 1953, Jonas Salk Papers.

182 **"Everybody and his brother ... as possible":** Thomas Rivers, minutes, National Foundation meeting, February 26, 1953, collection of March of Dimes Birth Defects Foundation.

PAGE

183 **"the first significant . . . or desired":** John Paul to Jonas Salk, January 28, 1953, Jonas Salk Papers.

183 **"Although it was nice . . . said by others":** Albert Sabin to Jonas Salk, February 9, 1953, Jonas Salk Papers.

187 **"Although progress . . . more confidence":** Jonas Salk, "The Scientist Speaks for Himself," in Carter, *Breakthrough*, p. 162.

192 **"Joe Smadel . . . their minds":** Thomas Rivers, undated recorded interview, collection of Richard Carter.

193 **"Since there is . . . around the corner":** Albert Sabin, "Present Status and Future Possibilities of a Vaccine for the Control of Poliomyelitis," speech before the annual convention of the American Medical Association, June 4, 1953.

195 **"Jonas was indeed . . . all at once":** Carter, *Breakthrough*, p. 179.

196 **"revealed to me . . . greater than giving":** Jonas Salk to Basil O'Connor, June 24, 1953, Jonas Salk Papers.

196 **"We understood . . . to Pittsburgh":** Carter, *Breakthrough*, p. 173.

200 **"I, for one . . . every time":** Albert Sabin, testimony, *Committee on Interstate and Foreign Commerce, House of Representatives*, "The Causes, Control, and Remedies of the Principal Diseases of Mankind," pt. 3, October 6 and 12, 1953, 83rd Congress, Washington, D.C.: United States Government House Hearings, 1953, p. 847 (hereafter, House Hearings, 1953).

200 **"when the question . . . this Committee' ":** John Paul, *A History of Poliomyelitis* (New Haven: Yale University Press, 1971), p. 424.

206 **"Our problem . . . most certain":** Jonas Salk, "Recent Studies on Immunization Against Poliomyelitis," *Pediatrics*, 12, no. 5 (November 1953), p. 482.

211 **"the medical writing . . . area":** Thomas Coleman, personal interview, April 9, 1986.

213 **"We had . . . very knowledgeable":** John Troan, personal interview, August 26, 1986.

215 **"God . . . so fast":** John Troan, personal interview, August 26, 1986.

217 **"You may be . . . mass production":** Jonas Salk to Robert Hull, March 13, 1953, Jonas Salk Papers.

217 **"on tissue culture . . . polio vaccines":** Bettylee Hampil to Jonas Salk, May 7, 1953, Jonas Salk Papers.

218 **"there are . . . at once":** Jonas Salk to Bettylee Hampil, June 26, 1953, Jonas Salk Papers.

218 **"all those . . . poliomyelitis":** Jonas Salk to R. H. Fitzgerald, November 3, 1953, Jonas Salk Papers.

219 **"The first automobile . . . vaccines ready":** *Science News Letter*, 65, no. 19 (May 8, 1954), p. 291.

219 **"They . . . research project":** Jonas Salk, undated recorded interview, collection of Richard Carter.

223 **"The entire program . . . Eli Lilly":** Jonas Salk to Basil O'Connor, December 1, 1953, Jonas Salk Papers.

PAGE

224 "You Connaught know . . . who knows": telegram, Basil O'Connor to Jonas Salk, October 28, 1953, Jonas Salk Papers.

226 "I can still . . . Smart man": Thomas Rivers, undated recorded interview, collection of Richard Carter.

229 "will it clearly . . . build up": Thomas Francis notes, "Meeting, NY: 1/11/54": Thomas Francis Collection.

236 "we would need . . . sterile": Melvin Glasser, personal interview, February 21, 1986.

242 "I think . . . State Department": Jonas Salk to Harry Weaver, August 11, 1953, Jonas Salk Papers.

243 "these investigators . . . stand out": Jonas Salk to C. E. A. Winslow, December 1953, Jonas Salk Papers.

244 "rather amused . . . his accuser": Jonas Salk to Aims McGuinness, December 14, 1953, Jonas Salk Papers.

244 "I would . . . inaccuracies": Jonas Salk to Aims McGuinness, January 7, 1954, Jonas Salk Papers.

245 "I completely agree . . . saved up. Albert": Albert Sabin to Aims McGuinness, December 15, 1953, Jonas Salk Papers.

246 "there has . . . to date": Jonas Salk to G. Foard McGinnes, January 4, 1954, Jonas Salk Papers.

246 "this 'thing' . . . processing": Fred Stimpert to Jonas Salk, January 29, 1954, Jonas Salk Papers.

249 "We have felt . . . which is": Victor Haas, testimony, House Hearings, 1953, p. 845.

251 "The Public Health . . . about polio": Thomas Rivers, undated recorded interview, collection of Richard Carter.

254 "In your honor . . . safety. Jonas": Jonas Salk to Basil O'Connor, March 29, 1954, Jonas Salk Papers.

255 "quoted . . . control study": "Daily Memo," April 1, 1954, Thomas Francis Collection.

WIDE-ANGLE: Polio Pioneers, 1954

263 "It was too quick": Annie Dillard, *An American Childhood* (New York: Harper & Row, 1987), p. 168.

263 "Everybody . . . just begun": Albert Sabin, testimony, House Hearings, 1953, p. 848.

268 "I went down . . . good or not": Leona Baumgartner, personal interview, August 19, 1986.

273 "I continued . . . extremely difficult": Bea Wright, "McCutcheon Transcript," p. 79, collection of March of Dimes Birth Defects Foundation.

PART FOUR: Proof by Numbers

277 "Between . . . and papers": Bruno Latour and Steve Woolgar, *Laboratory Life: The Construction of Scientific Facts* (Princeton: Princeton University Press, 1986), p. 245.

PAGE

284 **"alleged filmstrip"**: "Daily Memo," February 12, 1954, Thomas Francis Collection.

284 **"at the conclusion . . . carried out"**: Thomas Francis to Basil O'Connor, June 23, 1954, Thomas Francis Collection.

285 **"from health . . . widespread attitude"**: "Daily Memo," August 16, 1954, Thomas Francis Collection.

286 **"[Langmuir] . . . the inside"**: "Daily Memo," June 12, 1954, Thomas Francis Collection.

287 **"If it . . . suspicion"**: "Daily Memo," June 2, 1954, Thomas Francis Collection.

290 **"I would be . . . on the road"**: Jonas Salk to Basil O'Connor, May 1954, Jonas Salk Papers.

291 **"Dr. Salk . . . little information"**: "Daily Memo," July 12, 1954, Thomas Francis Collection.

292 **"Salk said . . . test areas"**: Thomas Francis Collection.

293 **"Good sailing . . . Donna"**: telegram, Donna Salk to Jonas Salk, August 26, 1954, Jonas Salk Papers.

295 **"I will not . . . J.E.S."**: Jonas Salk to Basil O'Connor, November 8, 1954, Jonas Salk Papers.

295 **"It is . . . eternity. J.E.S."**: Jonas Salk to Basil O'Connor, November 8, 1954, Jonas Salk Papers.

295 **"Van Riper . . . pretty good"**: Thomas Francis datebook, collection of Mary Jane Francis.

297 **"for me . . . my byline"**: Jonas Salk to Basil O'Connor, December 28, 1954, Jonas Salk Papers.

298 **"I liked . . . but themselves"**: Dorothy Ducas, personal interview, March 5, 1986.

300 **"If we get . . . to face"**: minutes, meeting of the Immunization Committee—Joint Advisory Vaccine Committee, December 18–19, 1954, p. 214, collection of the March of Dimes Birth Defects Foundation.

300 **"If we get . . . the vaccine"**: ibid., pp. 214–16.

300 **"the public . . . was over"**: ibid., p. 228.

300 **"The year . . . democracy works"**: Melvin Glasser, personal interview, February 19, 1986.

304 **"Ed Murrow . . . his eyes"**: Thomas Coleman, personal interview, April 9, 1986.

307 **"as flunkies"**: "Daily Memo," March 4, 1955, Thomas Francis Collection.

308 **"Tell Brandon . . . for granted"**: Thomas Francis datebook, March 14, 1955, collection of Mary Jane Francis.

308 **"one of . . . all time"**: Fred Friendly, personal interview, August 7, 1986.

312 **"Well, they've written . . . much attention"**: Dorothy Ducas, personal interview, March 5, 1986.

324 **"What the hell . . . with you"**: Carter, *Breakthrough*, p. 281.

324 **"It is . . . justifiably eager"**: Alan Gregg, "Possibilities, Probabilities, and Certainties," address delivered in Ann Arbor, April 12, 1955, collection of March of Dimes Birth Defects Foundation.

PAGE

329 "The sun . . . statement": Edward R. Murrow, *In Search of Light* (New York: Knopf, 1967), p. 279.

329–330 "The possibility . . . good luck": Edward R. Murrow and Fred W. Friendly, eds., *See It Now* (New York: Simon & Schuster, 1955), pp. 150–61.

PART FIVE: Political Science

333 "Because I have . . . luminous": F.R.S., "Notes of a Not-Watson," *Encounter*, 31 (July 1968), p. 61.

337 "A lot . . . original work," Thomas Rivers, undated recorded interview, collection of Richard Carter.

337 " 'Polio is conquered . . . no breakthrough": Albert Sabin, personal interview, February 20, 1986.

338 "Why did Jonas . . . colleagues": Alexander Langmuir, personal interview, January 22, 1986.

344 "The development . . . a Salk": Thomas Rivers, "Responsibilities in the Development of the Poliomyelitis Vaccine," address given in Ann Arbor, April 12, 1955, collection of March of Dimes Birth Defects Foundation.

345 "There were . . . April 12 material": Lorraine Friedman, personal interview, November 20, 1987.

347 "to build a film . . . medical research": Mark Selvaggio, "The Making of Jonas Salk," *Pittsburgh*, June 1984, p. 50.

352 "We could afford . . . no terrors for me": legislative meeting, May 4, 1955, Minnich Series (White House Office, Office of the Staff Secretary), Dwight D. Eisenhower Presidential Library.

353 "at Cabinet . . . Capitol Hill": Carl Brauer, *Presidential Transitions* (New York: Oxford University Press, 1986), p. 40n.

355 "The case for export . . . the supply": draft memo, Acting Secretary of Commerce to the President, April 21, 1955, Central File, Dwight D. Eisenhower Presidential Library.

355 "The whole effect . . . United States": John Foster Dulles to Oveta Culp Hobby, May 6, 1955, Central File, Dwight D. Eisenhower Presidential Library.

356 In view . . . set up": Charles F. Willis, Jr., to Governor Adams, April 14, 1955, Central File, Dwight D. Eisenhower Presidential Library.

359 "What the hell . . . in Idaho": Mahlon Bierly, personal interview, June 24, 1986.

362 "They were scared . . . was bad": Thomas Coleman, personal interview, April 9, 1986.

367 "The availability . . . field trial": Oveta C. Hobby, Hobby Collection, Dwight D. Eisenhower Presidential Library.

372 "3:15 P.M. . . . *Selah*": Thomas Francis datebook, collection of Mary Jane Francis.

374 **"a very special ... creativity"**: Mark Selvaggio, "The Making of Jonas Salk," *Pittsburgh*, June 1984, p. 50.

376 **"Let someone ... these people"**: Donna Salk, personal interview, November 20, 1987.

CLOSEUP: The Healthiest Generation in History

381 **"It was a ... kind of sensation"**: *Los Angeles Times*, January 13, 1985, sec. 2.

385 **"There was no rush ... any change"**: Albert Sabin, personal interview, February 20, 1986.

386 **"Not *a* vaccine ... *the* vaccine"**: ibid.

387 **"When ... checks' "**: Marilyn Chase, "Chic Disease," *Wall Street Journal*, September 28, 1987.

388 **"If one ... hundred years"**: "States Planting Seeds to Grow Crop of Scientists," *The New York Times*, March 15, 1989.

388 **"Failing to eliminate ... might not"**: Alice Steward Trillin, "For a Smoking Ban in New York City," *The New York Times*, January 24, 1987.

INDEX

Adams, Sherman, 355, 356
Advisory Group on Evaluation, 228
AIDS research, 389
AIDS vaccine, 387
Albert Lasker Awards, 364
Alex, Steve, 235, 260, 375
Allen, Jack, 213–14
American Academy of Pediatrics, 243
American Cancer Society, 69
American Heart Association, 69
American Medical Association, 193, 361
American Philosophical Society, 337
American Red Cross, 66, 69
Anderson, Ida, 303
Anderson, Linda Lou, 267
Ann Arbor announcement (4-12-55)
    media coverage, 315–19, 325
    planning, 306–10, 313–15
    scientific meeting, 315–16, 320–25
Arlington, Massachusetts, as field-trial
    site, 270
Armed Forces Epidemiological Board,
    126
Army Commission on Influenza, 105
Army-McCarthy hearings, 274
Association of State and Territorial
    Health Officers, 205, 252
Association for Research in Nervous and
    Mental Disease, 297

Baby Boom, 86–87
Barrows, Ray, 198, 235
Baumgartner, Leona, 23, 268
Bay of Fundy, 44–45
Bazeley, Percival L., 245
Becton, Dickinson and Company, 236
Beijerinck, Martinus Willem, 97
Bell, Joseph, 198, 204–5, 220

Belli, Melvin, 367
Bennett, Byron, 115, 323, 327
Benny, Jack, 75
Bierly, Mahlon, 359
Birthday Ball Committees, 70
Black children, participation of, in field
    trial, 273
Blakeslee, Al, 213
Blecha, John, 215
Blind controls, 202
Blood, Virginia, 235, 238, 271, 325
Bloom, Albert, 315, 318
B'nai B'rith, 84
Bob and Barbara, 237
Bodian, David
    advisor, National Institutes of Health,
        253, 325, 327, 365, 366, 372
    Ann Arbor announcement (4-12-55),
        317
    member, Vaccine Advisory
        Committee, 259
    research, 109, 110, 171
    research career, 129, 253, 327, 337,
        372
    Third International Conference on
        Poliomyelitis, 294
Bogart, Humphrey, 75
Boisen, Morton, 282
Boyd, Dr., 323
Brando, Marlon, 347
Brandon, Arthur, 306–7
Braseley, Ben, 293
Brodie, Maurice, 72, 132
Brodie vaccine, 72, 113, 145
Brown, Gordon, 281
Brown v. Board of Education, 273
Bureau of Biologics, 368
Burns, Bill, 215

Cagney, Jimmy, 75
Campbell, Angus, 281
Campobello Island, 45
Cant, Gilbert, 215
Cantor, Eddie, 73–74, 82, 319
Carpenter, Arthur, 68–69
Carrel, Alexis, 124–25
Carter, Richard, 196
Carver, George Washington, 36
Castle, Irene, 33
Celebration Balls in Honor of the
    President's Birthday, 70–71
Census Bureau, 252
Centers for Disease Control, 369. *See
    also* Communicable Disease
    Center
Chickenpox, 97
Cholera, 31
Churchill, Winston, 160
Clausen, Chris, 214
Cliffside Park, New Jersey, as field-trial
    site, 267
Cochran, Lucile, 141, 142, 293, 316
Coleman, Thomas, 211, 317, 341, 343–
    45, 347–48, 357, 362
Communicable Disease Center, 80, 285–
    86. *See also* Centers for Disease
    Control
Community Chest, 249
Connaught Laboratories (Toronto), 131,
    206, 217, 251
Cooke, Alistair, 344
Coolidge, Calvin, 49
Corcoran, Thomas, 63
Coué, Émile, 57
Coughlan, Robert, 209
Cox, James, 46, 49
Crick, Francis, 339
Crippler, The, 83
Culver, Bettyann O'Connor (daughter),
    170, 172, 372
Cutter incident, 359–67, 369, 371, 373
Cutter Laboratories, 221–22, 253, 356,
    366

Dail, Charles, 375–76
Davis, John W., 49
Davis, Morton, 387
de Kruif, Paul, 71, 256–58
Democratic Party, 67–68
De Neff, Wayne, 327
Denver, Colorado, as field-trial site, 272
Dietrich, Marlene, 319–20
Dietz, David, 242
Dillard, Annie, 264

Double-blind placebo-control studies,
    202–3
Dublin, Thomas, 198–99, 231–32,
    287–88
Ducas, Dorothy, 181, 297–98
    Ann Arbor announcement (4-12-55),
        307, 309, 311, 312
    director, public information, 81, 260,
        287, 289
    rebuttal to Winchell on safety, 257–
        58
    Salk vaccine field trial (1954), 237
Dukakis, Michael, 387
Dulles, John Foster, 355
Durant, Will, 50
Dusheck, George, 213–14

Eddy, Bernice, 252
Eisenhower, Dwight, 248, 350, 351–52,
    356–58
Eli Lilly and Company
    Ann Arbor telecast (4-12-55), 305,
        307, 308, 327–28
    Salk vaccine production, 177, 217,
        218, 221–22, 223, 356, 369
Emergency March of Dimes, 289, 300
Emmet, Marvin and Roosevelt, 46–47
Enders, John, 128, 129, 196, 288, 344
    Nobel Prize, 124, 293, 335
    research career, 125–31, 171, 172,
        217, 338
    and Salk vaccine, 143, 320, 365, 366
Epidemic Intelligence Service, at
    Communicable Disease Center,
    286
*Evaluation of 1954 Poliomyelitis
    Vaccine Trials,* 311–12

Family trial (1953), 189–91
Farley, James A., 70
Field, Marshall, 79
Field trials, 201–3. *See also* Salk vaccine
    field trial
Fitzgerald, R. H., 218
Fleming, Alexander, 190
Flexner, Simon, 34
Ford, Edsel, 71
Ford, Henry, II, 79
Formaldehyde inactivation, 338
Forrestal, James, 71
Fraley, Pierre, 213
Francis, Dorothy, 287
Francis, Thomas, Jr., 183–84, 225, 231,
    226–27, 284, 365, 391
    Ann Arbor announcement (4-12-55),

299, 302, 310–12, 320–24, 327,
344–45, 347
and Jonas Salk, 43, 103–6, 336
research career, 110, 122–23, 225
Salk vaccine field trial (1954), 225–29,
234, 239, 240, 245, 252, 258–60,
272–73, 280–82, 283, 284, 286–
87, 289, 290, 295–96, 350, 361
See It Now, 329
Third International Conference on
Poliomyelitis, 294
Francis Field Trial. *See* Salk vaccine field
trial (1954)
Friedman, Lorraine, 116, 139, 142, 177,
189–90, 316, 323, 327, 345, 377
Friendly, Fred, 303–4, 308
Fritz, Dr., 359

Gamma globulin, 193, 250
Gard, Sven, 294
Garland, Judy, 75
Garroway, Dave, 319
Gibran, Kahlil, 196
Gifford, Walter, 79
Gilot, Françoise, 377
Glasser, Melvin A., 201
on National Foundation debt, 300–1
operational director, Field Trial Unit,
198, 235, 236, 256, 287
Glen Ellyn, Illinois, as field-trial site, 267
Graff, Lou, 281, 307, 309–12, 317–19,
320
Gregg, Alan, 308, 317, 320, 329

Haas, Victor, 249, 325
Habel, Karl, 325
Hagerty, James, 357
Hammon, William McDowell, 143, 145,
171, 180, 193, 325
Hampil, Bettylee, 217–18
Harding, Warren G., 46, 49
Hatcher, Harlan, 306–8
Hayes, Helen, 271, 319–20
Health, Education, and Welfare,
Department of, 252, 354
Heifetz, Jascha, 75
Hench, Philip, 336
Herblock, 352
Hershey round-table meeting,
Committee on Immunization,
146, 173–74, 179–80
Hickey, Margaret, 182, 271
Hobby, Oveta Culp, 248, 357

Cutter incident, 363, 364–65, 367
distribution of vaccine, 351, 352,
354–55
licensing of Salk vaccine, 325–26,
350, 353
May 19, 1955, testimony of, 353
Secretary, Health, Education and
Welfare, 248, 357, 368
Hollywood community, 73–75, 319–20,
347
Horstmann, Dorothy Millicent, 171
House Committee on Interstate
Commerce, 252
Howe, Howard, 109, 110, 171, 301,
390
Howe, Louis, 47–49, 51, 59, 60, 63,
207

Immunity, 96–97
Influenza, 97
International Conference on
Poliomyelitis
Second, 172
Third, 291, 293–94
Iron lung, 40–42

Jacobs, Bill, 215
*Journal of the American Medical
Association (JAMA)*
rejection of Salk articles by, 291
report on Salk vaccine in, 177, 185
Jenner, Edward, 35, 97, 149
Jungeblut, C. W., 36

Kahn, Louis, 376
Kalen, Isidor, 32
Keefer, Chester, 353–54, 368
Keep Trying, 42
Kempe, Henry, 243–45
Kenny, Elizabeth, 38, 77
Kerr, Randy, 266–67
Knopf, Alfred, 344
Knopf, Blanche, 344
Kolmer, John, 72, 132
Kolmer vaccine, 72, 113
Koprowski, Hilary, 129–30, 171, 294
Korns, Robert, 282
Ann Arbor announcement (4-12-55),
317, 321
assistant director, Vaccine Evaluation
Center, 254–55, 260, 272, 282,
283, 284, 285, 286, 295
Kuhn, Thomas S., 168
Kumm, Henry, 198, 200, 288, 323

Laboratory of Biologics Control, 240, 248, 250, 251, 253, 254, 299–300, 361, 367, 368
Landsteiner, Karl, 34
Langmuir, Alexander, 199, 200, 285–86, 325, 337–38, 366, 369
Latour, Bruno, 278
Lauffer, Max, 107, 108
Laurence, Bill, 213, 315
Lawrence, David L., 101, 102
Lederle pharmaceutical company, 130, 171
Lederman, Leon, 388
Lewis, L. James, 115, 214–15, 315, 327
Lewontin, Richard C., 92
Lexington, Kentucky, as field-trial site, 267
Likert, Rensis, 281
Litchfield, Edward, 375
London, Howard, 314
Longworth, Alice, 71
Lovett, Robert, 45

MacArthur Foundation, 388
McCarthy, Frank, 347
McCarthy, Joseph, 160, 274
McEllroy, William S., 106, 107, 127
McGinnes, G. Foard, 145, 198, 235, 246, 253, 322
McGuinness, Aims C., 243, 246
Magnis, Herdis von, 181–82
Manual of Suggested Procedures, 238, 239
March of Dimes. *See also* National Foundation for Infantile Paralysis
    fund raising, 23–24, 74, 75, 76, 289, 300
    growth, 73–77, 84
Mariano, Joseph, 32
Martin, William, 139
Max Planck Institute, 374
May, Brian, 382
Measles, 97
Medium 199, 131, 217, 291
Meister, Joseph, 93
Mellon, A. W., Educational and Charitable Trust, 101
Mellon, Richard King, 100–1
Melnick, Joseph, 129, 200, 245
Merthiolate, in test vaccine, 292, 294, 295–96, 360
Microbe Hunters, 71
Milbank, Jeremiah, 71
Milzer, Albert, 243, 246
Minuse, Elva, 341
Moley, Raymond, 63, 174

Monkey Business, 191
Monkeys, in polio research, 120–24, 130–31, 133, 356
Montgomery, Alabama, as field-trial site, 273
Morgan, Isabel, 129
Morgan, Keith, 69–70
Muggs, J. Fred, 319
Muni, Paul, 347
Murdock, Thomas, 192
Murray, Roderick, 251, 366
Murrow, Edward R., interviews of Salk on *See It Now*, 303–5, 308, 328–30, 338, 341, 358
My Place to Stand, 42

Napier, John, 282
Nathanson, Neal, 366
National Academy of Sciences, 306, 336–37
National Congress of Parents and Teachers, 232, 234
National Council of Catholic Women, 84, 233
National Council of Jewish Women, 233
National Council of Negro Women, 84–85, 233
National Federation of Women's Clubs, 85
National Foundation for Infantile Paralysis, 24, 59. *See also* March of Dimes; *and under specific officers*
    board of trustees, 79
    Committee on Immunization, 143–50, 173–74, 179–80, 193, 199–201, 294–95, 298–301
    Committee on Research, 111, 114, 142
    Committee on Standards, 134
    Department of Public Information, 81, 237
    Educational Division, 85, 235
    finances, 65, 124, 249, 289, 300–1, 371
    fund raising, 66, 82, 83–85, 289, 300, 371
    O'Connor as president, 52, 54, 65–66, 73, 80–81, 112, 114–15, 169–70, 198, 300–1
    public relations, 205–10, 237–39, 371–72
    Radio and Film Department, 81, 83, 237
    research programs, 77–78, 98, 249, 370

Salk vaccine, 246, 247, 351
Salk vaccine field trial (1954), 198–99, 235–39, 270–71
significance of Baby Boom, 86–87
Statistical Services Division, 232
structure and operations, 64–68, 73, 79–85, 95, 161, 169–70, 193, 289, 300, 370, 371
Vaccine Advisory Committee, 193, 204, 258–60, 294–95, 298–301
virus-typing project, 109–19
Women's Division, 76–77, 87, 206, 238
National Institute of Health, 80, 99
National Institute of Microbiology, 248
National Institutes of Health. *See also* Ann Arbor announcement (4-12-55)
amount spent by, on polio research, 249
testing of Salk vaccine by, 177–78
National Society for Crippled Children, 69
National Tuberculosis Association, 69
Nehru, Jawaharlal, 303, 356
New Rochelle, New York, polio epidemic in, 32
1954 field trial. *See* Salk vaccine field trial (1954)
Nix, Robert, 188
Nixon, Richard, 386
Nobel, Alfred, 338
Nobel Prize, 335–39
No Time for Tears, 42

Observed-control field trial, 202
O'Conner, Doc (Dartmouth football coach), 53
O'Connor, D. Basil (Doc), 59, 60, 201, 372
Albert Lasker Awards, 364
Ann Arbor announcement (4-12-55), 308–9, 317, 320, 322, 324–25, 344
Cutter incident, 361
early life and career, 52–54
Eisenhower citation for Salk, 357
executive director, American Red Cross, 66, 69
and federal government, 248–49, 354–55
and Franklin D. Roosevelt, 54, 55, 56, 58, 61–62, 63
Hershey round-table meeting, Committee on Immunization, 146, 173–74, 179–80

and Jonas Salk, 171–73, 174, 186, 195–96, 220, 224, 374, 375
leadership style, 52, 62, 63, 66–68, 77, 233, 285
president, National Foundation, 52, 54, 65–66, 73, 80–81, 112, 114–15, 169–70, 198, 300–1
Salk vaccine, 180, 182–83
Salk vaccine field trial (1954), 23, 182–83, 220, 224–25, 227, 259, 260, 268, 288, 292, 351, 385–86
search for polio cure, 173–75, 179–80, 182–83, 192, 200, 207, 298–99, 351, 372, 385–86
Third International Conference on Poliomyelitis, 293
Warm Springs, 59–62
O'Connor, Elvira Miller (wife), 53, 372
O'Connor, Hazel Royale (wife), 372, 374
O'Connor, John (brother), 53, 54, 62
O'Connor, Sheelagh (daughter), 372
Okatie Farms, 121–22, 191
Olitsky, Peter, 125
On the Shoulders of Giants, 42
Operational Memoranda, 238–39
Oppenheimer, J. Robert, 303, 373–74

Palooka, Joe, 371–72
Park, W. H., 72
Parke, Davis and Company, and Salk vaccine production, 177, 216–20, 222, 246, 253, 351, 364, 366
Parran, Thomas, 101
Pasteur, Louis, 35, 93–94, 97, 149, 305
Pasteur Institute, 94, 135, 374
Patent, for Salk vaccine, 220, 338
Paul, John, 171
Hershey round-table meeting, Committee on Immunization, 145
research career, 75, 109, 110, 129, 200
Salk vaccine field trial (1954), 183, 184
Pauling, Linus, 335
Peabody, George, 57
Perkins, Frances, 51
Pickford, Mary, 76–77
Pitman-Moore Company, 221–22, 366
Pittsburgh, 100–1
Pitt vaccine, 349
"Plans for 1954," 194
Poliomyelitis
books written about, 42
diagnosis and treatment, 31, 34–38, 40–42, 96–98

Poliomyelitis (*cont.*)
  fears, 19–21, 31–32, 36–37, 155–57, 158, 386–87
  summer epidemics, 22, 31–35, 36, 39, 43, 45, 86, 160–61, 170–71
  worldwide, 383
Poliomyelitis Surveillance Unit of the Communicable Disease Center, 365
Polio patients, 38–42, 383
Polio Pioneers, 237, 265–67, 273. *See also* Salk Vaccine field trial
Polio Pointers for Parents (1954), 238
Polio research. *See also* National Foundation for Infantile Paralysis; Salk Vaccine Field Trial; Vaccine Evaluation Center; Virus Research Laboratory
  costs, 249
  Enders's breakthrough in tissue culture techniques, 126–27, 130, 217
  monkeys in, 120–24, 130–31, 356
  poliovirus-typing project, 110–19
Polio survivors, 38–42, 383
Poliovirus-typing project, 110–19
Polk State School, Salk Vaccine testing at, 137–39, 146, 176, 251
Popper, Erwin, 34
Post-polio syndrome, 383
Pray, Francis, 211
President's Birthday Ball Commission, 71–73
President's Birthday Balls, 84, 207
Presley, Elvis, 371
Preston, Dave, 235, 237, 311–12
Price, David, 192, 252, 325
Princeton Institute of Advanced Studies, 374–75
Protocol, 216
Public Health Service, 199, 249–52, 361
Pure Food and Drug Act (1902), 248

Quincy, Massachusetts, as field-trial site, 270

Rabies, 97
Reagan, Nancy, 83
Reagan, Ronald, 387–88
Research Supply Company, 191
Respiratory toilet, 41
Rise Up and Walk, 42
Rivers, Thomas Milton
  advisor, National Foundation for Infantile Paralysis, 113, 114, 142, 143, 145, 173, 247, 251, 301

Ann Arbor announcement (4-12-55), 317, 320, 322, 324, 327, 344
  and Albert Sabin, 147–48
  Salk vaccine field trial (1954), 182–83, 187, 194, 195, 219, 226–27
  research career, 71, 113–14, 122, 125, 131–32
  Vaccine Advisory Committee, 192–93, 259, 260, 298–99
R. K. Mellon Foundation, 101
Robbins, Frederick, 124, 126, 129, 335
Rockefeller, Nelson, 355
Rockefeller Institute for Medical Research, 34, 71, 113–14
Rocking bed, 41
Rooney, Mickey, 75
Roosevelt, Eleanor, 47–48, 49, 51, 60, 63, 207, 326
Roosevelt, Franklin D., 44, 62–63
  and Basil O'Connor, 54, 55, 56, 58, 61–63
  legal career, 46–47, 57
  paralysis, 45, 47–49, 56, 57
  political career, 46, 47, 49–50, 54, 62, 67, 74, 76, 174
  public image, 45–46, 49, 50–51, 57, 207
  Warm Springs, 57–59, 75
Rosenman, Samuel, 174
Ross, Lillian, 23

Sabin, Albert, 245, 264, 344. *See also* Sabin vaccine
  Ann Arbor announcement (4-12-55), 320, 337
  early life, 146–48
  Hershey round-table meeting, Committee on Immunization, 143, 144
  live-virus vaccine, 129, 131, 200, 301, 372, 373, 385–86
  National Medal of Science, 386
  research career, 99–100, 110, 125, 129, 146, 147, 171, 337, 372, 373
  Salk vaccine field trial (1954), 144–49, 183–84, 193, 199–200, 245, 255–56, 291, 294, 301, 366
"Sabin on Sunday" clinics, 386
Sabin vaccine, 149, 370, 384, 385. *See also* Sabin, Albert
Salk, Daniel (father), 316, 327
Salk, Darrell (son), 205, 316, 342–43, 357, 377
Salk, Donna (wife), 104–5, 205, 210, 293, 316, 341–42, 357, 376–77

Salk, Dora (mother), 316, 327
Salk, Herman (brother), 191, 218
Salk, Jonas Edward, 24, 101, 218, 293
  Ann Arbor announcement (4-12-55),
    322–24, 327
  and Basil O'Connor, 171–73, 174,
    186, 195–96, 220, 224, 357,
    374, 375
  belief in safety of vaccine, 171, 176,
    329
  celebrity status, 207–16, 345–46,
    373, 377
  Cutter incident, 359–67, 369, 371,
    373
  early life and career, 102–6, 108,
    110–11, 113, 147
  early vaccine trials, 133–34, 136
  family life, 104–5, 205, 293, 316,
    341–42, 357, 376–77
  Hershey round-table meeting,
    Committee on Immunization,
    145–46
  and National Foundation for Infantile
    Paralysis, 108, 145–46, 180, 220,
    259–60, 298–99
  National Foundation for Infantile
    Paralysis committees, 110–19,
    366
  poliovirus-typing research, 110–19
  professional relations, 103–6, 115–
    16, 145, 220, 224, 242–45, 294–
    301, 336–37
  public relations, 181, 207, 212, 214,
    215, 240–41, 297–98, 340–42,
    347–49, 361–62, 377, 387
  research career, 103–6, 110–19, 131–
    33, 180, 207, 240, 291–92
  Salk Institute, 375, 376, 377
  Salk vaccine field trial (1954), 194–
    96, 203–4, 206, 218–20, 222–
    23, 226, 246, 254–55, 260, 289–
    92, 294, 295–96, 300
  Salk vaccine production, 206, 219–
    20, 246, 247
  See It Now, 303–5, 308, 328–30,
    338, 341, 358
  special citation from President
    Eisenhower, 356–58
  Third International Conference on
    Poliomyelitis, 291, 293–94
  Virus Research Laboratory, 106–8,
    115–16, 127–28, 192, 241–42,
    376
Salk, Jonathan (son), 205, 316, 342–43,
  357, 377
Salk, Lee (brother), 316

Salk, Peter (son), 205, 316, 342–43,
  357, 377
Salk Hall, 102
Salk Institute for Biological Studies, 375,
  376, 377
Salk Soldiers, 348
Salk vaccine
  announcement. *See* Ann Arbor
    announcement (4-12-55)
  availability, 351–52, 384
  commercial production, 177
  early trials, 135–37, 254
    D. T. Watson Home for Crippled
      Children, 139–42, 146, 148, 176,
      188, 251, 361, 377
    Polk State School, 137–39, 146,
      176, 251
  importance, 390–91
  naming, 349
  opposition, 183–84, 199–200, 255–
    58
  patent, 220, 338
  price, 351
  public interest in, 179, 180, 181, 184,
    207–10, 340–41
  versus Sabin vaccine, 384
  safety, 146–49, 171, 176, 177–78,
    254
  worldwide, 355–56
Salk vaccine evaluation report. *See* Ann
  Arbor announcement (4-12-55)
Salk vaccine field trial (1954), 21–25,
  64
  costs of, 174
  design, 178–79, 194–95, 198–99,
    203, 225–35, 237–38, 267–74
  and Jonas Salk, 194–96
  Merthiolate problem, 292, 294, 295–
    96
  National Foundation for Infantile
    Paralysis role, 224–29, 235–39
  operations, 249–50, 270–73
  opposition, 149, 178–79, 183–84,
    194–200, 255–58
  participants, 159, 162–63, 233–34,
    238, 265–66, 268–69, 270, 273
  public relations, 255, 265, 267
  starting date, 177, 253, 260
  Vaccine Advisory Committee
    approval, 260
Salvation Army, 69
Sandburg, Carl, 303–5
Sanitary Fairs, 31
Sanitation, and development of polio,
  35–36
Sarah Mellon Scaife Foundation, 101, 108

Scaife, Alan, Mr. and Mrs., at Ann
    Arbor announcement, 316
Scheele, Leonard, 260, 325, 352, 363–
    64, 366, 369
Schenck, Joseph, 76
Schey, Hortense L., 32
Science reporting, 213–16
Scientific Glass Instrument Company,
    191
Scientific meeting. *See* Ann Arbor
    announcement (4-12-55)
"Scientist Speaks for Himself," 186–87,
    260, 361
Sebrell, William, 260, 295–96, 368
See It Now
    2-22-55 broadcast, 303–5
    4-12-55 broadcast, 308, 328–30, 338,
        341, 358
Shalom Farm, 191
Shannon, James, 253–54, 260, 295–96,
    366, 368
Sharpe and Dohme, 217–18, 221–22,
    366
Shearer, John B., 54
Shope, Richard, 366
Silverman, 213
Single-blind control, 202
Smadel, Joseph, 148–49, 325, 365
    manufacturers' protocols, 247, 251–
        52
    member, National Foundation for
        Infantile Paralysis committees,
        182, 192, 296, 366
Smallpox, 97
Smith, Al, 49–50
Smith, Joshua, 267
Smith, Kate, 75
Snider, Art, 318
Social Security Administration, 250
Sontag, Susan, 30
Spang Foundation, 128
Spock, Benjamin, 101, 162
Stanley, Wendell, 97
Statistical recordkeeping, 203
Stebbins, Ernest, 192
Stegen, Ed, 235, 315
Stella, Giovanni, 32
Stewart, Jimmy, 75
Stickle, Gabriel, 231–32
Stimpert, Fred, 217, 218, 246
Stockholm Pediatric Clinic, 34
Streeter, Thomas W., 53
"Studies in Human Subjects on Active
    Immunization Against
    Poliomyelitis," 177
Szilard, Leo, 374

Tammany Hall, 67
Theiler, Max, 182, 335
Third International Conference on
    Poliomyelitis, 291, 293–94
Tolchinsky, Eva, 281
Tolstoy, Alexandra, 344
Topping, Norman, 192
Tracheostomy, 41
Trippe, Juan, 79
Troan, John, 213, 214–15, 318, 327,
    328–29, 349
Truman, Harry, 364
Tuberculosis, 31
Tugwell, Rexford, 63
Turner, Thomas, 192, 325, 390
Tuskegee Institute rehabilitation
    facilities, 85
Typhoid, 31

Ubell, Earl, 213
United States Army, and field-trial
    evaluation, 105, 126, 288–89
United Way, 249
University of Michigan, 104, 306. *See
    also* Vaccine Evaluation Center
University of Pittsburgh, 101, 306
    School of Public Health, 101, 102
    Virus Research Laboratory. *See also*
        Virus Research Laboratory

Vaccines, 97. *See also* Sabin vaccine;
    Salk vaccine
    killed-virus versus live-virus, 128–29
    production, 128
    testing, 135–37
Vaccine Evaluation Center, 238. *See also*
    Ann Arbor announcement (4-12-
    55)
    Ann Arbor announcement (4-12-55),
        302, 306–10
    operations, 272–73, 281–85, 288–89,
        292
    origin, 178, 228, 280–82, 287–88
Van Riper, Hart
    Ann Arbor announcement (4-12-55),
        307, 317, 320, 321, 324–25
    medical director, National Foundation
        for Infantile Paralysis, 197, 198,
        235, 308, 327
    Merthiolate problem, 295
    and Thomas Francis, Jr., 225, 226,
        229
    Vaccine Evaluation Center, 228, 288
Virology, early, 35
Viruses, variety and instability of, 109
Virus Research Laboratory

funding, 108, 128, 134, 191
growth, 102, 107, 116–17, 190–91
Merthiolate problem, 295–96
Salk field trial (1954), 197, 254
secrecy concerning work, 142–43
staff, 115–16, 190, 245–46
virus studies, 123–24, 127–28, 130–31, 133, 195–96
Voight, Robert
Ann Arbor announcement (4-12-55), 317, 321
statistical director, Vaccine Evaluation Center, 252, 272, 281, 284, 292

Walker, Gale, 137–39
Walker, Jimmy, 62
Wall Street corporation, 67–68
Ward, Elsie, 116, 128
Warm Springs
under Arthur Carpenter, 68–69
under Basil O'Connor, 59, 60, 61, 62
financial needs, 70–71
and Franklin D. Roosevelt, 57–62
improvements, 68
as rehabilitation center, 73
Warm Springs Foundation
Celebration Balls in Honor of the President's Birthday for, 70, 71–72
creation, 59, 67
fund raising, 69–70
officers, 59
Watson, D. T., Home for Crippled Children, 140, 322
testing of Salk vaccine, 139–42, 146, 148, 176, 188, 251, 361, 377
Watson, James, 339
Weaver, Harry, 172, 173, 189, 344
Ann Arbor announcement (4-12-55), 321
field-trial plan, 181, 194, 195, 216–17, 218, 222, 226
and Jonas Salk, 220

research director, National Foundation for Infantile Paralysis, 111–14, 121, 138, 145, 193, 194, 198, 220, 322
round-table conferences as innovation of, 112, 143–44
Weller, Thomas, 124, 126, 129, 335
Wenner, Herbert, 282
White, E. B., 159
Whitelaw, Elaine, 77, 235, 238, 271, 272, 287, 325, 370
Wickman, Ivar, 34
Wilkins, Maurice, 339
Williams, Chet, 303
Wilson, Earl, 185
Wilson, Woodrow, 46
Winchell, Paul, 346
Winchell, Walter, 256–58, 359, 362
Women's Army Corps, 249
Woolgar, Steve, 278
Workman, William
Ann Arbor announcement (4-12-55), 320
director, Laboratory of Biologics Control, 146, 247, 295, 299–300, 315
field trial, 253, 292, 296–97
Hershey round-table meeting, Committee on Immunization, 251
licensing of Salk vaccine, 325–26, 350
vaccine safety, 254, 359, 360, 366
Wright, Bea, 238, 273
Wright, Jessie, 141, 293, 316
Wyeth Laboratories, 221–22, 359, 366

Yale Poliomyelitis Study Unit, 183
Young, Robert, 75
Youngner, Julius, 115, 245, 323, 327
Yurochko, Francis, 116

Zagury, Daniel, 135
Zinsser, Hans, 92, 125

Grateful acknowledgment is made for use of the following excerpts:

Quotations from interviews with Dr. Leona Baumgartner, conducted by the author, printed with permission.

Excerpt from *An American Childhood* by Annie Dillard. Copyright © 1987 by Annie Dillard. Reprinted by permission of Harper & Row Publishers, Inc.

Quotations from interviews with Lorraine Friedman, assistant to Jonas Salk, conducted by the author, printed with permission.

Excerpt from "Notes of a Not-Watson" by F.R.S. This article was first published in the July 1968 issue of *Encounter*.

Quotations from interviews with Dr. Alexander D. Langmuir, M.D., conducted by the author, printed with permission.

Quotation from *Laboratory Life: The Construction of Scientific Facts*, by Bruno Latour and Steve Woolgar. Copyright © 1986 by Princeton University Press. Reprinted by permission.

Quotation from " 'Honest Jim' Watson's Big Thriller About DNA," by Richard C. Lewontin. Reprinted by permission of *Chicago Sun Times*.

Quotations from the minutes of several National Foundation meetings held in 1953 and 1954, and from the transcript of an updated interview with Elaine Whitelaw and Bea Wright (McCutcheon Transcript). Printed by permission of Mr. Charles Massey, president, March of Dimes Foundation.

Quote from "The Dark Side of Survival: Polio Victims Outlast Money Meant for a 'Lifetime' of Care" by Robert W. Stewart, *Los Angeles Times*, January 13, 1985. Copyright © 1985 by *Los Angeles Times*. Reprinted by permission.

Excerpt from *See It Now*, edited by Edward R. Murrow and Fred Friendly. Copyright © 1955 by Edward R. Murrow and Fred Friendly. Reprinted by permission of Simon & Schuster.

Quotations from a letter from Thomas Rivers to Albert Sabin, December 2, 1946, Thomas Rivers Collection, American Philosophical Society, Philadelphia. Reprinted by permission.

Quotations from letters by Dr. Albert Sabin in the Salk Collection at the University Library of the University of California, San Diego. Printed by permission of Dr. Albert Sabin.

Quotations from interviews with Dr. Jonas Salk, conducted by the author, printed with permission of Jonas Salk.

Quotations from documents in the Salk Collection at the University Library, University of California, La Jolla. Printed by permission of Jonas Salk and Mrs. Donna L. Salk.

Excerpt from *Illness as Metaphor* by Susan Sontag. Copyright © 1978 by Susan Sontag. Reprinted by permission of Farrar, Straus & Giroux, Inc.

Excerpt from *Baby and Child Care* by Benjamin Spock. Copyright © 1946 by Benjamin Spock. Reprinted by permission of Pocket Books, Inc.

About the Author

JANE S. SMITH was born in New York City, where she was a Polio Pioneer. A graduate of Simmons College (B.A.) and Yale University (Ph.D.), she is the author of *Elsie de Wolfe*, a biography of the legendary interior decorator, and other works of fiction and literary criticism. She is currently a visiting scholar at Northwestern University's Center for Urban Affairs and Policy Research. She lives in Evanston, Illinois, with her husband and two children, and writes in a very small room with a very large window.